palgrave advances in development studies

Palgrave Advances

Titles include:

Jeffrey Haynes (*editor*)
DEVELOPMENT STUDIES

Forthcoming:

Michele Betsill, Kathryn Hochstetler and Dimitris Stevis (*editors*)
INTERNATIONAL ENVIRONMENTAL POLITICS

Terrell Carver and James Martin (*editors*)
CONTINENTAL POLITICAL THOUGHT

Michelle Cini and Angela Bourne (*editors*)
EUROPEAN UNION STUDIES

Palgrave Advances
Series Standing Order ISBN 1–4039–3512–2 (Hardback) 1–4039–3513–0 (Paperback)
(*outside North America only*)

You can receive future titles in this series as they are published by placing a standing order.
Please contact your bookseller or, in the case of difficulty, write to us at the address below
with your name and address, the title of the series and the ISBN quoted above.

Customer Services Department, Macmillan Distribution Ltd, Houndmills, Basingstoke,
Hampshire RG21 6XS, England

palgrave advances in development studies

edited by
jeffrey haynes
professor of politics, london metropolitan university

palgrave
macmillan

First published 2005 by
PALGRAVE MACMILLAN
Houndmills, Basingstoke, Hampshire RG21 6XS and
175 Fifth Avenue, New York, N.Y. 10010
Companies and representatives throughout the world

PALGRAVE MACMILLAN is the global academic imprint of the
Palgrave Macmillan division of St Martin's Press LLC and of
Palgrave Macmillan Ltd.
Macmillan® is a registered trademark in the United States,
United Kingdom and other countries. Palgrave is a registered
trademark in the European Union and other countries.

ISBN 13: 978-1-4039-1634-1 hardback
ISBN 10: 1-4039-1634-9 hardback
ISBN 13: 978-1-4039-1635-8 paperback
ISBN 10: 1-4039-1635-7 paperback

This book is printed on paper suitable for recycling and
made from fully managed and sustained forest sources.

A catalogue record for this book is available
from the British Library.

Library of Congress Cataloging-in-Publication Data
Palgrave advances in development studies / edited by Jeffrey Haynes.
    p. cm.
Includes bibliographical references and index.
ISBN 1-4039-1634-9 — ISBN 1-4039-1635-7 (pbk.)
    1. Developing countries—Politics and government. 2. Developing countries—
Economic conditions. 3. Developing countries—Social conditions. I. Haynes, Jeffrey.

JF60.P334 2005
320.9172'4—dc22   10049 70910   2004051402

10 9 8 7 6 5 4 3 2
14 13 12 11 10 09 08 07 06

Printed and bound in Great Britain by
Antony Rowe Ltd, Chippenham and Eastbourne

This book is dedicated to the memory of Marian A. L. Miller

table of contents

list of tables and figures

list of contributors

(1; 7; 15) Jeffrey Haynes, Professor of Politics, Governance and International Relations, London Metropolitan University, UK

(2) Björn Hettne, Department of Peace and Development Research, Goteborg University, Sweden

(3) Peter Calvert, Emeritus Professor, Department of Politics, University of Southampton, UK

(4) Mehran Kamrava, Associate Professor and Chair, Department of Political Science, California State University, USA

(5) Gautam Sen, Lecturer in the Politics of the World Economy, Department of International Relations, London School of Economics & Political Science, UK

(6) Robert Pinkney, Research Associate, Northumbria University, UK

(8) Howard Handelman, Department of Political Science, University of Wisconsin-Milwaukee, USA

(9) Lloyd Pettiford, Acting Head, Department of International Relations, Nottingham Trent University, UK; Pauline Eadie, PhD candidate, Nottingham University, UK

(10) James Chiriyankandath, Principal Lecturer, Governance and International Relations, London Metropolitan University, UK

(11) Shirin M. Rai, Professor of Politics, University of Warwick, UK

(12) Timothy M. Shaw, Professor of Commonwealth Governance & Development, Director, Institute of Commonwealth Studies, School of Advanced Study, University of London, UK

(13) Ian Taylor, Lecturer, School of International Relations, University of St. Andrews, UK

(14) Kato Lambrechts, Christian Aid, London; Chris Alden, Senior Lecturer, Department of Government, London School of Economics & Political Science, UK

part 1
concepts and theories

part I

concepts and theories

1
introduction
jeffrey haynes

At the start of a new century, poverty remains a global problem of huge proportions. Of the world's 6 billion people, 2.8 billion live on less than $2 a day and 1.2 billion on less than $1 a day. Eight of every 100 infants do not live to see their fifth birthday. Nine of every 100 boys and 14 of every girls who reach school age do not attend school. Poverty is also evident in poor people's lack of political power and voice and in their extreme vulnerability to ill health, economic dislocation, personal violence, and natural disasters. And the scourge of HIV/AIDS, the frequency and brutality of civil conflicts, and rising disparities between rich countries and the developing world have increased the sense of deprivation and injustice for many.

This quotation is from the back cover of the *World Development Report 2000/2001*, whose subtitle is 'Attacking Poverty'. The sentiments expressed suggest not only that development and inequality are global issues, but also that measures undertaken since World War II have failed to deliver broad-based development in many developing countries. Instead, many would agree, the current era is one of deepening inequality – both within and between countries. To comprehend the nature and causes of developmental and economic inequalities, we need to adopt a more sophisticated analysis than the simplistic categorisation of 'rich' and 'poor' states. We also need to 'unpack' what the concept of development actually *means*.

For many people, the initially vague and predictive term 'development' still struggles to acquire a precise meaning. Initially regarded as both a self-evident and prophetic concept, the widespread assumption in the 1950s and 1960s was that 'Third World' (or 'developing') countries would – almost inevitably – become 'developed' over time. At that time, conventional wisdom had it that over time *all* countries would *necessarily* move from a 'traditional' to a 'modern' state – via economic and technological progress. Following emergence of numerous new countries – especially in Africa and Asia, to join the existing long-independent yet still mostly 'underdeveloped' countries in Latin America, what became known as 'development theory' emerged to focus on studies of comparative political culture, and the difficult problems of nation-building and how to construct stable and workable institutions and administrations.

Now, 40 years on, what comes to mind when we think of the politics, economics and societies of the developing world (that is, the countries of Africa, Asia, Latin America and the Middle East)? While views no doubt differ widely, it is probably a safe bet to assume that, informed by sometimes unbalanced media coverage, some at least think primarily, or at least to a considerable degree, of negative images. Why? It may be because such information produced by various media sources – especially newspapers, television and radio – can serve to underline political, economic and/or social interactions that often appear to be played out in arenas characterised by political violence and instability, greed and corruption, avarice and malice. In other words, perceptions of what goes on in developing countries may be strongly informed by widely reported examples of political and economic conflict and societal disharmony. This is a way of saying that in many developing countries, especially in sub-Saharan Africa, what is known as 'the development process' appears to have gone awry in the last 10 or 20 years. However, it is also widely acknowledged that there are a number of 'development success stories' – notably various East Asian countries, such as Hong Kong, Singapore, South Korea and Taiwan.

The purpose of this book is to provide:

- understanding of the disparate theories concerning development, their assumptions and the intellectual forces underpinning them;
- material to analyse and evaluate current debates about development;
- intellectual tools to judge intelligently contemporary arguments concerning the problems and achievements of development policy in developing countries; and
- the ability to relate theories of development to contemporary policy issues

The book's focus is the post-Cold War era (that is, post-1989, the year of the fall of the Berlin Wall) for two main reasons:

- This period is notable for dramatic domestic political and economic changes that affected many developing countries. These include, but were not limited to: democratisation and democracy; neo-liberal economic reforms; calls for more and better human rights, especially for women and ethnic and religious minorities; in short, increased popular demands for better development outcomes.
- These years also saw an array of international trends and developments linked to development issues and outcomes. Many commenced with or were stimulated by events analytically connected to globalisation.

To attempt to explain different developmental outcomes, we need to seek explanations in relation to both domestic and external factors. Consequently, the book's initial premise is that the scope of politics in developing countries is usually broader than in the West. Methods of analysis now need to accommodate themselves to the reality of development issues more clearly and effectively than the familiar, if now comprehensively outmoded development theories – modernisation theory and dependency ('*dependencia*') theory. This is because neither modernisation theory, with its main focus on domestic factors, nor dependency theory, with its primary concerns in the external arena, are analytically adequate on their own to explain variegated development trajectories and outcomes in developing countries over time. In short, the book's contributors argue that the best, most convincing analysis to explain development outcomes in developing countries derives from a focus on both domestic and external factors and their interaction.

development theory and practice over time and space: the 1950s–1990s

To put recent occurrences regarding development into context, we focus in this section on changing perceptions of development over time, in three sections: the 1950s/1960s, the 1970s/1980s, and 1990s/early 2000s.

Although 'development' is often seen as a rather vague and rather general term, it began to acquire a more precise meaning for western social scientists after World War II. At that time, the key issue was the likely political and economic trajectories of 'underdeveloped' or 'developing' countries then emerging from colonial rule, initially in the

1940s in Asia (including, India, Ceylon, Pakistan, Nepal and Indonesia) and, from the mid-1950s, numerous countries in sub-Saharan Africa (starting with Sudan in 1956 and Ghana a year later). Over time, a new sub-discipline of political science – (political) development theory – evolved. It involved studies of comparative political cultures, nation-building and the construction of stable institutions and administrations. A second, related, issue that also emerged was the way 'underdeveloped' countries would deal with their pressing problems of economic and human development.

the 1950s and 1960s

Responding to a growing understanding of the complexity of development, various approaches evolved from the 1950s. Initially, modernisation theory, a specific way of thinking about development, gained credence with many Western governments, international financial institutions (IFIs), and analysts. The common starting point was a widespread – if as it turned out, somewhat simplistic – assumption that problems of poverty and human development would be solved by adequate investments in physical capital and infrastructure. However, despite the injection of huge quantities of foreign aid in many developing countries, many did not see much in the way of development. There was a failure to make much of a dent in global poverty – an outcome that made it clear that developmental outcomes depended on more than sufficient injections of capital. Of crucial importance for developmental outcomes, it appeared, was what governments did in policy terms with the assets at their disposal. And the specific types of policies that many government adopted were in turn linked to the degree of pressure to which their own people subjected them. While it seemed to many obvious that poor people throughout the developing world would benefit from opportunities for improved health and education, necessary policy shifts did not widely occur – not least because few governments were consistently and sufficiently pressurised by their own citizens. Put another way, while improvements in, for example, health and education, are important not only in their own right but also to help promote growth and development, they would often be resisted by some sections of society who believed that their own positions would as a result suffer unacceptably. In short, developmental decisions – especially those with major resource implications – are always highly *political* decisions; and typically vested interests seek to prevent them.

the 1970s and 1980s

Development disappointments in the 1950s and 1960s led in the 1970s to a new developmental concern: a shift to a focus upon a 'basic needs' strategy. Here the emphasis was on what many would regard as the foundations of development: to ensure that all people have basic necessities, including clean water, primary health care and elementary education.

In the 1980s, the aim of building 'human capital' was supplanted by an ideologically-driven developmental shift linked to changes in the developmental thinking of the key aid-providers: western governments and IFIs, whose policies coalesced around the theory and practice of what were known as 'structural adjustment programmes' (SAPs). Inherent in this shift was a 'downsizing' of the developmental role of the state and an increased faith in the ability of 'market forces' and 'economic efficiency' to bring about the levels of broad-based economic growth to deal with the problems of poverty and underdevelopment in the developing countries.

This way of thinking reflected the intellectual dominance in the 1980s of neo-liberalism, an economic and political philosophy ideologically underpinning the pro-market ideology and monetarist ideas of contemporaneously influential governments, especially those of Margaret Thatcher in Britain (1979–90) and Ronald Reagan in the USA (1980–88). The concept of neo-liberalism emphasised that, developmentally, the state's role should be downgraded and diminished – while that of private capitalists and entrepreneurs should be upgraded and augmented. Under pressure from Western governments and IFIs, notably the World Bank and the IMF, many governments of developing countries were encouraged to put in place neo-liberal policies, albeit with variable success. In sum, during the 1980s, much developmental emphasis was placed on improving economic management and on allowing greater play for market forces in many developing countries.

the 1990s and early 2000s

The ideological power of neo-liberalism was at its zenith in 1989–91 when the Cold War came to an end and the Eastern European communist bloc collapsed. To some observers these interlinked developments appeared to offer spectacular evidence of the superior power of both liberal democracy and capitalism over their long-term rival, communism. For several years, these linked events provided pro-market forces with apparently unstoppable momentum, and had immense economic and socio-political impacts on numerous developing countries. In many cases, economic changes coincided with, and often helped to stimulate, a shift towards democracy.

The neo-liberal development strategy became known as the Washington consensus, a nomenclature that reflected its pre-eminence among Washington-based opinion leaders (in the US government, the IMF and World Bank). However, critics of the Washington consensus model pointed out that the studiously pro-market view seemed to overlook the fact that only governments have the power to alter prevailing socio-economic realities through the application of appropriate policies and programmes and by constructing appropriate institutions. In other words, the market is not very good at allocating resources fairly; only governments can do that, and they need a range of appropriate institutions to accomplish their goals. But whether they are able to do this or not is strongly linked to the varying amounts of pressure put on governments by competing societal interests.

When it became increasingly clear that SAPs were not the expected panacea to ameliorate developmental shortfalls, there was a shift in developmental thinking, reflected in the concerns of the 1990 *World Development Report*. The Report suggested that the best way to deal with poverty in the developing world was through a two-pronged strategy, involving: (1) promotion of labour-intensive growth through economic openness and investment in infrastructure, and (2) general provision of basic services, especially basic health and education. Over time, as the 1990s progressed, it became clear to all but the most blinkered observers that Washington consensus policies would not be the whole answer to developmental shortfalls in the developing world. This was because its measures – notably SAPs – had failed to stimulate development across the board in the ways that its proponents had claimed it would. The result was that the international development community was faced with an overall gloomy development picture, characterised in many developing countries by rising poverty and polarising inequality. As a result, at the end of the 1990s, the international community set itself the challenge of a renewed onslaught on poverty and related dimensions of human deprivation in the developing world, reflected in the United Nations' Millennium Development Goals, declared in September 2000, with a deadline of 2015 to achieve its objectives. Seven goals were announced (http://www.developmentgoals.org/):

- Eradicate extreme poverty and hunger
- Achieve universal primary education
- Promote gender equality and empower women
- Improve maternal health
- Combat HIV/AIDS, malaria, and other diseases

- Ensure environmental sustainability
- Develop a global partnership for development

At the time of completion of this book (late 2004), there was much scepticism – from both academics and development professionals – that (m)any of the goals would be achieved. In particular, there was doubt about the extent to which the richest countries – that is, the industrially developed nations – would take their proclaimed developmental role seriously, and actively seek to achieve the goals agreed by the UN in 2000.

the book's framework

The book is divided into three parts. The first part, comprising chapters 1–3, is entitled 'concepts and theories'. The second part, made up of chapters 4–11, is called 'development and domestic factors', while the third part is named 'development and globalisation', and contains chapters 12–14. Chapter 15 is the concluding chapter.

Focusing on principles and practices of development, and primarily written for second- and final-year university undergraduates, this book features up-to-date analysis and data throughout. The primary purpose is to present focused analysis of recent political, economic and social developments in the countries of the developing world – Africa, South Asia, East and South East Asia, the Middle East, and Latin America – and explain why things have turned out developmentally as they have done. In order to explain development outcomes, both domestic and international factors are examined in all chapters and, where appropriate, their interactions highlighted.

The overall aim of the book is to examine the breadth, nature, range and complementarity of some of the most pressing and topical issues that affect developing countries. Consequently, as well as theoretical and conceptual issues of development, the chapters of the book focus upon, *inter alia*: the theory and practice of globalisation (especially economic and political dimensions); economic growth and developmental consequences; democratisation and democracy; religious and ethnic competition and conflict; human and women's rights; and the socio-political impact of environmental damage. These themes and issues also exemplify two further concerns of the book: (1) defining the boundaries, and examining the concept, of 'development', and (2) examining methods deployed by the sub-discipline over time to understand economic and political developmental outcomes in the developing world.

As already suggested, the context of the book is that global trends of the last few years – notably globalisation, with its two main economic (liberalisation) and political (democratisation) foci – have affected all developing countries. We argue that no up-to-date analysis of development outcomes in the developing world can legitimately ignore the phenomenon of globalisation. However, there is often a lack of precision in specifying precisely what globalisation *is*. Having spawned innumerable conference papers, articles, book chapters and books, much interest in the concept stems from two key events that took place over a decade ago. First, the collapse of the USSR in 1991, along with the contemporaneous disintegration of the Eastern Europe communist bloc, was an epochal event whose full significance is still unfolding. Second, the demise of Europe's communist countries did not start, yet certainly encouraged, both the 'third wave of democracy' and a global trend towards economic liberalisation and demands for increased human rights, developments examined in the book.

Another important issue to emerge in recent years has been the challenge to the 'Washington consensus', a set of beliefs that dominated development thinking in the 1980s and much of the 1990s. The Washington consensus exemplified the hegemony of neo-liberal thought and rational choice assumptions in explanation and policy recommendations. From the 1990s, however, interest has grown again in institutions, both formal and informal, and their role in shaping economic and political practices, and in politics in shaping institutions. Since that time, a large amount of research has emerged from various sources including the World Bank and various independent academic researchers. The overall thrust of this research has been to raise important questions about all sorts of policies and practices and the wider implications for development. In particular, attention focused on two main topics in relation to the groups of developing countries:

- appropriate 'rules of the game' – that is, formal and informal institutions – how they can be constructed and implemented;
- conflicting sets of institutions (essentially clientelistic *versus* Weberian rule-governed bureaucratic behaviour) and how – individually and collectively – they can influence policy and practice.

The role of institutions in facilitating or retarding development is the second key theme explored in several of the book's chapters. The point is that whether we are talking about regions or gender, religion or human rights, we are necessarily interested in similar issues, concerned with questions about rules and procedures, with outcomes moulded by often unequal power relations between various – ethnic, religious, rural/urban, gender-based – groups. Consequently, to understand developmental outcomes over time within developing countries requires taking into account the characteristics of both their formal and informal institutions. Referring to *formal* political institutions, what I have in mind are the permanent edifices of public life found in virtually all states:

- laws;
- public offices;
- political society; and
- elections.

Informal institutions, on the other hand, can be conceptualised as: 'dynamics of interests and identities, domination and resistance, compromise and accommodation' (Bratton and van de Walle 1997: 276). Analytically important *informal* institutions include:

- civil society;
- historically-produced societal behaviour (political culture); and
- interactions between various interest and societal groups, including class divisions and state power.

During the third wave of democracy from the mid-1970s to mid-1990s, various informal institutions were judged to be significant for developmental outcomes in democratising countries. Attempts to establish democratic political structures and processes in new democracies – of which there were many in the developing world – marked a phase whereby a range of political and newly politicised actors searched for new, binding, democratically legitimate rules of political competition and engagement (Haynes 1997). Rueschemeyer, Stephens and Stephens (1992) argue that these kinds of relationships were pivotal in explaining developmental outcomes in various kinds of state. This is because the nature and characteristics of relationships between various groups – for example, large-scale capitalists, the bourgeoisie, the middle classes, industrial workers, landlords, and peasants – profoundly affect developmental outcomes. Put another way, a country's political trajectory – for example, towards or away from democracy – is typically influenced by various historically determined structures, often driven by particularistic chronicles of capitalist development (Cammack 1997).

the chapters

The individual chapters of this book focus – often implicitly – on the chances of achieving developmental progress of the kind envisaged in the Millennium Development Goals. In each, however, there is a focus upon:

- the analytical importance of both domestic and external actors, including those associated with the phenomenon of globalisation; and
- the importance of – both formal and informal – institutions for the achievement of development goals.

Following this introductory chapter, in chapter 2 Björn Hettne's main focus is on both the concept of, and ways to achieve, 'development'. He explains that while 'development' is an old idea, it is also an integral part of the modern project. He shows that the latter comes from the ideological tradition of seeing society as an object to be changed by rational, purposive human action, a worldview that grew strongly over time in Western Europe.

More recently, such a view was recently incorporated into 'development studies', that is, the academic field devoted to the study of the modernisation of 'underdeveloped' societies that has developed since World War II. Hettne notes that in the early phase of theory-building this incorporation took what he calls an 'essentialist' form that, he claims, was close to a form of 'fundamentalism'. Now, however, he suggests that the intellectual climate is, generally and for good reasons, more sceptical towards many manifestations of Grand Theory, including development theory. Now, he avers, we live in a postmodern era, as well as a post-development one. Nevertheless, thinking about development constitutes a rich tradition in social science, encompassing important theoretical debates as well as an ambition to reflect a global experience of societal changes in different parts of the world.

Hettne points out, however, that it is rather difficult to summarise this debate in terms of clear-cut results or a blueprint for 'development'. Consequently, his survey of thinking about development over time starts from the assumption that, in order to make sense of successive schools of development theory, we need to contextualise them historically – rather than perceive them in terms of a simple and clear linear evolution of ideas over time. His analysis extends to a discourse on development that relates chances of success to the security problems – both domestic and external – currently facing developing countries in the context of globalisation. He also stresses the importance of building appropriate political, economic and social institutions. This is a necessary focus, not least because development is rarely considered an issue by itself outside professional circles dealing with development aid. However, he contends, security is now, due to the worldwide development crisis, an integral part of the development discourse.

Theorising about development, Hettne makes a distinction between what he calls *mainstream* and *counterpoint* views. The former refers to the predominant view that focuses on both a general modernisation and, more specifically, on economic growth from either state or market perspectives. The *counterpoint* stance refers to mainly oppositional, sometimes 'anti-modern' ideas, which emanate principally from 'below', that is, from civil society organisations, and which stress the importance of informal institutions in the context of achievement of proclaimed development goals. Such ideas often refer – implicitly or explicitly – to a claimed superiority of small-scale, decentralised, ecologically sound, community-centred, human and stable models of societal development. Such ideas often struggle, however, fully to enter the development discourse, reflecting the fact that they are typically expressed by, or on behalf of, those normally excluded from the development process. In sum, these sets of ideas – mainstream and counterpoint – are contrasting positions within a particular development discourse, and carry different amounts of weight in terms of discursive power.

Turning to globalisation, Hettne suggests that the notions of *globalisation* and *chaos* are closely related, concerned with the problem of development beyond the nation-state system. For him, the key question is: 'What could be the meaning of development in a globalised world, where the nation-state is declining, and people have to act in a vacuum, where global inequalities are increasing, where "new wars" multiply, and the poverty problem in the predominant aid philosophy is contained rather than resolved?'

Hettne is sceptical about development aid, arguing that in the current era of globalisation, it has been largely reduced to a 'civil form of intervention in collapsing states and what has been called "complex humanitarian emergencies", that is, fundamental security crises'. He suggests that a way out of this dilemma is both to link policy areas in a coherent way, and to increase levels of coordination between the donor community and recipient societies. In this way, it might be possible to go from emergency aid to *global development*. The counterpoint is expressed by an emerging global civil society normally critical of globalisation in its current, market-led form (that is, 'globalism'). As Hettne points out, 'governments, as in earlier times, have to manage the social consequences of market-driven economic development, but fail to do so in a globalised condition'.

Peter Calvert focuses in chapter 3 on the state and its developmental role. He points out that, as noted above, the primary role of the state's institutions in development was under attack during much of the 1980s and 1990s. During those decades, the prevailing economic orthodoxy was the 'Washington consensus', with its intellectual and conceptual foundations in the notion that the state 'should' play only a minimal developmental role, principally to secure or ensure a 'level playing field' for private interests. Anything more than that, so the argument went, would unhelpfully distort the free working of the market and, as a result, hinder rather than help economic development. From the early 1990s, when it was formally adopted, the Washington consensus helped to guide the developmental policies of the leading IFIs, the IMF and World Bank. Over time, however, renewed discussion ensued on the central role of the state and its institutions, in both stimulating – that is, creating the conditions for – and, in policy terms, presiding over trajectories of economic development. This renewed institutional focus came about as a direct result of the fact that a group of important developmental successes – East and Southeast Asia's Newly Industrialising Countries (NICs) – had achieved developmental success via a highly significant role for the state.

It became clear during the 1990s that failure of economic development, particularly but not exclusively in sub-Saharan Africa, the world's poorest and most underdeveloped region, was not, as previously thought, the result of states being *too strong* but rather, because of the plethora of *weak* states. That is, the 'hollowing out' of the state left many governments in the developing world fatally weakened, to the point that many could no longer even successfully achieve the main economic functions, such as, 'maintaining a stable currency and guaranteeing the security of bargains in the market'. In contrast to the strong, developmental states of the Asian NICs, hollowed-out states – especially common in sub-Saharan Africa – suffer from debilitating practical weaknesses. Such weak, often fragmented, states have little or no say in shaping economic and political reforms, and find themselves subject to various external – supranational, international, and transnational – pressures over which they have little or no control. In short, it is now widely recognised that the issue of state capacity is crucial to development outcomes.

However, as Calvert also notes, all governments – whether of rich or poor countries – are now to some degree prisoners of economic forces beyond their control, most of which are linked to the controversial issue of globalisation. On the other hand, it also seems clear that democratically elected governments are generally more successful than any form of non-democratic government both in fostering economic development and maintaining its progress. Calvert concludes his survey of the role of the state in development over time by averring that, 'to be successful, a developmental state may not need to be a *democratic* state, at least initially, but it must be a *democratising* state'.

The fourth chapter is by Mehran Kamrava. Building on the themes of democracy and development and the importance of getting institutions right for developmental successes, Kamrava's chapter examines twin processes: democratic transition and consolidation. He starts with a brief definition of democracy as a kind of political system, articulating common characteristics of democratic political systems. He goes on to explain that definitions of democracy often vary, as they tend to be based on differing kinds of democratic system. This is a way of saying that not all democracies are similar in institutional make-up nor can rely upon sharing a clearly supportive political culture. Kamrava's discussion of various kinds of democratic systems leads him to examine democratic transitions in the developing world, of which there were dozens in the 1980s and 1990s, and problems of consolidating democracies, often because of institutional weaknesses. However, certain conditions are said to facilitate democratic transitions, although they can take various forms and patterns. It is important to be clear, however, that *transition* to democracy is only part of the story. The next stage, democratic *consolidation*, is a different and often more difficult-to-achieve state of affairs; it has proved very hard to bring about in numerous developing countries over time. To achieve democratic consolidation requires both development and embedding of appropriately democratic institutions. And this has proved to be a very difficult – albeit essential – step.

Kamrava details what is needed to consolidate democracy: institutional arrangements and considerations that can overcome two interrelated sets of challenges. One is economic and often arises from a specific set of ubiquitous policy prescriptions in the developing world in the 1980s and 1990s: structural adjustment programmes (SAPs). The second concern is to focus on the nature of the pacts – that is, the informal institutions – covering the relationships between outgoing, pre-transition elites and their incoming, post-transition counterparts. The overall point is that no political system, whether democratic or not, is assured of permanence; in particular, newly established democracies are often precarious. As a result, the future of democracy in the developing world is nowhere assured, while some regions – notably the Arab countries of the Middle East – have achieved little or no progress so far.

Kamrava examines the impact of globalisation on the chances of democratic consolidation in the developing world. He notes that developing countries' increasing economic integration into global markets – while sometimes strengthening emerging elements with civil society, at the same time fostering transparency and free flows of information, and encouraging increased economic and political accountability – can over time erode the staying power of authoritarian rulers. For example, certain regions in the developing world – notably, Latin America and East Asia – are more economically integrated globally than some other regions, such as the Middle East, sub-Saharan Africa or Central Asia. As a consequence, Kamrava avers, those regions evincing deeper levels of globalisation appear to correlate closely with recent shifts to democracy; in other words democratisation has gone furthest in Latin America and East Asia precisely because of those regions' openness to globalisation forces, coupled with pressures from below emanating from civil society. In the Middle East and Central Asia, on the other hand, patterns of economic development have so far neither encouraged emergence of an autonomous and powerful private sector or middle class, nor resulted in significant openings to globalisation. The result is that, on the whole, economic development in the Middle East and Central Asia has served, not as a democratisation catalyst, but instead as a hindrance and obstacle to its chances of success.

Moving from political to economic development, Gautam Sen examines in chapter 5 variable developmental outcomes over time in the regions of the developing world. He explains that the topic of development economics is actually inseparable from the study of economics itself, whose roots are traceable to the preoccupations of various classical political economists, such as Adam Smith and David Ricardo. From soon after the end of World War II, increased focus was applied to the issue of development economics, largely because of the onset of decolonisation in various parts of the developing world. This led to the emergence of numerous new countries, all of them economically 'underdeveloped'. Sen explains that the main focus of development economics is how to address the urgent task of combating poverty in emerging nations, a problem identified with the very task of nation-building itself and the importance of getting the state's institutional mix right.

Sen also explains that while the post-war record of economic progress in developing countries is uneven, there is a dramatic contrast in performance between the Asian NICs and *all* sub-Saharan African countries (with the partial exception of South Africa). Rates of economic growth in most Latin American countries fall somewhere between the two extremes; with many regional countries now enjoying higher absolute per capita incomes compared to the immediate post-war period. Overall, Sen explains, there is a significant minority of developing countries that have stagnated or suffered a decline in absolute incomes owing to a combination of negligible economic improvement and population growth. In addition, there are noticeable differences in income distribution among countries, with Asia exhibiting more egalitarian patterns than elsewhere. To explain the divergence he points not to the inequalities of the global economic system so much as to the importance of a strong, purposive state in achieving commendable development outcomes.

Sen's chapter provides a challenge to a set of interrelated approaches, disciplines and debates which comprise established IPE, with relevance beyond the global South. For him, both state-centrism and an over-emphasis on formal and legal sectors are now misplaced in terms of both analysis and prescription. It seems increasingly clear, he contends, that to achieve economic and developmental successes during an era of pronounced globalisation, what is required from developing-country governments is the achievement of 'flexible, innovative coalitions or partnerships involving a range of non-state actors'. This perspective challenges established notions, focused in a set of social science disciplines around the state and market. Sen concludes by noting that, more than before, successful, sustainable governance of the international political economy requires creative networking amongst a range of actors located variously in flexible production and outsourcing arrangements, franchise agreements and supply chains. This underpins the fact that globalisation necessitates continuous adaptation at regional, national and local levels for all developing countries.

We have already noted that the 'third wave of democracy' was an important factor in explaining the shift from authoritarian to democratic rule in many parts of the developing world in the 1980s and 1990s. It is important, however, to bear in mind that this shift to democracy was by no means uniform; many developing countries still have non-democratic governments in power, especially in the Middle East (including North Africa) and Central Asia. The most common form of non-democratic political system in the developing world is one that involves a key role for the armed forces. In chapter 6, focusing on the political role of such forces in the developing world, Robert Pinkney begins by examining the political history of armed force. He then reviews the institutional role of the armed forces over time in the context of the politics and development of the developing countries. He starts from the premise that there has been a generally important role of armed force in politics among many such countries.

From there, he moves to an examination of the various ways that military force has been wielded over time – 'by whom, why and with what consequences for the political process' – in pursuit of political goals in developing countries. Pinkney also examines ideologies and interests of those wielding military power and their impact on the direction, competence and stability of government. In this context, it is important to note the changes wrought by the end of the Cold War and the contemporaneous rise to analytical prominence of globalisation. On the issue of the political power of the armed forces in this context, Pinkney notes that now people with guns have to face a world that, at least rhetorically, demands democratic governance; consequently, he looks at the prospects for civilian political control in the developing world. It might be expected that, within this environment, processes of globalisation would push the doors of democratisation open more widely – not least because many developing countries would be expected to have less scope to resist external pressures to democratise. However, as Pinkney points out, things are not quite that simple: globalisation may reduce the importance of national frontiers, but it also facilities the easier movement of both arms and soldiers.

Jeff Haynes' focus on religion in chapter 7 works from the premise that modernisation and development failures have contributed to resurgence of religious identity in many parts of the developing world. But modernisation did not impinge upon an otherwise blank or uniform cultural and political situation; rather, the struggle to develop modern political institutions and a developed economy often conflicted with pre-modern social norms and traditions. Sometimes, but by no means invariably, religious schisms led to serious societal, political and developmental conflicts. However, Haynes notes, it is difficult accurately to predict where or when religious conflict will erupt by reference to a simple religious fragmentation model. Sometimes serious societal conflict erupts in religiously and ethnically *homogeneous* countries – such as Somalia – but not in a neighbouring state – Tanzania – with much higher apparent levels of religious and ethnic fragmentation. What seems to be important is the level of governmental skill in achieving and maintaining a fair level of social solidarity, as in India. When competence is high in this regard, then potentially serious cultural schisms can be transcended and attention paid to development issues.

Like religion, ethnic rivalry and sometimes conflict is often associated with unwelcome development outcomes in many developing countries. In chapter 8, Howard Handelman explains that, since the end of World War II, most notably in sub-Saharan Africa, South and Central Asia, and the Middle East, ethnic strife, more so than class conflict or other types of social cleavage, has been the major source of political friction and violence. Although accurate data is understandably hard to come by, Handelman estimates that since the end of World War II, 60 years go, ethnic conflict has resulted in the deaths of around 20 million people in the developing world. Most of those killed lived in Asia (especially, Afghanistan, India, Indonesia, Sri Lanka, Iraq and Turkey) and sub-Saharan Africa (notably, Angola, the Democratic Republic of Congo (formerly Zaïre), Ethiopia, Mozambique, Nigeria, Rwanda and Sudan).

Handelman explains that there was a surge in ethnic bloodshed in the 1970s and 1980s, and many observers believed at the time that ethnic hostilities would continue to grow. This prediction, however, turned out to be ill-founded, as the level of ethnic protests and rebellion in the world declined from the early 1990s, after rising steadily during the previous half century. On the other hand, Handelman notes that it is highly likely that ethnic conflict in parts of the developing world will continue to be a factor in political and economic development outcomes for the foreseeable future. To what extent is globalisation a significant factor in this regard? Handelman suggests that to reduce the amount of ethnic conflict it would be necessary to deal with both external *and* internal factors:

- more mature political leadership;
- stronger national political institutions; and
- enhanced mechanisms for international peacekeeping through the United Nations and other multinational, including regional organisations.

Only with these factors in place might we expect to see maintenance or even acceleration of the recent trend toward reduced ethic hostilities in the developing world.

In chapter 9, turning to the issue of development and the natural environment, Pauline Eadie and Lloyd Pettiford focus upon the effects of economic development on the natural environment in the developing world. They explain that looking at the relationship between the natural environment and economic development in the developing world reveals a truly complex and fascinating picture. Environmental outcomes, they explain, increasingly reflect the impact and interaction of both domestic and external factors. In this regard, they note not only forces associated with economic globalisation, such as multinational corporations, but also the impact of powerful international IFIs, including the International Monetary Fund and the World Bank. But this does not imply that states in developing countries are powerless to affect environmental outcomes in their territories.

Eadie and Pettiford point out that there are two key institutional issues to take into account when thinking about environmental issues and development outcomes. On the one hand, there is a school of thought that suggests that developing countries are in effect victims left with no choice but to despoil their environment in a desperate bid to win a game whose rules have been determined by someone else. On the other hand, significant local factors – such as population policy, institutional effectiveness, and levels of corruption – are also analytically pertinent, as they have important effects on environmental and developmental outcomes.

They argue that the current relationship between the natural environment and development looks in many developing countries particularly problematic. On the other hand, they also stress that the issue is not clear cut. This is not least because the effects of increasing resource use on a finite planet will almost certainly 'boomerang' back on humanity for ever. Those states currently without political power may be seen to hold environmental trump cards. Eadie and Pettiford suggest that this is partly because efforts to take these trump cards away or prevent them being played will undoubtedly be made by rich and powerful international forces. On the other hand, currently triumphal capitalism may eventually be compelled to accept that its historical externalizing of the environment is highly problematic; and this may eventually lead to more meaningful strategies of reform and intervention, and ultimately possibly even radical solutions to environmental problems. However, if this happens it seems that radical solutions are more likely to come through necessity (due to harsh environmental conditions) than through the planned creation of a better society. It is not a reassuring scenario.

Like the natural environment, human rights are another key issue area to focus upon when assessing development outcomes in the developing world. In chapter 10, James Chiriyankandath explains that since the end of the ideological standoff that characterised the Cold War, like the environment human rights has become one the chief themes of international discourse. Yet this has not (yet) resulted in great advances in the realisation of rights, certainly in the developing world. He contends that this is primarily because human rights remain contested and the terrain on which they have to be realised is extremely uneven. In addition, he explains, the language of rights continues to be used by states more to justify their practices rather than determine their actions. He gives as an example the fact that powerful western states may well use the issue of human rights as a way to express criticism of some developing countries while at the same time be apparently willing to accept human rights 'abuses' among their allies in the developing world.

But this is not to suggest that the West has had things all its own way. In recent years, some developing countries have sought to develop alternative, allegedly more culturally appropriate, conceptions of human rights. For example, during the 1990s governments of some East Asian states collectively promoted the notion of distinctive 'Asian values' to try to discredit western criticism of their record on human rights and political freedoms.

Chiriyankandath's chapter starts with a brief review of the evolution of the modern western conception of human rights. He goes on to consider the spread, manly via the United Nations system, of a global conception of human rights after World War II, which impacted upon the growing number of developing countries. He also traces and explains the debate about the problems of cultural relativism. In relation to globalisation, Chiriyankandath's chapter considers the rise of humanitarian interventionism in the post-Cold War era, as well as the scope for the incremental strengthening of human rights in the developing world via national non-governmental organisations and state and regional institutions.

Moving from human rights in general to those concerning females in particular, in chapter 11 Shirin Rai outlines key feminist interventions in the debates on development. She suggests that these interventions collectively broaden understanding of the practical and strategic needs of both women and men in different contexts. The feminist engagements with theoretical debates and development policy-making structures have over time helped to secure a valuable and critical space for women within various development projects. She adds, however, that these interventions worked and largely continue to work within the liberal framework, and that this makes certain strategies of empowerment of women feasible, while at the same time closing off other alternative spaces.

Rai argues that a focus on power relations within any socio-economic system must address not only issues of empowerment for women, but also the power relations within which both men and women work and live. She contends that feminist movements have achieved a great deal: not only politicising gender within countries, but also within the international system more generally. For Rai, this is an important achievement that has had practical ramifications. For example, the World Bank now explicitly proclaims gender to be an important developmental issue. She notes that this has changed the Bank's developmental emphasis, in turn reflecting over time sustained pressure from a variety of women's organisations, both domestically and internationally based. Their combined pressure served to put the Bank in a difficult position, while encouraging it to engage fully in the gender debate and the role of women in development. Moreover, in the 1990s, gender inequality became an important issue for assessing human development – and this was directly linked to pressure exerted from domestic, regional and international sources, notably the women's movement. Rai concludes however by suggesting that talk of apparent progress in relation to gender and development should come with 'health warnings'. This is because changes in project funding and even perhaps some new, admittedly important, policy initiatives, do not necessarily make for necessary paradigmatic shifts in neo-liberal economic thinking that feminist economists have long been demanding.

The third part of the book is explicitly concerned with the implications of globalisation for development outcomes. In chapter 12, Tim Shaw discusses the evolution of the global political economy after World War II and the implications for development outcomes in the developing world. He explains that to a significant degree the development chances of many developing countries – especially in sub-Saharan Africa, the key focus of his chapter – are integrally linked both to the international economic positions that such states inherited at independence and to what state institutions have done since then to try to improve things developmentally. In recent years the issue has become increasingly contextualised by the issue of globalisation.

Shaw suggests that contemporary policy responses in relation to development increasingly entail attempts to try to transcend orthodox assumptions still prevalent in established disciplines and even interdisciplinary fields such as development or security studies. The implication is that institutional policy responses at all levels – both from state and non-state actors – necessarily need to be creative in a world that comprises not only nearly 200 states, but also countless competing companies, regions and sectors. Shaw concludes by highlighting that development outcomes for the developing countries must take into account the notion of what is now a *global* political economy, informed and influenced by, *inter alia*, corporate codes, innovative partnerships, economic causes of conflict, and informal and illegal sectors.

In chapter 13, Ian Taylor examines the impact of various manifestations of globalisation on the development chances of the developing world. He argues that what is needed to enhance development outcomes is an alternative vision regarding global development. This would necessarily not only question deeply the nature of the inequitable global trading system but also fundamentally rethink aspects of its rules-based regime in order to benefit the least developed countries and the poorest people. In other words, Taylor avers, a thorough overhaul of the international financial system is a necessary prerequisite if the South as a whole is even to begin to pursue and achieve development. This is because in a world characterised by increasingly 'footloose' capital, it seems impossible for most developing states to acquire the necessary capacity to make rational long-term use of national resources for developmental ends. In addition, the current high levels of subsidies for agricultural producers in the North should be addressed – because these structures not only effectively close off the North's markets to African and other developing countries' exports, but also as a result help block strategies for rural poverty alleviation.

Taylor concludes by arguing that the reformist and essentially neo-liberal line inherent in the overall message emanating from the South, part and parcel of the current globalisation discourse, is deficient as it neglects major structural issues in the global economy. Consequently, it is very likely to be counter-productive. The point is that it is simply inadequate developmentally to predicate such calls around 'growth' alone – and hope that, as a result, development will somehow occur. Thus the reformism that informs most of the intercourse of the developing world with the North is almost certain to fail to address developmental aspirations. This is because it fails to advance any concrete agenda regarding the asymmetric power relations between North and South. This inequality, Taylor reminds us, is a – if not, *the* – main cause of *maldevelopment*, a huge obstacle for the success of developmental projects. In this sense, globalisation – a concept that Taylor defines as 'the political and economic reconfiguration of power on a global scale' – is having a clear impact on the developmental opportunities of the South. The problem however is that as long as the rulers of developing countries remain wedded to the twin hegemonies of neo-liberalism and the globalisation discourse of 'no alternative', then the lack of new ideas regarding development and global transformation are inherently linked to a necessarily limited and short-term reformist vision. Taylor notes that this state of affairs is most unlikely to question fundamentally the current economic and political relations that characterise an increasingly unequal world and, as a result, will perpetuate the crisis of development under conditions of neo-liberal globalisation.

The contemporary rise of both regionalism and regionalisation is often said to be a key manifestation of globalisation. In chapter 14, Kato Lambrechts and Chris Alden use the terms regionalism and regionalisation respectively to describe (1) the political project of building a community of states and the regional expression of global processes of integration, and (2) changing structures of production and power in a given geographic area. They explain that, historically, these processes have exercised enormous influence over the strategies adopted by developing countries to extricate themselves from their relative weakness in the international trade, political and production system and from the cycle of poverty that has, in most cases, formed a key facet of their post-colonial inheritance.

To contextualise the domestic, regional and global factors that have influenced these twin processes, Lambrechts and Alden's chapter maps out key theories of regionalism and regionalisation, and discusses their impact on developing countries' policies in relation in particular to Latin America, South East Asia and sub-Saharan Africa. They explain that these theories serve as key analytical tools that are necessary to comprehend motives for region-building among developing countries, as well as difficulties that they uniformly face in seeking to achieve closer cooperation.

Lambrechts and Alden conclude that regionalism – theoretically, a demonstrably successful strategy for promoting economic development and political independence among developing countries – often remains in many respects an elusive goal. Examining the record over time, Lambrechts and Alden contend that it may be that attainment of the kind of development aims characterising regionalism are fundamentally compromised by – perhaps even incompatible with – the requirements of the political aspects of the project. It also appears that, linked to the onset of rapid globalisation and the concurrent adoption of the tenets of neo-liberalism as a global standard by the IFIs, aid donors and most developing countries, the 'nationalist impulse underlying many regional projects has been subsumed within the framework of variants on open regionalism'. In addition, most developing countries have experienced tremendous socio-economic, and often political, changes since independence. This has led to an unprecedented diversification of development amongst what was, at least roughly, once a relatively homogeneous grouping. Nevertheless, repositioning and reassessment of the costs and benefits of cooperation – both with other developing countries and across the North–South divide – appears to be a rational response by many developing countries as they seek to confront challenges posed by globalisation.

Finally, in chapter 15, the book's concluding chapter, Jeff Haynes summarises the main themes of the foregoing chapters, and suggests possible future development trends among developing countries.

2
discourses on development
bjÖrn hettne

introduction

Development is an old idea, but nevertheless an integral part of the modern project, that is, the ideological tradition of seeing society as an object to be changed by rational, purposive human action, a worldview that grew particularly strongly in Europe. This view was more recently incorporated in development studies, the academic field devoted to the modernisation of 'underdeveloped' societies. This incorporation took an essentialist form, in the early phase of theory-building close to fundamentalism. Today the intellectual climate is, for good reasons, more sceptical towards Grand Theory in general, and perhaps development theory and social engineering in particular. We are said to live not only in a postmodern era, but also a post-development one. Nevertheless, thinking about development constitutes a rich tradition in social science, encompassing important theoretical debates as well as an ambition to reflect a global experience of societal changes in different corners of the world. It is, however, difficult to summarise this debate in terms of clear-cut results or a blueprint for 'development'. This overview therefore rests on the assumption that, in order to make sense of successive schools of development theory, it should be historically contextualised rather than understood as a linear evolution of ideas. Furthermore, the discourses on development are here also related to security problems; not least because development is rarely considered an issue by itself outside professional circles dealing with development aid. From being more indirectly linked, security is now, due to the worldwide development crisis, an integral part of the development discourse (Senghaas 2002). The security problem can also only be understood contextually. Hence, our focus is on successive discourses, where there are continuities as well as discontinuities.

First, some conceptual clarifications. By *discourse* we simply mean the broader academic and public debate on an issue, in this case the problem of 'development' and 'underdevelopment', a debate reflecting a particular historical context. The discourse is delimited through an official, politically-recognised agenda with a generally accepted understanding among theoreticians as well as practitioners of what the debate is all about and, thus, what can be excluded as being of no relevance. This is what makes control over discourses a dimension of power.

Turning to theorising on *development*, a distinction is made between *mainstream* and *counterpoint*, the former referring to the predominant view, focusing on modernisation and economic growth from either a state or a market perspective. The latter refers to certain oppositional, sometimes 'anti-modern' ideas from 'civil society', typically arguing for an inherent superiority of small-scale, decentralised, ecologically sound, community-centred, human and stable models of societal development. Often such ideas, struggling to enter the discourse, are expressed by, or rather on behalf of, those who are being excluded from the development process. However, equally often these ideas may represent nostalgia for lost privileges. Mainstream and counterpoint are thus (in a dialectical sense) contrasting positions within a particular development discourse and carry different weight in terms of discursive power. However, counterpoint ideas may modify the mainstream through co-option and remind us that modernisation was not automatic, and far from uncontested.

Finally, by *security*, I mean a reasonable level of predictability at different levels of the social system, from local communities to the global level. It includes change but not chaos. It can be seen as the opposite of durable disorder. *World order* refers to the rules of the game in which development, including trade and investment, takes place internationally. These rules increasingly include the issue of intervention by force in countries suffering a security crisis (humanitarian emergencies), often closely associated with development crises.

Let me also introduce two historical perspectives applied in this analysis that have a bearing on the meanings of development. The first is that the current world order is in transition from a Westphalian international system, which originated in Europe in the first part of the 17th century. This was a 'messy' period in European history, due to the fact that one political order was dying while a new was about to be born. This also resembles today's situation. Ultimately, from the 17th century a new political order grew out of the king's power, and led to the sovereign, territorial state, which in turn implied the end of local power centres as well as the end of continental, all-European political and economic structures. A complex multi-level order was thereby grossly simplified. The state ultimately became responsible for what came to be called development, and the nation-state territory became the privileged area in which development was to take place and welfare to be created.

The pendulum between centralism and decentralism did not disappear in the new system of Westphalia, in spite of the fact that its logic was based on anti-hegemonic principles and, if necessary, anti-hegemonic struggle. Throughout European history there have been several efforts to create hegemony or dominion, provoking anti-hegemonic wars. These hegemonic attempts have come from the once dominant nations, France and Germany; whereas England and Holland have been guardians of the principle of balance of power (Watson 1992). Marked by inter-state competition, the international system created a 'modernisation imperative'. Now, however, this system is changing towards either a neo-Westphalian or a post-Westphalian system, depending on how strong the transnational institutions are allowed to become (Hettne and Odén 2002). Consequently the meaning of development is also changing.

The second historic perspective applied here is that associated with Karl Polanyi and his theory of economic history. This is informed by an expansion and deepening of the market, followed by a political intervention in defence of society. The expansion of the market marks the first, and the societal response, the second movement. It is important to note that political forces and actors engineer both processes, albeit through different dynamics. The 'first movement' contains an institutionalisation of market exchange on a larger scale than before, which implies both a widening (in terms of scope) and a deepening (in terms of production factors) of the market mechanism. The 'second movement' contains all kinds of counter-movements caused by the dislocations and disturbances (disorder) associated with market penetration into new areas. As Polanyi (2002 [1957]) put it, society defends itself, and the way to organise this defence is ultimately through political intervention by the state. The development problem is quite different in the first and the second movement. The critical and alternative perspectives (the counterpoint) become more prominent in the second movement as the limitations of mainstream development became evident.

The specific historical point of departure is the 'development problem' in the context of capitalist development and mercantilist nation-building, more particularly the economic and military rivalry among sovereign territorial states in 19th-century Europe. This competitive context shaped the development problem in the first discourse, *development and power*, which was concerned with the problem of uneven development and 'backwardness' among sovereign states in a competitive states-system, and the resulting security implications for individual countries as well as for the international system as a whole. The balance of power which was established stimulated both national and international market expansion, industrialisation and, subsequently, welfare. The counterpoint was expressed by social groups that resented economic and political centralisation undermining their earlier autonomy.

The second discourse, *the geopolitics of poverty,* started after World War II. It concerned global poverty and 'underdevelopment', as a threat to the post-war world order in the context of the emerging Cold War and US hegemony. The development issue was now subsumed under altogether different security concerns: the struggle for power between the superpowers (the USA and the Soviet Union) and, at the same time, competition between two different socio-economic systems. This facilitated a 'great compromise' between national regulation and international free trade. None of the theories specifically addressing the problem of underdevelopment constituting the second discourse proved to be of much instrumental value for development in the poor areas of the world even if they provided a conceptual framework within which this relative failure could be explained. They were ultimately replaced by orthodox forms of modernisation, expressed in the policy of *structural adjustment,* a 'purified' modernisation paradigm of 'disciplined' economic development. The counterpoint position can best be described as a merger of leftist and environmentalist ideas but with inspiration from earlier counterpoint positions.

The third discourse, *globalisation and chaos,* the current one, is concerned with the problem of development beyond the nation-state system. The key question is: What could be the meaning of development in a globalised world, where the nation-state is declining, and people have to act in a vacuum, where global inequalities are increasing, where 'new wars' multiply, and the poverty problem in the predominant aid philosophy is contained rather than resolved? Development aid has here been reduced to a civil form of intervention in collapsing states and what has been called 'complex humanitarian emergencies', that is, fundamental security crises. One way out of this dilemma has been to link policy areas in a coherent way and to increase the level of coordination both from the donor community and the recipient societies. This is one way to go from emergency aid to *global development.* The counterpoint is expressed by an emerging global civil society that is normally critical of globalisation in its current, market-led form (that is, 'globalism'). Governments, as in earlier times, have to manage the social consequences of market-driven economic development, but fail to do so in a globalised condition.

In concluding this overview, an effort is made to define global development as an improvement in the quality of international relations by means of new political institutions, and as an issue to be studied through global social theory, rather than development theory. This could turn out to be the fourth development discourse. In what follows these discourses will be described in greater detail.

The chapter is concerned with the following key issues:

- To make sense of successive schools of development theory, they should be historically contextualized rather than understood as a linear evolution of ideas;
- Development as a security issue; and
- Distinctions between *mainstream* and *counterpoint* theories of development.

To do this, the chapter focuses on four discourses:

- The first discourse: *Development as power*;
- The second discourse: *The geopolitics of poverty*;
- The third, and current discourse: *Globalisation and chaos*, concerned with the problem of development beyond the nation-state system;
- The emerging fourth discourse: *Towards global development?*

the first discourse: development as power

A convenient starting-point for analysing the European development experience, on which development theory was founded, is the emergence of nation-states and the international system that, initially, they constituted. The predominant approach to international relations – that is, to consider the international system as a form of 'anarchy' – took shape during the 'modern' phase in European history, which, as mentioned above, started with the peace of Westphalia (1648), following a 30 years' war (Tilly 1975). Thus began the 'Westphalian era' of territorial, sovereign states, a period of state-formation and mercantilist nation-building during which 'development' became a 'national interest', even an imperative for state survival. The major threat was that of peripheralisation.

The discourses are not unrelated to each other. Today the paradigm for development is the neo-liberal orthodoxy and the belief in the unrestricted market. The roots of this way of thinking can be found in the doctrine of harmony of interests, expressed in its classical form by Adam Smith in his *The Wealth of Nations*. The European development experience is, nevertheless, largely mercantilistic (Senghaas 1985). Few European countries actually developed in accordance with the way the World Bank and the International Monetary Fund (IMF) now recommend underdeveloped countries to develop (Hettne 1993). In the 19th century there emerged a sharp development differential due to the industrial revolution in England, which made this particular country 'the workshop of the world'. The 'development problem' was then 'industrialise or perish', a dilemma most authoritatively formulated by the German economist Friedrich List, who therefore can be called the 'father' of development economics (Senghaas 1985), in opposition to the British (Ricardian) theory of comparative advantage and free trade. In order to challenge the dominant industrial power, protectionism and support for 'infant industries' was needed, according to the Listian theory of how to 'catch up' with the strong powers.

Peace, understood as 'absence of war', was synonymous with a balance of power, focusing on military security at the level of the state. Internal conflicts were related to the process of nation-building, which implied the imposition of a uniform order upon heterogeneous local communities. Other internal conflicts, for instance food and tax riots, were related to the deepening of the market system to include all factors of production, thus reducing social security embedded in the 'traditional' social structure.

Development in an anarchical system implied a strengthening of the material base of the state through industrialisation, a process remarkably similar from one (successful) country to another, and reinforced by the security interests of the ruling elite. In the mainstream model, there is consequently potential conflict, primarily between competing states within the inter-state system, and, secondly, between state power, on the one hand, and restive, unassimilated social and ethnic groups challenging the legitimacy of the state, on the other. The concept of the nation-building project is a key to understanding what mainstream development (the modernisation imperative) essentially came to be about. Similarities in the pattern of economic development did not reveal inherent tendencies in history towards 'modernity' but rather security imperatives for the emerging states, making industrialisation necessary simply for military reasons. To this should be added that the 'expansion of Europe', which also became an 'expansion of international society' (Bull and Watson 1984; Watson 1992), was a competitive process, involving a number of core states struggling for hegemony, with crucial repercussions in the rest of the world, subsequently divided into colonial empires. In a global perspective the first discourse thus coincides with the era of colonialism in Asia and Africa and neo-colonialism in Latin America. This is the historical background to the second discourse.

The state-building process in Europe was violent; therefore, people gradually learned to conceive 'their' state as protector, and the rest of the world as a threat. The realist logic was born. Similarly, the Soviet state was consolidated by war against both internal and external enemies. This was the modernisation imperative as it appeared to the Russian revolutionaries and it led to an extreme variant of the modern project. The emergence of the Soviet system was the result, and implied the division of the world into two hostile blocs, two socio-economic systems and two development ideologies.

Another important factor in development thinking is the crisis in capitalist development manifested in the Great Depression of the 1930s, which provoked the ideological radicalism implied in the second movement. Interventionism therefore also became part of the mainstream, and as such it formed part of the received wisdom from the first to the second discourse.

There was, however, also a conscious anti-modernist debate about *not* 'catching up' or imitating, since industrialisation implied the sacrifice of values inherent in 'traditional society', a position taken for instance by the Russian 'narodniks' or 'populists' (Kitching 1982) and representing the counterpoint in the debate on development (Hettne 1995). For the classical sociologists, the transition from *Gemeinschaft* (community) to *Gesellschaft* (industrial civilisation) was taken to be painful for the individual. To Karl Marx alienation was a necessary consequence of the capitalist mode of production. Max Weber pointed out that the irreversible rationalisation of modern society made it dull and unbearable because it lost its 'charm' (*Entzauberung*). Anarchists and utopian socialists looked for more or less radical solutions to the anomie created by the new industrial order, but the most articulate position was represented by the *narodniks*, or Russian populists (Walicki 1969). The *narodniks* argued against industrialism as a large scale and centralised form of production and for similar reasons they were also against the state as a centralised political institution. However, the political weakness of this position can be seen in relation to the crucial link between industrialisation and conventional (military) security in the first discourse: 'industrialise or perish'.

the second discourse: the geopolitics of poverty

The second development discourse emerged with the bipolar post-war order after 1945. This was characterised by a global security complex involving not only competition between two political and socio-economic systems, but also by a nuclear 'terror balance' that served to rule out war between major powers. At the same time it imposed a straitjacket on the other regions of the world, artificially divided according to the bipolar logic. Thus, all conflicts were interpreted in Cold War terms. This was an hierarchical world order of centres and peripheries, which together with bipolarity shaped the general pattern of conflict.

This new conflict pattern also shaped the post-colonial world, described by President Truman of the USA in his often quoted 'Four Points' inauguration speech of 1949. He referred to the 'underdeveloped areas' of 'hunger, misery and despair' that, Truman said, constituted a potential threat to what was to be called the 'free world' (Rist 1997). For great powers this was always the main rationale behind development aid, whereas the smaller and more neutral countries could afford to develop a more extravagant 'Third Worldist' position.

Also on the economic front new wars were avoided through what Ruggie (1998: 72), has termed the 'compromise of embedded liberalism'. Such a *great compromise*, which can be defined as a political deal between opposing forces that define a particular world order, has significant structural implications. Most importantly, it was a compromise between economic liberty and free trade outside the nation-state, and economic regulation for the purpose of full employment and social peace inside. This was the ideology of Keynesianism rooted in the years of economic depression. The result in terms of economic growth was dramatic. Thus the second discourse coincided with what both Hobsbawm (1994: 8) and Ruggie (1998: 77) refer to as the 'Golden Age'.

In the Cold War both superpowers defined security in terms of bloc stability, which had the effect of drastically limiting the principle of sovereignty, particularly for the decolonised 'Third World' or 'developing countries'. The latter responded, first, with their little-appreciated Non-Aligned Movement (NAM) and, subsequently, in the 1970s, with equally futile demands for a New International Economic Order (NIEO).

In the post-colonial era (that is, the post-1950s), state-building became a global process, and the nation-state a universal political phenomenon. In this particular respect the second discourse was a generalisation of the first. The anti-systemic guerilla struggle, often ethno-national but labelled 'communist insurgency' by the West, was the typical form of war during this period, particularly in Africa and Latin America. But there were also inter-state tensions, for instance in East Asia, South Asia and the Middle East. Here we find rivalries and occasional wars which can be related to balance-of-power politics, regional security complexes, reminiscent of the 19th-century European states system. These tensions had a clear impact on the development discourse, pushing the countries towards mainstream approaches, by focusing on modernisation and industrialisation, and therefore marginalising counterpoint positions in development thinking which might have benfited rural areas and ethnic minorities.

The reconstruction of Europe after the World War II provided the model for state-directed *modernisation* of the 'new nations'. Development economics of an interventionist kind, inspired by Keynesian theory and experiences from the Great Depression of the 1930s, was the core of this paradigm. Its counterpart was in the so-called 'non-capitalist development' or 'socialist-oriented' strategy of the rival Soviet bloc. This strategy played down the need for revolutions and gave heavy industry the role of the leading sector. Development was seen in an evolutionary perspective, and the state of underdevelopment was defined in terms of observable economic, political, social and cultural differences between rich and poor nations. Development implied the bridging of these gaps by means of an imitative process, in which the less-developed countries would gradually assume the qualities of the industrialised nations through an active interventionist state. This was the art of nation-building inherent in the modernisation paradigm.

The neo-colonial implications of this model led to the rise of the *dependency paradigm*, reflecting the subordinate economic position of the non-European areas in the world system as well as the limited political sovereignty implied in bipolar domination. In this perspective there were within a given structure certain positions which regularly and more or less automatically accumulated material and non-material resources, whereas other positions were deprived of these resources. Development for one unit could therefore lead to underdevelopment for another, depending on how the two units were structurally linked. Poverty was seen as a structure rather than as a particular stage (backwardness) as in the first discourse.

These rival mainstream approaches, which dominated the debate in the 1970s, were in turn challenged by the counterpoint, or 'alternative' theoretical positions, grounded in environmentalism, endogenous and indigenous development, eco-development, ethno-development, human development, feminist theorising, and the like. Its main concern was the many problems created by mainstream development, as well as with those social groups and classes excluded from development. *Another Development* was defined as need-oriented, endogenous, self-reliant, ecologically sound and based on structural transformation (Nerfin 1977).

The ideas can be summed up and reformulated in the three principles of territorial development, ecological sustainability, and cultural pluralism (Hettne 1995). They can also generally be described as 'the voices of the excluded'. The 'green' ideology (as it was termed in the North) can be seen as a modern synthesis of neo-populist and neo-anarchist ideas, revived in the 1960s and forming part of the New Left movement in the USA and in Europe. Later they merged with ecology, peace and feminist movements both in the North and in the South. These ideas bear a certain resemblance to the classical populism and anarchism in urging for community (*Gemeinschaft*) and in their distaste of industrial civilisation (*Gesellschaft*).

The development theories, mainstream or counterpoint, associated with political interventionism were more or less unsuccessful, except for a handful of 'developmental states' in East and South East Asia. These states more or less closely followed the recommendation to 'catch up' developmentally (rather inspired by the First Discourse), and supported by the West for geopolitical reasons. Elsewhere state intervention was more politically motivated and legitimised through the ideals of welfarism in the West. However, many countries indulged in overspending which soon led them into financial crises and towards accepting economic and political conditionalities, ultimately following from this dead end. Forced by these conditionalities, the developing countries gradually began to open up. In the Soviet bloc '*perestroika*' was introduced in 1985, enforcing the general process of liberalisation. The discourse (according to some even 'history') came to a close. Since radical development theories proved to be of limited instrumental value for development, the failure led to a 'crisis' or 'impasse' in development theorising (Shuurman 1993).

Through what was called a 'counter-revolution' in development economics, which took up momentum in the early 1980s (Toye 1987), the non-interventionist, anti-Keynesian, neo-classical approach, at first associated with 'Thatcherism' and 'Reaganomics', became predominant, paving way for structural adjustment programmes (SAPs; with or without a human face) and privatisation, orchestrated by the Bretton Woods institutions. In this way the domestic bases for continued globalisation were created and secured. This marked the end of the Great Compromise and the Golden Age and the beginning of the Washington Consensus.

The counter-revolution was partly ideology, partly a resurgence of realism, particularly as far as political realities in many 'Third World' countries were concerned. It is undeniable that many politicians and 'rent-seeking' bureaucrats were enriching themselves rather than developing their countries, thereby becoming 'development obstacles'.

The SAPs were therefore a useful, but far from sufficient, means to achieve sustained economic growth, and in many cases they were actually a 'prelude to systemic crisis' (Duffield 1998, 2001) and an end to genuine nation-building.

Development policy thus formed an integral part of the nation-building project in the second discourse, which can be seen as a legacy from the first discourse with its strong focus on the tasks of European state formation. By the creation and productive use of the welfare state the idea was to achieve an integrated and consolidated nation-state, with a sufficient degree of legitimacy. In many developing countries, movement towards internal coherence was interrupted, and neither the investment nor the welfare funds could be maintained. Instead many of these countries became increasingly militarised, with large sums spent on 'security' for the political elite, paving way for the collapse of both state and civil society – and subsequent chaos or disorder.

the third discourse: globalisation and disorder

Globalisation is sometimes said to be the current form of development. However, there is no consensus on what we mean by that concept. What is certain is that it will have a great impact on development and the development discourse. The literature on globalisation has (by Held et al. 1999) been divided into three categories: hyperglobalisers, sceptics and transformationalists. The former believe that we live already in a global economy, a thesis that sceptics reject as a myth.

The transformationist thesis is that all states and societies are going through a profound transformation as they adapt to a globalising world. Globalism or 'global adjustment', the current hegemonic development paradigm, implies as its ideological core the growth of a world market, increasingly penetrating and dominating 'national' economies. Since this process is synonymous to increased efficiency and a higher 'world product', globalists consider 'too much government' as a systemic fault. Good governance is consequently often defined as less government. Thus, the current ideology of globalism argues in favour of a particular form of globalisation, namely neo-liberal economic globalisation. It is a simplification, however, to identify globalisation with neo-liberalism. Other political contents should in principle be possible. There is a struggle for the political content of globalisation. Stronger regions would, for example, shape the form and content of globalisation in different ways, depending on the political trends in the respective regions.

The purpose of political order, according to the globalist vision, is to facilitate the free movement of economic factors. This is seen not only as a natural but also as the most beneficial condition for development and welfare. Any attempt to isolate oneself from market forces is, according to the liberal view, a sentence to stagnation for a country or even a region. The optimum size of an economy (and therefore its ultimate form) is the world market. All other arrangements, for instance regional trade agreements, are only second best, but acceptable to the extent that they are stepping stones rather than stumbling blocks to the world market.

---

box 2.1   globalisation and the market

Contemporary globalisation (Held et al. 1999) can be seen as a further deepening of the market system, which (including its disturbing social repercussions) is now taking place on a truly global scale. We should not expect a uniform response to this 'great transformation', but, as history shows, many forms of adaptation and resistance. So far the globalist (neo-liberal) hegemony has been powerful. Highly contrasting political forces converge on the same neo-liberal economic policies. It is not much of an exaggeration to say that, whereas a five-year plan was a must for a developing country expecting to receive international assistance in the second discourse, it would in the third discourse have disqualified that country from receiving aid.

In accepting the neo-liberal ideology of globalism the state becomes the disciplining spokesman of external economic forces, rather than the protector of society against these forces, which was the classical task of nation-building, culminating in the modern welfare state. The retreat of the state from these historical functions also implies a changed relationship between the state and civil society (civil society is the totality of citizens' organizations engaged in a range of broadly social and/or political pursuits) (Tester 1992; Chandhoke 1995) and, in particular, a tendency for the state to become alienated from civil society. Inclusion as well as exclusion are inherent in the networking process implied in globalisation, and benefits occurring in one place are negatively balanced by misery and violence in another. Particularly in the South, there is an ongoing informalisation of the economy and fragmentation of society. The fundamental problem with globalisation is the selectivity of the process. Not everybody is invited to join. The exclusivist implications lead to 'politics of identity', as loyalties are being transferred from civil society to 'primary groups' (defined as the smallest 'we-group' in a particular social context), competing for scarce resources in growing development crises.

Development, as a crucial part of modernity, was traditionally seen as a rational progressive process organised by the state. The idea that the world is instead moving into global chaos (Sadowski 1998) has been forcefully presented by a school of thought represented by Robert Kaplan (1994) and Samuel Huntington (1993). Others apply a theory of chaos borrowed from science, which seems to imply that the social system can be made to move in unforeseeable directions through minor changes occurring anywhere in the system. A related postmodern line of reasoning acknowledges the fact that globalisation has undermined the nation-state order, but tries to identify some sort of logic in this seemingly turbulent situation in which domestic chaos can go on for decades, thus no longer being abnormal. Conventional view has it that disintegration of the state implies non-development, but some studies of 'real' substantive economies suggest a more complex picture of emerging 'local' (or rather 'glocalised') economies, delinked from state control, run by a new type of entrepreneur, supported by private military protection, and drawing on international connections (Chabal and Daloz 1999). All this is possible, since the state is becoming unable to legally define and protect various assets and resources situated within the 'national' territory (Duffield 1998).

The postmodern global condition is often described (and celebrated) by the key concept *difference*. The turbulence following from globalisation gives rise to different forms of state: fundamentalist, 'ethnocratic', warlord, militarised, microstates. The emphasis on contextualisation underlines not only historical but also geographical differences. Each region in fact deserves its own framework. The crisis for the African nation-state, the problem of 'failed states', would perhaps have occurred without the impact of globalisation, simply owing to inherent difficulties in the nation-building project; but when it happens it happens in a context of ideological globalism, firmly pushing for minimal government. The poor who do not dominate the state, or the not-so-poor who face the end of patronage, rely on collective identities which not only enhance solidarity within the group but can create hatred towards outsiders. Those who can't control the state turn to 'warlord politics' (Reno 1998). There is sometimes little difference between the old 'kleptocratic' state bureaucracy and the new militarised entrepreneurs. Elsewhere one can still discern a difference between the conventional nation-state strategy of maintaining sovereign rule over the national territory and local strategies of reserving local assets for local entrepreneurs disregarding claims from the official, but no longer de facto existing, nation-state.

In contrast to the point made above regarding the second discourse, the rival political projects in the third discourse are no longer necessarily nation-state projects. It is nevertheless interesting to note that the new entrepreneurs rationalise their behaviour in accordance with the hegemonic economic ideology. Liberalisation and privatisation are really on the agenda. Neo-liberalism and warlordism thus seem to travel well together. Thus the description of such situations as state disintegration, 'black holes', and 'failed states' is somewhat simplified. It is not the state that disappears. It is everything else that changes. A new political economy is emerging, both local and global at the same time.

Even if 'new wars' are usually defined as 'internal', the new situation is actually characterised by the erosion of the external–internal distinction. As a state is dissolved, most clearly in the case of Zaïre (now the Democratic Republic of Congo), it can no longer be territorially defined, and occasionally neighbouring states are drawn into clashes among themselves, underlining the increasingly irrelevant distinction between 'internal' and 'external'. The phenomenon is obviously on the increase and may, as noted above, not only be a simple passing crisis for the state, but a 'durable disorder' or, in metaphorical terms, 'a new medievalism' (Cerny 1998). This can be described as some sort of regression into pre-Westphalianism – a world with a drastically reduced role for the nation-state as we know it. The overall significance of this route is a downward movement of authority from the state to subnational regions, localities and social groups, while supranational forms of governance remain embryonic. As I stated at the beginning of this chapter, I see disorder as a problem of insecurity and belonging to the broad security discourse, including security threats that come from inside society.

In terms of 'development' *durable disorder* can mean a generalised warlord economy with limited influence of external forms of authority on the local power-holders and social forces. The mode of development possible in such a context may at best be some sort of 'primitive accumulation'. Obviously the standard definitions of development from the second discourse are hard to apply in this situation. Development aid has in this context been reduced to a civil form of humanitarian intervention, and the major reason for intervention is violent conflict; to prevent it, to manage it, or to reconstruct societies in post-conflict situations. Post-conflict reconstruction is a new development experience of massive social engineering, completely different from the physical rebuilding of war-torn societies (for instance in post-World War II Europe), in which the inner societal coherence is still intact. The black-hole syndrome,

tarian emergency', includes not only physical destruction
lusion, depletion of 'social capital', erosion of civil society,
titutions and decline of civility. It is a destruction of the
oral substance of society. In view of the fact that the pre-
conflict structure generated tensions that led to conflict, post-conflict
'reconstruction' is of course a most inappropriate term.

The complex rebuilding (or rather the creation of a new equilibrium)
cannot be done by outside actors alone, but normally it cannot be done
without them either. Local actors have become paralysed by mutual
hostility and fear, apart from lacking necessary resources, destroyed
by the war. There is thus no alternative but to build on the combined
efforts of external intervenors and remaining 'islands of civility' (Kaldor
1999) to combat hate, suspicion, corruption and criminality. There are
already manuals based on early experience produced by NGOs which,
as a result of the 'new wars', have got a new task and new role in global
governance (Duffield 2002). There is, however, as yet little actual research
to build on.

---

box 2.2   globalisation and humanitarian intervention

In the globalised world there emerged, as a result of the spread of chaos, a qualitatively new
discourse on intervention called 'humanitarian intervention', which implied a coercive involvement
by external powers in a domestic crisis with the purpose of preventing human rights abuses and
promoting democracy and 'good governance'. It can be seen as an extension of international
development assstance. The recent focus upon human security rather than state security is significant for
understanding the change of the security and development discourse and the fundamental challenge to
sovereignty. Implied in concepts such as 'human security', 'human development', 'human emergency',
and 'humanitarian intervention' is the idea of a transnational responsibility for human welfare.

Intervention is a key issue in the new discourse. In international
law there are only two *legal* types of intervention: (1) where a conflict
constitutes a threat to international peace, and (2) where the behaviour
of the parties to a conflict fundamentally violates human rights or
humanitarian law. The practice of external intervention in domestic
affairs has so far been rather restricted. A counter-sovereignty operation
is not compatible with what was originally stated in article 2 of the UN
charter: 'Nothing in this charter shall authorize the United Nations to
intervene in matters which are essentially within the domestic jurisdiction
of any state.' However, the *legitimacy* factor with respect to intervention
in 'domestic affairs' has in the last decade grown stronger relative to the
legality factor, and consequently the number of interventions in response
to 'complex humanitarian emergencies' has also increased.

The different cases of external intervention that we have seen so far have different degrees of legitimacy, not unrelated to the behaviour of the parties to the conflict. The more barbarian the behaviour of the warring parties, the more urgent and the more acceptable (legitimate) the external intervention will appear to public opinion. More recently the discourse has again changed from 'humanitarian intervention' to 'war against terrorism'. The full implications of this, as far as the future world order is concerned, are yet to be seen. The war against Iraq was not compatible with international law and may be a turning point as far as liberal interventionism is concerned. The future of development cannot be understood without taking September 11 into consideration. A new context is emerging in which the US hegemony, rooted in multilateralism, is transformed into dominance, expressed in unilateralism, 'the unipolar movement' and the security doctrine of pre-emptive warfare. Development thinking reappears in a rude, caricatured form of 'nation-building' under conditions that remind us of colonialism and 'the white man's burden'.

Development has thereby been reduced to be what development workers have to do, and what they do they usually do in situations of crisis and conflict. Since these situations are globalised, and 'national development' has lost much of its meaning, development theory is necessarily merging with International Political Economy into 'Global Studies'. Globalisation, however, constitutes processes of both inclusion and exclusion; thus the alternative tradition in development theory can still be defined as incorporating demands from 'the excluded' but it is, in the era of 'post-development', no longer so clear into what they are supposed to be included. An additional alternative development dimension in a context of societal disintegration is the model role of remaining 'islands of civility' in a sea of civil war (Kaldor 1999). In spite of failed states and horrific conflicts, development thinking forms part of the 'modern project', retaining its normative approach and its belief in the rational human being. The third discourse is not concluded, or perhaps we could rather say that it is paving the way for a *fourth* discourse, focused on the project of global development.

the fourth discourse: towards global development?

Global development necessitates a further strengthening of the societal dimension of world order. Global development, so defined, would mean that standards applied in most (non-failed) domestic systems are increasingly taken as norms in the international system as well. The

Cancun meeting (held in September, 2003) showed, through the overt clash of interests, that we are far from this goal. The world-order crisis discussed above also underlines this.

---

box 2.3   global development

Global development can be defined as an improvement in the quality of international relations, which traditionally are described as 'anarchic', or at best as 'anarchical society' (Bull 1977), that is, more than anarchy but less than community. Humanity does not yet constitute a political community, much less a political actor. Humanitarian intervention has been carried out in the name of humanity; by militarily cooperating states; sometimes in a formal UN context, sometimes in what is called a 'plurilateral' form. This is sometimes complemented by various non-military forms through international NGOs, representing what somewhat prematurely is referred to as 'global civil society'.

We are thus talking about alternative futures, beyond the current crisis, which unavoidably implies normative perspectives as well as global social theory. A global social theory must first of all be global, which must be distinguished from universal. Global implies that a variety of societal experiences from around the world are taken into account. The great achievement of development studies has perhaps been to create such a worldwide empirical base for building a global theory by providing so much concrete knowledge of local development- and under-development situations from the world. No other social science specialization can match this. These various situations, which have to be contextually understood, are coexisting worlds, not stages in a 'natural history' of development as modernisation.

Regarding globalisation, there are already too many definitions for this concept to be a useful research tool. This is not to say that the definitions, distinctions and elaborations of this phenomenon, proposed in the literature, do not make good sense. We live in a globalised condition, but this condition cannot be understood by the concept of globalisation, which is merely an expression of this condition; in fact a measure of ignorance. We would need global social theory to explore the global condition further. The globalisation debate signifies a crisis in social theorising – and development theory in particular. This theoretical crisis in turn derives from the crisis of the nation-state. A crisis of the nation-state does not imply its disappearance, but a change of its functions: for instance a reorientation from welfare states to competition states, a change which is perceived as a crisis by many of those who experience it, as well as by some of those who analyse it. We may also witness an 'unbundling' of state functions through the emergence of supranational protective and interventionist structures strengthening the societal dimension of world order. To say that the nation-state remains an important actor, which is what everybody says today, does not mean that a social science based on its primacy still makes sense.

One attempt to get out of the conceptual prison has been the concept of governance. In the globe-talk of the international financial institutions (IFIs) 'good governance', as was noted above, simply means less government. I nevertheless think that the concept can be useful to explain processes of decision-making and implementation that take place also on other levels than the national, and with governments playing a reduced role. Global governance thus implies multi-level governance, and there is a need for global social theory to make sense of it. Global governance is the content of world order, which I define in structural and institutional terms; for instance unipolar versus multipolar, unilateral versus multilateral, and different forms of legitimisation. These can be ordered in a scale from international law to the pursuit of national interest. The qualitiative dimension of global governance, encompassing a number of basic human values, is, I suggest, what global development is all about.

In the present context, the historical process of market expansion is a worldwide process, which is likely to make the social and political counter-movements vary even more in the different regions of the world, and therefore become even harder to predict. This new double movement, of which the second part has hardly begun, has been interpreted as a 'second great transformation' (Hettne 1997, 2000). The question then arises if the dialectics between the first and second movement will lead to a new great compromise, shaping the world order, which at present is on a unilateral course.

Theoretically there are of course various future options of world order. For the present purpose we are more concerned with 'ideal models' than 'hybrid forms'. The liberal view of globalisation, which still enjoys a hegemonic position, stresses the homogenising influence of market forces towards an open society. Liberals normally take a minimalist view on political authority. The original historical background for this argument was mercantilist regulation, but subsequently the 'negative other' took the form of *planning* (or other non-market forms of economic and social organisation). To interventionist thinkers, concerned with the content of the 'second movement' – that is, to politicise the global – the liberal project is not realistic; these critics tend to see the unregulated market system as analogous to political anarchy. Many of the classical theorists (whether conservative or radical) held that the liberal ideology of ever-expanding and deepening markets lacked ethical content. Similarly, the morality of the market system can, according to contemporary critics of 'hyperglobalisation', only be safeguarded by some kind of organised purposeful will, manifested in a return of 'the political', or 'reinvention of politics' (Beck 1997), for instance in the form of new social movements and a 'new multilateralism' (Cox 1997, 1999; Gill, 2000). The second movement or the return of the 'political', may appear in various forms. One possible form, assuming a continuous role for state authority, is a reformed 'neo-Westphalian order', governed either by a reconstituted UN system, what can be called *assertive multilateralism*, or by a more loosely organised 'concert' of dominant powers, assuming the privilege of governance (including intervention) by reference to their shared value system focused on order. This we can call *militant plurilateralism*.

Even if the UN is the only legitimate world actor in security crises there exist many flaws due to its anachronistic structure. The Westphalian logic makes it non-operative in a post-Westphalian context. The multilateral model in a strengthened, more 'assertive' form is based on radical reforms in order to upgrade the UN as a world-order model. For instance, the Security Council would be made more representative, and the General Assembly should have representatives also from civil society. A strengthened Economic and Social Council would take primary responsibility for global development (International Commission on Global Governance 1995). The proposed reforms were intended to increase the efficiency and the legitimacy of the global institution. Instead the UN entered its worst crisis ever, after the unilateral attack on Iraq.

A more appropriate form for the return of 'the political' is a post-Westphalian order, where the locus of power moves up to the transnational level. The state can be replaced or complemented by a regionalised order, that is, the *new regionalism* (Hettne et al. 1999/2001), or by a strengthened global civil society supported by a new 'normative architecture' of world-order values (Falk 2002). 'Global cosmopolitanism' emphasises the role of community on the global level as well as the formation of global norms. However, from a realist perspective it needs institutionalisation. The most likely candidate for such a role, although it does not appear to be imminent, is the interregional organisation facilitating multiregional governance, the major alternative to unilateralism.

It can be argued that the European model, owing to its strong focus on the role of institutions in Europe's own integration process as well as on the importance of institutionalised interregional relations, represents a potential world order. The relevant contrast and currently predominant trend is US unilateralism, contradicting basic principles in the European Union (EU) external policy. The short-term implications of interregionalism can be judged from the ASEM (Asia Europe Meeting) experiment. As shown by the ASEM process the institutionalisation of interregional relations, not to speak of multi-regionalism, is very slow and affected by sudden changes in the geopolitical environment. ASEM is only one example. The EU is in the process of building interregional relations with all regions of the world. The overall purpose of interregionalism is to make the external environment of Europe, that is, the rest of the world, more stable and more predictable. The significance of this experience is that trans-regional institutions have the potentiality of shaping, through intersubjectivity and mutual learning, the outlook of regional civilisations towards compatible patterns of coexistence, ultimately through multiculturalism and multi-regionalism (Hettne 2003).

From a global development perspective, there is, however, still a striking governance gap. The concept of global governance is by itself a recognition of the possibility of a rules-bound order, a refutation of the anarchy model of international relations as well as the utopia of the self-regulating market. What can be put in their place? The need is for a new great compromise. Such a compromise should provide the framework for *global development*, which in a globalised world is the relevant form of development. The disrupting social consequences of deterritorialisation implied in the process of market-led globalisation generate political forces to halt and modify the process of globalisation in order to guarantee territorial control, cultural diversity and human security. In order to promote global development there must, instead of cultural homogenisation and structural polarisation, be an inter-civilisational dialogue on the level of the macro-regions; such a dialogue would necessitate a reasonably symmetric power base for regionally-based civilisations; instead of asymmetry and polarisation, the structural gap between regions must be bridged, and the vertical structure of the world order horizontalised through the strengthening of weak and incoherent regions in the periphery. Of importance is also that intermediate regions are capable of advancing their interest in changing the structure, rather than simply adapting to the received pattern, of comparative advantages. For this the building of transnational and interregional institutions are needed.

To conclude:

- This overview has not provided a consistent and permanent definition of development.

- This is because there can be no fixed and final definition; only suggestions of what it should imply in particular contexts.
- In sum, development is still part of the unfulfilled modern project, defined as critical, reflexive and potentially universal.

3
changing notions of development: bringing the state back in

peter calvert

The trouble with the French is that they have no word for entrepreneur.
(attributed to President George W. Bush in Ivins 2002)

introduction

The role of the state in development was under attack for two decades: the 1980s and the 1990s. The prevailing economic orthodoxy, the 'Washington consensus', was that the state had only a minimal role to play, in ensuring a 'level playing field' for private interests. Anything more than that, it was argued, would distort the free working of the market and so hinder rather than help economic development. Adopted in 1991, the 'Consensus' helped guide the developmental policies of the international lending agencies, the International Monetary Fund (IMF) and World Bank (WB) for most of the time since then. However towards the end of the 1990s, discussion again focused upon the central role of the state in stimulating as well as presiding over economic development in the Newly Industrializing Countries (NICs). At the same time it was realised that the failure of economic development, particularly but not exclusively in sub-Saharan Africa, was not, as previously thought, caused by the *strength* of the state but rather by its *weakness*. The 'hollowing out' of the state left it fatally weakened, to the point at which it could no longer even successfully achieve its primary economic functions of maintaining a stable currency and guaranteeing the security of bargains in the market.

During the 1980s and 1990s, the main context of the debate was the capacity of externally encouraged economic reform programmes to stimulate development in the developing world. It is increasingly clear, however, that such programmes have not generally been successful. There is no doubt that the direction of development may be influenced by a variety of external agencies, such as the US Agency for International Development (USAID), the World Bank or the IMF. But it is equally clear that it is also affected by internal considerations, including what powerful vested interests want. Vested interests are just one indigenous obstacle to development, others include various structural factors, including: a lack of industry and infrastructure; low literacy, poor education and low school enrolment; rapid population growth and urbanisation; little administrative capacity; poor financial institutions; archaic social structures; and serious internal societal conflicts. Such matters fall largely within the competence of the state to make better – or worse. In fact, the very fact that the state has the undoubted ability to make such matters worse is one of the strongest arguments for its ability to make them better. This chapter, therefore,

- seeks to revisit the notion of the 'development state'; and
- argues for the historical and current importance of the state in development.

For many people, the initially vague and predictive term 'development' still struggles to acquire a precise meaning. For most people it still means first and foremost economic growth, as measured by the increase over time in gross domestic product (GDP), and/or GDP per capita. It is also associated with other economic phenomena, such as: industrialisation, enterprise and occupational differentiation. By industrialisation we mean an increase in the role of manufacturing industry in the economy. Latterly, however, the role of industrialisation has been challenged. The advanced industrial countries (AICs) have been moving into a post-industrial age, characterised by the decline of traditional heavy industry and the apparently unending growth of the tertiary (services) sector. Some economists argue that under modern conditions, newly industrialising economies (NIEs) may be able to move directly to the post-industrial era, as, for example, when British banks out-source much of their customer relations to call centres in India. The ability of Indian entrepreneurs to take advantage of the possibilities offered by information technology and the availability of large numbers of educated workers able to speak English fluently may be taken as an example of the second phenomenon, enterprise. Via entrepreneurial efforts, enterprise leads to the foundation of new businesses, the spread of factories and the concentration of the population in urban centres, where they become available for work. It is also an example of the third, occupational differentiation. Occupational differentiation offers the possibility of new ways of earning one's living in a changing society. It is also associated with a range of social, political and cultural changes, although as in the case of improvements in health or the extension of education, there is still serious debate about the direction of causation.

However some would argue that economic development is not just economic growth, but self-sustaining growth. This in turn involves specific structural changes in the mode of production, technological advancement, social and political reform and a general amelioration in the well-being of the population at large. A major objection to this view is the impact of globalisation; in today's world it is none too clear that a concept such as self-sustaining growth has any real meaning, since all economic processes are now subject to influences and even interruption from outside the state boundary. Explanations as to why economic growth takes place in some areas and not in others have, at least since World War II, had to take into account external as well as internal decisions. As things stand today, the free movement of capital, the weakness of most currencies and the volatility of exchange rates combine to leave individual governments at the mercy of forces which they only dimly understand and which are in any case largely beyond their capacity to control.

---

box 3.1   max weber and development

The first attempt to explain the way in which development occurs in some places and not in others was that of the economist and sociologist Max Weber. It was his essay on *The Protestant Ethic and the Spirit of Capitalism* (Weber 1974) that established a tradition of ascribing to religion or religious beliefs a special role in fostering or inhibiting economic growth. However Weber himself failed to lay sufficient emphasis on the structural requisites of development. Wanting to develop is not enough, as the failure of industrialisation in Cuba in the 1960s shows. Structural conditions have first to be fulfilled, such as the ready availability of raw materials, and means of transport both to bring the raw materials to the place of manufacture and to take the finished product to the place of sale. In any case Weber's implied criticism of Roman Catholicism in southern Europe looks much less convincing today in the light of the relative economic success of Italy and Spain, Brazil and Chile. Thus even in Latin America it would now be difficult to uphold the thesis convincingly.

Max Weber's idea – that religion (or perhaps ideology) plays an essential role in fostering development – dies hard. The influence of Islam in fostering fatalistic attitudes and anti-commercial or anti-materialist values (particularly the condemnation of all lending at interest) has more recently been invoked as part of the explanation for the relative economic backwardness of the Arab states of the Middle East. This is despite the huge advantages many such states enjoy in the form of rich endowments of gas and petroleum. Yet the fact is that, despite some variations, Middle Eastern states operate under serious physical disadvantages in lacking economic resources other than petroleum. In addition, they share the problems of other developing states in being subject to antiquated traditional governments or (as, for example, in Iraq) the predatory militarists who – until 2003 – replaced them. Further, the Confucian ideals that were in the past blamed for the relative economic backwardness of China have more recently been invoked as an explanation for the successful economic development of Hong Kong, Taiwan and Singapore. In the latter, the state has consistently emphasised both the role of education in equipping its citizens to compete in the world marketplace and of Confucianism as the source of the 'Asian values' of discipline and order.

development and modernisation theory since 1945

For the first twenty years after 1945, self-sustaining growth was not an issue because relatively few countries were autonomous and many of those were primarily engaged in post-war reconstruction. For the first new states development was initially regarded as both a self-evident and a prophetic concept. The universal assumption in the 1950s and 1960s was that 'developing' (or 'Third World') countries would – almost inevitably – become 'developed' over time. This was because, conventional wisdom had it, all countries *necessarily* moved from the 'traditional' to the 'modern' via economic and technological progress.

This era of state-led economic growth was exemplified both by the leaders of the newly industrialising economies (NIEs) of Asia and by the 'cepalistas' in Latin America (who derived their nickname from the Spanish acronym for the United Nations Economic Commission for Latin America: CEPAL; now CEPALC). Both regarded it as the essential role of the state both to own and to manage key industries and services, according to a predetermined plan, with a view to promoting the systematic and successful economic development of their countries. The state also became the banker of last resort, providing investment capital on a selective basis where overseas investors were unable or unwilling to do so.

Mexico, although atypical in other respects, is regionally typical in the concentration of state ownership and investment (Cypher 1990). By the 1970s nearly every major industry except cement production

box 3.2 walt rostow and development

The US economic historian, Walt Rostow (1960), argued that existing advanced economies were differentiated from others by having achieved self-sustaining economic growth. Before they could reach the 'take-off' point at which sustained flight became possible, however, three factors had to be in place: development of the necessary science and/or technology, accumulation of the necessary capital and control by a political elite oriented towards development. Subsequently this was further refined by the convergence theorists into a view that all societies that industrialise will tend to develop very similar social systems and that industrialisation itself is only a stage in the development of post-industrial society (Kerr 1962; Bell 1973).

was state-owned and managed by parastatal organisations. Nacional Financiera, SA (NAFINSA) was the prime agency in directing capital where it was expected to have a significant developmental effect. Emerging new states in Africa and Asia in the 1960s, joining existing 'developing' countries in Latin America, also followed this pattern. Various forms of 'African socialism' went further still in giving the responsibility for growth almost exclusively to the state. One of the earliest examples, Ghana, showed however that it was all too easy for ambition to outrun performance. Money invested in roads, airlines, ships, and the like was often wasted because the infrastructure simply did not exist to make use of it productively (Jones 1976). After 1975 the Mexican economy became increasingly dominated by the production of petroleum and failed to become a major player on the world stage. Argentina, according to Walt Rostow, had been on the point of 'take-off' in 1930 but had failed to achieve self-sustaining growth, while Brazil, with all its obvious advantages in terms of abundant resources, continued to suffer from high rates of inflation which negated rates of annual growth of the order of 7 to 9 per cent.

At the 'developmentalist' stage, belief in the primary role of the state in economic development was supported on the one hand by Marxism and the legacy of Soviet industrialisation in the 1930s and on the other by Alexander Gerschenkron's (1962) theory of 'relative economic backwardness'.

The main examples Gerschenkron used were the United States, Germany, Japan and Russia – the four great industrial success-stories. In each case, the primary reference was to a specific time: for the USA, the era from Alexander Hamilton (1791) down to the Civil War (1861–65); for Germany, the era of Friedrich von List and Graf von Bismarck (1841), for Japan, the Meiji Restoration (1880); and for Russia the era of 'war communism' (1920s). Gerschenkron's argument was that in each of these cases the patterns of finance of industrialisation could be understood as

---

box 3.3   gerschenkron and development

Gerschenkron measured an economy's relative backwardness partly in terms of psychological and physical distance from Great Britain, the first industrial nation, and partly in terms of the ability and willingness of banks to mobilise risk capital and to assume an active ownership role in other firms ('universal banking'). He also advanced a number of reasons for relative economic backwardness based on historical experience in Europe, the USA and Japan. These included the roles of agriculture, of original capital accumulation (colonialism and banks), of technology, of market expansion, and above all, that of the state (industrialisation imperative, protectionism).

---

responses to relative economic backwardness. Retained profits and private investors would dominate in well-advanced countries. Bank finance and entrepreneurship would be important in conditions of moderate backwardness. In extreme backwardness the state would be the key to industrial investment.

Though many of Gerschenkron's arguments have not withstood the criticism of their basis in European economic history, especially in terms of his key cases, Germany and Russia (Sylla and Toniolo 1991), his concept of 'substitutes for prerequisites' has been a most useful contribution. By this he meant to stress that backwardness often stemmed from the absence of factors that served as preconditions for development in more advanced countries. Thus he highlighted the importance of examining the ways in which, in conditions of backwardness, substitutions for the absent factors could be and had been achieved (Gerschenkron 1962: 46), implying a greater role for large firms and complex bureaucracies in those countries.

However, relying on the state to spearhead the escape from backwardness also incurs risks.

- Not only Ghana, but in fact the vast majority of developing countries during this period, fell far short of their ambitious plans.
- State-owned enterprises are notoriously subject to agency problems that undermine productivity performance (for example, Mexico).
- The state itself may be predatory and unable credibly to commit itself not to expropriate the returns from private-sector investment (e.g., Egypt, Iran, Iraq), while rent-seeking behaviour tends to flourish in circumstances of centralised industrial policy and protected markets (for example, India).
- Many developing countries have/had weak governments unable successfully to maintain the necessary tight control on costs and outcomes (Nigeria, Ghana).

- It has often proved easier to manipulate the statistics than to secure genuine economic development (many Central American countries).

In the meantime development theory also began to take on board the relevance of political culture, nation-building and construction of stable institutions and administration. A key text was the structural-functionalist manifesto of Gabriel A. Almond and James S. Coleman, *The Politics of the Developing Areas* (1960). It was not long before the dominant view emerged that not only was the state essential to economic development, but also, unfortunately, it would very likely be an authoritarian state. Some such as Samuel P. Huntington (1968) saw the armed forces as necessary agents of modernisation and seemed prepared to accept that. Others, such as Al Stepan, Philippe Schmitter and Guillermo O'Donnell, disliked the notion of an authoritarian state but in varying degrees saw it as an historical necessity (Stepan 1973; Schmitter 1995; O'Donnell 1988).

The early 1970s were the high-water mark of dependency (*dependencia* in Spanish) theory and of its critics. The dependency theorists rejected the notion of a common path towards developed status. They saw the existing state as at best an obstacle to development and at worst a key part of the architecture within which the 'Third World' was exploited by the advanced industrial countries (see, for example, Cardoso and Faletto 1979). At its worst, this would mean that once certain countries, the states of the so-called 'core', had developed, all others on the 'periphery' of the world system would be precluded from doing so. The existing state, therefore, had to be smashed to make development possible, though it would be impossible to do this without a social revolution that in most cases was not immediately forthcoming. However most politicians were not so pessimistic and many felt that, at least in the meanwhile, the developing countries could and should work together to try to adjust the terms of trade in their favour. This effort reached a peak with the call led by the presidents of Mexico and Venezuela for a New International Economic Order (NIEO) and the adoption in 1974 by the General Assembly of the UN of a non-binding Charter of Economic Rights and Duties of States (CERDS).

This apparent success foundered amid the impact of the first 'oil shock' on the international system in the early 1970s. Much of the Middle East had missed out on the thirty years of post-war development; at least in any sense which benefited the majority of its inhabitants. If state activity was in itself a measure of economic development, the Middle East should have been much more developed than it actually was. But

the area has an inadequately educated, poor population and an agricultural system characterized by small pockets of high productivity in a landscape of low yields and by the inefficient use of scarce capital. However ironic it may seem in retrospect, the leaders of the state saw the need for intervention in order to avoid wasting scarce resources
(Richards and Waterbury 1996: 175)

By creating a massive governmental machine to control their mainly exiguous populations, they instead imposed on them a massive additional cost. Hence where they could, they came to develop a fatal dependence on a single resource, oil, to make good the deficiency. The fact that this resource was concentrated in a few, authoritarian states, controlled by small elites, fatally weakened their individual bargaining power. The advanced industrial countries (AICs) underwent only a brief period of recession before the international oil industry was able to announce huge potential discoveries in other parts of the world. The Charter remained a dead letter, the AICs scrambled to try to salvage their pre-eminence and in many countries development came to a complete halt as they struggled to pay off the debts they had rashly incurred on the assumption that they would be able to pay them.

There are a number of criticisms that can be made of most dependency writing.

- It has a tendency to ignore significant differences between states.
- It was developed to explain Latin American circumstances and thus is not really historically applicable to other parts of the world.
- It tends to embody what Kamrava (1992) terms 'latent conspiratorial assumptions'.

But for our present purposes its main failing is that it assumes that all states in the core will be strong states, and all in the periphery will be weak – that is, what Myrdal (1968) referred to as 'soft states': with neither the administrative capacity nor the political skill to carry out their developmental project.

A similar pessimism afflicted the neo-liberals. However by the mid-1970s they were already confident that all other models had failed and were arguing that the state had a wholly negative effect on development. The remedy, they claimed, was to take the state out of the business of economic management altogether, and to open up the internal market to competition, to sweep away protectionist barriers, and remove restrictions on the movement of capital. For Latin America the 1980s proved to be a 'lost decade', for Africa a decade which failed to justify expectations, so there were already places where the new message – that the state still had an important developmental role – was taken seriously. Nevertheless, after 1991 neo-liberal ideas achieved hegemony via their adoption as fundamental principles by the international lending agencies, in the form of what became known as the 'Washington consensus' (see also chapters 1 and 2).

the developmental state

Since 1989, international trends and developments, begun or stimulated by events connected to the end of the Cold War, have awakened concern about the impact of globalisation on developing states. This in turn has helped stimulate a fundamental re-examination of developmental processes. In many developing countries this has been accompanied by the rediscovery of the notion of the developmental state.

The term 'developmental state' seems to have originated with Chalmers Johnson's study of Japan in the thirty years of rapid post-war development (Johnson 1982; see also Johnson 1995). It was later extended to the other newly industrialising economies of Asia (White 1984; Deyo 1987; White and Wade 1988), becoming in the process a model for the development of yet more states, including Thailand and Indonesia. The idea of the developmental state has two components: one structural, one ideological.

- Structurally, the developmental state is organised to promote economic development, accumulation and industrialisation.
- Ideologically, it has a mission to promote economic development, and 'establishes as its principle of legitimacy its ability to promote sustained development, understanding by development the steady high rates of economic growth and structural change in the productive system, both domestically and in its relationship to the international economy' (Castells 1992: 55).

The popularity of the model stems from the undoubted fact that certain economies have been able, since 1945, not only to develop but to reach advanced industrial status. The model also appeared to be applicable to a wide range of societies and states in East and South East Asia; not only to Japan itself, and to South Korea (Amsden 1989; Minns 2001) and Taiwan, but also to a lesser extent to the 'little tigers': Singapore (Low 2001), Malaysia and Hong Kong (Castells 1992; Weber 2001). Not only did they prove successful but with success their more authoritarian features were muted, and in many cases greater wealth was accompanied by a substantial measure of democratisation. Hence their example helped bring about elsewhere popular demands for better development outcomes, affecting many other would-be developing countries. This in turn led to dramatic domestic political and economic changes in other parts of the developing world. These included: economic reforms in the direction of the market economy, democratization and democracy, and calls for better human rights, especially for women and minorities.

The interesting question is: Why were the lessons offered by Asia's developmental states not understood earlier? There seem to be two reasons. On the one hand there was a tendency among their advocates to emphasise the authoritarian features of the East Asian experience, and in particular the suppression of local autonomy and the disregard of legislatures in favour of a strongly bureaucratic state, although this was in fact not universally true. For example, Japan started with a democratic system imposed by US occupation and both South Korea and Taiwan moved away from the Stalinist model of a command economy and also more recently embraced democracy (Xia 2000: 2). At the least it was thought that specific features of East Asian network society gave it a comparative advantage in an era in which industry was increasingly dominated by information technology (Castells 1996: 173). The apparent failure of state-led economic growth in democratic India, also, did not encourage the view that the model could or should be exported (Ahrens 1997; Herring 1999).

In the West the Japanese and South Korean experience was edited for public consumption by the advocates of the free market, to suggest that it was reliance on market forces and the adoption of market-driven export-oriented development strategies that led to efficient exploitation of the cheap labour which formed, it was argued, those countries' comparative advantage (Balassa, 1971; Little et al., 1970). This view was enshrined in the early 1980s in the official view of the World Bank (1981). The most important consequence of this, however, was to consolidate the view that the promotion of development was solely a matter for economic policy rather than political and economic institutions. Under this view, development could be secured simply by opening the economy up to international trade and investment and maintaining a balanced budget and a stable money supply, managed only by the control of interest and exchange rates.

The most telling critique of the role of the state from the political Right, however, has focused not on the value of cheap labour but on something much harder to identify: the role of the entrepreneur. In the past a variety of theories has been put forward regarding the part played by entrepreneurship in economic development. The Weberian view saw the entrepreneurial urge as at least in part the product of social exclusion. The social-exclusion argument certainly has some validity: the state may in fact inadvertently play a positive role in promoting entrepreneurship by acting to exclude key groups (such as immigrants) from power. This has the effect of forcing them in turn to act as entrepreneurs and occupy sectors of the economy in which the oligarchy has not taken an interest. For example, in Argentina late-19th-century society was captured by a military landed elite; it was the mass of new immigrants who were excluded from access to land that became the main force behind the significant development of artisan production and early industrialisation. Unfortunately after 1930 the gains of this early period were to be frittered away by a series of military or military-backed governments.

Marxian debates over the role of 'national capital', on the other hand, treated capital simply as a structural prerequisite for development; hence the state, which had access to unlimited quantities of capital, could promote development more effectively than any private individual. (It is an irony indeed, that one of the few really saleable products of a Marxist state has been the Kalashnikov, which in the hands of state and non-state armies has done so much to hold back the development of the Middle East.)

An emphasis on the importance of entrepreneurship does not necessarily mean that the state has no role to play, however. Policies can influence the supply of entrepreneurs in the economy and the allocation of their resources, and public interventions can influence accessibility to resources, technology and markets. How to optimise the design of the state machinery in order to facilitate economic development is therefore the main practical problem. In the thirty years between 1945 and 1975 a number of states achieved impressive economic growth. West Germany rebuilt its industries to become a leading economic power. France transformed itself from a largely agrarian to a largely industrial economy. But it was Japan's economic recovery after 1945 that was to be the model both for the 'Asian Tigers' and for the 'Third World' more generally. State-directed planning, not the random processes of the market, informed this process, through the agency of the powerful Ministry of Trade and Industry (MITI). The logic behind the process was the orderly development in turn of communications, primary production and heavy industry. In the case of post-war Japan the government did not try to manage the entrepreneurial process; taking things as they were and having set the

---

box 3.4   schumpeter and development

It is Schumpeter (1950) who most clearly asserts the key role of the entrepreneur in economic development and who plays down the role of the state. Schumpeter portrayed entrepreneurs as the critical agents for economic change and development. The entrepreneur introduces new goods and services into the market, develops new methods of production, opens up new markets and sources of supply of raw materials, and pioneers new forms of business organisation. In 'follower' economies, national entrepreneurs might be expected to play a crucial role in adapting technologies to local needs and promoting structural changes which alter the national position in the international division of labour. An obvious problem therefore, which cannot be easily dismissed, is that states do not seem to be very good at choosing entrepreneurs. The choice of heads of state industries in developing countries is inevitably politically motivated; they are most often cronies of leading politicians and at the least members of the oligarchy. Unfortunately such people seldom seem to be natural risk-takers; they have too much to lose and too little to gain.

---

goal to be achieved companies were encouraged to find solutions. Japanese companies were also encouraged to look out for opportunities to compete in the export market either by exploiting their comparative advantage in manufacturing better-quality products, such as, cameras, at a lower price, or, as in the case of the desktop computer, the transistor radio and the games machine, exploiting inventions made elsewhere for purposes which their inventors had not originally envisaged.

Two characteristics of the Japanese organisation of production were particularly significant in this process. On the one hand, industries were encouraged to group in giant conglomerates, so that introducing new products, or even whole ranges of products, was relatively free of risk. There was everything to gain and little to lose. On the other hand, every individual member of the firm was encouraged to assume personal responsibility for his or her part of the production process, to ensure the highest standards in the finished product and to recommend innovations wherever possible. Thus workers were engaged in a constant process of self-criticism and product-improvement, and to some extent the entrepreneurial function was collectivised. The result was a system that was highly efficient in exploiting existing inventions and making them available to a mass public at rock-bottom prices. It also avoided reproducing the social divisions and the pattern of institutionalised conflict that frustrated the best intentions of management and labour alike in, for example, the United Kingdom.

As we have already noted, much of the criticism of the role of the state in economic development has its roots in a generalised suspicion of the state and a touching, if unfounded, belief in the good intentions of private investors. We should note, therefore, that in purely economic terms it seems to make no difference whether investment comes from the state or from private individuals; comparing the two shows that the distinction 'does not materially affect the results' (Barro and Sala-i-Martin 1999: 441–2).

Although the East Asian economic crisis of 1997 was seen abroad, and particularly in the United States, as heralding the end of the developmental state model, it is evident that some disillusion had already set in rather earlier. Economists were already concerned about the unreliable nature of much of the evidence on which the model was based (Wade 1992). At the beginning of the 1990s the Japanese economy was stagnant. Savings ratios were the highest in the world, but, even with interest rates at zero, investment and consumption had levelled off and in 1994 Paul Krugman (1994) launched a scathing attack on the whole notion of Asia's exceptionalism in a key article in *Foreign Affairs*. He argued that the East Asian states had indeed been successful in mobilising resources, savings and investment, but it had been achieved by 'perspiration rather than inspiration', and efficiency levels had been low. The implication was that when the developing economies lost their comparative advantage, by no longer suffering from their initial poverty and the low wages workers had been eager to accept during the first period of growth, they would no longer be able to compete with economies that had continued to adjust. The crisis itself merely acted to confirm views that had been most of a political generation in the making (Fine 1999; Lukauskas and Rivera-Batiz 2001; Root 2001).

the developmental state as a democracy

How can the state best be structured to promote favourable developmental outcomes? Is it sufficient for it to meet certain minimum standards of 'good governance'? Or is a working democratic system a necessary condition of advanced development? And is the need to engage the general public in the task of monitoring governmental performance something fundamental to the notion of a development state? These key issues must be addressed today if the concept of the developmental state is to continue to have value. In addition, if it is to be applied, institutional structures have to be identified through which the goals of the developmental state can be realised.

Since the crisis of development in the 1980s it has been belatedly realised that the political conditions for development need to be embedded in a political system capable of responding to such crises. The command economy of the former Soviet Union achieved spectacular results in a limited number of areas, but it did so at a very high cost and was inherently wasteful because it lacked the effective capacity for self-criticism. Mikhail Gorbachev, on assuming the leadership of the Soviet Union, recognised its essential weakness, the fact that there was no real, authentic basis for judging how the economy was actually working. He made a desperate attempt to stave off the collapse of the Soviet system through the application of *perestroika* (restructuring) and *glasnost* (openness) and this, paradoxically, hastened its collapse. But the basic critique was sound. The problem was that to achieve results, it was necessary to operate within a totally different political context. In short, a successful developmental state was either a democracy to start with, or was forced to become one once the process of growth was well under way (Robinson and White 1999).

The development of Japan and the other 'Tigers' occurred, it must be remembered, at precisely the time (1945–75) that rapid economic growth was also taking place in the United States, Germany, France and the other advanced industrialised countries. The authoritarian features of the East Asian states, therefore, do not appear to have been helpful, and may well be quite irrelevant. It has not proved possible to show a significant relationship between democratization and economic growth (Barro and Sala-i-Martin 1999; Gastil 1987). However there are four main aspects of democratic states which seem to support the view that they have been exceptionally successful in generating economic growth and a high standard of living for their citizens. These are:

- judicial fairness;
- good governance;
- democratic accountability; and
- political stability.

Each will be considered in turn, together with some assessment of the types of institutional structures most likely to achieve them.

First, the strongest association with economic development seems to be with *the rule of law and judicial fairness*. In research carried out in the mid-1990s, an increase in the rule of law (as defined) by one standard deviation was associated with a rise in growth rate of 0.8 per cent per annum (Barro and Sala-i-Martin 1999: 439–40, citing Knack and Keefer 1994). Although the measurement of a concept such as rule of law is somewhat arbitrary and the direction of causation uncertain, this looks intuitively right. Successful trading nations centuries ago realised the importance of an impartial judiciary to determine disputes between traders and to hear appeals from customers who believed that they had been the victims of malpractice. Only a strong state can guarantee a free market.

But a strong state can all too easily be captured by special interests. The growth of regulatory capitalism in the West in the past decade has shown that even in open societies the pressure to intervene for this reason or that, is all but irresistible. Mechanisms which have successfully defended the rule of law in the past have included the independence and self-regulation of the legal profession, the involvement of lay persons in the administration of justice and a properly paid and well-trained police force. However legal systems cannot simply be borrowed from other countries, or, more precisely, if they are borrowed, they do not work (Seidman 1978). As the case of Colombia shows, unfortunately, where very large sums of money are involved, key individuals are effectively above the law. In such circumstances the majority of economic activity may take place in the 'black economy', resulting in the waste or even total loss of the greater part of the revenues that could have been devoted to economic development. But pressure from the United States for action against the 'drug barons', including attempts to extradite Colombian citizens for trial in the United States, have been conspicuously unsuccessful, and have indeed eroded the credibility of government without bringing any compensatory economic advantage.

Second, the notion of *good governance* originated with the World Bank and the IMF. Both, under the terms of their Charters, are supposed to be purely economic institutions. They are not supposed to make political decisions, and they are prohibited from intervening in the internal politics of the countries with which they deal. However during the 1980s it was increasingly realised that without significant structural reforms to the governments of 'Third World' states they simply could not be expected to perform the functions necessary to a successful economy. Such functions include: audit of governmental operations, efficient collection of taxes, and eradication of corrupt practices. Far too much of the money advanced by the IMF vanished down a 'black hole' with very little to show for it. Worse still, some countries had clearly developed a drug-like dependence on further subventions, promising every time to meet their obligations next time and inevitably failing to do so. The notion of 'good governance' emerged, therefore, to describe a set of administrative requirements for success. Requiring states to make the necessary changes gradually became a requirement of loans from the international financial institutions (IFIs), but this form of conditionality, significantly, became known as 'political conditionality'.

Third, an obvious way of achieving some of the technical goals of good governance was via the creation of *mechanisms of democratic accountability*. Authoritarian states have repeatedly claimed legitimacy on account of their supposed ability to direct economic development, and at one time the claims of the armed forces to special competence in this respect were taken at face value. In the case of South Korea, the first steps towards its evolution into a newly industrialised economy (NIE) were taken under the military dictatorship of General Park. But with increased prosperity the pressure for a controlled move to democratic government became irresistible, and in any case experience has shown that sustained economic growth cannot be attained under an authoritarian system, as the lack of accountability of the typically closed elite permits the unchecked growth of rent-seeking behaviour and corruption. Thus the military government in Argentina between 1976 and 1983 'squandered billions on impractical construction schemes (unfinished highways, the 'Russian mountains'), subsidising financial speculation and personal corruption' (Calvert and Calvert 1989: 278).

But democratic systems cannot continue to work in the absence of what Evans (1995) terms the 'embedded autonomy' of business and industry, of regional or local government, of the mass media or of political parties. Minimum requirements for these would appear to be: a written constitution, multi-party democracy, free and fair elections under a generally accepted system of allocation and legal guarantees of the freedom of speech and of the press, broadly construed. The importance of an independent system of audit of state expenditure, too, should not be overlooked. France has an exceptionally powerful bureaucracy, which laid the foundations for France's *trente glorieuses* under the much-criticised and turbulent Fourth Republic. But it is segmented into autonomous bodies, subject to the audit of an independent corps of financial experts and open to challenge by an independent system of administrative law. Unfortunately efforts to transplant such a system, even in former French colonies, have collapsed when the expatriates who initially managed them have been withdrawn.

The fourth issue – that of political stability – is difficult to assess. Certainly development is the product of economic activity. Before development can take place therefore the structural and procedural conditions must be in place for the arena of economic activity, a market, to exist and to function effectively. When – as in Somalia, occupied Palestine or occupied Iraq – this is not the case, the result is the collapse of the economy and severe economic hardship. However research suggests that political instability as such has only a limited negative effect on economic activity (Barro and Sala-i-Martin 1999: 435), and this requires an explanation. One of the reasons may well be that people's notions of what constitutes stability are very varied. Another is that in uncertain circumstances, they prioritise what is important to them, earning their living, feeding, clothing and housing their families, and minding their own business.

However the effect of political instability is negative, and this has implications for investment. Unstable governments that behave unpredictably frighten off investment; hence if they wish to develop, they have little alternative but to use the resources of the state. Investors are notoriously chary of political instability, and rightly so, since rates of return have to be very high indeed to outweigh a possible total loss of capital invested. For this reason, in the past many business people have chosen to do business with authoritarian regimes, because they wrongly believed that those regimes were stable. Of course the problem with authoritarian government is that, lacking legitimacy, it cannot provide for a successful political succession; this can be guaranteed only by a constitutional order that facilitates an orderly succession of democratic governments. And in recent years there have been some high-profile challenges to the legitimacy of foreign investment under authoritarian regimes, as, for example, with Shell in the Ogoni lands in Nigeria and the deal by which an Australian company obtained permission to drill in the Timor Gap while East Timor was illegitimately occupied by Indonesia. So the realisation has gradually dawned that, although authoritarian regimes may last a long time, they are dynamically unstable and may collapse unexpectedly.

This makes democracy a much more reliable system, even if frequent changes of government limit the ability to plan for the long term. However the minimalist definition of democracy, choosing political leaders by a process of contested election, is not enough. Even in sophisticated states with a long history of democratic contestation the political process all too often throws up demagogues, or, at least, populists swept to power by the meretricious allure of simplistic solutions. Institutionally, therefore, a stable democracy requires predictably periodic elections, a fair electoral system and a limited number of broadly-based political parties through which leaders can be recruited and trained.

conclusion

From what we have seen in this chapter, it would seem that the concept of the 'developmental state' is still useful and, indeed, is now enjoying something of a revival (Woo-Cumings 1999). At the same time, the changes associated with the so-called 'Third Wave' of democratisation, have given it a more secure basis than many had previously thought possible. But persuading governments, even democratic governments, to create the necessary institutions to foster economic growth is not going to be easy. Democratic governments have a notoriously short time-horizon and the essence of effective economic development is the allocation of resources over a long term according to agreed criteria. In addition, all governments today suffer from a 'democratic deficit' inasmuch as they are to a greater or lesser extent prisoner of economic forces beyond their control, such as globalisation. However the experience of democratic states is that they are more successful in fostering economic development and maintaining that process of development than any other form of government. We conclude that to be successful, a developmental state may not need to be a *democratic* state, at least initially, but it must be a *democratising* state.

part 2

development and domestic factors

4
democracy and democratisation
mehran kamrava

introduction

The 'third wave' of democracy (Huntington 1991) that extended from the mid-1970s to the mid-1990s resulted in the emergence and spread of democratic political systems in areas that once seemed quite inhospitable to democracy. As history has repeatedly demonstrated, crafting a workable and resilient democratic polity is a highly complex and delicate endeavour. In fact, the growing crop of relatively new democracies – most of which are clustered in the countries of the developing world – are neither all equally democratic nor assured of immunity from reversals. The process of transition to and consolidation of democracy is one fraught with pitfalls, and the possibility of democracy's breakdown is a real danger for democratising or newly democratised systems.

This chapter examines the twin processes of democratic transition and consolidation in the developing world. In doing so, it begins with a brief definition of democracy as a political system and the characteristics that such a system must necessarily entail. Definitions of democracy often vary based on the precise nature of the democratic system in question, as not all democracies are similar in institutional make-up or can rely upon or share a clearly supportive political culture. Discussion of varieties of democratic systems in turn leads to examination of democratic transitions, especially conditions that facilitate them, the various forms and patterns they are likely to take, and the nature and sequences of the dynamics that are often involved. *Transition* to democracy, of course, is only half of the equation, the other half being *consolidation*. The chapter therefore then moves to a discussion of democratic consolidation, focusing once again on the dynamics involved in this phase. In addition to institutional arrangements and considerations, the strength of a newly established democracy is likely to be tested by two, somewhat interrelated, sets of challenges. One set of challenges is economic – more specifically arising out of the implementation of structural adjustment programmes – while another revolves around the nature of the pacts between outgoing, pre-transition elites and the incoming, post-transition ones replacing them. No political system, not even a democracy, is ever assured of eternal life, and the lives of newly established democracies are all the more precarious. The chapter will end with a look into the future of democracy by examining some of the obstacles that still block its emergence in regions such as the Middle East, and, in places where it does exist, by examining the possibilities of its resilience or reversal.

defining democracy

From a historical perspective, the birth of democratic political systems is a relatively recent development that can be traced to New Zealand in the 1890s and Australia soon after (Lijphart 1999: 49). However, even in these two cases the designation 'democratic' is open to questioning – since in New Zealand women were initially barred from running for public office (until 1919) and, in Australia, the native aborigines could not vote in federal elections until as recently as 1962. As these two cases demonstrate, democracy may be defined either narrowly or broadly, and there is often tremendous variation in the scope and depth of the democracy that is found in 'democratic' political systems. This section begins with a simple, 'minimalist' definition of a democratic political system. This definition is in turn used to delineate between the different types of democratic political systems that are distinguished from one another on the basis of their institutional make-ups and their political culture underpinnings.

Robert Dahl offers perhaps the most straightforward definition of a democratic political system in his seminal book *Polyarchy* (1971: 3). For Dahl a democratic political system must feature eight important institutional guarantees:

- freedom to form and join organisations;
- freedom of expression;
- right to vote;
- eligibility for public office;
- right of political leaders to compete for public support and votes;
- access to alternative sources of information;
- free and fair elections; and

---

box 4.1   schumpeter and democracy

A couple of decades before Dahl, Joseph Schumpeter (1950: 269) had defined democracy in similar, institutional terms: 'the democratic method is that institutional arrangement for arriving at political decisions in which individuals acquire the power to decide by means of a competitive struggle for the people's vote.'

- 'institutions for making government policies [that] depend on votes and other expressions of preference'.

Such definitions of democracy see it as a system in which political power is somehow shared and is diffused between the official institutions of power – that is, the state – and the people – that is, society.

---

box 4.2   what is democracy?

In essence, democracy is a system in which established institutions and procedures enable society to participate in and determine the life of the state through routinely scheduled elections and other structural forums that are specifically designed for political expression and participation. Society is politically empowered and exercises that power in accordance with established rules and procedures as outlined in a constitution and/or political tradition. The key to democracy, therefore, is the balance of power between state and society as enshrined in constitutional and other legal mandates.

By themselves, these and other similar definitions of democracy describe only the most general operations of political systems that can be classified as 'democratic'. Although not necessarily incorrect, such definitions do not describe some of the more important and fundamental institutional and cultural traits that distinguish different types of democratic systems from one another. Democracies, in fact, can be divided into different categories along two important, distinct, but somewhat interrelated axes. One axis is *structural* and revolves around the institutional means through which regularised input from society is channelled into the political system. More specifically, from an institutional perspective, democracies may be divided into what Arend Lijphart (1999) calls 'majoritarian' versus 'consensus' democracies. Another axis along which democracies may be divided revolves around the *depth* and practical meaning of political democracy for social actors. Here distinctions can be made regarding the nature and extent of the limits on citizens' liberties within the political arena. Some democracies, in simplest terms, are more profoundly democratic than others, not just in institutional terms but also in essence and spirit.

The institutional differences that distinguish democracies into the two broad clusters of majoritarian and consensus models are often the most noticeable features of democratic political systems. According to Lijphart (1999: 2),

> the majoritarian model concentrates power in the hands of a bare majority – and often even merely a plurality instead of a majority . . . whereas the consensus model tries to share, disperse, and limit power in a variety of ways. A closely related difference is that the majoritarian model of democracy is exclusive, competitive, and adversarial, whereas the consensus model is characterized by inclusiveness, bargaining, and compromise; for this reason, consensus democracy could also be termed 'negotiated democracy'.

---

box 4.3   lijphart and consociational democracy

In an early, seminal, article Lijphart (1969) used the label 'consociational' to describe what he later called 'consensus' democracy. Lijphart maintains that Westminster-type democracies offer the best examples of majoritarian democracies – especially as in Britain, New Zealand, and Barbados – where, among other things, there tends to be a fair amount of social and ethnic homogeneity. Consensus-model democracies, often found in countries with deep ethnic divisions, may be found, among other places, in Switzerland, Belgium, and, more recently, the European Union.

Lijphart (1999: 3–4) maintains that the primary differences between majoritarian and consensus democracies can be clustered along the two dimensions of 'executives–parties' and 'federal–unitary'. On the 'executives–parties' dimension, majoritarian democracies tend to concentrate power in a single-party majoritarian cabinet while consensus democracies often feature multi-party coalitions in which power is shared and diffused; majoritarians tend to have two primary and electorally significant political parties while consensus democracies are often multi-party systems; consensus democracies have proportional representation while majoritarians have disproportional representation; and, while pluralist interest groups compete with one another in majoritarian systems, in consensus models one often finds coordinated and corporatist interest groups whose efforts result in compromise and consensus. Along the 'unitary–federal' dimension, majoritarian democracies often have unitary and centralised governments while consensus democracies have federal and decentralised systems; while in majoritarian models legislative power is concentrated in a unicameral legislature, strong bicameralism is predominant in consensus models; majoritarian models have relatively flexible constitutions, while consensus ones have rigid constitutions that cannot be easily amended; consensus models feature strong judicial review and equally strong central banks, whereas in majoritarian models central banks are more dependent on the executive and judicial review is often the purview of the legislature itself.

While profoundly important, Lijphart's analysis remains isolated to the broader institutional features of democracies. Undoubtedly, institutional characteristics greatly impact on the extent to which a democracy invites and welcomes electoral input into the political process. At the end of his exhaustive study, Lijphart (1999: 301–2) comes to the important conclusion that 'the overall performance record of the consensus democracies is clearly superior to that of the majoritarian democracies'. Nevertheless, institutional characteristics notwithstanding, the depth to which a democracy is politically meaningful for the average citizen can vary not just in degree but, more importantly, also in quality and nature. More specifically, some democratic political systems, while featuring all of the characteristics outlined by Dahl and others, remain devoid of a meaningful social base and continually operate at an elite level, for a distinct class of social and economic elites. In simple terms, these are democracies for the elite and by the elite, with the bulk of the population taking on the role of bystanders and observers. Surely they can vote, and they frequently do, but the essence of the system remains elite-oriented. For lack of a better term, these polities may be called 'quasi-' or 'pseudo-democracies'.

Whether parliamentary or presidential (see Box 4.4), pseudo-democracies tend to have narrow social support bases and, for systems calling themselves democratic, feature rather confined political arenas. In the Turkish and the Israeli political establishments, for example, the military plays an unusually influential role, and significant segments of the population – the Kurds and Islamists in Turkey and the Palestinians in Israel – are often subject to official or unofficial political restrictions of various kinds. Not surprisingly, pseudo-democracies are frequently vulnerable to populist eruptions and/or the emergence of populist political personalities whose democratic credentials are suspect at best. As ostensibly democratic political systems, pseudo-democracies invariably feature universal suffrage. At the same time, however, as elite democracies they inhere a certain level of popular resentment and mistrust on the part of the electorate toward an establishment that is generally perceived as corrupt and unresponsive. Consequently, presidential or parliamentary elections at times may facilitate the rise to power of a populist individual

---

box 4.4   pseudo-democracies

Pseudo-democracies may assume either a parliamentary or a presidential form, examples of which include Turkey, Israel and India for the former and many of the new democracies of Latin America – especially Argentina, Venezuela, and Peru – for the latter. In each of these two limited types of democracies, the primary difference lies in the extent to which executive power and privileges are shared within the elite. In parliamentary pseudo-democracies, the legislature and the political parties that constitute it offer institutional forums through which concentrated power is shared and circulated within social and economic elites. These elites in turn use the institutional and procedural accoutrements of democracy – such as elections, party politics and the parliament – to maintain and perpetuate their privileged political and economic positions *vis-à-vis* the rest of society. In presidential pseudo-democracies, in contrast, power tends to be far more concentrated within the hands of the chief executive, and the inner circle of elites and confidants on whom he or she relies tends to be far narrower. Guillermo O'Donnell (1994) has labelled this type of a system a 'delegative democracy', in which the electorate delegates – or, more accurately, abrogates – near absolute power and responsibility to an elected Caesar for a predetermined length of time until the next presidential elections come around. 'The president is taken to be the embodiment of the nation and the main custodian and definer of its interests. . . Accountability to (courts and legislatures) appears as mere impediment to the full authority that the president has been delegated to exercise' (O'Donnell 1994: 59–60).

---

or party, recent examples of which include Alberto Fujimori in Peru, Hugo Chavez in Venezuela, and the former Refah Party and its leader Necmettin Erbakan in Turkey (Kamrava 1998).

Two factors appear to be critical in the emergence of pseudo-democracies. The first factor, which will be discussed in greater detail in the following section, has to do with the manner in which a democratic transition occurs. In broad terms, democratic transitions that are generated 'from above' – where previously non-democratic elites, on their own and under reasonably favourable circumstances, initiate measures to pre-empt the possibility of being swept out of power – often result in the establishment of democratic political systems with significant limitations attached to them. In these cases, non-democratic elites seek to devise post-transition guarantees that either maintain their continued privileges or, at the very least, ensure their immunity from prosecution for past deeds. Therefore, the 'democratic bargain' that is struck often features considerable limitations in terms of exactly what is and what is not permissible in the new system.

Transitions from above are not, however, always doomed to usher in pseudo-democracies. Moreover, even highly vibrant, liberal democracies need to impose some limitations on the types of political activities considered permissible. This is where a second factor comes into play, namely the role of the middle classes. Again, since this topic will be explored in greater detail below – in relation to the consolidation of democracies – only a few preliminary observations are offered now. Of primary importance is the degree to which the middle classes feel secure enough in their economic standing to have time to devote to politics. If the middle classes feel chronically insecure – perceiving that their economic status is only skin deep and that they have to take on two or three jobs in order to maintain their class standing and their living standards – then they are more likely to leave the field of politics to those with sufficient means to indulge in it. Being involved in politics, in other words, is a luxury which few members of the middle classes can afford; their time and efforts instead are consumed by the more immediate and mundane concern of earning a decent living. For a political system to be meaningfully democratic, a vibrant, sizeable and reasonably secure middle class appears to be key.

democratic transitions

So far, the question of how democracies come about has only been indirectly touched on. Democratic transitions in the developing world deserve particular attention given the specific circumstances within which they occurred in the late 20th and early 21st centuries. Transitions 'from above', mentioned earlier, are only one mode of democratisation. Even then, there are often a series of factors and developments that prompt non-democratic elites to gradually turn power over to successors. No doubt, opportunism and 'reading the writing on the wall' may play a part in the decision to give up power. But there are often far deeper dynamics at work. It is to the examination of these dynamics that this section turns.

At the broadest level, democratic transitions come about as a result of two developments:

- particular patterns and consequences of economic development; and
- the emergence of civil society.

As the following pages will argue, by itself civil society is insufficient to bring about processes of democratisation. Civil society can, however, tilt the balance of power away from the state and in favour of society. Nevertheless, the contest over power between the state and society remains an essentially political one. Civil society may enhance society's sense of the self, its capacity for action, and its confidence to take on the state. But by itself civil society does not initiate the transition process. Quite frequently, transition processes are initiated because of cracks in the political and economic arrangements through which non-democratic states rule.

By nature, developing countries feature processes of economic development that are inimical to democratic openings. More specifically, most though not all developing countries face what Eva Bellin (2002: 4) has called the 'developmental paradox'. Societal autonomy and the empowerment of social actors in relation to the state are key to the onset of pressures for democratisation. Developing states foster economic and industrial processes that constrain the autonomy of social actors in the short run while, in the long run, enhancing their prospects for empowerment and autonomy from the state. As Bellin (2002: 4) points out:

> by sponsoring industrialization, the [authoritarian] state nurtures the development of social forces ultimately capable of amassing sufficient power to challenge it and impose a measure of policy responsiveness upon it. In short, the very success of the state's strategy leads to the demise of the state's capacity to dictate policy unilaterally.

(On this point, also see chapter 3.)

While this developmental paradox may in the long run foster conditions that favour democratic openings, it is not a natural by-product of economic development in just any developing country. It is, rather, a specific outcome of development processes unleashed by 'developmental states'. Chalmers Johnson (1999) defines developmental states as those that combine the market-rationality of capitalist economies of states like the United States with the ideological-plan economies of states similar to that of the former Soviet Union. 'In the plan rational [developmental] state, the government will give greatest precedent to industrial policy; that is, to a concern with the structure of domestic industry and with promoting the structure that enhances the nation's international competitiveness' (Johnson 1982: 18–19). Developmental states, at least in their successful form, are preponderant in East Asia, with Japan, South Korea and Taiwan being paradigmatic cases. Elsewhere in the developing world, only the Chilean and to a much lesser extent the Argentine and the Brazilian states come close to being considered developmental, although all three were more aptly classified as 'bureaucratic-authoritarian' in their pre-democratic days (O'Donnell 1973). (Also see chapter 3 for a discussion of developmental states.)

In other parts of the developing world, most notably in the Middle East, in Central America and the Caribbean, and throughout Africa, the dynamics of economic transformation and development have been decidedly different. Whatever the inter- and intra-regional differences in the economic development of each of these remaining parts of the developing world, the one more or less consistent feature in all of them has been the state's ability to withstand being swept away as a result of the consequences of the development that it itself fostered. A partial exception is South Africa, although its democratic transition was as much a result of the relentless struggle of the African National Congress (ANC) against a morally bankrupt and internationally isolated state as it was a consequence of economic development and the rise of a small but articulate group of middle-class, black revolutionaries (DeFronzo 1996: 291–332).

economic development and democratisation

Regarding the relationship between economic development and democratisation, two key, interrelated developments should occur. First, there needs to emerge a sizeable middle class that is financially autonomous of the state. Second, and concomitant with the first development, there needs to be a private sector that also retains a meaningful level of economic and political autonomy from the state. These two factors are, of course, organically linked. By definition, the middle classes outside of the government service (that is, financially autonomous from the state) belong to the private sector. But there are also important qualitative differences between the two, namely in levels of economic power and organisational resources. Their natural overlappings notwithstanding, the two groups serve the process of democratic opening in two distinct ways, with elements from the middle classes doing so *subjectively* while the private sector do so *objectively*.

The subjective ways in which the middle classes help the cause of democratisation is through their explicit or implicit support for non-state initiatives and non-state-dictated sources of identity, especially as represented through professional associations and non-governmental organisations (NGOs). While such activities on the part of the middle classes, if permitted by the authorities, ultimately erode the institutional, objective bases of the state, they also help spread in society the ideals of self-empowerment, political independence (from the state), local activism, and civic responsibility. The middle classes, in other words, are critical components of civil society, so long as they have the political autonomy and the financial and organisational resources necessary to mobilise themselves into professional associations and other civil society organisations.

This is not to imply that the oppositional potential of the middle classes is overwhelmingly, or even largely, subjective and devoid of direct institutional significance. In fact, this is far from the case. Through their membership in NGOs and professional associations, members of the middle classes – many of whom are responsible for the initial establishment of such alternative institutions – directly challenge the functions and performance of state institutions in specific areas, be it in the provision of particular services or the fostering of a sense of confidence that the state had long taken away. Nevertheless, these middle-class-driven organisations contribute more to the larger societal context and atmosphere within which democratic openings occur rather than serve as the actual catalysts for authoritarian withdrawals.

The defection of the private sector from the 'authoritarian bargain', however, can be far more directly consequential for the overall strength and the institutional integrity of the state. Authoritarian states, as we shall see presently, rely on authoritarian bargains of various kinds, many of which revolve around the incorporation and complicity of the private sector. For the private sector's defection to be politically consequential, it needs to have first amassed formidable economic muscle and organisational and financial strength of its own, and, even if it initially owed its good fortunes to the state and its corporatist largesse, it must first break away from the state's tentacles and become politically autonomous.

Much, then, depends on the viability and resilience of the bargain struck between authoritarian state leaders and key social actors whose financial and/or organisational resources the state needs to co-opt for its own purposes. At the very least, even if the bargain does not explicitly co-opt these resources, it needs to mollify their potential for political opposition if it is to persevere. Looking at authoritarian bargains in broad strokes, we see why they unravelled in pre-democratic Latin America, and to a much lesser extent in East Asia, especially in South Korea and Taiwan, while they continue to persevere in the Middle East.

In Brazil and Argentina, the state adopted the import-substitution industrialisation (ISI) strategy for development, through which it sought to placate middle-class demands for consumer durables and, more importantly, direct targeted benefits to domestic and international investors who were part of its corporatist equation (Franko 2003: 59–61). From about the 1950s to the late 1970s the bargain worked, as military-led states fostered impressive industrial growth, kept the middle classes economically content, and held the domestic opposition at bay through indiscriminate repression. But in the face of inadequate domestic exports or other natural resources (such as hydrocarbon reserves) to finance ISI, Brazil and Argentina had to resort to massive borrowing from international lenders, confronting balance-of-payment and debt crises by the early 1980s (Waterbury 1999: 334–5). The structural adjustments that were subsequently dictated by the so-called Washington Consensus alienated the very groups who were once the beneficiaries of ISI – the middle classes and the investors – resulting in the unravelling of their authoritarian bargains (Haggard and Kaufman 1995: 33). The Argentine military state, itself suffering from internal discord and lack of cohesion, resorted to one last desperate measure to rally middle class support when it invaded the Falkland Islands in 1982. But its failed venture only expedited its collapse and the retreat of the ruling generals back into the barracks.

In Argentina, the military state simply collapsed. Similarly hasty withdrawals from power also occurred in Bolivia and Peru, as well as in the Philippines, followed subsequently by elections, the democratic veracity of which are still open to debate nearly two decades later. In Brazil and Uruguay, where the military exited from power under more favourable economic and political circumstances, it was in a better position to negotiate the terms of its withdrawal, already having committed itself to some political liberalisation before the elections of the mid-1980s (Haggard and Kaufman 1995: 69).

In East Asia, meanwhile, developmental states were able to foster and in turn rest on what some observers have called 'conservative coalitions'. According to David Waldner (1999: 138), 'conservative coalitions are narrowly based coalitions supporting collaboration between the state and large business; significant segments of the population are excluded from these coalitions, and deliberate efforts are made to maximize side-payments to popular classes.' The South Korean and Taiwanese state elites (and the Japanese elites before them) enjoyed high levels of internal cohesion. Against a backdrop of deep-seated economic nationalism (Woo-Cumings 1999: 6), these elites, secure in their incumbency as they were, could devise economic policy without significant pressure from the popular classes (Waldner 1999: 4). Following the Japanese model, the Taiwanese and South Korean states devised elaborate agencies, as well as formal and informal mechanisms, to promote the growth and success of the private sector: Korea's Ministry of Trade, Industry and Energy (originally called the MTI), and Taiwan's Council for Economic Cooperation and Development (later renamed CEPD), successfully replicated the work of Japan's Ministry of International Trade and Industry, the MITI (Weiss 1998, 55–9). So long as the state's policies resulted in the growth of private-sector capital, the private sector remained ambivalent toward democratic reform. However, when 'the state began to cut back on its sponsorship of private sector capital and the latter's need for state support also declined. . .the private sector began to exhibit remarkable enthusiasm for political reform and democratization' (Bellin 2002: 163). By the early 1990s, both the South Korean and Taiwanese states, and in a somewhat more precarious way also the Thai state, could be considered democratic.

The situation in the countries of the Middle East could not have been more different. Almost uniformly, regional states differ from those in East Asia and Latin America in three significant ways. They:

- initially lacked elite cohesion;
- have relatively easy access to economic resources; and
- are comparatively 'unglobalised', that is, they are relatively unaffected by globalisation.

These variables combined to produce authoritarian bargains that so far have been able to withstand major challenges, undergoing only minor modifications. Consequently, when unravelling authoritarian bargains characterise regime change in East Asia and Latin America, many Middle East states remain bastions of authoritarianism.

First, especially unlike the states of East Asia, those in the Middle East, with the exception of Israel, had little or no initial elite cohesion. To a large extent, this was a product of the region's colonial interlude from the early 1920s to the late 1940s, when indigenous political institutions were unable to emerge and gain a hold. When independence came abruptly after the end of the World War II – and in Algeria in 1962 after a long and bloody war of national liberation – political aspirants competed with one another for dominance by seeking to cultivate support among specific social groups. As Waldner (1999: 36) maintains, 'intense elite conflict impels one of the competing elite factions to incorporate a mass base: the state bargains with popular classes, exchanging material benefits for popular support.'

The incorporation of the masses into the political process might have undermined the state's economic performance, but it also gave it a facade of 'street democracy' that masked, albeit often unsuccessfully, its innately authoritarian nature. At the very least, it balanced out the grievances of the groups excluded from the bargain (such as workers and peasants) with support from those who were included (for example, civil servants). As many once inclusionary states aged, they resorted less and less to street theatre to keep up democratic pretences. However, they could not significantly reduce the high levels of side-payment they were disbursing to their societal constituents. In fact, over time, a relationship of mutual dependence developed, between the state on the one side and certain key societal constituents on the other, with neither being able fully to escape the relationship. Precisely who these societal groups comprise differs from one Middle Eastern country to another. Across the board, however, the middle classes are uniformly targeted for incorporation, especially through expansive civil services and state-owned enterprises (Richards and Waterbury 1996: 210–11). Other targeted groups often include organised labour, especially in Algeria and Egypt (Pripstein Pousney 1997), or wealthier members of the private sector, as in Iraq (Farouk-Sluglett and Sluglett 2001: 242) and Turkey (Waldner 1999: 71–2).

Second, especially unlike Latin American states, those in the Middle East are often able to rely on rentier economies, a phenomenon discussed extensively in the political-economy literature of the region. Briefly, rentierism is the result of earning high profits from economic activities that do not require proportionately high levels of productivity. For example, the extraction and export of oil is a relatively easy task compared to the amount of revenues and profits accrued from selling it abroad. In the Middle East, in fact, oil has become a primary source of rent for most of the region's governments, and the 'oil monarchies' (Gause 1994) of the Persian Gulf in particular have become rentier states *par excellence*. But rent-seeking is not limited to the export of primary products at highly profitable rates. As Peter Evans (1995: 34) maintains, 'rationing foreign exchange, restricting entry through licensing procedures, and instituting tariffs or quantitative restrictions on imports are all ways of creating rents.' In oil-poor Jordan, for example, a rentier economy has emerged around massive infusions of foreign aid and worker remittances (Piro 1998: 63).

Rentierism has given Middle Eastern states extractive autonomy from society. In Jordan and elsewhere in the Middle East, the state has been able to provide for the population without demanding much in the way of revenues in return (Piro 1998: 60). Direct forms of taxation in the Middle East, for example, remain 'ludicrously low in most Arab states in which a personal income tax exists, and in a good number of them such a tax does not even exist' (Luciani 1995: 217). More importantly, by and large, the state in the Middle East has been able to avoid the vulnerabilities of debt-ridden Latin American states by continually financing the incorporation of groups dependent on it. Even the recurrent economic recessions of the 1980s and the 1990s failed to completely dislodge the rentier underpinnings of Middle Eastern economies, although they did necessitate certain economic liberalisation measures (Harik and Sullivan 1992). Ultimately, however, as the once-fractured state elites have over time become more cohesive, half-hearted economic liberalisation measures were neither followed up nor (involuntarily) yielded meaningful political liberalisation, notwithstanding outside observers' hopes (Korany et al. 1995; 1998).

Third, globalisation has had a comparatively lesser impact in the Middle East – with the exception of Iraq and the US-led invasion of 2003 – compared to other regions of the developing world, save Africa. There is a strong correlation between high levels of economic and normative globalisation and the prospects of democratic transitions (Simensen 1999: 394–5). However, literally all states in the Middle East, with the exception of the region's two democracies –Turkey and Israel – rank consistently low on all indices of globalisation. Outside of the oil sector, in fact, foreign direct investment has been low in the Middle East as compared to levels in either East Asia or in Latin America (World Bank 2003: 312).

Authoritarianism and comparatively low levels of globalisation in the Middle East assume a mutually reinforcing relationship with one another. In the Middle East overall and within a number of specific Middle Eastern countries in particular, state leaders have greeted globalisation with considerable scepticism, seeking at most to allow it in a 'trickled', highly controlled manner. The official fear of and resulting restrictions on information technology that is apparent in all authoritarian states of the Middle East attests attempts to control the flow and nature of globalisation (Teitelbaum 2002). For now, with the institutional underpinnings of dictatorial rule continuing to exhibit remarkable resilience, the potential that globalisation would erode authoritarianism in the Middle East

---

box 4.5   the middle east and globalisation

There are a number of reasons for the lack of impact of globalisation on most countries in the Middle East. Among the most important are the fact of weak domestic markets and uncompetitive private sectors, as well as strong opposition from so-called 'moralisers' who see globalisation as a threat to cultural authenticity, religious and/or ethnic identity, and their countries' national interests (Henry and Springborg 2001: 19). Far more important, however, is the fundamental threat that globalisation poses to the grip that authoritarian leaders have on the reins of power. By nature, globalisation requires transparency in economic transactions, free flows of information, a credible banking system, and civil society empowerment. Each of these phenomena alone, and especially in combination, can be lethal to authoritarian states. Not surprisingly, regional authoritarian 'bunker' states — such as Algeria, Qaddafi's Libya, Baathist-era Iraq, Asad's Syria, and the Sudan, as well as the region's 'bully praetorian' republics of Egypt and Tunisia — seem most wary about globalisation (Henry and Springborg 2001: 20–1).

seems highly unlikely to be realised. And, by the same token, so long as authoritarian rule remains the norm prospects for the region to undergo globalisation – like Latin America or East Asia – seem bleak.

We can see that economic development has a paradoxical relationship with democratisation. There is no linear relationship between industrial development and democracy. The causal relationship between the two is far more nuanced and context-specific. After looking at the relationship between capitalist development and democracy in Europe, Latin America and the Caribbean, Rueschemeyer et al. (1992: 284) come to the conclusion that 'factors such as dependent development, late and state-led development, international political constellations and events, and international learning, all conspired to create conditions in which the combination of causes and thus the paths to democracy (and dictatorship) were different in different historical contexts and in different regions'. If in the process of economic development, the middle classes and the private sector gain autonomy from the state on the one hand and organisational and financial resources and strength on the other, they can emerge as powerful actors in the push for state accountability and democratisation. Specifically, private-sector defection from authoritarian bargains can prove fatal to the longevity of state elites, as it did in East Asia and in much of Latin America.

In sum, increasing economic integration into global markets – which tends to strengthen emerging elements with civil society, foster transparency and free flows of information, and ultimately encourage greater economic and political accountability – can over time erode the staying power of authoritarian state elites. Much deeper levels of globalisation in Latin America and East Asia correlate closely with their greater preponderance of democratisation. In the Middle East, however, patterns of economic development have neither fostered the emergence of an autonomous and powerful private sector or middle class, nor have they resulted in significant levels of globalisation. Consequently, by and large, economic development in the Middle East has served as both hindrance and obstacle to democratic transitions rather than a democratisation catalyst.

civil society and democratisation

This extensive focus on the political economy of democratisation is not to suggest that civil society is unimportant. In fact, in recent years, considerable scholarship has been devoted to exploring the relationship between civil society and democratisation (Gellner 1994; Gill 2000; Hall 1995; Tester 1992). A number of experts have pointed to the prevalence of civil society in regions such as Latin America or Eastern Europe as one of the main reasons for their greater levels of democratisation compared to the Middle East or Africa, where civil society is often less developed (Gyimah-Boadi 1996; Lewis 1992). Regarding the Middle East specifically, it is often argued that the region's democratic deficit is due to the fact that civil society either does not exist, or, where it does, it is too embryonic and fragile to be of serious consequence. It is, therefore, important to explore the precise nature of the relationship between civil society and democratisation, and to see what consequences, if any, arise from civil society's regional predicament.

Philip Oxhorn defines civil society as

> a rich social fabric formed by a multiplicity of territorially and functionally based units. The strength of civil society is measured by the peaceful coexistence of these units and by their collective capacity simultaneously to *resist subordination* to the state and to *demand inclusion* into national political structures. The public character of these units allows them to justify and act in open pursuit of their collective interests in competition with one another. Strong civil societies are thus synonymous with a high level of 'institutionalized social pluralism'.

In addition, 'because they are self-constituted, the units of civil society serve as the foundations for political democracy' (Oxhorn 1995: 251–2).

It is important to note a subtle – but important – distinction to be drawn between *civil society* and *civil society organisations* (CSOs). CSOs are the constituent components of civil society; Oxhorn (1995: 251) calls them 'a multiplicity of territorially and functionally based units'. CSOs are the various individual groups and organisations whose collective efforts over time – and the effects of the horizontal and often also the organic links that develop among them – make it possible for civil society to emerge. Frequently, CSOs are issue-specific and issue-driven, and as such have a strong sense of corporate identity. They are also politically, institutionally and financially independent from the state and guard their autonomy jealously. In fact, they often come into existence as the very result of the state's inability, or unwillingness, to perform those functions which society relies on it to perform. CSOs therefore emerge in response to specific exigencies created by state inaction or impotence – for example, state inability to ensure citizens' physical security, or its lack of sufficient attention to spreading literacy or job skills. Therefore, the emergence over time of CSOs, followed later by civil society, is

---

box 4.6   linz and stepan on civil society

Juan Linz and Alfred Stepan (1996: 7) define civil society as 'that arena of the polity where self-organizing groups, movements, and individuals, relatively autonomous from the state, attempt to articulate values, create associations and solidarities, and advance their interests.' However, they argue, civil society is a tremendously helpful but ultimately insufficient element of democratic transitions. 'At best, civil society can destroy a nondemocratic regime,' but for democratic transition – and especially democratic consolidation – to occur, civil society needs to be politicised and transformed into 'political society', that is 'that arena in which the polity specifically arranges itself to contest the legitimate right to exercise control over public power and the state apparatus' (Linz and Stepan 1996: 8).

---

contingent on the nature and extent of the relationship between state and larger society.

Since a democratic transition will not be made possible until an authoritarian regime is confronted with a crisis of power, CSOs, and even civil society are, *in themselves*, politically inconsequential if they do not directly weaken state power. What CSOs and civil society do is to give social actors an unprecedented sense of empowerment and self-actualisation. But social empowerment is not the same as a regime's institutional weakening and a consequent vacuum of official power. By itself, therefore, civil society does not lead to democratisation. The existence of civil society is not even a prerequisite for democratic transition. However, in cases where it does exist, civil society not only greatly facilitates the transition to democracy but, more importantly, facilitates democracy's deepening in society once a new, democratic state has been established. In fact, as Linz and Stepan (1996) maintain, it is at the stage of democratic consolidation that civil society makes its greatest and most important contribution. Civil society does, nevertheless, provide the larger societal and cultural context within which collapsing states are replaced by democratic ones.

democratic consolidation

The term, 'democratic consolidation' refers to the evolution and embedding of a democratic system, tracing a trajectory from a procedural, quasi-democracy to a sustained – and sustainable – liberal democracy. Huntington (1991: 266–7) views democratic consolidation in terms of the passage of a period of time or the peaceful turnover of elected officials in two electoral cycles. A democracy may be viewed as consolidated, he maintains, if it successfully and peacefully goes through two elite turnovers following democratic elections. Instead of affixing a specific – and somewhat arbitrary – period before a democracy can be considered consolidated, it might be more accurate to conceptualise democratic consolidation in terms of *depth* and the evolution of a democratic system from a *procedural democracy* to a *liberal democracy*. As the earlier discussion of quasi-democracies demonstrated, a political system may have all of the institutional and procedural trappings of a democracy while remaining devoid of a democratic essence and spirit. O'Donnell (1994: 56) correctly makes a distinction between *consolidation* and *endurance*; a quasi-democracy, he maintains, may endure without being consolidated. As conceptualised here, quasi-democracies may be institutionally *consolidated*, but have not (yet) acquired the societal *depth* and resonance – those civic components (Linz and Stepan 1996: 7) – traditionally associated with liberal democracy.

Because democratic consolidation is a continuing and dynamic process, it is difficult ever to consider a democratic political system 'consolidated'. By nature, any democracy requires built-in institutional safeguards and constant vigilance – in the form of judicial review, or checks and balances, separation of powers, or any combination of these – to ensure against the possibility of a breakdown or a reversal. There are two critical elements in democratic consolidation. The first revolves around democratic constitution-making and the establishment of viable, workable democratic institutions. A second critical element is the new system's level of legitimacy and its ability to effectively deal with emerging challenges to its performance.

The first element is procedural and revolves around the designing of a workable constitution that is democratic, is institutionally viable, and, at the same time, is not so alien from the country's political and historical tradition as to require a prolonged period of political socialisation. Constitutions may be divided into two general types:

- 'preservative', that is, seeking to preserve the political order – as is the case with the British constitution; and
- 'transformative' , that is, seeking to change and transform the previous order (Sunstein 2001: 67).

The transformative mode characterises the constitutions of new democracies, which face the most serious challenges in terms of workability and innovation. Their task is made more difficult as they have to devise a delicate and viable balance of power both between the state and society and within various state institutions. As the examples of the Weimar Republic in Germany (1919–33) and the French Fourth Republic (1946–58) showed, designing democratic systems that are at once both democratic and workable is extremely difficult. There are three important issues to deal with:

- How to ensure the fair representation of all of the different political tendencies without making the legislature dysfunctional or giving disproportionate influence to small parties;
- How to manage the powers of the legislature and the executive and balance the relationship between them;
- What kind of electoral system is best?

These and similar questions are seldom raised in the transition process but become extremely important and consequential later. To this day, the relatively well-established democracies of Israel and New Zealand continue to tinker with their electoral systems, both having recently decided to have the prime minister elected by direct, popular vote while still otherwise retaining their parliamentary systems.

For new democracies, where consolidation is a tenuous and embryonic phase, issues associated with institutionalisation can be particularly problematic. In Argentina in 1994, for example, former president Carlos Menem forced through a constitutional amendment that enabled him to remain in office longer than the constitution originally permitted. In the late 1990s, Hugo Chavez went so far as to add a whole new branch to the Venezuelan government in an attempt to strengthen his personal power-base. Earlier, in the mid-1990s, Alberto Fujimori had engaged in similar machinations in Peru. The challenge is not to ensure that all elected officials have impeccable democratic credentials. Even in long-established Western democracies there may be elected officials who would subvert the democratic process if they could get away with it. Former British prime minister Margaret Thatcher's restrictions on the BBC's coverage of the Northern Ireland conflict, and the US attorney-general John Ashcroft's inconsistent adherence to constitutional guarantees to civil liberties in light of the so-called 'war on terror' are prime examples. The question is why can Menem (Argentina) or Chavez (Venezuela) get away with it, but Thatcher and Ashcroft, for the most part at least, cannot? Apart from the obvious factors of age and tradition as enjoyed by the older democracies, there is also the critical element of legitimacy. This is the second crucial factor in consolidating new democracies.

New democracies face numerous challenges and difficulties in the post-transition period, not all of which they can anticipate or are properly equipped to deal with. Most new democracies face two immediate challenges. One is how to deal with figures from the former regime

– to confront the evils of the past head on and somehow go through a national process of political cleansing, or to try and forget the past and instead look to the future. South Africa's Truth and Reconciliation Commission, convened to hear reports of human rights violations committed in the country between 1960 and 1994, is a classic case of an attempt by a new, post-transition regime to confront the sins of the past to try to make certain they would not happen again. The Commission, whose proceedings were nationally televised, provided a forum for both blacks and whites to talk about the crimes that had been committed against them, or which they had committed themselves, and to forgive or beg for forgiveness as the case might be. Other 'truth commissions' were also established in Peru and in Sierra Leone in order to help the national 'healing process' in each case. In a number of other cases – as in Argentina, Uruguay and Chile – the pacts that made democratic transition possible featured guarantees of immunity from prosecution for those who had committed human rights abuses in the past, almost always former army officers and commanders.

A second, more immediate challenge is the economy. More specifically, new democracies often find themselves rolling back the extensive tentacles of the state as inherited from the pre-democratic days and instituting far-reaching economic liberalisation and structural adjustment programmes (SAPs). Particular national differences notwithstanding, SAPs – the exact details and implementation of which are often prescribed or mandated by the IMF and the World Bank – tend to share several common characteristics. Most notably, SAPs entail the removal of state subsidies from inefficient state-owned or state-supported industries, often resulting in lay-offs and rises in unemployment. Similarly, new democracies often remove or substantially reduce price subsidies on foodstuffs and other basic consumer goods, thereby precipitating sharp price increases. Increasing international demands to open up the economy to outside investments and to remove protective tariff barriers tend to further exacerbate economic difficulties. These include even more price hikes, the demise of older internationally uncompetitive domestic industries, and rising domestic unemployment among labour forces whose skills are not yet sufficient or fit for new market realities.

Simultaneously, since SAPs often entail the sale of state-owned enterprises (SOEs) and the awarding of government contracts to private capital, post-transition periods often result in a sharpening of glaring differences in class standing as represented through purchasing power and economic status. It is often the well connected and the wealthy who are the primary beneficiaries of government contracts, the sale of SOEs, and trade liberalisation. Especially in the previously closed markets of East European countries, an entire class of entrepreneurs has emerged which imports foreign goods for the wealthy. The middle and the lower classes, in the meanwhile, find their living standards declining and their purchasing powers eroded. In simple terms, the rich get richer and the poor get poorer. (See the chapters in this book by Sen and Taylor (chapters 5 and 13) for further discussion of this topic.)

Not surprisingly, if these conditions persist, before long the urban middle classes begin to long for 'the good old days' and start to lose faith in the new, democratic system. The ensuing consequences can be highly detrimental for a new democracy. Given today's global environment, despite the serious economic difficulties they face, outright overthrow of new democracies seems highly unlikely. If for no other reason, therefore, the global environment will serve as a safeguard mechanism against the collapse and breakdown of East European and Latin American democracies. *Procedurally*, at least, these democracies appear to have been consolidated. However, the economic challenges they face often directly translate into voting preferences as the electorate is likely to vote for those offering quick fixes and populist platforms regardless of their real intentions or their democratic credentials. This is precisely the reason that the likes of Chavez and Fujimori found their way into presidential palaces in Latin America. In Eastern Europe, the electorate has repeatedly voted into office the same crop of ex-communists against whom it rebelled only a decade or so ago.

In sum, as long as structural economic difficulties persist in new democracies and are not properly addressed, the possibility of reversals and the ascension of non-democrats to office by democratic means remain a distinct possibility. Democracy as a political form and a system may not be overthrown or break down *per se*. But the resilience of its liberal nature remains highly vulnerable to serious challenges from within. In nearly all of today's contemporary democracies, lack of consolidation in the form of institutional breakdown is rather unlikely, though by no means impossible. What is far more likely to happen, however, is an increasing shallowness and loss of depth and substance, whereby a newly democratic system becomes even less substantive.

conclusion

All political systems are characterised by a certain distribution of power and resources between the state on the one side and society on the other.

- In *democracies*, the balance of power is institutionally and procedurally tilted in favour of society, since at regular intervals society – via elections – chooses the leaders of the state and exercises its influence on their agendas and policies. Exactly how meaningful and embedded this societal political participation is varies from case to case – or it can vary in the same case from one period to another. It depends on both the institutional make-up of the system and the degree to which the electorate cares or can afford to get involved in politics.
- A *democratic transition* is the process whereby the state–society balance of power shifts from one of state dominance and unresponsiveness and results in the emergence of developments and forces that politically empower society on a routine and regular basis.
- *Democratic consolidation* occurs when society's political empowerment acquires depth and goes beyond the narrow circle of socially isolated elites. Consolidation, of course, is a continuing process without a final end. Even if unconsolidated, however, the prospects for the current crop of new democracies appears bright, from an institutional perspective if nothing else. Nevertheless, substance and facade are two quite different things.

5

the political economy of development

gautam sen

This chapter examines:

- influential theories of economic development;
- reasons why some countries – and regions – have developed, but not others; and
- the reasons for debt and financial crises in the developing world from the 1980s.

introduction

The idea of economic development is intimately associated with the study of economics itself, traceable to the preoccupations of classical political economists before and after Adam Smith, David Ricardo and others (Bardhan 1993: 129–42; Martinussen 1997; Meier and Stiglitz 2001). However, development economics, as a subject of enquiry, came into its own at the end of World War II, with the onset of African and Asian decolonisation. It addressed the urgent task of combating poverty in emerging nations and was also identified with the very task of nation-building itself. Economic development became the *raison d'être* of the state in the newly independent countries, even when other ideological claims to legitimacy like religion and ethnicity informed it.

The post-war record of economic progress in developing countries is uneven, but there is a dramatic contrast in performance between a significant number of Asian countries and much of the continent of Africa. Rates of economic growth in most Latin American countries have fallen behind the most successful countries of Asia, but they continue to exhibit the higher absolute per capita incomes with which they began the post-war period. However, there is a significant minority of

89

developing countries that have stagnated or suffered a decline in absolute incomes owing to a combination of negligible economic improvement and population growth. In addition, there are noticeable differences in income distribution among countries, with Asia exhibiting more egalitarian patterns than elsewhere (World Bank 1993).

economic analysis of development

We start by examining some of the key theoretical contributions made to the economic analysis of development in the 19th century and first half of the 20th.

In the 19th century, it was widely believed that trade protection was essential for industrialisation. This idea was inspired by the views of figures such as Alexander Hamilton and Friedrich List, who saw a need for protection to shelter domestic industry from foreign competition (Evans et al. 1985, Evans 1995; Sen 1984). Subsequent debates on how to bring about industrialisation in backward agrarian economies took place in the context of Soviet industrialisation from the 1920s. That programme culminated in the ruthless expropriation of an agricultural surplus to finance industrialisation in the infamous five-year Stalinist economic plans, which nevertheless achieved spectacular industrial successes (Nove 1972). In the USSR, post-World War II policies on economic development were coloured by the example of the rapid progress of Soviet industry during the 1930s, which occurred during a time of economic crisis in the capitalist world.

After World War II, the key theoretical conceptualisation was the adaptation of what was known as the 'Harrod-Domar model'. This outlined the central role of capital accumulation and productivity for economic growth. In this formulation, the fundamental determinant of the rate of economic growth was the savings rate and the incremental capital-output ratio. However, it depended on a number of restrictive assumptions and the concept was later extended in the pioneering work of Robert Solow in 1956.

Subsequent work identified two additional factors to explain growth, the contribution of human capital and the dynamics of endogenous growth for productive activity. While the relevance of human capital accumulation was already recognised in Solow's model, it was given greater attention in subsequent decades. The importance of endogenous sources of growth was highlighted in the path-breaking work of Paul Romer.

---

box 5.1   robert solow on development

Robert Solow's innovation was to include labour as a factor, while the role of technology was highlighted as an independent variable and crucial catalyst for economic growth. The critical prediction of Solow's model (1970) was of convergence between developing and advanced economies through capital inflows into the former – because capital in developing countries has a higher marginal productivity, since they have less of it. However, convergence proved elusive and the so-called residual (total factor productivity) was ascribed a large share of the contribution to economic growth. Moreover, Solow's model relies on efficient markets, which are often lacking in developing countries.

Arthur Lewis (1954) identified the existence of a dual economy and the potential for transferring surplus labour from agriculture to the manufacturing sector as the vehicle for accelerating economic growth. Although subsequently criticised for overestimating the extent of unproductive labour in agriculture and inadequate recognition of the capital inputs required to complement it, Lewis' dual economy model remains an important backdrop for the analysis of economic development.

policy recommendations for achieving economic growth

These and other theoretical insights informed policy recommendations for achieving economic growth and hence development.

The analysis of the factors on the supply side, necessary for economic growth, does not identify the wider permissive conditions for the accumulation of physical and human capital and successful technological advance (Cohen and Soto 2002). These *permissive* conditions for the supply side of the economy require an understanding of the impact of the international economy, which comprises an important aspect of the demand side of the growth equation and also has an impact on supply (for example, as a source of capital and technology). These issues have been crucial for debates about development policy since World War II.

Many such debates concerned the nature of *market failures* that would justify corrective *state intervention*. While few observers questioned the need for state intervention in economic development, opinion was divided on:

- how much state intervention; and
- the appropriate policies.

We can note divisions between:

- a conservative, pro-market view; and

- a more interventionist perspective. (Note, however, that few now espouse Soviet-style central economic planning in the post-Cold War era.)

Some observers have also been concerned to point out the presence of political factors that frustrate or, indeed, assist economic development. But the current mainstream view is that development economics is a subject amenable to standard neo-classical tools of analysis.

An early proposal was that state intervention was necessary to ensure 'balanced growth' (Rosenstein-Rodan 1984). It was argued that investment needed to occur contemporaneously in a number of sectors – since investments in different sectors were interdependent owing to supply-demand linkages. As a result, they needed to be coordinated in order for each to achieve optimum production levels – because there are increasing returns to scale in the relevant output range for producers. Some believed that markets in developing countries could not ensure such coordination because of high start-up costs in latecomer countries (Bell 1998: 818–25). The issue of interdependence and concomitant externalities was considered especially acute in relation to infrastructure projects owing to the lumpiness of investment in them.

Accompanying the interventionist implications of 'balanced growth' policies was a lack of confidence in international trade, partly because of the experience of the economic depression immediately before World War II. It was this scepticism towards the international economy that underpinned the far-reaching proposals put forward by Raul Prebisch (1984), the first director-general of the Economic Commission on Latin America (ECLA). His 'structuralist' analysis viewed the problem of underdevelopment in relation to its reciprocal interaction with the developed world and argued that development entailed industrialisation. He and, subsequently, Hans W. Singer (1984) held that primary commodity exporters were condemned to experience a secular decline in their terms of trade, accompanied by chronic balance of payments crises. For both men, the preferred policy package was to shift production towards manufacturing, with its higher income-elasticity of demand. Consequently, they therefore favoured state-led import-substituting industrialisation (ISI) to escape both the low-level equilibrium trap of commodity production and the bias of skewed income distribution in developing countries towards importing manufactures. Their aim was the rapid promotion of domestic manufactured goods production and the means to produce them – that is, capital goods.

Critiques of both these perspectives underpinned the subsequent debate about development policy that ended with the neo-classical counter-revolution in the 1980s, culminating with IMF structural adjustment programmes and its intellectual crystallisation in the 'Washington consensus' (Toye 1993: 93–152). (Also see chapters 1, 3 and 4 for discussions of the Washington consensus.) Before this, Hirschman (1984) had argued that, instead of balanced growth, it was desirable for economic growth to be 'unbalanced'. Even earlier, Chenery (1968) rejected the scepticism towards the international economy and proposed that national economic development should be integrated with it, in order to benefit from comparative advantage.

development outcomes in developing regions

asia

After World War II, in a period spanning four decades until the 1980s, the most noteworthy economic transformation occurred in East Asia in the so-called Asian Tigers and other high-performing Asian economies (HPAEs), followed by the more recent economic successes of the People's Republic of China, South East Asia – especially Malaysia and Thailand – and India (World Bank 1993). More generally, there was a sharp break in the fortunes of a significant number of countries across the developing world at various points in the decade after the quadrupling of oil prices in 1973.

The HPAEs achieved middle-to high-income status in three decades, beginning in the mid-1960s. The rapid advance of South Korea, Taiwan, Hong Kong and Singapore was followed by the impressive gains of other Asian economies. Growth rates in a significant number of Asian countries, including China, but excluding Japan and India, a more recent entrant among high performers, was around 7 per cent a year over three decades. The result was a dramatic global shift in manufacturing production from the US, Japan and Europe to Asia. Exports played an important role in Asian economic growth and foreign direct investment (FDI) was also an important contributor in South East Asia and China (some others, like Mexico, also gained), countries that followed the original Asian Tigers of East Asia (World Bank 1993; United Nations 1998).

The economic success that subsequently occurred in Malaysia, Thailand, Indonesia, and to some degree the Philippines was followed by high rates of growth in nearby former communist regimes like Vietnam and Cambodia, which constituted the second tier of Asian countries to advance. However, the financial crisis of 1997 deflected a number of

---

box 5.2   china's strong economic growth

The spectacular advance of the original group of Asian Tigers was followed by the rapid economic transformation of China after 1979 (Sen 2002). A swathe of southern China has now achieved remarkable economic growth, attracting huge amounts of FDI, principally from overseas Chinese communities in Asia. The initial economic success of China that underpinned the later phase of explosive economic growth began with agrarian reform and the inauguration of so-called township village enterprises (TVEs) that achieved high rates of productivity growth.

The subsequent phase of FDI-led export growth was remarkable. Access to the US market allowed China to take advantage of prodigious supplies of cheap, proficient labour and foreign expertise to achieve sustained export-led growth. Despite some doubts about statistics on growth and FDI (it remains the second largest recipient of FDI in the world) and concern over the viability of state-owned industries, as well as the associated bad debts being carried by banks, few countries have attained its economic success with such rapidity.

---

countries, including Thailand, Malaysia, South Korea and Indonesia, while others – including Russia and various Latin American countries – experienced deleterious 'contagion effects'. However, the long term trend in economic growth remains positive in the Asian region, despite the severe socio-economic dislocation suffered by Indonesia in particular in recent years.

India's dirigiste economy, which had been experiencing falling growth in successive decades of planning that began in the early 1950s, experienced a sustained acceleration of economic growth in the late 1980s, which has been maintained since. The average annual GDP growth rate has been around 6 per cent a year, with an even sharper rise in exports and a fall in the percentage of population below the poverty line (Deaton with Dreze 2002). Feeble attempts at domestic deregulation and liberalisation in the late 1980s were intensified in the aftermath of a serious balance of payments crisis in 1991 and resort to IMF borrowing (Mohan 2004; Krueger 2002a; Jalan 2003). India in 2004 enjoyed the status of the second-fastest-growing economy in the world, after China. The Indian economy has had particular success in software exports and is an increasingly popular destination for FDI for some industries – for example, call centres and back-office services like clerical support – and is demonstrating prowess in other areas, such as auto-parts fabrication.

In sum, many of the developing-country success stories are to be found in Asia. We can explain this outcome by allusion to the ability of mostly strong states to take advantage of global conditions for domestic benefit.

latin america

Following the quadrupling of oil prices in the 1970s, economic growth in much of Latin America, under a regime of import-substitution, reached a turning point. This development policy had delivered modest growth in real incomes in Brazil and Mexico, though not in Argentina. However, with the exception of some of the smaller countries annual growth rates of GDP had been slight, though Brazil itself did achieve spectacular growth rates during the late 1960s and early 1970s. But Latin America entered a period of severe economic crisis during the 1980s, experiencing a succession of debt crises that began with the Mexican debt default of 1982 and endemic real output losses.

A degree of stability was subsequently restored, although at high social cost, with debt-restructuring and economic reform. The economic situation currently remains unpredictable, despite periods of economic stability. Argentina's economy collapsed yet again in 2001 and is currently (2004) undergoing a renewed IMF-sponsored programme of adjustment. Brazil is struggling to stave off a balance-of-payments crisis by resorting to high interest rates that are, however, damaging both investment and growth. Of the larger countries, Mexico seems to have escaped periodic economic setback since joining the North American Free Trade Agreement (NAFTA), while Chile is also achieving high rates of economic growth.

In sum, Latin American countries have experienced variable developmental outcomes in recent years. Many observers contend that part of the reason for this is that the region's governments have showed erratic ability in dealing with both domestic and international problems.

sub-saharan africa

The record of economic growth of most of sub-Saharan Africa (SSA) was reasonably good between 1960 and the onset of the oil price rise of 1973. However, by the 1980s most regional countries had suffered a major reverse at some point, followed by chronic stagnation lasting into the early 1990s. In a recent study by Pritchett (1998), half of the 21 countries he examined – amounting to 80 per cent of the region's population and GDP – experienced reasonably high growth before a prolonged period of stagnation began. The others had stagnated with growth rates below 1.5 per cent a year. Subsequent recovery was modest. For the period as a whole, the average annual growth of per capita incomes has been 0.9 per cent, compared to 3.9 per cent in the best African performers (Botswana and Mauritius) and in East Asia, and 2.4 per cent compared to developing countries as a group.

In sum, the dominant characteristic for most SSA countries for most of the period has been sharp oscillations in growth patterns. In addition, growth rates in the non-oil Middle East and North Africa have not on the whole been encouraging.

Table 5.1 Average annual percentage growth of GDP in selected developing countries and regions

Country	1980–1991	1990–2001
Korea	8.7	5.7
Singapore	5.3	7.8
Hong Kong	5.6	3.9
East Asia & Pacific	6.1	7.5
Thailand		3.8
Malaysia	2.9	6.5
Indonesia	3.9	3.8
Philippines	-1.2	3.3
Vietnam	Not available	7.6
Cambodia	Not available	4.8
China	7.8	10.0
India	3.2	5.9
Chile	1.6	6.4
Brazil	0.5	2.8
Mexico	-0.5	3.1
Argentina	-1.5	3.7
Peru	2.4	4.3
Latin America & Caribbean	-0.3	3.1
Sub-Saharan Africa	-1.2	2.6

Source: World Bank 1993, 2003.

explanations for the divergence in growth performance among developing regions and countries

The experience of East Asia is usually counterposed to intrusive state-regulation and import-substituting policies in much of Africa and Latin America, as well as in countries like India. The principal contrast has been with the setback suffered by a majority of Latin American and African countries during the 1980s – a period sometimes referred to as the 'lost decade' for development. This was a time when problems of indebtedness, followed by default and structural adjustment programmes, entered the popular discourse in crisis-prone economies. However, despite contrasts in circumstances and some notable differences in policies between the developing countries of Asia and Latin America, Brazil was one of the best performing economies in the world and others, like Mexico, managed to achieve respectable targets until the mid-1970s (Kaufmann and Stalling 1989).

The debate about the reasons for the divergence in economic performance between Asia, on the one hand, and most other developing countries on the other, with some exceptions, has been about policy choices and the differing conditions they encountered. The original issue was the relative efficacy of states versus markets and a corresponding contrast in the impact of import-substituting industrialising (ISI) and export-led policies on economic performance. This was the so-called 'closed economy pathology', curbing static and dynamic gains from international specialisation by channelling investment in accordance with political priorities. Nevertheless, for the resource-poor economies of Asia labour-intensive production for export was a logical choice while more prolonged ISI was broadly consistent with the resource-rich endowment for the larger countries of Latin America. However, serious differences of opinion persist on the impact of international economic openness on economic growth.

Growth accounting has sought to identify the associated correlates of economic growth (Cohen and Soto 2002). But such mechanical exercises cannot explain how positive individual factors come into play and operate to induce growth. For example, it is possible to disaggregate the sources of economic growth into its components (capital, labour and factor productivity), but this does not explain relative rates of saving in different countries or the return on capital that spurs investment. It is therefore necessary to return to the issue of policy choices that condition these factors and how such choices come to be made.

In the case of successful *Asian* economies, physical as well as human capital accumulation and labour supplies overwhelmingly account for recorded economic growth (Krugman 1994; Young 1994). According to a number of studies, the role of factor productivity in East Asian growth (TFPG) has been negligible, but Rodrik (1997) questions this conclusion. According to him, labour-saving capital-deepening is likely to have occurred in East Asia and the comparison made by Paul Krugman with 'extensive Soviet-style growth' is misleading. East Asia experienced a rise in TFPG unlike the Soviet Union, where it actually declined over time. East Asian governments have also achieved great advances in human capital formation. By contrast, lower levels of domestic capital accumulation have been a constraint for the worse-performing economies of Latin America and Africa. Of course growth in factor supplies alone, both capital and labour, do not assure economic growth, as the experience of Soviet-style economic planning has confirmed.

One study highlights three main reasons for *sub-Saharan Africa's* poor growth performance: relatively slow capital accumulation, low productivity rises and high population increases. The ratio of investment to GDP averaged 9.6 per cent in SSA compared to 15.6 per cent in other developing countries. The stock of human capital in SSA is also comparatively modest and its relative position has deteriorated over time, especially in secondary education. But the crucial factor has been slow physical capital formation and population increases because that has depressed capital per worker, with negative consequences for growth rates (O'Connell and Ndulu 1999).

Depending on the base year and whether or not a weighted or unweighted average is chosen, the growth performance of *Latin America* during the post-war period can seem poor or rather better. However, an unweighted average that makes allowance for the relatively good performance of Brazil and Mexico, which comprise 36 per cent and 28 per cent of the region's GDP, respectively, demonstrates generally poor growth rates, especially compared to those of East Asia (Randall 1997; De Gregorio and Jong Wha-Lee 1999). Latin American ISI relied on imported capital goods, unlike India, which espoused similar policies in other respects, leading to dependence on borrowing and eventual macroeconomic instability. It led to unsustainable fiscal deficits, external debt, high inflation and volatile exchange rates (Collier et al. 2000).

The ultimate factors that account for Latin America's poor growth performance, as opposed to the immediate reasons that underlie it, can be identified as low investment and high inflation. Decomposing the sources of growth in the region highlights the impact of low investment, though it is, ultimately, a symptom of a deeper malaise. Inflation in Latin America has been high for much of the past 30–40 years and suggests poor macroeconomic management. The rate of terms-of-trade growth also correlates positively with growth. Other factors like FDI, government expenditure, political instability and enrolment ratios do not appear to be statistically significant. The impact of financial repression on economic growth seems to depend on the quality of regulation rather than liberalisation *per se*.

The universal role of increased factor supplies in accounting for economic growth is consistent with the basic interpretation of the models of Harrod-Domar, Robert Solow, Arthur Lewis and other policy prescriptions discussed above. The role of human capital accumulation is less obvious from growth-accounting exercises though it is considered relevant. It may possess greater importance than growth-accounting exercises suggest because it is crucial for technological adaptation (Hausman and Rodrik 2003). The negative impact of inflation, highlighting macroeconomic management, is noteworthy, as the Latin American example underlines. But what are the underlying socio-political features that account for the divergence in the accumulation of factor supplies and their ability to generate economic growth? The answer is that they combine with economic policy choices to explain the divergence in growth performance between the successful economies of Asia (and a few elsewhere for periods of time) and the majority in Latin America and Africa.

politics

The debate is not merely couched in terms of markets versus states and openness versus autarchy. Nor is it about good governance and reliable property rights alone. These questions are relevant, but it is also about specific policies that institute the supply-and-demand conditions to facilitate profitable investment. Market mechanisms have an important role to play in allocating investment, but entrepreneurial success requires nurturing by determined state action to correct market failures, since such failures are endemic in developing countries. Thus, the quality of state institutions and the panoply of interests in civil society within which it is embedded is absolutely critical for the making of policy choices that facilitate economic development. Furthermore, other well-established and dominant states interact with often-weaker states in developing countries to determine its behaviour. In addition, the international economic environment may prove a greater or lesser facilitator or inhibitor of economic development during particular historical periods.

State autonomy is a necessary but insufficient first step in instituting the ability to become a successful developmental state. The state could still be a creature of domestic interests inimical to development or find it difficult to espouse policies favouring development. On the whole, democratic states are more vulnerable to competitive redistributive domestic politics, though this turns out not to be an insurmountable barrier to economic progress, as the recent history of Indian economic growth underlines. India is and remains a society deeply fractured vertically and horizontally and economic decision-making is deeply politicised (and associated corruption is rife), but in the 1990s it achieved annual growth rates of around 6 per cent.

Authoritarian states, which might, at first sight, be thought better able to resist societal pressures, are also embedded in a nexus of societal interests that can prevent sustained attention to the goal of economic

---

box 5.3   external intervention and development outcomes

Some developing countries, especially those possessing strategic raw materials and/or geopolitical significance (for example, many Middle Eastern countries, including Iraq) may be especially vulnerable to foreign intervention. This is of decisive importance in explaining why economic development failed in so many developing countries for prolonged periods after World War II. External intervention during the Cold War was widespread and designed to deny influence to rivals (Gaddis 1997: 152–220). It often resulted in the creation of incompetent predatory states and dominance by local political elites wedded to parochial interests and alienated from the wider aspirations of their own societies. The outcome was numerous Latin and African military dictatorships, opposed to minimal reforms necessary for achieving development goals (see chapter 6 for further discussion of these issues). Other countries remained arenas of chronic competition to secure political control, preventing serious attention to development issues. Weak states unable to reassure Cold War protagonists (Ethiopia and Zaïre [now the Democratic Republic of Congo]) were likely to 'invite' intervention because of their very vulnerability to subversion. The ability to assert autonomy (India) or guarantee loyalty to a particular side to the conflict (East Asia) was a better guarantee of being able to function with some degree of autonomy, since it forestalled attention by powerful countries to alter an uncertain status quo.

---

development (O'Donnell 1973). Many authoritarian governments in Latin America in power during the 1960s and 1970s courtesy of Cold War politics, were nevertheless unable to embark on reform and implement economic policies appropriate for economic transformation owing to opposition from established domestic interest groups. Ultimately, the state needs some degree of insulation from wider societal forces below to be in a position to embark on the kind of long-term choices that immediate aspirations can easily frustrate. The key is insulation rather than democracy or authoritarianism *per se* – since the historical experience of Latin America and Africa suggests that the latter alone does not guarantee economic transformation and the former does not completely frustrate it, although pluralist politics can slow the pace of change. (Note that India's privatization of downstream activities in the petroleum sector were halted in September 2003 by litigation in the Supreme Court instigated by a device known as public-interest litigation that allows unaffected third parties to the policy to claim *locus standi*.)

institutions

We have noted that the successful developmental state needs

- to enjoy immunity from excessive external interference; and
- insulation from undue domestic politicisation.

in order to implement decisions that have a pay-off in the medium and long term. Only when these initial conditions have been met can the question of appropriate policy be posed. The autonomous developmental state, according to common consensus, is the principal vehicle for creating an appropriate institutional framework (that is, structure) and ensuring that they are actually able to function (that is, process). The importance of the latter needs to be recognised because countries often have good legislative provision that fails in practice due to resource constraints, inefficiency and corruption.

Institutional arrangements can compensate for imperfect information, risk and moral hazard. Another cognate trajectory of institutional economics identifies the transaction costs of greater complexity, as specialisation becomes more anonymous with increasing scale due to economic development, and opportunistic behaviour threatens cooperation. Such institutions can be informal, though formal arrangements tend to dominate eventually as development proceeds. As a result, the developmental state has usually played a role in credit markets, for example in the leap from a mercantile to an industrial economy. Similarly, the enforcement of property rights is usually regarded as a must (Bardhan 2000). However, one needs to recognise the complexity of actual historical experience, which highlights a variety of processes and outcomes. The economic transformation of South Korea and Taiwan during the 1960s and 1970s was achieved with rather heterodox forms of governance and China has experienced explosive economic growth since the early 1980s without enacting formal property rights. Nor has improved governance in Latin America during the 1990s been correlated with improved economic performance generally (Hausman and Rodrik 2003).

impact of the international economy

The other side of the neoclassical prescription has been the avoidance of the closed-economy pathology that the orthodoxy considers a barrier to static and dynamic gains from trade, retarding the acquisition of technology and impeding the import of capital goods. The evidence of the apparent association of economic growth with increased trade, predicated on economic openness, is considered to be convincing evidence against protection. This analytical conviction is a key aspect of the prolonged post-war debate on the merits of an open economy. However, critics argue against the intrinsic logic of economic openness as a necessity for successful investment and economic growth, judging increased trade to be a function of economic growth rather than its systematic, linear cause.

The principal opposition to the open economy model espoused by mainstream economists and international economic institutions is on infant-industry grounds. Rodrik (1997) explains that temporary monopoly power facilitates technological innovation and creation of new products by holders of intellectual property rights (through patents) in advanced countries. In his view, unless firms in developing countries are able to enjoy comparable temporary market power through protection (which may mean subsidised credit, tax incentives or temporary monopoly as well as trade restrictions) there is no long-term incentive to adapt novel technologies and bring new products to the market. Ease of entry can, in fact, be regarded as a deterrent to investment because firms embarking on a new line of production need to appropriate rents to discover the true costs of production and finance their own learning.

Such a process is central to development since experimentation establishes which products are profitable within a large choice set. The mere fact of being a labour-abundant economy does not indicate which products, among a potentially wide variety of labour-intensive products, might be chosen for investment, and thus entails high risks and uncertainty. Sanjaya Lall (2001) and others reiterate the complementary point that adapting to technology and absorbing tacit knowledge is a complex and error-prone process that requires shelter from competition.

In sum, the state has usually played a critical role in successful economies by ensuring infrastructure provision, allocating credit to preferred sectors and promoting the accumulation of human capital. The allocation of credit has been a vehicle helping entrepreneurs to choose investments from the large choice set referred to above, though both failures and successes have occurred. The countries of South East Asia (Thailand, Malaysia and Indonesia in particular) chose FDI as the vehicle for export-led growth, unlike the dominant pattern in South Korea and Taiwan. The drawback of this pattern of development has been the absence of indigenous technological dynamism as a source of economic growth (Lall 2000).

historical experience: explaining developmental success among the asian tigers

It is now widely accepted that the economic success of Asian countries, especially the pioneering group of four (South Korea, Taiwan, Singapore, Hong Kong), can be attributed to a combination of favourable contingent socio-economic circumstances and superior state policies. It might be argued that some of the permissive conditions for economic development

---

box 5.4   the state and development

The role of the state remains controversial, from the failure of the socialist experiment, on the one hand, to the presumed superiority of laissez faire for economic growth, on the other. Planned economies under socialism curbed consumption, but high investments failed to deliver sustained growth because productivity stalled in the absence of market allocation of priorities and private performance incentives. The highly dirigiste economies of the Middle East and North Africa also failed to achieve economic growth despite high levels of investment in physical and human capital because the state distorted investment priorities and educated labour was also seriously misallocated (Collier et al. 2000). By contrast, Hong Kong is held up as an example of a high-growth laissez-faire economy. (On the role of the state in development, see also chapter 3.)

---

in the two larger economies, South Korea and Taiwan, had been established before World War II. Indeed the latter countries may be considered to belong to an intermediate category that possessed some features similar to countries in need of reconstruction rather than being completely underdeveloped, since they had already experienced some degree of socio-economic transformation earlier.

Three sets of factors significantly affected the development trajectory of South Korea and Taiwan:

- antecedent conditions;
- policy choices; and
- the international context.

Unlike the majority of developing countries, South Korea and Taiwan experienced land reforms under the aegis of the US occupation at the end of World War II, which underpinned subsequent productivity, and the concomitant supply of labour and domestic purchasing power (Olson 1976).

South Korea and Taiwan experienced some economic development during colonial occupation and already possessed a degree of educational attainment, although literacy rates were low in Taiwan. (On the Japanese impact on Taiwan, see Howe 1996: 335–65.) The bureaucracy was also committed to national goals and relatively uncorrupt. Both societies also exhibited a nationalist commitment to economic development, fuelled by competition with communist neighbours. In a general sense, they were well-established societies, with associated pride in their own identity. Ethnic and religious homogeneity curbed the kind of destructive social and political rivalries evident in more fractured societies. Finally, both were dictatorships that were, in addition, unlike many other similar authoritarian governments, relatively insulated from civil society and pressures from below.

Both South Korea and Taiwan espoused interventionist economic policies – a position at odds with the official view that took shape after the 1980s. This blamed the economic setbacks suffered by Latin American and African countries on decades of state-intervention and import-substitution policies. As a result, orthodox macroeconomic policies were advocated, accompanied by a dramatic reduction in the role of the state as well as open economic policies to secure economic prosperity. By contrast, the East Asian NICs directed investment into preferred sectors by controlling the price of credit, instituted trade protection and repressed labour. South Korea and Taiwan also imposed detailed regulation on FDI and in the case of South Korea only constituted a modest proportion of gross domestic investment. What these countries undertook successfully was nationalist economic development, with considered attention to the acquisition and adaptation of technology, with asset-ownership largely in the hands of domestic firms (Amsden 1989; Wade 1990).

South Korea and Taiwan received significant US economic aid during the first decade or so after World War II and access to the US market was made available to them because of their critical role in US Cold War politics. A crucial phase of East Asian economic advance in the 1960s and early 1970s coincided with the expansion of the world economy caused by the expansionist US policies resulting from the Vietnam war and President Lyndon Johnson's great-society programmes. It is worth noting that state intervention has persisted and greater economic openness did not occur until the late 1980s.

---

box 5.5   ranis on economic development

Ranis (1991) put forward a four-stage analytical grid for evaluating the experience of economic development among developing countries after World War II. According to Ranis, developing countries experienced four stages of development. They began as poor primary exporters, then graduated, in the second stage, to ISI in light consumer products, which they also exported. At the third stage a critical divergence in strategies took place. The original four East Asian countries (South Korea, Taiwan, Hong Kong and Singapore) pressed ahead with exports while Latin America and some other countries pursued a strategy of deepening ISI, by attempting to create a capital-goods industry. The contrasting results were evident in the fourth stage, with Asia experiencing sustained economic expansion and rising wages (and living standards) through exports, and ISI-oriented countries descending into stagnation and external debt as the deepening of ISI proved a costly failure. Ranis' characterisation outlines other necessary conditions for successful economic growth, but the explanation for the differing outcomes is the crucial policy choice at the third stage (see also Haggard 1990).

The vulnerability of the Latin American and African ISI strategy was exposed when oil prices rose in 1973 and they resorted to borrowing in order to maintain fiscal spending. It finally succumbed to external shock when oil prices began to rise again in 1979, followed soon by high US interest rates when President Reagan embarked on the costly 'star wars' missile defence programme, without a commensurate increase in taxes. The servicing cost of international debt, borrowed on floating rates, began climbing sharply with a concomitant fall in world demand (when a rise was needed to increase exports in order to defray higher debt-servicing) provoked by higher interest rates and worsening terms of trade. The Mexican debt default of 1982 was quickly followed by debt crises in other Latin American and African countries. The response was intervention by the IMF and World Bank in exchange for official lending and rescheduling of existing debt.

Table 5.2 Impact of Exogenous Shocks on External Debt of Non-oil Developing Countries (Billion US$)

Effect	Amount (billion US$)
Oil price increase in excess of US inflation (1974–82 cumulative)	260
Real interest rate in excess of 1961–80 average: 1981 and 1982	41
Terms-of-trade loss, 1981–82	79
Export volume loss caused by world recession, 1981–82	21
Total	401
Total debt increase, 1973–82	482

Source: Cline 1983: 13.

'third world' debt and structural adjustment

What was known as the Third World debt crisis dealt a crippling blow to the interventionist ISI strategy of economic development. In 1970 15 heavily indebted countries had a total external public debt of approximately $18 billion, amounting to just below 19 per cent of GNP. By 1987 the same nations owed approximately $407 billion, or 47.5 per cent of their GNP. Interest payments over this period rose from $2.8 billion to over $36 billion. Debt-service obligations (including principal and interest in foreign currencies) was 1.5 per cent of GDP and 12.4 per cent of export earnings in 1970. By 1987 these figures had risen to 4.3 per cent of GDP and 24.9 per cent of export earnings. The figures for a number of countries, including Argentina, Brazil, Mexico and Peru in 1980 were worse (Ferraro and Rosser 1994: 332–55). It was this unsustainable burden of debt that had led to IMF and World Bank structural adjustment programmes, combining an economic stabilisation programme with policy-reform package. As Clines (1983) noted, higher oil prices in 1973–4 and again in 1974–80 were key reasons for the external debt crisis that affected many developing countries from the early 1980s; there were also high interest rates, falling export volumes and prices, linked to the global recession of 1981–2. These factors afected domestic economic management and led to adverse effects on credit markets.

---

box 5.6   features of structural adjustment programmes (saps)

Structural adjustment was the response to these macroeconomic shocks, characterised by large current-account deficits up to and exceeding 10 per cent of GDP and, in some cases, double-digit monthly inflation (Taylor 1992). The involvement of the IMF was in the form of a 'stand-by' arrangement, which is a line of credit tied to a macroeconomic programme set out in a Letter of Intent. The credits and policy guidelines agreed are referred to as *conditionality* and the loans are available when the performance criteria specified in the Letter of Intent are satisfied.

The package involves fiscal contraction, higher prices for products supplied by state agencies, and tax increases. A revision of the exchange rate is required, usually devaluation, and monetary policy is tightened. Curtailment of state intervention in domestic markets, including public investment and planning, lowering of trade barriers and easing of exchange controls are all recommended. Finally, wage restraint and revision of subsidy and transfer programmes are thought desirable.

High inflation is the prime target of stabilisation and the principal point of disagreement with the alternative structuralist perception of economic shock. The orthodoxy blamed over-expansion and excess demand for the economic crisis. By contrast, structuralists asserted that inflation occurred because distributional conflict, highlighted by shifts in relative prices, and rules of price formation that expanded the conflict into price increases throughout the system – a propagation mechanism. It may be argued that the causes of inflation approximate the monetarist model better if markets are price-clearing (food products and services) and indexation of nominal payments is not widespread. If mark-up or administered pricing and wage indexation is the norm the structuralist explanation fits better. However, the IMF argues that flexible prices are the norm, mark-ups and indexation are epiphenomena of excess money creation when there is inflation.

On the question of austerity, the IMF argued that demand restraint would not reduce output if the price level fell. If prices of traded goods are held by the law of one-price austerity it must lead to a fall in the prices of non-traded goods and therefore improve the trade account by cutting import demand and stimulating exports. According to the IMF, increases in interest rates do not lead to a fall in output while critics have asserted that they are almost certain to do so because they drive up working-capital finance costs. However, the import content of investment and output is also important. It was almost two-thirds for investment in sub-Saharan Africa, one-third elsewhere and about one fifth for output, which therefore becomes more expensive with devaluation (Taylor 1992). The structuralists argued that the mode of adjustment matters; if, for example, output is close to the upper bounds because of capacity constraints or foreign-exchange availability, austerity would lead to a fall in output. They suggest that less unequal income distribution would allow adjustment without necessarily leading to a fall in output.

On devaluation the question was whether or not it can occur without a fall in GDP, with the Fund arguing that it would improve GDP via exports within a year, while the structuralists insisted that a fall in output needed to occur first. However, the latter acknowledge that if the exchange rate is seriously over-valued a remedial depreciation is strongly called for. It is also necessary to look at other necessary conditions for an increase in exports, such as institutional support. It was argued that in Africa it benefited large foreign-owned companies in the export sector disproportionately rather than the majority of small-scale producers. There was, in addition, disagreement about the consequences of exchange liberalisation, which the Fund thought removed distortions while structuralists argued it prompted capital flight (Collier and Willem 1999).

A World Bank (1994) study of African countries that adopted far-reaching policy reforms concluded: 'the policy packages to address the adverse external shocks and severely overvalued real exchange rates of the early 1980s had high payoffs'. Others found the evidence on the impact of devaluation on growth and the structure of exports inconclusive though exchange-rate adjustment itself was impressive (Gylfason and Radetzki 1991). Supply responses were very poor and exports of manufactures did not expand. The explanation for the lack of success in export diversification is that many African countries had modest industrial production and export bases and suffered from structural rigidity, low skill capacity, and poor infrastructure (Sowa 1994). In some cases – for example, Zambia and Côte d'Ivoire – de-industrialisation appears to have taken place.

The IMF denies that its policies created widespread poverty, arguing that intervention occurs when a crisis is already unfolding and socio-economic conditions are likely to worsen in any case. But there was recognition that an initial contraction worsened the condition of the poor and pushed others into their ranks, though public provision could counteract it. One major study identified significant improvement in the position of the poor owing to the adoption of specific policies in the context of an adjustment programme (for example, in Uganda) (Collier and Willem 1999). By the late 1980s, IFIs had generally acted to improve safety net provision in response to sustained public criticism (Nelson 1989). There was also acceptance that adjustment policy might be sequenced better (price deregulation and the switch to cash crops in Zambia, for example, failed, because of inadequate transport) and there was acknowledgement that premature financial liberalisation negatively affects economic performance.

Lance Taylor (1992) evaluated 18 studies of structural adjustment programmes (SAPs) conducted by the World Institute for Development Research and concluded that there were no spectacular successes in SAPs – and outcomes have ranged from the moderately successful to the disastrous (Taylor 1992). Leading economists like Jeffry Sachs (1989) and William R. Cline (1983) have argued that the IFIs' approach to resolving the debt crisis failed to take into account the external causes of the crisis (such as the need of banks to recycle petrodollars).

In Sachs' (1989) view the solutions pursued were essentially directed at internal adjustment of indebted countries and were hugely deflationary, with real wages in Mexico, for example, declining by half between 1980 and 1988. It also precipitated violent protest in countries like Peru, which experienced sharp contractions, with long-term consequences. Eventually, partial debt forgiveness, in the form of Brady bonds and improved economic performance, reduced the debt ratio (Edwards 1995). Cline (1991) notes that the return of investor confidence and the normalising of interest rates were critical for economic recovery in Mexico, rather than savings on the external obligations. Nevertheless, indebtedness remains endemic to the modern international political economy, as subsequent events in Asia and Argentina were to demonstrate.

The political nature of structural adjustment can be judged from Waterbury's (1999) recommendation either to outwit domestic interests with bribes when required, or to reshape fundamentally the domestic coalition, as in Turkey in the 1980s. This was followed by the institution of an open economy. But Callaghy (1989) points out the crucial role of states in economies, and the contradictions in seeing it as the principal obstacle to development and simultaneously requiring it to execute far-reaching acts of change in adjustment programmes. Callaghy was also critical of the obsession with markets and export-led growth on the grounds that they had no historical precedent.

In sum, the issue of structural adjustment needs to be situated in a wider context of relations between dominant economies and weak ones. The IMF itself now recognises that structural adjustment compromises sovereignty, a situation that should not be prolonged.

the financial crises in asia and latin america in the 1990s and their aftermath

latin america

The impact of major financial crisis that befell Asia's hitherto successful economies in 1997 is the counterpart to the experience of Latin America and Africa during the decade of the 1980s. The Asian crisis was preceded by the financial crisis in Mexico in 1994–95, resulting from investor anxieties about elections and a sharp drop in capital inflows, followed by a credit expansion, which was probably ill-advised, and a mild devaluation. A steady erosion of reserves occurred, plummeting to $6 billion, forcing a float of the currency. It soon became clear that short-term bond liabilities ($28 billion of so-called *tesobonos*), due in months, exceeded foreign-currency reserves and could no longer be honoured. Mexico could not borrow from private lenders to make the repayments and was in danger of defaulting, though the bonds only comprised 10 per cent of its pre-crisis GDP. The crisis was overcome by a $50 billion US guarantee, in exchange for the surrender of oil revenues if funds were actually drawn down.

A reform package and subsequent export expansion to the US market stimulated economic recovery (Frieden 1991). Argentina also faced an election in May 1995, months after the Mexican crisis, and suffered a rapid loss of bank deposits that turned into a panic. It resulted in a liquidity crisis that was only overcome through a bail-out by official lending from the IMF, World Bank, Inter-American Development Bank and some private creditors. Like Mexico, Argentina suffered a sharp temporary contraction and reasonably swift recovery in the two following years and a restoration of capital inflows (Radelet and Sachs 1998).

Even now, nearly 10 years on, many regional economies in Latin America are still relatively weak.

asia

The Asian crisis that arose two years later in 1997 was distinctive because it arose from private-sector debt and much of the pre-existing economic analysis was of public liabilities. Capital inflows into Asia had grown substantially, but were not being invested in high-return activities to credit-worthy borrowers. The incremental capital-output ratio in South Korea and Thailand rose in successive years between 1990 and 1996, but exports remained competitive, though they declined with falling world demand (ADB 2002b).

Since foreign borrowing was intermediated by domestic banks rather than in the form of FDI there was greater vulnerability to a liquidity crisis. In Thailand banks and finance companies raised low-interest yen-denominated loans to engage in real-estate speculation and their foreign liabilities rose from 6 per cent of deposits in 1990 to a third by 1996. Korean corporations were highly leveraged as well, with a debt-to-equity ratio over 400 per cent for the 30 biggest *chaebols* (big industrial conglomerates), compared to approximately 160 per cent for US corporations as a whole.

The foreign exposure of Korean banks and Indonesian corporations was also rising in this period. The ratio of short-term debt to overall external liabilities as well as foreign reserves rose sharply between 1994 and 1997 and remained high in Indonesia subsequently. The short-term debt-to-reserve ratio in Korea, Indonesia and Thailand reached 150 per cent in June 1997, though Malaysia and the Philippines were not as badly exposed. The ratio of M2 money to reserves was high in Asian countries and indicated the potential for a run on their foreign-exchange reserves should there be a loss of confidence in the local currency, since they had fixed exchange rates (World Bank 1998).

Thus, the conditions for a financial crisis in Asia were becoming fortified. Financial institutions and corporations borrowing in foreign currency, without adequate hedging, were vulnerable to currency depreciation. In addition, the relatively low cost of foreign borrowing proved irresistible even after taking into account exchange-rate risks. This was reinforced by the regulatory and tax advantages of obtaining loans from 'offshore' financial markets. A significant proportion of the debts being incurred were also short term, though the assets acquired were long term, exposing borrowers to a potential liquidity crunch that could be similar to a run on a bank. A rapid rise in equity and real-estate prices prior to the financial crisis had also made a sharp deflation probable. Finally, as noted earlier, the allocation of credit was poor owing to political interference and resulted in increasingly visible problems in banks and financial institutions.

Once the crisis broke in mid-1997 it was unstoppable, because as investors rushed to exit, currencies depreciated, making more institutions insolvent, further reducing the prospects of repayment and thereby prompting further capital flight. Floating exchange rates were unavoidable in the face of such irresistible market pressures despite concern to avoid a self-defeating spiral of depreciation and inflation. But the descent into a vicious circle was compounded by hesitancy in responding to the crisis and evidence that information on international reserves had been withheld, damaging credibility.

The IMF-supported intervention comprised three elements: major financing packages ($36 billion for Indonesia, $58 billion for South Korea and $17 billion for Thailand) and attempts to curb further capital flight; an unprecedented package of structural reforms; and macroeconomic policy measures to overcome the crisis itself (Lane 1999). But the financial package was not available at the outset when it would have been more effective, rather than through the established method of successive tranches to ensure adherence to adjustment policies.

In South Korea and Thailand, stabilisation proved successful by mid-1998, with real interest rates peaking at 20 per cent and 15 per cent respectively, before nominal and real rates returned to pre-crisis levels. In Indonesia monetary policy failed to maintain its course as liquidity expanded massively to prevent a collapse of banking and inflation accelerated. Interest rates remained negative and only in late 1998 did market conditions stabilise, though earlier monetary tightening, with a temporary surge in interest rates, would almost certainly have caused less damage.

Much of the blame for the fragility of Asian financial systems can be attributed primarily to inadequate supervision and regulation, against a backdrop of financial-sector liberalisation. The liberalisation of capital accounts was badly sequenced, encouraging short-term borrowing and borrowers underestimated exchange risk because exchange rates were inflexible. Domestic credit expansion had also become unsustainable due to lax monetary policies. And both borrowers and lenders had been imprudent, owing, in part, to bad risk management, lack of information and the implied government guarantee of a fixed exchange rate. This is what the World Bank referred to as a 'time bomb' (World Bank 1998; Aghion 2001).

The deliberations following the Asian crisis were twofold. The first related to the causes of the crisis and the need for appropriate structural reforms and the second was a re-evaluation of the response to it. The most important set of policy measures related to domestic supervision and regulation of the financial sector. As a corollary, measures were taken to improve governance and competition, which entailed reform of state-sponsored monopolies and more robust competition laws. There was also recognition that markets needed assurance of transparency in financial and economic data available. Strengthening of international surveillance with closer scrutiny of the financial sector and focus on international standards was thought desirable. Finally, trade reforms were thought important to prevent beggar-thy-neighbour responses to the crisis.

The importance of maintaining sound macroeconomic policies was reiterated. But the question of the appropriate exchange-rate regime remained unresolved and the possible merits of discouraging short-term capital inflows (such as implemented in Chile) left open. The need to avoid a liberalisation regime that restricted long-term capital investment while encouraging short-term inflows, especially before the domestic financial system had been strengthened, was considered important. The decision of Malaysia to impose capital controls to stem outflows, though seen as a betrayal of previous commitments, did not reduce short-run FDI inflows (Stiglitz 1999). However, it has been argued that they were unimportant for the subsequent recovery because they were imposed when it had already commenced (Dornbusch 2001). More to the point, it is believed that imposing such controls merely encourages exit at the first sign of trouble in any subsequent financial crisis.

Measures to restore economic viability were accompanied by social-sector reforms, which were undertaken in response to concerns about the poor and vulnerable. Income transfers were raised and policies were implemented to assist the unemployed and mitigate the impact of price increases on poorer households, through continuing subsidies on food and energy, transportation and ensuring access to health and education provision. However, given the severity of the economic crisis social policy measures could not measure up to its magnitude, especially in Indonesia, which experienced a radical breakdown of social order that remained a serious concern in 2004.

Unemployment in Indonesia rose over from 2.3 per cent in 1996 to 17.1 per cent in 1998 though the rise was less dramatic in South Korea and Thailand (6.8 per cent and 6.5 per cent respectively, rising from 2 per cent over the same period). In the year following the crisis in the region industrial production was a quarter below the level the previous year and income losses over the period amounted to a trillion US dollars (Stiglitz 1999; Barro 2001). The World Bank itself acknowledges that social spending might have been more expansionary given the contraction in private-sector spending. The overall progress on reducing poverty during the decade after the debt crises subsided in the late 1980s has been uneven, with progress in Asia, but only modest gains in Africa and Latin America; and a worsening in the transition economies (see Figure 5.1).

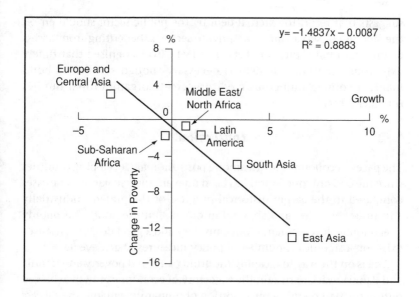

Source: Collier et al. 2000: 5

Figure 5.1 Growth and Poverty Reduction, by Region, 1988–97

---

box 5.7   stiglitz's criticisms of stabilisation programmes

Criticisms of the stabilisation programme and structural reform package, some of which have been recognised by the IMF itself, include the impact of the extent to which monetary policy was tightened. Joseph Stiglitz (1999) and others have argued that unduly rigorous monetary policy turned liquidity problems into an insolvency crisis. Firms that had been viable earlier could not operate under the high interest rates designed to staunch the outflow of capital; smaller firms were especially adversely affected. Stiglitz also laments the adverse unaccounted effects on social and organization capital that large economic declines impose.

Finally, Argentina's currency board (effectively surrendering national monetary policy to the US Federal Reserve) did not suffice to avert another debt crisis in 2001, accompanied by social and political upheaval. The dynamics of debt were an important factor in the crisis, but confidence in the sustainability of debt in Argentina was intertwined with maintenance of a currency board and doubts about either guaranteed destruction of both. And sound fiscal and structural policies are both demanding but necessary, and a currency board is not a panacea – overvaluation hurt the Argentine economy (with a strengthening dollar and devaluation of the Brazilian *real*) while debt mounted. The Argentine experience suggests that resort to external debt by the public sector should err on the side of conservatism if the private sector is benefiting from access to international capital markets. The IMF also recognised that timely exit from unsustainable debt is necessary though syndicated bond loans, involving numerous creditors, create organisational hurdles (Krueger 2002).

conclusion

The pace of economic growth among post-colonial, developing countries since the end of World War II has been uneven, spectacular in some cases compared to the earlier historical progress of the present industrially advanced countries, and abysmal in others. But the political economy of economic development is not a mystery and a great deal of consensus exists on a significant number of policy measures to achieve it.

Asia is on the way to escaping the grind of age-old poverty and if India and Bangladesh can sustain the trajectory of economic growth achieved during the past decade a huge portion of humanity will join the success stories of the rest of Asia. Latin America has emerged with greater stability from the setbacks of the 1980s, the major exception being the recent experience of Argentina. Periodic setbacks seem to offer painful additional real-world lessons about the specific difficulties associated with particular policies. Recent experience in Asia and Latin America has reaffirmed the need for sound macroeconomic policies and strong financial institutions and regulation in globalised financial markets.

The debt crises that have recurred periodically have prompted re-thinking about the conditions for economic stability and concern about underlying threats to the viability of an interdependent global economic and financial system itself. The Asian debt crisis caused some surprise because public finances and the balance of payments in the region were relatively sound. Subsequent analysis has suggested that debt crises were not perverse and could, possibly, have been anticipated and policy recommendations have been suggested, despite disquiet at the penchant of markets for turning a liquidity crunch into a crisis of insolvency. However, despite the dramatic collapse of Asia's economies and the spread of crises to Latin America and Russia greater stability did return relatively quickly to most of Asia.

The analysis of factors explaining economic growth has grown in sophistication and complexity. Broadly, there is greater appreciation of market mechanisms for sustaining the accumulation of capital to promote economic growth. But a supportive state, as opposed to one unduly truncated for ideological reasons, is considered essential by most professional observers (World Bank 1997b). There is agreement that there is a need for mature institutions and the good governance that allows them to function. Such institutions are necessary to uphold contracts, provide other public goods like education and infrastructure and constrain arbitrary behaviour by agencies of the state.

Sound economic management, combining effective fiscal and monetary policies, which curtails inflation and does not 'crowd out' private investment is deemed essential. The nature of the trade-off between desirable, growth-enhancing public investment and private spending remains a subject of debate. However, crucial disputes remain unresolved about appropriate policy responses to economic crisis.

The importance of market mechanisms and appropriate economic incentives for achieving economic growth is now widely accepted. The drawbacks of state-ownership for efficiency (and even equity) are recognised. There is less conviction concerning the tolerable extent of foreign ownership of the local economy despite the widespread contemporary encouragement to FDI (UNCTAD 1999).

The Uruguay Round Agreement of 1994 that resulted in the establishment of the World Trade Organisation (WTO) was a far-reaching treaty that foreclosed many trade policy choices, generally favouring greater international openness. But misgivings linger about the appropriateness of such openness to trade for development, as recorded earlier. The recent disputes about trade policy that thwarted progress at the Cancun round of WTO talks in September 2003 stemmed from a mixture of resentment about the functioning of the agreement itself and determination to concede as little as possible for the future until it is satisfactorily addressed. It remains to be seen the direction that such talks will take in future.

6
the power of the gun: armies and armed force

robert pinkney

introduction

Political authority in most countries rests ultimately on the ability of rulers to coerce their subjects. Any collapse of such authority generally requires superior force on the part of the regime's opponents, or at least their greater skill and determination in wielding force. Where the 'developing' world differs from the West and the erstwhile Soviet bloc is in the tenuous control that the government or any group in society has over armed force. While the army has occasionally occupied centre stage in western countries, civilian control over the military has been the norm. In much of the developing world, in contrast, military coups, military governments and extensive military influence over policy have been common, for reasons which we shall explore presently.

Three models of civil–military relations are suggested in Table 6.1. In the *liberal democratic model* power depends on public support, especially through the ballot box, and is maintained in the first instance through control of the machinery of state. Elected politicians may use parliamentary majorities, and their authority over public officials, to impose their legislative and executive will. Beyond the formal structures, there is a need to collaborate with economic (and other) elites in view of the sanctions which these can bring to bear. Military and police force, we suggest, are lower down the hierarchy of resources because the government's legitimacy is not usually challenged, though such force can be deployed effectively when required, whether against suffragettes and Irish nationalists before 1914 or by the then British prime minister, Mrs Thatcher, against striking miners in the 1980s.

Table 6.1 Means of obtaining and maintaining political power in different political systems: a hierarchy of resources

	Liberal democratic model	Totalitarian model	Praetorian model
Key to power	Public support	Control of state/party apparatus	Control of armed force
Tools for maintaining authority, in order of importance	1. Control of machinery of state 2. Interaction with economic elites 3. Military and police force	1. Military and police force 2. Control of the economy 3. Public affirmation	1. Interaction with the 'developed' world 2. Tenuous control over the machinery of state 3. Patron–client relations

In the erstwhile *totalitarian model*, adopted for example in Nazi Germany from the early 1930s until 1945 and in the Soviet Union from 1917 until the 1980s, state violence might appear to have been more important. However, it was actually control of the state/party apparatus that made possible control of coercion. Hitler and Stalin did not attain public office because they controlled armed groups; they controlled the army and police because they held public office. Their authority was then bolstered by state control of the economy and by mobilising mass support.

The *praetorian model*, in its extreme form, assumes that every man is his own soldier and that political power depends on which armed group gains control of the machinery of state. Once they have gained control in a relatively impoverished developing country, their nation's poverty will normally require such a group to establish a relationship with the countries of the 'developed' world – which will at least prevent foreign invasion or economic ostracism, and at best attract aid and investment. The current (2004) Musharraf regime in Pakistan is a case in point. As in Pakistan, the insurgents can then exercise tenuous control over the state, although with little of the legitimacy that liberal democratic or even totalitarian rulers can enjoy, and with the constant threat of other armed groups displacing them. Lacking public support and unable to coerce all the people all the time, they try to consolidate power through a system of patron–client relations which provide material rewards for supporters and punishments for opponents. Note that we are *not* suggesting that the majority of developing countries are necessarily close to the praetorian model, although Uganda under General Amin (1971–79), and more recently the Democratic Republic of the Congo (formerly Zaire), Liberia, Sierra Leone, Burundi and Rwanda, have all been at times closer than most. Yet for reasons explained elsewhere in this book (see chapter 1), political institutions typically enjoy less popular legitimacy in many developing countries than in the West and, lacking the disciplined structures of totalitarian countries, armed force is likely to play a major role in trying to resolve political conflict.

Having noted the generally important role of armed force in politics, our task is now to examine the various ways in which this force has been wielded in the developing world over time, by whom, why and with what consequences for the political process. This chapter begins by briefly plotting the history of armed force. It will go on to look at the ideologies and interests of those wielding military power and their impact on the direction, competence and stability of government. We then move on to the post-Cold War environment in which people with guns have to face a world that, at least rhetorically, demands democratic governance, and look at the prospects for civilian control. Within this environment, the process of globalisation might be expected to push the doors of democratisation open more widely, as developing countries have less scope for resisting outside pressures but, as globalisation reduces the importance of national frontiers, it also facilitates the easier movement of arms and soldiers.

the heyday of military government

> The army differs in function from the society that surrounds it and its function requires that it be separated and segregated. It requires a common uniform and this immediately distinguishes it from the civilian masses. It requires separate housing, in purely military quarters, the barracks. It requires a systematised nomadism, moving from one garrison to another. It demands a separate code of morals and manners from that of the civilian population ... all this tends to enhance military solidarity by making military life self-centred. It is easy, even, to inspire contempt for one's contemporaries – the civvies   (Finer 1962: 9).

If these observations of Finer's are correct, it is easy to understand why armies have frequently decided that they are better qualified to rule than civilian politicians, and why they have frequently had the ability to impose such rule. But closer inspection may suggest that the number of armies fitting Finer's description is limited in time and space. Before the 20th century, few armies would have possessed the sense of corporate identity, or 'professionalism', that the description implies; and few would have contemplated establishing a military government, that is a government comprised mainly of serving officers and relying on the army as its main power base. Many rulers won power through armed force before the twentieth century, and subsequently used elements of force to retain power, but for the most part the process of government remained a civilian one, working through and with institutions such as legislatures, bureaucracies, political parties and interest groups.

Even in Latin America, where most countries gained independence much earlier (the early 19th century) than Africa, Asia or the Middle East, military intervention before the 1920s was concerned more with deposing or replacing governments than with the more mundane business of running them. Philip (2003: 64–6) traces the beginnings of military government in the region mainly up to the 1920s, by which time armies were relatively disciplined bodies with a monopoly of the use of force. They offered a progressive, honest force, in contrast to corrupt, oligarchic civilian rulers, and generally resisted the lure of both communism and fascism. From these beginnings in Latin America, the phenomenon of military government spread to much of Africa, Asia and the Middle East after the colonial powers had handed power to nominally independent, but often weak, governments in the decades after 1945. I calculate that 56 countries experienced military government at some time between 1960 and 1990 (Pinkney 1990: 11–12), yet by the beginning of the 21st century the number of existing military governments could be counted on the fingers of one hand. Like the cinema organ and the motorcycle sidecar, military government appears to have been very much a 20th-century phenomenon.

How does one explain this dramatic rise and fall, and what is its significance for the political role of armed force at the start of the 21st century? On the rise of military government, much of the early academic debate focused on the relative importance of military strength and civilian weakness, with some additional allowance for the role of external subversion (Finer 1962; Huntington 1968; Janowitz 1964). Military government is only possible if a relatively coherent army exists, and Philip's description of Latin America in the 1920s suggests that the emergence of more professional armies was important. But a strong army is not a sufficient condition for military government, or we would have military governments all over Western Europe and North America. Much hinges on the weaknesses of civilian governments and civil institutions generally, which may lack both the legitimacy to enlist public support in resisting the military (see Table 6.1), and the resources to maintain a political system in which the military are kept in their place. A rudimentary army of barely 200 soldiers was sufficient to displace a civilian government in Togo in 1963, yet it is difficult to conceive of a much larger and more complex army in Britain contemplating the overthrow of civil government, let alone succeeding in such an exercise. We can attribute this to the greater legitimacy accorded to civilian government in Britain, by soldiers and civilians alike, or to a political structure in which the respective rights and roles of soldiers and civilian politicians are more clearly delineated. This is Luckham's (1971: 8–34) 'objective control' model, where armies may enjoy internal autonomy but accept their ultimate subordination to an elected government. But the contrast still requires us to explain why Britain arrived at such a state of affairs while Togo did not.

Broadening the question from Britain and Togo to the 'developed' and 'developing' worlds generally, we can approach it from at least two directions: the bases of political conflict in society and civil–military relations. The former approach requires us to modify the notion of battle lines being drawn between 'soldiers' on one side and 'civilians' on the other. It also leads us to ask whether the military belongs to, or might want to align itself with, particular groups in society in opposition to other groups which threaten their interests.'In a world of oligarchy, the soldier is a radical. In a middle class world, he is a participant and arbiter; as mass society looms on the horizon he becomes a conservative guardian of the existing order' (Huntington 1968: 221).

This generalisation of Huntington's provides a rough explanation of military perspectives, though obviously not all soldiers in a given army will think alike. We have already hinted at the presence of radical soldiers confronting landed elites 'in a world of oligarchy' in Latin America in the 1920s. The Middle East in the 1950s presents a similar picture. By the 1960s and 1970s, in the wake of industrialisation and the rise of an organised working class, many Latin American soldiers saw a threat 'to the existing order' and turned their fire on actual or aspiring leaders of left-wing governments. This might suggest that the interests of army officers (and it is generally the officers who determine the role of the army) are bound up with those of a larger professional middle class which wants to break free from the constraints of the traditional elites in the early states of development. But officers later become fearful of working-class demands for greater social equality, especially in the context of the Cold War where left-wing movements might be seen as advancing Soviet interests. But if particular social groups want to defend or advance their interests, why do they enlist the support of the military, and why do the military support them on their own initiative, in some countries but not in others? A simple answer would be that in liberal democracies the ballot box and scope for participation in decision-making provide adequate alternatives to conspiring against the government.

The reasons why liberal democracy exists in some parts of the world but not in others are beyond the scope of this chapter (the issue is extensively discussed in chapter 4), but we can note here the importance of social and economic development.

---

box 6.1   armed force, development and power

All 20 countries – other than Spain – to which the United Nations Development Programme (UNDP) gives a higher 'human development' ranking have been democracies since at least the 1950s, whereas over a third of the countries with a lower ranking than Spain have experienced military government (Pinkney 1990: 11–12; UNDP 2002: 149–52). Indeed if one eliminated the very small states with virtually no standing armies and the states where totalitarian control before 1990 precluded military intervention, the proportion would be considerably greater than a third. A greater scarcity of resources will generally make for a more desperate struggle for power, with elites trying to hold on to their disproportionate share by fair means or foul, and non-elites often resorting to violence in the absence of effective constitutional channels. In some cases non-elites will create their own rebel forces, or governments representing elites will deploy national armies within the letter of the law. But in many cases armies will intervene, often with substantial prompting from civilian allies and sometimes foreign powers, in the belief that there is no other way of altering the existing distribution of power, or of countering threats to it.

The above analysis risks the criticism that armies are merely portrayed as appendages of particular social groups, rather than distinctive institutions with their own views of the world. A complementary approach is to take civil–military relations as the starting point and consider the 'boundaries' between the army and society. This was the pioneering approach used by Luckham (1971: 8–34).

It would be tempting to equate the categories noted in Box 6.2 with different degrees of social and economic development, with the most 'developed' countries having the most effective and clearly differentiated armies, but this is not always the case. Pakistan occupies 138th place on the UNDP human development index, yet its army is probably more clearly differentiated from civil society in terms of role and ideology than that of El Salvador in 104th place. A history of more than a century of British tutelage, followed by over half a century facing a perceived threat from India, has probably contributed to an army that fits Finer's description of an institution with its own morals and manners, distinct from the civilian population, whereas the El Salvador army has faced fewer external foes to unite it. The officer corps' preoccupations have

---

box 6.2   luckham and the political roles of the military

Although Luckham's typology could be criticised for creating too many pigeon-holes for the limited number of pigeons, three of his types illustrate well the diversity of military roles. First, there is the 'garrison state' in which extensive military power enables the armed forces to demand as large a share of decision-making as they require, as in Greece in the 1960s and early 1970s. Military government here will be a no-nonsense form of authoritarianism, with minimal scope for civilian participation or consultation. This model probably assumes the existence of an army with a degree of cohesion and resources beyond the scope of most developing countries. Chile and South Korea might have come close to it, but they fit more easily into the second category. This is the 'guardian state', where military power is lower but the military still have some self-steering capacity in the absence of strong civil institutions. In addition to South Korea, Luckham cites Pakistan and Turkey. Here soldiers may have greater difficulty in crushing dissent than in the garrison-state model, but they still have a clear perception of their own interests and substantial ability to pursue them. Third, there is the 'praetorian state' where civil and military institutions do not always have clearly defined roles, and military factions pursue power and influence in shifting coalitions with particular civilian factions. Much of Central America and tropical Africa would fit this model.

---

been more with protecting the social class from which it is drawn, and the El Salvador army has often looked more like the military wing of the landed elite (Ayub Khan 1967; Gardezi and Rashid 1983; Karl 1986: 9–36). A similar contrast could be made between the armies of Turkey (85th on the human development index) and Venezuela (69th), which in this context I am regarding as a 'typical' example of a Latin American country where, like El Salvador, the army is more bound up with civilian – and especially class – conflict. The Turkish army was heir to the Ottoman warrior tradition, and had distinctive views on how the polity should be ordered, whereas the Venezuelan army appears more engulfed in conflicts within civilian politics (Dikerdem 1987: 12; Dekmejian 1982: 45).

Armies promoting their own distinctive corporate interests and armies promoting broader class interests do not exhaust the range of possibilities. Huntington's distinction between the 'world of oligarchy' and 'mass society' assumes an evolving class structure in which the landed elite is faced with pressures from the middle class, which subsequently faces pressures from the working class. This may be a recognisable pattern in Latin America, or even parts of the Middle East, but in most of sub-Saharan Africa class structures are much more fluid. Here control over the machinery of state, or access to those who control it, is more important than social status. Liberia and Sierra Leone are extreme examples of this. There are therefore few distinctive social classes for the military to adhere to, in contrast to Latin America, yet African armies, most of which were created hastily at independence, do not have the sense of corporate identity found in Turkey or Pakistan. Military government is therefore less likely to be concerned with radicalism, conservatism or distinctive military values, and more with immediate calculations of benefits for oneself, one's colleagues and one's ethnic group. This is not to say that some African soldiers do not have strong political ideals, but the whole social and political setting makes it unlikely that military intervention will either create or avert major changes in society.

Combining the perspectives of social and economic development, conflicts between social classes, and the internal evolution of armies themselves, we can make five general, if not universal, propositions about the significance of armies in the working of the political process.

- In most 'developed' countries, armies are of relatively marginal interest to political scientists. For the most part the army is just another interest group with 'insider' status, able to wield influence but mainly in conformity with accepted rules.
- In developing countries the sheer unpredictability of the behaviour of armies makes them an interesting subject, as they take advantage of the ill-defined rules of the political game and exploit the weaknesses of civil institutions.
- Where class differences are particularly pronounced, there is force in Huntington's portrayal of soldiers as radicals challenging landed elites or conservatives fending off a rising working class. This is important because the army is often the most effective, if not the only, instrument for determining the fate of a particular social configuration. In the absence of free elections, who but armies under General Neguib and Colonel Nasser (who in July 1952 forced King Farouk to abdicate) and Colonel Gadaffi (who in 1969 led a *coup d'état* that overthrew King Idris) could have replaced right-wing monarchies in Egypt and Libya with 'modernising' left-wing governments? In the absence of moderating forces to establish consensus, who but armies under General Pinochet in Chile in 1973 or General Suharto in Indonesia in 1965 could have replaced left-wing governments with governments more to the liking of the middle class and the United States?
- The role of the army in politics is much more than one of aligning itself with particular social groups, especially where the army has had the time, common experiences and resources to evolve its own distinctive worldview. In such cases it may intervene in politics not just to trim the sails of particular social groups but to assert its own interests and values, as in our examples of Pakistan and Turkey.

- Where distinctions between social groups are more blurred on account of a more rudimentary economy, and where armies have little distinctive corporate history, military intervention may be frequent, given the weakness of civil institutions. But it will seldom contribute to any great social transformation, even though it may enrich or impoverish particular individuals. This has been the pattern in much of tropical Africa.

To sum up, we have suggested in this section that the rise of military government was facilitated by the emergence of a greater sense of corporate identity within the military, and by conflicts in society which political actors could not or would not resolve by peaceful means. Weaknesses in the polity and society made military intervention easier, but the nature of the subsequent military government in any country depended on the extent to which the army had a distinctive set of interests and values, and on its perception of who its friends and foes were in the wider society. By the 1980s military government looked like a well-entrenched form of government over much of the globe. But its survival depended on the ability of soldiers to prove that they were more competent rulers than civilians, on their ability to keep their own military constituency happy, and on a belief that their interests and objectives could be served only if they remained in power. We shall now consider the challenges to these abilities and beliefs.

after the cold war: the demise of military government?

Military government is a rarity in the post-Cold War world, but the decline of military government began long before 1990. It was partly a victim of a general decline of authoritarian rule which also swept away many personal dictatorships and one-party regimes. Explanations of this trend would be another diversion from our main concerns, but in many cases authoritarianism turned out to be yet another experiment that failed to yield greater material prosperity, public order or human happiness, just as the hopes raised by economic planning, development administration, attempted industrialisation, large-scale farming, and possibly structural adjustment and free markets, have also been dashed. Authoritarians were unlucky in that they presided over a period of economic decline (though with exceptions in East Asia) hastened by falling export prices in much of the 1970s and 1980s, over which they had little control, but they also lacked the political structures for executing any scheme of social or economic transformation. Many authoritarians were skilled in looting public resources and eliminating their opponents, but few will be remembered for promoting economic growth, setting the unemployed to work or making the trains run on time. Unable or unwilling to deliver any tangible benefits to most of the people, they had to rely increasingly on coercion, but even coercive resources were in limited supply against populations who had accorded their rulers little legitimacy in the first place and who now saw little reason to obey authority. The ending of the Cold War then tilted the balance still further against authoritarian rulers. On the one hand they could no longer invoke the Soviet system (on which they sometimes erroneously claimed to model their own rule) as a superior means to development rather than pluralism, while opposition activists took heart from the toppling of tyrants much stronger than those at home. On the other hand, Western powers no longer saw any need to underwrite authoritarian rulers who, for all their brutality, might once have been bastions against communism.

In the specific case of military government, there is the added factor of a limited 'shelf life', irrespective of economic conditions or external pressure. General Suharto's regime in Indonesia lasted over thirty years (1965–98), but the normal life span of a military regime is much less than twenty. While traditional monarchies can survive for centuries if they enjoy public legitimacy, and single-party regimes can last for several decades by mobilising the masses, military regimes by their nature tend to be stop-gaps. Their claim to legitimacy is not their own inherent virtue but the assertion that only they have been able to remove, or avert the emergence of, an undesirable government, and only they can remedy the deficiencies in the polity or the economy. This raises the paradox that if they then succeed with their remedies, they are redundant and the people demand a return to normal politics; yet if they fail, as they more frequently do, they can no longer claim to have superior qualities to civilian politicians and there is again pressure for them to stand down.

In addition to pressures from society, the internal dynamics of the army also set a time bomb ticking under the life of a military government (Baloyra 1987: 9–10, 38–43, 297; Finer 1985: 24–5). Unless an army is exceptionally well disciplined (perhaps the case of Pakistan) or has a clear vision of a long-term reform programme (Egypt and Libya), there is likely to be tension between the minority of soldiers enjoying the fruits of political office and the majority remaining in barracks. The greater the fear that soldiers within this majority will oust the current soldiers in government through a counter-coup, the greater the possibility of the soldiers in government seeking an exit from politics to preserve their lives and liberty, provided they can retain the wealth they have acquired and secure immunity from prosecution.

Pressures from both society and the army may curtail the life of an individual military government, but there was nothing before the 1990s to prevent the emergence of a succession of short-lived military governments interspersed with periods of civilian rule. This was the pattern in Latin America from the 1920s, and more recently in much of West Africa, Central Africa and Pakistan. What is remarkable about the period since 1990 is that, with a few exceptions, the civilian 'interludes' have continued indefinitely. The post-Cold War pressures we have described:

- ending of the hopes raised by the Soviet experiment;
- cessation of western need to support 'anti-communist' authoritarians; and
- promotion of democracy as a form of western triumphalism

have all made military government, like other blatant forms of authoritarianism, illegitimate in the eyes of both indigenous populations and external donors. A blind eye may sometimes be turned where the regime rules a country of strategic importance, as in Pakistan under the current ruler, President (formerly General) Musharraf), or at the other extreme where it is considered too insignificant to merit foreign intervention, as in The Gambia in 1994, when a military *coup d'état* overthrew an elected ruler. But these are exceptions to the general rule.

the legacy of military government: weak states and unconsolidated democracies

What, then, has replaced military rule, in the fifty or more of our 56 countries that once experienced it? The actual figures are imprecise because there is room for disagreement on whether a regime has really been civilianised. The process was unambiguous in countries such as Brazil and Chile, where the rulers in the 1980s had little choice but to permit elections which were then won by politicians not favoured by the military, but there are more dubious cases like Algeria and The Gambia in the 1990s where virtually the same soldiers continued ruling in a similar way after holding rigged elections. If we regard military government as having ended after a relatively free election has been held, and any soldiers or ex-soldiers who remain in the government rule mainly through civilian political institutions, then the number of surviving military governments at the time of writing (late 2004) is probably reduced to a handful of Asian and African countries: Myanmar/Burma, the Central African Republic, Libya, Pakistan, and possibly the borderline cases of Algeria, The Gambia and the Sudan.

The successor regimes are at least as varied as the military regimes they have replaced, but what is common to most of them is that violence, or the threat of violence, continues to have a role in politics. Next we explore three broad aspects of post-military government:

- the break in political continuity that military intervention wrought;
- the changes in the balance of civil-military relations; and
- the 'unconsolidated' nature of the democracy in what are generally weakened states, often unable to control violence within their borders.

The break in continuity occurs in the sense that an incoming military government will probably have suspended the constitution, banned some or all political parties, replaced uncooperative bureaucrats and ignored or persecuted interest groups of the 'wrong' political persuasion. There have been exceptional cases like Uruguay where most of the pre-coup landscape has subsequently been restored, but more frequently the rules of the political game have been rewritten to suit the needs and beliefs of the military. When the military returns power to civilians, once-dominant political groups may be put in the shade on account of the military's preference for alternative ideologies, social classes, or ethnic or religious groups. The once-dominant groups may be disqualified from holding political office, or handicapped by the ways in which elections are conducted, or excluded from political consultation. In the early 2000s, trade unions and left-wing parties no longer enjoy the prominence they once did in Latin America, and the ethnic balance has shifted from north to south in Nigeria and Uganda. The heirs of King Farouk have little chance of returning to rule Egypt. If policies are followed that meet with the disapproval of the military, the mere fact that they have intervened in the past may provide a sufficient warning to successor politicians. In practice the warning is usually reinforced by constitutional or legal provisions that entrench the power and privileges of the military, and which were a necessary part of the bargain for military withdrawal from government.

This takes us back to the thorny area of civil–military relations. Whether the ending of military government and the post-Cold War pressures for democratisation have tilted the balance in favour of democratic civilian control over the military is a matter of controversy, as indicated in Table 6.2.

Table 6.2 Civil–military relations since the Cold War

Democratic control over the military?	The military as a rogue actor?
Democratic and post-Cold War values lead to the military being reduced to a more **subordinate role**. Civilian politicians recognise the professionalism of soldiers, rather than using them for narrow political purposes.	There are new or growing **social problems** e.g. civil unrest, drugs and crime, especially with growing poverty. The army is often brought in to tackle these problems, though with little success. The involvement of the military implies **a continued role for force as a political instrument**.
Past experience shows that **the military is not good at governing**, and few people want soldiers to return to government.	Conscription has been ended in most countries. **This may make the army more remote from society.**
Pressure for retrenchment may **reduce the capacity of the military**.	Long-standing problems of **inadequate civil control over the military** continue. Civilian governments may lack the will or expertise to control the military. Guerrilla insurgency gives the military a pretext for demanding freedom to act autonomously. There is frequently a **lack of integration of the military into the political system**.
There is a greater expectation of western governments **imposing sanctions on governments brought to power by military coups**. But does this work?	

The argument that there is now greater democratic control over the military today than there was before the wave of coups from the 1960s to the 1980s is based on two main points:

- the military's loss of credibility as a political actor in the light of experience of brutal yet ineffective military government; and
- the general post-Cold War environment which requires democratic governance and retrenchment in the public sector, including the defence budget (Fitch 1998: 59; Huntington 1996: 3–12; Luckham 1995: 49; Malan 2000: 150).

Huntington (1996) paints a broad picture of improved civil–military relations as one of the major achievements of the 'new democracies', with an acceptance by both soldiers and civilians that objective control of the military is in the interests of both sides, and is a relatively inexpensive goal to pursue. The limited ability of the military to resolve political problems is now widely recognised, so the military are able to return to a more specialised professional role. Fitch (1998) and Malan (2000) both focus on the restraining hands that neighbours place on military intervention, or on authoritarian tendencies generally, in a global environment where democracy is back in fashion. In this way, authoritarian takeovers have been aborted or reversed in Guatemala, Peru, Lesotho, Niger, Burundi and Sierra Leone, although some of these successes have been short-lived.

An alternative approach focuses more on the reality of countries faced with poverty, instability and conflict rather than the outward appearance of democratisation at home underwritten by powerful democracies abroad. In contrast to Huntington, Rial (1996: 47–65) argues that the military have generally resisted executive and legislative control, and that civilian politicians lack the expertise to exercise such control, and would anyway gain few political rewards from it. Military links with civil society remain weak. Beyond the inadequate links between soldiers and politicians (which may have become weaker still as new generations of politicians emerge who have not undergone conscription), loom societies wracked by growing poverty, civil unrest, drugs and crime, and in parts of Latin America the survival of well-organised guerrilla movements. Under these conditions, soldiers become less concerned with national defence and more with internal order. In the latter field, it may be difficult for civilians to prevent the military from defining their own role, often free of any democratic control (Rial 1996: 47–65; Philip 2003: 77–8, 83). It is frequently soldiers who decide how to deal with street children, whether to set up counter-insurgency campaigns, and whether to prosecute, or profit from, the drugs trade. As the major contestants in the Cold War have withdrawn their own or their proxy troops from many areas, especially in Africa, this has allowed simmering conflicts to explode. In response, either neighbouring armies have been sent to fish in troubled waters, or international peacekeeping forces have been despatched in an attempt to keep the lid on conflicts based on ethnicity, religion or simply greed. These sojourns abroad have enabled many soldiers to engage in profitable business activities, which makes them even more reluctant to submit themselves to political control.

These conflicting perspectives might suggest that we should not be asking whether armies are now stronger or weaker, but in which areas they have gained or lost influence. In terms of controlling the whole political process, as in Chile under General Pinochet or Uganda under General Amin, armies have clearly had to concede defeat to civilians. As powers behind the throne, or as rogue actors who can decide which areas of policy they will control, the picture is more complicated. Nearly all military governments will insist on certain conditions for handing power back to civilians, though the bargain they can strike will depend on whether they are departing from a position of strength or weakness. General Pinochet could give up power in Chile with the advantages of a united army, an expanding if inegalitarian economy and a large number of allies in the civilian elite, whereas General Galtieri had to make a hasty withdrawal in Argentina after a humiliating defeat in the Falklands War of 1982.

---

box 6.3   exiting power: the military and post-power arrangements

Nearly all outgoing soldiers will insist on immunity from prosecution from any misdeeds during their term of office. Beyond that, they may demand varying degrees of autonomy, adequate budgetary allocations, control over areas of policy which they regard as their prerogative and possibly representation in state institutions (Hunter 1998: 299–322). Some of these privileges will be written into the constitution, some will be acknowledged implicitly as the price to be paid to prevent further military intervention, and some emerge, for example the abandonment of attempts to prosecute Argentinian soldiers, as the realities of power are recognised. In much of Africa, and more recently in Pakistan, soldiers divesting themselves of their uniforms have won elections to head nominally civilian governments, sometimes by rigging elections and sometimes because their preceding periods in power have given them a head start in terms of money and power bases.

All this might suggest that the legacy of military rule has been to tip the balance in civil–military relations in favour of the military but, as Hunter (1998: 307) suggests, we need to consider not just the degree of military power but the extent to which it is actually used. It may be that soldiers genuinely want a quieter life away from politics, unless there is an immediate threat to their lives, liberty or careers, or that public opinion will no longer tolerate governments that give too much ground to the military. And if the ultimate sanction of a military coup becomes almost unthinkable, the lesser means of applying military pressure may become less effective.

Our third aspect of post-military government, unconsolidated democracy within weak states, might be seen as a phenomenon that stretches beyond countries that have experienced military government (see chapter 4 for a discussion of this issue). In recent years India and Sri Lanka have experienced growing political violence as well as Pakistan; Mexico as well as Guatemala, and Kenya as well as Uganda. The ending of the Cold War, globalisation and pressures for free-market economics, all of which are discussed elsewhere in this book, have led to the emergence of weaker states with fewer resources for buying friends or punishing foes (for discussion of these topics, see chapters 1, 4, and 13). Ideologies such as nationalism, socialism and non-alignment no longer provide even the fragile basis for legitimacy which they did formerly, and increasingly impoverished people respond to more-and-more ineffective states by retreating into self-help, often within their own ethnic or religious communities (Kaldor and Luckham 2001: 48–69). (See chapter 7 for a discussion of the role of religion in development, and chapter 8 for that of ethnicity.) In some cases this may involve little more than worthy projects to provide schools or water supply in the absence of state provision, but in other cases a sense of group identity leads to violent conflict with other groups. This development has been aided both by the more ready availability of arms which globalisation has facilitated and by a greater western reluctance to police conflicts in faraway lands.

On the other hand, 'electoral democracy' may survive, in the sense of rulers having gained or held power through competitive elections. Even the current rulers of Algeria, The Gambia, Liberia and Pakistan can claim a democratic mandate in that sense, in contrast to most of the dictators of the 1970s, but at worst such democracy is a sham and at best it remains 'unconsolidated'. Little consensus exists on the rules of political conflict, and institutions for mediating such conflict are weak or non-existent (Schmitter 1995: 11–41). Of all the countries under authoritarian rule in the 1980s, there is near-unanimity in the literature that only Uruguay has achieved democratic consolidation, although Chile, Argentina, South Africa and Ghana (probably in that order) may have travelled a considerable distance along the road (Pinkney 2003: 181–3).

We must avoid the temptation to label the above developments as exclusively post-Cold War ones, any more than they are exclusively post-military-government. The legacy of military government exists alongside other, long-standing, legacies. Ethnically-disadvantaged groups have been engaged in guerrilla warfare in much of Latin America for several decades, and Zaïre (now the Democratic Republic of Congo), has been plagued by violent internal conflict ever since independence in 1960, often exacerbated rather than constrained by the Cold War protagonists. It would be better to think of experience of military government, the ending of the Cold War, globalisation and increased poverty as different tributaries that have fed into the violence that characterises many countries today, though the tributaries frequently criss-cross each other. Experience of military government is relevant to the extent that it creates a precedent for violent challenges to authority, though military government might of course be a symptom of societies unable to resolve their differences by peaceful means. In the early 2000s, countries such as Côte d'Ivoire, Liberia and Sierra Leone, all of which had histories of relatively orderly government before experiencing their first coups, have not been able to build new peaceful orders, whereas violence has been much more contained in Malawi, Tanzania and Zambia where no successful military coups have ever occurred. But even if a developing country avoids military government, it can hardly escape the criss-crossing tributaries of globalisation and the impact of the ending of the Cold War.

---

box 6.4   globalisation and military power

Globalisation leaves already enfeebled governments, presiding over poor countries, with even less ability to control their own destiny, as a slight shift in world markets can destroy a country's economic base. The ending of the Cold War reinforced these trends, as the victors insist on retrenchment and 'free trade' for 'developing' countries while preserving protectionism at home. On one side of the equation, governments have fewer resources to spend on maintaining order or rewarding supporters. On the other their constituents, who see few tangible benefits in return for their votes and few potential benefits for voting for any alternative if policies are decided in Washington or Brussels, are now better able to secure arms and manpower to challenge enfeebled national armies. As Cerny (1999: 18) argues, violence today is less the province of national governments, and more the domain of ethnic groups, drugs cartels, mafias, mercenaries and private armies linked to firms and other sub-state or cross-national organisations.

We must however be careful not to exaggerate the contrast between the old and the new, or indeed the extent of violence. In some 'developing' countries, notably in Eastern and Southern Africa outside Zimbabwe, the incidence of political violence is little greater than in most of Europe, and in much of Latin America political conflict can be seen as a continuation of the age-old struggle to seek equilibrium between the claims of civilian politicians and regular armies. But it is difficult to dispute Cerny's assertion that the more fragmented forms of violence are on the increase. A continuum of relations between armed force and politics is sketched below.

- **Praetorianism** Much of the population wields arms and a 'national army' is either non-existent or ineffective. Political power depends on which transitory armed groups can take control of the machinery of state. Examples include Democratic Republic of Congo, Sierra Leone and Liberia.
- **Civil war** Armed groups, even if weakly structured and ill disciplined, are distinguished by some territorial, ethnic, religious or ideological base. Examples include Cambodia, the Sudan and Sri Lanka.
- **Limited rebellion** The national army is unable to dislodge rebels who control a limited part of the national territory, but there is no immediate threat of national disintegration or the violent overthrow of the regime. Examples include Peru and Uganda.

- **Military autonomy** Recognisable national armies exist but are subject to tenuous political control. Soldiers may use their advantage of armed force to set up businesses and plunder resources. Examples include Nigeria and Turkey.
- **Uncertain military veto** There is limited consensus on the proper role of the army, and limited legitimacy is conferred on civil authority. Soldiers intervene in politics in unpredictable ways. Examples include many states in Central and West Africa.
- **Military government** The national army is a sufficiently coherent entity to take control of the state (though prolonged control may make it less coherent). Examples include Libya, Myanmar, Pakistan and possibly Algeria.
- **Institutionalised military veto** There is a tacit understanding of the areas of government policy which the military are likely to resist. Examples include Argentina, Brazil and Chile.
- **Objective control** The military are subordinate to civilian authority. Examples include all 'developed', western countries ('the western model').

Our analysis so far has tried to explain why many countries have moved closer to the first five categories since 1990. Within them, and especially within the first three, the whole concept of armed groups is a difficult one to handle. Terms such as 'insurgent', 'bandit', 'terrorist', 'rebel' and 'warlord' indicate the diversity of groups with which we are now dealing. Some of these groups may have recognisable political objectives, such as protecting Christians from Muslims in the Sudan, some may make dubious claims to political objectives, and others have more immediate objectives such as cattle-rustling or drug-trafficking. Some groups may thus create little more than a 'law and order' problem, albeit often a serious one, but others come more into the realm of 'politics' because they are seeking to defend or advance the interests of particular groups, or even to take control of the machinery of state, as in Liberia, Sierra Leone and Rwanda. But where they succeed, they do not become 'military governments' in the narrow sense, because they do not constitute national armies, and 'government' may consist of little more than plundering whatever resources they can.

We have moved to a stage where we are witnessing not just new or expanding types of violence, but types of violence that are increasingly dysfunctional to state and nation-building. Kaldor and Luckham (2001: 58–9) make the point that the 'total wars' of the first half of the twentieth century helped to build stronger states as the war effort required mass mobilisation, control of the economy and adequate welfare provision to give the poor a stake in society. Rather than being fought directly by the Cold War protagonists, many major wars between 1945 and 1990 (excluding Korea, Vietnam and most of the terminal anti-colonial struggles) were fought by proxy. These wars sometimes led to a descent into near-anarchy, as in Angola and the Congo, but in many cases they strengthened both the external patrons and the client governments. State authority was probably enhanced in Indonesia, Mozambique and much of Central America either through the need to build a post-war consensus between clearly identifiable factions, or through the military might of the victors. Such authority might even be seen as a prelude to building democracy. In contrast, the growing conflicts implicit in our first three categories are dysfunctional for the building of state authority, democracy or civil society. Kaldor and Luckham speak of the unravelling of the formal political and economic sectors. Warlords who wield power obtain revenue through theft from civilians and foreign donors, from illicit trade and from foreign governments that benefit from this trade, while neighbouring governments help to keep the wars going, presumably because it is easier for them and their soldiers to plunder a country's wealth when it is in a state of chaos (Kaldor and Luckham 2001: 58–61). Such an account would help to explain why the search for peace in the Democratic Republic of Congo, Sierra Leone and Liberia has been so difficult.

the search for civilian control

Most democrats, and probably most people who value political order if not democracy, would like the relationship between armed force and politics shifted away from our first seven categories and towards objective control: that is a system in which armies enjoy operational autonomy and institutionalised means of interacting with their governments, but are ultimately subordinate to the democratic will of the people through their elected representatives. Are there any signs that we are moving towards this goal, and are there any solutions available which would bring us closer to it?

In the course of this survey, we have noted some optimistic voices. Huntington detected a move towards objective control and greater military professionalism, and Fitch mentioned external pressures to deter military intervention in Latin America (Huntington 1996: 3–12; Fitch 1998: 59). We could also note the relative restraint shown by armies in recent political crises, in contrast to their higher profile in earlier times. The Guatemalan army did not condone the behaviour of a populist president flouting the constitution in 1993, and the Chilean army kept off the streets at the time of the arrest of General Pinochet in 1998. The removal of Presidents Collor and Fujimori in Brazil and Peru in 1992 and 2000 respectively was executed with minimal military involvement. Perhaps even more remarkable was the restraint shown by the Argentine army in 2001 when the government was brought down by one of the country's severest economic crises. In recent years in Africa, civilian protesters chased the military out of office in Côte d'Ivoire, and in Mali and Malawi the military took the side of civilian democrats against authoritarian rulers. In Ghana there is now a contrast between the constant fear, and the ultimate reality, of military intervention in the Second and Third Republics of 1969–72 and 1979–81, and the restraint shown by the military in the Fourth Republic, even after the defeat in 2000 of the party favoured by the military (Pinkney 2003: 200–1).

But in most of the countries mentioned in the previous paragraph there is a degree of differentiation between civil and military institutions, even if it stops short of objective control. We have seen that in many other countries violence is the common currency, and it is not issued solely or even mainly by a distinctive national army. Even where this is not the case, there is often a real possibility of a greater fragmentation of the armed forces. In the face of these hazards, the existing literature does not offer a lot of comfort in terms of solutions. There is near-unanimity that civilian governments should avoid the temptation of 'finding something to keep soldiers occupied', whether in public works, welfare provision or policing, partly because soldiers may resent being treated like odd-job men and may rebel against such impositions, and partly because they are ill-qualified for such roles. Involvement in combating the drugs trade or crime in general is singled out, on the grounds that soldiers may use or provoke greater violence than policemen, or may get involved in corrupt activities on the wrong side of the law (Fitch 1998: 184; Malan 2000: 157; Hunter 1998: 309). Peacekeeping abroad may perhaps offer a role more suited to military capabilities, however (see Box 6.5).

Beyond the narrow literature on civil–military relations are arguments that violence and political chaos are the product of years of impoverishment fuelled by exploitation by global capital and indigenous elites alike, and that only a reversal of this process will make orderly democratic government possible. Increased and properly targeted aid, debt relief and fair trade could all be invoked in support of this. It is difficult to disagree with such a proposition, but the unlikelihood of such a major turnaround in western policy might make it sensible to stick to a narrower focus.

---

box 6.5   the military and peacekeeping abroad

Peacekeeping abroad tends to be more popular with both governments and armies. It enables governments to put a distance between themselves and troublesome soldiers, and often provides soldiers with illicit means of supplementing their earnings, but there is both a limit to the number of peacekeeping missions available and a danger of the 'peacekeepers' seeking to prolong conflicts out of self-interest. Academics who are bold enough to offer positive solutions, and not just warnings of what to avoid, face an uphill task. Kaldor and Luckham (2001: 64–5) want to rebuild and professionalise armies, police and security forces, and subordinate them to democratic authority, but it is not clear how one would reach such a state of affairs in countries where governments have a very limited capacity. Fitch is also keen on professionalism which, he argues, requires commitment to defend democracy, 'not the state or some ideal conception of the fatherland'. Military training should include instruction in democratic theory (Fitch 1998: 184). It is not clear what would happen if the soldiers' conceptions of democracy conflicted with those of their political masters.

---

conclusion

Lack of space, and not just moral cowardice, prevents the canvassing of any alternative solutions in this chapter, but it does seem that demanding greater professionalism or democratic civilian control is putting the cart before the horse. Many countries are in the violent state that they are because their governments have lost any basis for control, whether through democratic legitimacy or force, and it seems curious to urge them to pursue solutions that they would have pursued long ago if they had had the capacity to do so. Governmental authority might be strengthened if it acquired a greater popular legitimacy as the government came closer to responding to the people's aspirations, however imperfectly. Or, less plausibly, it might be strengthened by a foreign power coming in and trying to root out the causes of, and opportunities for, violence. Mozambique and Uganda might be cited as countries which, whatever their shortcomings, have moved some of the way to strengthening the bonds between government and governed and thus reducing violence. The second solution remains a gleam in the eye of post-imperialists, though it might yet be attempted if the current anarchy spreads further.

Another line of approach might be to ask "What are armies and armed force for?" Do we really need large standing armies in countries where there is little prospect of an enemy attack in the foreseeable future? A more rational solution might be to have a much smaller standing army, restore conscription and keep the conscripts in a reserve force at the end of their term in readiness for any emergency. This would be politically unpopular with both the would-be conscripts and the regular soldiers threatened with redundancy, and it might be fanciful to imagine orderly queues of recruits answering the call to arms in countries where people show little inclination to obey the law, but such an approach might draw the teeth of the rebel groups which at present attract many impoverished youths. It would be more effective if complemented by more rigorous attempts by western governments to stem both legal and illegal arms sales to both governments and rebel groups, unless a clear case can be made on grounds of national security. This again risks the charge of wandering into a fantasy world in which tigers can become vegetarians, and governments can acquire beliefs and skills for which they previously showed little inclination. The task of resolving political conflicts by non-violent means is, if anything, more complex than at the height of the Cold War. The military regimes of the 1980s were often more brutal and repressive than anything seen before in the countries they ruled, but at least a relatively disciplined, professional army was removable from office through negotiations between the military hierarchy and party leaders. Political systems faced with a more diffuse exercise of violence today may find the establishment and maintenance of a democratic polity, based on trust and consensus, a much more difficult process. To get the current diversity of violent groups to change their ways will require a substantial amount of time, skill and luck. Most of the solutions proposed so far probably have only a limited chance of success, but it is frightening to contemplate the consequences of not attempting any solutions at all.

7
religion and development
jeffrey haynes

The aim of this chapter is to provide readers with:

- intellectual tools to judge intelligently contemporary arguments concerning interactions between religion and politics in the developing world;
- the ability to relate such issues to contemporary policy issues, including development outcomes.

Ever since the Cold War ended and the Soviet Union collapsed, people have speculated about political and developmental outcomes in the countries of the global South. But how exactly are things changing? What do these changes, if they are in fact occurring, mean for peace, prosperity and justice in the developing countries? This chapter seeks to address such questions – by focusing on the ways that religion impacts upon development outcomes in the developing world.

Academics, policy-makers, the media and development professionals increasingly appreciate the roles of religion in relation to the following:

- religion has an important function in engendering and influencing values, which in turn can affect the formulation of underlying policy considerations and policies of states;
- depending on circumstances, religion can both exacerbate and resolve political conflicts;
- some religious groups eschew political involvement.

The chapter focuses on the various relationships between religion and politics over time in the developing world. The aspiration is to provide a commentary on what has taken place, and is currently happening, to the spheres of religion and politics. In sum, the chapter provides a comparative treatment of the issues noted above – so that readers will be able to appreciate and comprehend the rich variety of particular national and regional situations that inform outcomes involving religion and politics in the countries of the developing world. The overall purpose of the chapter is an introduction to the topic, with the intention to stimulate further examination and discussion of the issues it discusses.

introduction

Ever since the 1970s, commentators have noted what many see as widespread involvement of religion in politics, especially in many countries in the developing world. It is often noted that religio-political conflict, for example, in Nigeria, is exacerbated by/and or contributes to political instability and conflict, as well as development failures. This chapter examines the relationship between religion and politics in the developing world, and is structured as follows. First, it examines the relationship between religion and modernisation. Second, it offers a typology of political religion. Third, it examines the relationship between religious mobilisation and political action.

The chapter also seeks to shed light upon the relationship between religion, politics, conflict and identity in the developing world, and the extent to which such issues have impacted upon development outcomes. The focus will predominantly be on mass culture rather than elite preferences because no states are currently governed by actual or claimed theocratic regimes apart from a handful in the Muslim world (Saudi Arabia, Iran, and, arguably, Sudan). In many developing countries, on the other hand, opposition groups frequently include among their leaders religious figures.

The chapter advances three main arguments:

- Developments associated with modernisation – that is, socio-economic and political change involving urbanisation, industrialisation, and centralisation of government – are crucial to an understanding of the political role of religion in the developing world.
- Far from fading from political relevance, religion has, on the contrary, assumed important – although variable – mobilising roles in recent years in many developing countries.

- The nature of a religious vehicle will not only be accountable by reference to structural and systemic attributes and developments, but will also reflect the particular characteristics of the culture(s) that produce and use it.

It was once widely assumed that nations would invariably secularise as they modernised. Loss of religious faith and secularisation dovetailed with the idea that technological development and the application of science to overcome perennial social problems of poverty, environmental degradation, hunger and disease would result in long-term human progress. However, the lack of uniform success in this regard was one of the factors behind the recent renaissance of religion's role in politics, not only in the developing world, but also more widely. Examples over the last 25 years include

- Iran's Islamic revolution of 1978–80;
- Christian fundamentalists' involvement in political and social issues in various countries, including the United States (Haynes 1996 and 1998);
- Protestant evangelical sects in various parts of the developing world, including Latin America, with variable political connotations;
- sometimes intense conflict between: Hindus and Muslims in India, Buddhists and Hindus in Sri Lanka, and Muslims and Christians in former Yugoslavia;
- In India, Sikh separatists in Punjab and Muslim militants in Jammu-Kashmir;
- the role of Islamic and Jewish religious fundamentalist groups in the context of the continuing Israel–Palestinians dispute.

In short, religion has had considerable impact upon politics in many regions of the developing world. Religion may be used as a vehicle of opposition or as an ideology of community self-interest. In the first category can be included various kinds of religious entities, including: 'culturalist', fundamentalist and syncretistic groups. Each of these types of group is examined in the chapter.

These various religious reactions are the result of real or perceived threats – either from powerful, outsider groups, or from manifestations of unwelcome symptoms of modernisation (such as the perceived breakdown of moral behaviour, alleged over-liberalisation in education, and, more generally, changing social habits in the context of modernisation). In addition, widespread governmental failures to push through programmes of social improvement has encouraged the founding of local community groups in many developing countries, groups that tend to organise themselves around sets of religious ideas. In sum, religious actors can lend themselves to a variety of ecclesial, ideological and political uses, some of which are oppositional or antipathetical to incumbent governments, while others – for example, many fundamentalist evangelical Protestant movements, especially in Latin America and sub-Saharan Africa – are not. It is however important to note that whatever role religion adopts, there is an ambivalence: its role depends on both the developmental and political contexts within which it acts. As a result, both context and contingent events can play a key role in emergence or strengthening of countervailing tendencies: for example, the rise of evangelical Protestantism in recent years in Latin America should be seen in the context both of developmental failures and of the decline from hegemony of the Roman Catholic Church. We start by examining what is perhaps the key contextual issue in relation to the political and developmental roles of religion in the developing world: the problematic issue of the relationship between religion and modernisation.

religion and modernisation

One of the most resilient ideas about societal development after World War II was that nations would inevitably secularise as they modernised. The idea of modernisation was strongly linked to urbanisation, industrialisation and an accompanying rationalisation of previously 'irrational' views, such as religious beliefs and ethnic separatism. Loss of religious faith and secularisation dovetailed with the idea that technological development and the application of science to overcome perennial social problems of poverty, environmental degradation, hunger and disease would result in long-term human progress. With the decline in the belief in the efficacy of technological development to cure all human ills came a wave of popular religiosity with political ramifications.

To analyse and explain this wave of apparently unconnected developments we need to confront at the outset an issue consistently ignored in political analysis. How do religious values, norms and beliefs stimulate and affect political developments, and vice versa? For example, historical analysis would point to the close relationship over time between the top hierarchy of the Roman Catholic Church and successive less-than-democratic governments in Latin America, yet in the 1980s and 1990s some Church officials emerged as champions of democracy (Haynes 1998 and 2002). Senior members of the Roman Catholic hierarchy, on the other hand, retained their roles within the ruling triumvirate, along with senior military figures and big landowners and capitalists. How do we explain the contemporary divergence of views between senior Catholic figures and many priests on the ground in Latin America?

Among followers of Islam throughout the Muslim world, that is, some fifty countries stretching from Morocco to Indonesia, we can note a similar process. Often, senior Islamic figures remained close to secular rulers, while political challenges to the status quo were often led and coordinated by lower- and middle-ranking Muslims. A similar type of schism was also observable in Thailand and Myanmar (Burma) where senior Buddhists were often supportive of military(-supported) regimes, while junior figures attacked them for their corruption and political incompetence. Thus, a common denominator in these events was the close relationships between senior religious figures and secular political and economic elites. Those closest to the people, on the other hand, those involved in religious issues at community level, often found themselves responding to popular pressures for change that cut across horizontal class stratifications, vertical ethnic or regional differences, and/or the urban–rural divide. In short, what emerged were often serious rifts between rulers and ruled, with religion frequently a focal point for demands for change.

Before going further it is necessary to inform the reader what I mean by the term 'religion'. In this chapter I use it in two distinct, yet related, ways. First, in a material sense it refers to religious establishments (that is, institutions and officials), as well as to social groups and movements, whose *raisons d'être* centre on various religious concerns. Examples include the conservative Roman Catholic organisation, Opus Dei, the reformist Islamic Salvation Front of Algeria (FIS), India's Hindu-chauvinist Bharatiya Janata Party ('People's Party'), and, in Latin America, both Protestant evangelical groups and Roman Catholic communitarian organisations influenced by the radical ideas of liberation theology. Second, in a spiritual sense, religion pertains to models of social and individual behaviour that help believers to organise their everyday lives. In this sense, religion is to do with the ideas of:

- **transcendence** – that is, it relates to supernatural realities;
- **sacredness** – that is, it is a system of language and practice that organises the world in terms of what is deemed holy; and
- **ultimacy** – that is, it relates people to the ultimate conditions of their existence.

Because of the importance placed here on the explanatory value of the role of modernisation, it is appropriate at the outset to say a little about it. Throughout the developing world, with the important exception of post-revolutionary states, such as China and Iran, the general direction to which social change has taken place is usually referred to as either 'modernisation' or 'westernisation'. That is, social change is understood to lead to significant shifts in the behaviour and prevailing choices of social actors, with such particularistic traits as ethnicity or caste losing importance in relation to more general attributes such as nationalism. In this context, growth of formal political organisations – such as political parties – and procedures – such as 'the rule of law' and the use of the ballot box to choose governments – is thought to reduce the central role of other kinds of political practices – such as clientelism and patronage. In short, it was widely contended that the advent of social change corresponding to a presumed process of modernisation would eventually lead to a general jettisoning of older, traditional values and the adoption of other, initially alien, practices in developing countries. In many respects, however, the adoption of Western traits in many developing countries was only skin deep: for example western-style suits for men rather than traditional dress; symbolic trappings of statehood – a flag, constitution and legislature; and a western lingua franca. However, the important point is that social change was rarely even throughout such societies, while social and political conflicts often remained likely due to the patchy and partial adoption of modern practices. It became clear that rather than enhancing chances of development, instead social changes linked to modernisation destabilised, and created a dichotomy between those who sought to benefit from wholesale change and those who preferred the status quo. Over time, new social strata arose whose position in the new order was ambiguous. For example, recent rural–urban migrants in Middle Eastern, sub-Saharan African, Latin American and Asian countries often found themselves effectively between two worlds, without an effective set of anchoring values. Such people were often open to political appeals based on religious precepts.

More generally, religion is an important source of basic value orientations in most developing countries. It may have a powerful impact upon politics within a state or region, especially in the context of ethnicity, culture or (religious) fundamentalism. As Handelman explains in chapter 8, ethnicity relates to the perceived shared characteristics of a racial, linguistic or cultural group. In some cases, religious beliefs can reinforce ethnic consciousness and inter-ethnic conflict in the developing

---

box 7.1 ___ religious fundamentalism

Religious fundamentalism is defined by Marty and Scott Appleby (1993: 3) as a 'set of strategies, by which beleaguered believers attempt to preserve their distinctive identity as a people or group' in response to a real or imagined attack from those who apparently threaten to draw them into a 'syncretistic, areligious, or irreligious cultural milieu'. Such defensiveness can develop into a political offensive that aims to alter prevailing social, political and sometimes economic realities that characterise state–society relations in individual countries.

---

world (but not only there, think of more 'developed' contexts, such as Northern Ireland, former Yugoslavia and Russia).

Religion also relates to politics in ways that are themselves linked to individual societies' particular historical and developmental trajectories, both 'traditional' and 'modern'. In 'traditional' societies the relationship between religion and politics is always a close one. Political power is underpinned by religious beliefs and practices, while political concerns permeate to the heart of the religious sphere. Rulers are not only political heads but also religious leaders, individuals whose well-being is thought to be closely linked to 'their' people's health and welfare.

It was long assumed that processes of modernisation would invariably lead to a high degree of secularisation and a practical, although not necessarily symbolic, separation of politics and religion. Over time, however, it is increasingly recognised that such a process is neither simple nor clear cut. For example, Queen Elizabeth II of the United Kingdom is a constitutional ruler who is also formally the head of the Church of England. In practice, however, she is much less politically powerful than most state presidents; from a religious point of view her role is practically moribund, yet symbolically it still has some importance. On the other hand, the late King Hassan II of Morocco (1929–99) was imbued with a high degree of religious authority that also gave him great political influence and status. His religious authority derived from his role as Al Amir al Mumineen ('Commander of the Faithful'). Many Moroccans believed that King Hassan was a direct descendent of the Prophet Muhammad himself. King Hassan was able to use his religious standing to offset challenges to his position from various sources, including an Islamist threat from those seeking an 'Islamicisation' of Morocco's politics and society.

The current – although ailing – Saudi monarch, King Fahd, also has a significant religious title 'Protector of the Holy Places' (Mecca and Medina). Yet, Fahd 'protects' them as the head of a modern state, rather than as leader of a religious community alone.

---

box 7.2   religio-political power in saudi arabia

For King Fahd, the role of religion (in an institutional sense) in the upholding of his power is limited: in Saudi Arabia, there is no elected assembly, no written constitution, and no advisory body of religio-legal scholars (the *ulama*) to give the king's authority an Islamic gloss. In addition, there is no public scrutiny of decision-making and the political processes. Instead, Fahd rules by way of his own absolutist political and tribal authority rather than because of his religious credentials, although the latter are useful in bolstering his position. (Note, however that the ailing Fahd is not really now (2004) running the kingdom. His half-brother, Crown Prince Abdullah, has been de facto ruler since Fahd suffered a stroke in 1995.)

Somewhere in the middle of the two extremes – that is, virtual absence of religious authority (Queen Elizabeth II) and rulers that have much of it (Kings Fahd and Hassan) – we can note King Bhumipol Adulyadej of Thailand (b.1927). In Thailand, *theravada* Buddhism is the state religion according to the constitution of 1968. Consequently, King Bhumipol must profess and defend the Buddhist *dharma* (the moral and physical order of the state) and the community of monks (*sangha*). He must also, however, reach a *modus vivendi* with the military because of its traditional role as power broker (see chapter 6 for an extensive discussion of the political roles of the military in the developing world).

We can conclude this section as follows:

- Monarchical systems, linked to traditional forms of rule, exist in the developing world but are rare.
- Political systems are common whose leaders have authority derived from their ability to win and hold on to power, normally via elections.
- Most contemporary leaders and governments in the developing world are not formally connected with one particular set of religious beliefs.

We can also note that since the early 1970s, religion – in both material and spiritual senses – is said to have enjoyed a strong rejuvenation – even resurgence – in many developing countries. Let us next examine a typology of political religion in the contemporary developing world.

a typology of political religion in the developing world

Attempts to salvage the secularisation model have interpreted evidence of burgeoning religiosity in many contemporary political events to mean that we are witnessing merely a fundamentalist, antimodernist backlash against science, industrialization, and liberal Western values ... Religious fervour is often dismissed as ethnic hostility ..., typically explained away as an isolated exception to unremitting trends of secularization and seldom recognized as part of a larger global phenomenon   (Sahliyeh 1990: 16).

The quotation suggests two areas where religion is of particular importance in understanding political and social developments in the developing world: in relation to ethnicity issues and to 'religious fundamentalism'. Yet this is only part of the story. We also need to be aware of the political importance of both religious 'syncretism' and of community-orientated religious groups, in order to understand what has been happening in recent times in relation to religious-political interaction, and hence development issues, in the developing world.

We can note four types of religion-inspired entities: 'culturalist', 'syncretistic', 'fundamentalist', and 'community-orientated' – that have variable impacts upon political and developmental outcomes in the developing world.

1. *Culturalist groups* emerge when a community, sharing both religious and ethnic affinities, perceives itself as a powerless and repressed minority within a state dominated by outsiders. The mobilisation of the opposition group's culture (of which religion is an important part) is directed towards achieving self-control, autonomy or self-government. Examples include Sikhs in northern India, southern Sudanese Christian peoples (such as the Dinka and the Nuer fighting both Islamisation and Arabisation), Tibetan Vajrayana Buddhists in China, and Muslim Palestinians living in Israel's Occupied Territories. In each case, the religion followed by the ethnic minority provides part of the ideological basis for action against representatives of a dominant culture that the minority perceives wants to undermine or even eliminate them.

2. *Syncretistic groups* have religious worldviews that draw on a number of different religious traditions. They are found predominantly among certain rural dwellers in parts of the developing world, notably sub-Saharan Africa and Latin America. They typically feature a number of elements found in more traditional forms of religious association, such as ancestor worship, healing and shamanistic practices. Sometimes ethnic differentiation forms an aspect of syncretism. Syncretistic communities use both religious and social beliefs to build group

solidarity in the face of what they see as a dangerous external threat, often the state itself. Examples include the cult of Olivorismo in the Dominican Republic and Sendero Luminoso in Peru, whose ideology, a variant of Maoism, also utilises aspects of indigenous – that is, pre-Christian – cultural-religious beliefs in order to attract recruits and supporters from among the peasants of Ayacucho. Other examples include the Napramas of north-eastern Mozambique who combine traditional and Roman Catholic beliefs, and were temporarily successful in defeating the South African-supported guerrilla movement, the Mozambique National Resistance (RENAMO) in the early 1990s; and the two 'Alices' – Lakwena and Lenshina – who led syncretistic movements, respectively in post-colonial Uganda and Zambia. Both groups were informed by religious ideologies that fused mainstream Christian faith and traditional beliefs against their governments in pursuit of regional autonomy.

3. *Religious fundamentalists* of various kinds have in a common a perception that their way of life is under threat from hostile forces, typically the state. Consequently, they aim to reform society in accordance with religious tenets and, in some cases, to change laws, morality, social norms and sometimes political configurations. They aim to create a traditionally-orientated, less modern(ised) society. Religious fundamentalists tend to live in population centres – or are at least closely linked with each other by electronic media. They often fight against their governments because the latter's jurisdiction encompasses areas which the former hold as integral to the building of an appropriate society, including education, employment policy (of men rather than women) and the nature of society's moral climate. Religious fundamentalists may also struggle against both 'nominal' co-religionists whom they perceive as lax in their religious duties, as well as against members of opposing religions whom they perceive as their enemies. Examples of religious fundamentalist groups in the developing world are found among followers of Christianity, Islam, Judaism, Hinduism and Buddhism.

4. Finally, *'community-orientated' groups* utilise aspects of their religious faith to inspire their members toward self-help improvements in their lives; this may or may not have an overtly political dimension or involve conflict with government. Prominent in this category are local community groups, mostly Roman Catholic in inspiration and inspired by the ideas of liberation theology, which emerged from the 1960s in Latin America, the Philippines and some sub-Saharan African countries. In addition, owing to the oppression associated with the

dictatorships that were common in Latin America until the 1980s, some national religious hierarchies – such as the Roman Catholic Church in Chile – emerged as significant sources of opposition, seeking to protect local communities from malign governments.

However, in Latin America, like elsewhere in the developing world, processes of modernisation – such as urbanisation – served to dislocate millions of people from their ties to local communities. This necessitated the reforging of personal relations, including religious ones, thus opening the way to renegotiation of allegiances to traditional institutions. Put another way, the recent strong growth of Protestantism in Latin America is said to be tied to the regional phenomena of urban migration and social dislocation. Politically, the evangelical Protestant churches have a variety of stances: from a disinclination to participate in politics, on the one hand, to strong political involvement – sometimes, as in Guatemala, to the extent of sponsoring candidates for political office. From a religious perspective, what the Protestant churches seek is parity with the long-hegemonic Roman Catholic Church.

In conclusion, these four broad categories of religio-political entities – culturalist, syncretistic, fundamentalist and community-orientated groups – are not mutually exclusive. For example, some fundamentalist groups may also be community orientated, while a number of culturalist groups may also be syncretistic in orientation. The purpose of differentiating between them in what is inevitably a somewhat ideal fashion is to seek to identify the nature of their relationship both with other religious groups and government.

religious mobilisation and political action

Each of the four types of religious groups discussed in the preceding section has two factors in common:

- Leaders of each type of group seek to utilise religious precepts to present a message of hope and a programme of action to putative followers.
- The religious groups may or may not be oppositional in character. In some cases, leaders try to capitalise upon pre-existing dissatisfaction with the status quo in order to focus and direct organised societal opposition.

It is important to note, however, that not all of the four types of groups are overtly political. While fundamentalist and culturalist groups are inherently antipathetic towards government, community-orientated and syncretistic groups tend to be more diffuse in character: many are rurally-based and much more concerned with self-help issues than seeking to express opposition to government and its policies. This section of the chapter examines the relationship between religious mobilisation and political action.

Culturalist groups are informed by individualistic cultural perceptions. Political culture is an important variable in analysis of culturalist groups, as it suggests underlying beliefs, values and opinions that a people holds dear. It is often easy to discern close links between religion and ethnicity. Sometimes, indeed, it is practically impossible to separate out defining characteristics of a group's cultural composition when religious belief is an integral part of ethnicity. Both are highly important components of a people's self-identity. For example, it would be very difficult indeed to isolate the different cultural components – religious and non-religious – of what it means to be a Sikh, a Jew, a Tibetan, or a Somali.

It is important to note, however, that not all ethnic groups are also collectively followers of one particular religion. For example, the Yoruba of south-west Nigeria are divided roughly equally between followers of Islam and adherents of various Christianities, including Roman Catholicism and evangelical Protestantism. Yoruba group self-identity is tied closely to identification with certain geographically specific areas; religious differentiation is a more recent accretion, traceable in part to the impact of colonialism. It does not define 'Yoruba-ness' in relation to other ethnic groups. The Ibo of eastern Nigeria, on the other hand, are predominantly Christian; very few are Muslim. While this singular religious orientation was largely a result of European colonialism, Christianity became an integral facet of Ibo identity in relation to predominantly Muslim groups who mostly reside in the north of the country. Many Ibos came into contact (and conflict) with northern Muslims as a result of their migration to the north in pursuit of economic rewards. In a subsequent civil war between 1967 and 1970, the Ibo secessionists used hatred of Islam as part of their rallying propaganda. They sought to depict the north of the country as exclusively Muslim, when the true proportion was in the region of 60–70 per cent of the population. In the civil war, Christian middle-belt peoples (including, the Tiv, Idoma, Igalla and Southern Zaria) formed the bulk of the federal infantry; while Yorubas (both Muslim and Christian) took many posts in the federal technical services.

We have already noted that culturalist campaigns seek to further one particular cultural or ethnic group in relation to either the power of the state or that of other groups within the state. The driving force for such movements is a striving for greater autonomy and a larger slice of the 'national cake' in relation to other groups perceived to be enjoying more than their fair share. India became the locus of a number of culturalist challenges to the status quo in the 1980s and 1990s. During the 1980s, politicisation of communal tensions expanded into rural areas where they had been more or less unknown before; they became especially pronounced in various southern states and in the northern state of Jammu-Kashmir. Moves towards separation and autonomy within Indian society were accompanied by a linear increase in communal violence. Developing from isolated incidents involving only limited numbers of combatants, serious, large-scale clashes erupted between communal groups. In the 1980s, such communal violence came to characterise relations between Sikhs and Hindus, through terrorist acts on the part of Sikhs and, in the aftermath of Prime Minister Indira Gandhi's assassination in 1984, Hindu destruction of Sikh life and property in many northern Indian cities. Political support in Punjab for a Sikh homeland of 'Khalistan' has only polarised the issue, as the central government has refused to concede Sikh demands for greater autonomy and decentralisation of power within the federal system.

Turning to the second category, religious fundamentalism, we can note that the character and impact of fundamentalist doctrines is located within a nexus of moral and social issues that revolve around state–society interactions. A key factor behind the evolution of recent fundamentalist movements in the developing world has been a perception on the part of both leaders and followers that their rulers are performing inadequately and, often, corruptly. Religious fundamentalism is often (but not always – Buddhist and Hindu 'fundamentalisms' are exceptions) strongly related to a critical reading of religious texts, and the relating of 'God's words' to believers' perception of reality. The significance of this from a political perspective is that it supplies already restive peoples with a ready 'manifesto' of social change leading to a more desirable goal, which their leaders use both to berate their secular rulers and to propose a programme for radical reform of the status quo.

It may be relatively easy for fundamentalist leaders to gain the support of those who feel that in some way the development of society is not going according to either God's will or that of the community's best interests. Among fundamentalist groups, those emanating from a Muslim context are often regarded as having the most important political consequences.

Some such groups propose (or practise) armed struggle to wrest power from government, some believe in incrementalist change through the ballot box, while others seek to achieve their goals by way of a combination of extra-parliamentary struggle, societal proselytisation and governmental lobbying. However, despite tactical differences, Islamic fundamentalist groups share two broad ideas: (1) politics and religion are inseparable and (2) Muslim (*sharia*) law should apply to all Muslims. Many Islamic fundamentalists believe also that Muslims as a group are the focal point of a conspiracy involving Zionists and western 'imperialists' whose joint aim is to wrest from them Muslim lands and resources (especially oil). In addition, western multinational corporations' 'control' over Arab oil, plus Israel's denial of full rights for its (largely Muslim) Arab Palestinian constituency, also provide 'evidence' for Islamic fundamentalists' claims of a western conspiracy to belittle and deprive Muslims.

Islamic fundamentalist groups recruit most of their members from a range of professions and backgrounds. Such people tend to come from lower-middle- or middle-class backgrounds, and are found predominantly among the following occupations: teachers, university students and graduates (especially from scientific and technical backgrounds), military and police officers, and shopkeepers. Many such fundamentalists live in urban areas, albeit with recent experiences of rural dwelling. The arguments and appeals of their leaders are couched in theological language, but the chief concerns of followers are often social, economic and developmental issues that require, they believe, fundamental political changes. In other words, to bolster and strengthen their theological and religious terminology is a range of political, economic and developmental grievances that collectively account for such groups' widespread appeal in many Muslim countries. In sum, Islamic fundamentalist groups seek participation in what are essentially closed political and economic systems – often dominated by cohesive political and economic elites, and frequently including senior military personnel (Bromley 1994).

In recent years, Islamic fundamentalist parties have registered electoral successes in several Middle Eastern countries, including Turkey, Algeria, Jordan and Tunisia. Islamists in these countries (with the exception, controversially, of Algeria) have gained seats in legislatures in recent times, a development that helped to sustain public support for their movements' aims and objectives. The effects of this have been two-fold: on the one hand, pressure is kept up against the governing elites which may lead to further concessions while, on the other, Islamist victories help both to sustain the support of the existing followers – while making it more plausible for others to add their weight to fundamentalist campaigns for political and economic changes. In addition, practical steps to increase such groups' societal influence have included staging demonstrations against IMF-supported structural adjustment programmes, Israel's treatment of the Palestinians, state failures to implement (or implement quickly enough) the incorporation of *sharia* law into the legal systems and, finally, corruption among political office holders (Haynes 2002).

Our third category, syncretistic religious groups, are widely found in sub-Saharan Africa. During the colonial era, such groups often flourished in rural areas in the wider context of dissatisfaction with aspects of colonial rule. On occasion, erstwhile ethnic foes – such as the Shona and the Ndebele in colonial Rhodesia (now Zimbabwe) – combined to try to resist British colonialism. Religious identifications were an important facet of such organisation, with spirit mediums using so-called 'medicines' to enhance warriors' martial efforts. Such figures created a national network of shrines to provide an agency for the transmission and coordination of information and activities, a structure that was re-established during the independence war of the 1970s. The use of 'medicine' had earlier helped galvanise the anti-colonial Maji-Maji rebellion of 1905–7 in German-controlled Tanganyika (now Tanzania). At this time, the diviner and prophet, Kinjikitili, gave his followers 'medicine' supposed to render them invulnerable to bullets. He anointed local leaders with the *maji* ('water') which helped to create solidarity among about 20 different groups and served to encourage them to fight together in the common anti-colonialist cause. In addition, in northern Uganda, the cult of Yakan flourished among the Lugbara people; it centred on the use of allegedly magic 'medicine', which galvanised the Lugbara in their short war against Europeans in 1919 (Allen 1991: 379–80). The list of such syncretistic groups could be extended; the point however is already, I hope, clear: many cults arose in Africa during the colonial era, led by prophets, stimulated by colonialism and the social changes to which it led. They employed local religious beliefs as a basis for anti-European protest and opposition.

After colonialism, similar cults continued to appear: clearly their existence could not only be explained by the stresses and strains occasioned by colonial rule. Beliefs associated with the followers of syncretistic leaders, such as Alice Lenshina and Joseph Kony in Zambia in the 1950s and 1960s, and the violence these beliefs engendered, can be located within a general background of upheaval which occurred as a result of the end of colonial rule (Allen 1991: 379). Such figures can be explained as a response to extreme social trauma, a manifestation of collective despair at an unwelcome political and developmental outcome.

Both Lenshina and Kony skilfully fashioned an ideology of resistance that used a blend of both pre-Christian and Christian religious beliefs to create potent forces. What this suggests is that in many rural areas of Africa – places threatened by crisis and the problem of profound social instability – when there was a sufficient degree of communal solidarity, prophet-led resistance was influential in organising communities in self-defence.

Given the lack of clear class differentiation in many rural African societies, the appeal of religious syncretist ideologies has a wide currency. Oppressed and defeated peoples sometimes turned to the metaphysical in pursuit of their struggles against external force and domination. It seems clear that such movements were not merely a reaction to either colonialism or discrete post-colonial political developments. Rather, they were concerned with cultural, political, economic and developmental tensions that had existed before colonialism (and which the latter helped to politicise), and which resurfaced in the post-colonial epoch, as one ethnic or religious group sought to achieve hegemony over all others. Groups who resorted to religious symbolism as political ideology were generally those who not only felt that they had been mistreated or abandoned by their governments, but were also people marginalised developmentally by both colonial and post-colonial governments.

The fourth category of religious expression is the community-orientated groups found among the peoples of Latin America. We can note the importance of both Roman Catholic and Protestant groups. Recently, the impact of the spread of evangelical Protestantism in Latin America helped facilitate the growth of related community groups that, like their Roman Catholic counterparts, may function as conduits of community solidarity and mobilisation.

The origins of the Roman Catholic Basic Christian Communities (BCCs) can be traced back to moves towards popular community development, encouraged by radicalised grassroots clergy, which developed from the early 1960s in many Latin American countries, for example Brazil. These priests organised their followers for both developmental and spiritual purposes, guided by a vision of the Christian promise of redemption that directly linked the temporal sphere with the spiritual. That is, present-day social change was seen as integral to people's chances of longer-term spiritual redemption. Concretely, this meant the full participation of ordinary people in the shaping of their own lives, including developmental outcomes. Profound dependence and passivity had to be replaced by full participation and self-determination in both economic and political spheres. To achieve these goals, radical priests

---

box 7.3   protestant churches in latin america

Despite claims to the contrary, it is too simple to portray evangelical Protestantism in Latin America as simply a right-wing phenomenon. Instead it covers a range of political and social opinions. The US Christian religious right may have a certain demonstration effect, but at home it functions in a religious and political context totally different from that of Latin America. In short, there is no clear evidence that evangelical Protestant churches in Latin America are funded or guided from the USA. In fact, quite the contrary: in many cases, their members support the work of the churches by providing regular payments from often meagre incomes. However, despite some similarities between the churches – such as, a concern with morality and family – their differences (such as, background, methods, demands and prospects) are often more significant. For example, in Peru, where the Protestant field is smaller and less Pentecostal than in many other countries of the region, there was a sudden entry into politics in 1990 that owed a lot to a secular initiative (the Fujimori campaign). Another example comes from Guatemala, the most Protestant country in Latin America, where in the 1990s both Protestant presidents (Rios Montt and Serrano) were already politicians before their conversions. As a result, Protestantism entered politics through its penetration of the ruling class. At the same time, in the rural areas of the country where the indigenous Indians mostly live, Protestant congregations became a focus of both community organisation and manifestations of ethnic identity. This is by no stretch of the imagination a simple manifestation of 'right-wing' politics.

---

became spokesmen for a programme with two main aims: participatory democracy and practical development, that is, to deliver desirable social goods, including electricity, schools, health posts, clean water, roads and latrines. Over time, some BCCs produced leaders of mass movements, such as trade unions and the Brazilian Labour Party, important actors in the process of popular mobilisation that ultimately helped to undermine the credibility and viability of the country's military dictatorship, forcing it to hand over power to elected civilians in 1985 (Medhurst 1989: 25).

Typically, BCCs are small, face-to-face groups of 15 to 20 families (60–190 people), frequently bonded by physical proximity and poverty. They meet periodically, perhaps once a fortnight or once a month. Because of a serious shortage of Catholic religious professionals on the ground throughout Latin America, priests' efforts have focused on getting communities to operate on their own. This means in practice that BCCs demonstrate a diversity of both religious beliefs and roles and practices. Three functions of BCCs are common. First, there is Bible study – the occupation that usually brought such communities into existence in the first place. The Bible can be interpreted from either a fundamentalist or reformist viewpoint. That is, the Bible can be used as a justification either to attack the status quo or to support it; Bible study *per se* is ideologically free. Bible-study sessions typically last an hour or more, and involve reading selected passages, followed by collective discussions. The latter are typically combined with prayer sessions and perhaps a communal meal. Second, the BCCs often have a real sense of developmental goals that require communal action in pursuit of various projects, including educational, health and environmental goals. Third, BCCs seek to change their members' self-consciousness. Sometimes, as in Chile, there is little need to develop people's self-consciousness or even to use Bible study as a means of achieving politicisation. It is unfortunately only too clear to many poor people, especially under the military government of General Pinochet (1973–90), that the exercise of power in Chile is for the benefit primarily of the rich and powerful.

More generally, BCCs' political orientation has been linked to the types of people who joined them, and their precise functions varied according to the nature of the regime under which they operated. In Chile, for example, local BCCs were often radicalised by a series of increasingly politically repressive and economically stringent measures – whose net effect was seriously to disadvantage the developmental chances of the poor. As a result, some BCCs became vehicles for those who wished to change society to empower the poor, those who were unrepresented – or at least seriously under-represented – both politically and developmentally.

The most dynamic period in many BCCs' existence was the long era of military rule in Latin America in the 1970s and 1980s. In his assessment of BCCs in El Salvador, Rodolfo Cardenal (1990: 245) notes that

> The primary factor in the base Christian communities was the characteristic awareness of having overcome the alienating aspects of traditional popular religiosity. They rejected not what was popular, but rather the separation of religious values from the real and distressing problems of life which, furthermore, they discovered opposed popular Christian religiosity.

In other words, during military rule in El Salvador, BCCs became vehicles of what was known as 'liberation theology', partly because of the absence of alternative means of mobilisation. In conservative Colombia, on the other hand, Catholic bishops vigorously attacked democratisation within the churches, reserving special fire for liberation theology, the 'popular church', and autonomous BCCs (Levine 1990: 26). A different kind of example comes from socialist-oriented Nicaragua in the 1980s, home of numerous BCCs, most of which were wedded to a radical vision of a Christian-socialist future. A few others were politically opposed to the regime (Serra 1985).

Perhaps the primary developmental benefit of BCCs in Latin America was in their contribution to establishment and evolution of a sense of citizenship, primarily among lower-class participants. This is because BCCs typically functioned as vehicles for what was known as 'conscientisation', principally among poor people, by far the largest participants in the BCCs. In many Latin American countries, it is necessary to note, most poor people had long been entwined in a patron–client mentality that had traditionally defined class relations in their societies; now, often for the first time, there was a chance that collective effort might lead to a better world – one of their own making. Working together with pastoral agents to press local officials for developmental improvements, such as sewers, streetlights and land reform, BCCs learned that sometimes the best way to achieve their goals was not by appealing as individuals to powerful figures and bureaucratic authorities, but by working together.

In conclusion, BCCs in Latin America cannot easily be pigeon-holed ideologically; some could be labelled 'left-wing', others could not as they were more conservative. As already noted, some of the most politically radical were found in Chile during the period of the Pinochet-led dictatorship. There, many BCCs served as solidarity organisations, and provided a haven for many of those who had lost their jobs because of opposition to Pinochet's government. In Sao Paulo, Brazil, on the other hand, many BCCs showed a tendency to become vehicles for middle-class political activity, especially before the return to democracy in Brazil in 1985. More generally, since the return to democratic politics in Latin America in the 1980s and 1990s, there has been a strong growth in several countries in the region of Protestant evangelical churches. Critics charge that these groups are no more than American 'Trojan horses', the most recent examples of an increasingly determined US attempt to submerge Latin American culture beneath a layer of alien, born-again Christian propaganda.

We do not have space to enter into a full discussion of these foreign churches in Latin America. It will have to suffice to make no more than a few points concerning their aims and orientations, especially in the context of globalisation. First, there is no clear evidence that such churches are funded and guided from abroad; in fact, quite the contrary: many church members support the work of the church by regular payments from often meagre incomes. Second, the ironical result of re-democratisation in Latin America was to bring it home to many people that the formal process of electing political representatives did not necessarily result in clear improvements to their own lives. Under these circumstances the creation of church groups which would function as community-solidarity groups fulfilled many people's religious and, increasingly, material needs. Popular evangelical church ministers often came from the same class and culture as their congregations; Catholic church religious professionals, on the other hand, were sometimes viewed as culturally different, representatives of a class which could never know the hopes, fears and aspirations of poor people. Finally, many converts to Protestantism came not from groups who participated in BCCs, but rather from the large majority of people who viewed themselves as culturally part of the Catholic Church but who, in reality, were never active in the Church's congregation. What this represents is not so much an 'invasion of the US sects'; rather, as Berryman (1994: 10) notes, the 'Protestant coming of age marks the end of Catholic religious hegemony' in Latin America. The Catholic hierarchy is unsurprisingly opposed to this development in many Latin American countries, and as a result, has found it expedient to portray the growth of Protestantism as a US-controlled imperialistic move.

conclusion

Over the last thirty years or so religion has had considerable impact upon development outcomes in many parts of the developing world. Confidence that the growth and spread of urbanisation, education, economic development, scientific rationality and social mobility would combine to diminish significantly the socio-political position of religion was not well founded. Two broad trends were noted. First, religion was used as a vehicle of opposition or as an ideology of community self-interest. In the first category were the culturalist, fundamentalist and, to some degree, the syncretistic, religious entities. Threats emanating either from powerful, outsider groups or from unwelcome symptoms of modernisation (breakdown of moral behaviour, over-liberalisation in education and social habits) served to galvanise such groups. Second, failure of governments to push through programmes of developmental improvements encouraged the founding of local community groups who developed a religious ideology of solidarity and development, often without much help from religious professionals.

We also noted that religious traditions – for example, Roman Catholicism and evangelical Protestantism in Latin America – can lend themselves to a variety of ecclesial, ideological and political uses. Some are oppositional or antipathetical toward governments, while others (such as many of the fundamentalist evangelical Protestant movements, for example) are not.

More generally, developments described in this chapter collectively suggest that one of the most resilient ideas about societal development after World War II – that nations would inevitably secularise as they modernised – was misplaced. It was understood that modernisation, involving urbanisation, industrialisation and rationalisation of previously 'irrational' views including religion, would lead to the development of a new kind of society. Loss of religious faith and secularisation dovetailed with the idea that technological development and the application of science to overcome perennial social problems of poverty, environmental degradation, hunger and disease – in short, developmental issues – would result in long-term human progress. However, what became clear was that technological development and other aspects of modernisation left many people with a feeling of loss rather than achievement. One result was a wave of popular religiosity, often with political ramifications.

To analyse and explain what became a widespread development throughout much of the developing world, it was necessary to look at different manifestations of burgeoning religiosity. Two areas where religion was of particular importance in understanding political and social developments in the contemporary era was in relation to culturalist issues and religious fundamentalisms, as well as community-orientated religious groups and those reflecting religious syncretism. In relation to the latter, its importance was noted in two particular contexts: colonial and post-colonial African societies, where central government often failed to protect local communities, or to deliver economic development or social cohesion.

More generally, we have noted much involvement of religion in political and developmental issue in the developing world over time. The recent political impact of religion falls into two – not necessarily mutually exclusive – categories. First, if the mass of people are not especially religious then religious actors tend to be politically marginal. However, in many developing countries, most people are religious believers. Unsuccessful attempts by many political leaders to modernise their countries have often led to responses from various religious actors. Often, religion serves to focus and coordinate opposition, especially – but not exclusively – that of the poor and ethnic minorities. Religion is often well placed to benefit from a societal backlash against the perceived malign effects of modernisation. In particular, various religious fundamentalist leaders have sought support from ordinary people by addressing certain crucial issues. These include the perceived decline in public and private morality, and the insecurities of life, the result of an undependable market where, it is argued, greed and luck appear as effective as work and rational choice.

And what of the future? If the issues and concerns that have helped stimulate what some see as 'a return to religion' – including socio-political and economic upheavals, patchy modernisation, and increasing encroachment of the state upon religion's terrain – continue (and there is no reason to suppose they will not), then it seems highly likely that religion's political and developmental role will continue to be significant in many parts of the developing world. This will partly reflect the onward march of secularisation – set to continue in many countries and regions, linked to the spread of globalisation – which will be fought against by religious professionals and followers, albeit with varying degrees of success.

8

ethnicity and ethnic conflict

howard handelman

introduction

In much of the developing world – most notably Africa, South Asia, Central Asia, and the Middle East – ethnic strife, more so than class conflict or other types of social cleavage, has been the major source of political friction and violence during the past half-century. Indeed, since the middle of the 20th century ethnic clashes have led to the death of perhaps 20 million people in such countries as Afghanistan, India, Indonesia, Sri Lanka, Iraq, Turkey, Angola, the Democratic Republic of Congo (formerly Zaïre), Ethiopia, Mozambique, Nigeria, Rwanda and Sudan. Note, however, that firm data on deaths due to ethnic massacres or purposeful starvation are generally unattainable in any country with substantial numbers of dead, and worldwide estimates are obviously even more difficult. Some thirty years ago, Harold Isaacs (1975: 3) estimated that ethnic bloodshed had cost some ten million lives since the end of World War II. Massive ethnic violence since the early 1970s in Sudan, Mozambique, Angola, Congo, Rwanda, Burundi, Ethiopia, India, Iraq, Guatemala and elsewhere have likely at least doubled that figure.

Donald Horowitz (2001: 10–11) finds that for every person killed in ethnic riots, roughly one hundred people have been displaced as refugees. He estimates that rioting between Muslims and Hindus in India and Pakistan, following partition in 1947, killed more than 200,000 people and created an estimated 10 million refugees (others put the death toll at 500,000 or more). In 1997–98 alone, Africa contained more than 9.3 million 'internally displaced placed persons' (that is, people forced to flee their towns and villages, but still living in their own country), most of them trying to escape ethnic hostilities (Oucho 2002: 223). Millions more lived as refugees in adjacent countries. In addition, Alex Argenti-Pillen's (2003) research on Sri Lankan women widowed by the civil war between Sinhalese and Tamils – and often witnesses to frightful atrocities – analyses a less well-documented consequence of extreme ethnic violence. Many of these women suffered from post-traumatic-stress syndrome and other psychological disorders. As ethnic conflict continues to rage today in countries such as India, Indonesia and Sudan, it is easy to view it as an intractable part of the developing world's political landscape. But, in fact, ethnic rivalries elsewhere, although still quite relevant to national politics, have been resolved or at least contained in nations such as Malaysia, South Africa and Trinidad. Further, in various countries, including Mozambique and Sri Lanka, there is now at least hope that decades of bloody ethnic warfare can be ended.

This chapter asks why people identify with a particular ethnic group and why they are often antagonistic toward other ethnicities. It focuses upon the following questions: What causes ethnic groups in some nation-states to live together relatively amicably while elsewhere they have vested unspeakable horrors on their neighbours? and What accounts for the high incidence of ethnic violence in many less developed countries?

To answer these questions, we will examine specific conflicts between races, nationalities, religions and tribes in the developing world in order to better understand their causes. Finally we will discuss various political efforts to reduce ethnic animosities and will analyse recent trends in ethnic relations in Africa, Asia and the Middle East.

ethnicity defined

In essence, 'an *ethnic group* is a group of people bound together by a belief of a common kinship and group distinctiveness, often reinforced by religion, language and history'(Byman 2002: 5; Weber 1978: 389). Ethnicity is a shared identity that brings people together while setting them apart from other groups in their proximity. Generally the group's specific sense of identity has an objective basis. For example, Chinese and Malays in Singapore *do* have different physical characteristics, as do blacks and whites in South Africa. Muslims and Hindus in India, as well as Jews and Muslims in Israel, *are* obviously separated by differing religious beliefs. (For a discussion of religion see chapter 7.)

Even objective ethnic bonds and distinctions are typically shrouded in myth. The qualities that a particular ethnicity shares and the factors that distinguish it from other ethnic groups are frequently exaggerated, while distinctions *within* ethnic groups often are sometimes overlooked.

---

box 8.1   problems of defining ethnicity

Defining ethnicity and identifying people's ethnic affiliation are often elusive and controversial tasks. Recent scientific research suggests that even race, the most physically obvious of ethnic distinctions, has little biological significance (DNA, for example, differs little across races). Other ethnic identities are even more problematic and many are simply invented. In this chapter we will first define what we mean by ethnicity and then analyse several types of ethnic categories – from race to tribe – which have engendered intense political and social tensions, and often racked the developing world with violence.

Thus, poor Hindu villagers in Kashmir may believe that they share more goals with the region's powerful Hindu landlords than they do with neighbouring Muslim peasants. Rioting Hausa farmers in northern Nigeria may kill fellow villagers who are Ibo, while supporting urban, middle-class Hausa politicians with far different – that is, richer – lifestyles. Although Hutu militants in Burundi and Rwanda, Kurdish activists in Turkey, and Tamil extremists in Sri Lanka insist that their own tribe or nationality has a common origin and share objective characteristics, in reality most ethnic groups are fairly diverse and are rather subjectively defined. To a large extent, then, ethnic identity is a social construct, a way that certain groups over time have come to view themselves as distinct from other ethnicities. Each ethnic group 'share[s] a distinctive and enduring collective identity based on a belief in a common descent and on shared experiences and cultural traits' (Gurr 2000: 10–11). Similarly, Chazan et al. (1999: 108) define ethnicity as 'a subjective perception of common origins, historical memories, ties and aspirations'. But generally, even when based in fact, these identities and histories are also partially created or embellished upon by entrepreneurial politicians, intellectuals and journalists who gain some advantage by 'playing the ethnic card'. Thus, Benedict Anderson's (1991) description of nations as 'imagined communities' applies to most ethnic identities.

Ethnicity plays a central role in a country's politics only when people feel that their own group's interests are distinct from – and often in opposition to – those of other ethnicities, and when they also believe that those ethnic distinctions are more salient than other social cleavages such as class. Thus, for example, although it is often assumed that African tribes have 'a fixed, centuries-old primordial consciousness' in fact, most tribal identifications became politically significant only in the last century in response to major social changes. 'The process of ethnic self-identification occurred [at that time] because of the impact of colonial interventions

box 8.2   ethnicity and myth

Sometimes ethnic identities are created wholesale out of myths and imagined differences, either in error or out of political expediency. For example, during South Africa's apartheid era (1948–1994), the government, in its efforts to enforce white rule, created the ethnic category of 'coloureds' to refer to people of mixed racial backgrounds. But since some coloureds and whites looked totally alike, the authorities had to create absurd methods for categorising them. The 'pencil test' allowed bureaucrats or police to place a pencil in a person's hair. If the pencil fell out, that individual would be classified as white. If not, they were labelled coloured! Thus someone might live for decades as a coloured only to be reclassified at some point as a black (or white), thereby having a different salary and legal status than before. Yet, even after the abolition of apartheid and the achievement of majority rule in 1994, millions of South Africans continue to identify themselves as coloureds.

and the intense competition over power, status, economic resources, and social services happening in the late colonial and postcolonial periods' (Chazan et al. 1999: 109).

In the Belgian Congo, colonial administrators, missionaries, explorers and anthropologists erroneously lumped together people from the upper Congo River into an imaginary tribe called the Ngala (or Bangala). After a number of decades, the 'myth of the Bangala' took on a life of its own as migrants from the upper Congo settling in the capital city of Kinshasa mobilised politically under the artificial tribal name that the Belgians had given them (Young 1976: 171–3; Anderson, C. et al. 1974).

In sum, real or imagined common history, traditions, and values not only bind together a group's members, but also distinguish them from neighbouring cultures and may encourage group conflict (Rothchild and Olorunsola 1983: 20). Thus, J. E. Brown's cynical definition of a nation can be applied to many other ethnic identities: 'A group of people united by a common error about their ancestry and a common dislike of their neighbors' (quoted in Friedman 1996: 1). In times of great change and uncertainty (such as national independence or economic modernisation), intellectuals and politicians are likely to create historical myths that give their own ethnic group a sense of security in the face of perceived challenges from competitors. In the words of Serbian peace activist Vesna Pesic, ethnic hostilities are caused by a 'fear of the future, lived through the [real or imagined] past' (quoted in Lake and Rothchild 1998:7).

multi-ethnic states in the developing world

By definition, then, ethnicity is not a politically salient factor in ethnically homogeneous countries. It only becomes politically relevant when ethnic identity can be used to unite 'us' against 'the others'. For example, in Mexico one could hardly rally support for a movement that promises to defend the rights of *Latinos* (Hispanics) against all other Mexicans, since virtually every Mexican *is* a Latino. But when millions of Mexicans who had migrated to the United States faced discrimination at the hands of the Anglo (white) majority, many of them flocked to *Chicano* (Mexican-American) civil-rights groups such as *La Raza Unida* (the United Race). Similarly, for decades whites in South Africa formed their own political parties and brotherhoods to perpetuate their dominance over the black majority. In Iceland, however, whites (nearly all of the population) would have no interest in a white-supremacy party.

Thus, if the world were composed exclusively of relatively homogenous countries – such as South Korea, Japan or Uruguay – ethnically based wars might continue *between* sovereign states, but there would be no internal (*within-state*) strife based on communal antagonisms. Indeed, the underlying cause of internal ethnic tensions is that boundaries for 'nations' (referring here to distinct cultural-linguistic groups such as Malays, Chinese or Tamils), races, religions and tribes so often fail to coincide with boundaries for states (self-governing countries) (Ra'anan 1991: 4–7). For example, the absence of an independent state to house the Kurdish nation has aroused continuing friction in Turkey, Iraq and Iran. Similarly, Sikh militants in India's Punjab region have demanded their own independent country. In such cases, ethnic and political boundaries do not coincide. And when an ethnic group feels that it has been denied its fair share of political and economic power, it frequently will turn to protests or even warfare. An examination of the world's ethnic maps, particularly those of less developed countries, reveals how frequently sovereign states house multiple ethnic groups. In the mid-1970s a review of 132 countries worldwide indicated that only 12 (9 per cent) were ethnically homogeneous (populated by a single ethnic group), while another 25 (19 per cent) were principally populated by a single ethnic group. Thus, the remaining 72 per cent of all countries had substantial minority group populations. In fact, in 39 countries (30 per cent of the total) no single ethnic group accounted for even half of the population (Said and Simmons 1976: 10). That pattern is most marked in sub-Saharan Africa, where almost every country is composed of several ethnic (tribal) groups. For example, Nigeria, the continent's most populous country with some 120 million people, has more than 200 such linguistic communities (Omoruyi 1986: 120).

In conclusion, three factors seem to contribute to the developing world's high incidence of ethnic conflict.

- Countries in sub-Saharan Africa, South Asia, and South East Asia are more likely to house multiple ethnic groups that can be mobilised politically.
- Economic resources are generally scarce in those regions, so politics can become a virtual life and death struggle for land, food, natural resources, jobs or government assistance. For example, in Rwanda, one of the world's most densely population nations, fierce competition for land intensified tensions between Hutus and Tutsis in the early 1990s (Prunier 1995).
- Political institutions in many developing countries – such as parliaments, political parties, interest groups and bureaucracies – are not yet adequately equipped to mediate and ease ethnic frictions.

the effects of decolonisation and modernisation on ethnic relations

Because so much of the past half-century's ethnic violence has taken place in newly independent countries, many people have associated ethnic warfare with the failures of European colonialism or the more recent problems of social and economic underdevelopment. We should, however, note that even though the world's most economically developed countries have apparently put the most extreme forms of ethnic hostility behind them, it is necessary to remember that the worst genocide of the 20th century – the Nazi Holocaust – took place in a comparatively developed country. More recently, religious and racial violence in, for example, Northern Ireland and the United States, further demonstrate that bloody ethnic violence is not limited to developing countries. Similarly, the Yugoslav experiences of the 1990s also show that ethnic hostility and conflict is not limited to Africa and Asia.

A corollary to that view is the conviction that national independence and subsequent socio-economic development – including urbanisation, higher literacy and improved living standards – would ameliorate ethnic tensions. To be sure, the colonising powers frequently created boundaries in Africa and Asia that joined incompatible ethnic groups together in countries such as Nigeria, Indonesia and the Democratic Republic of Congo. More sadly, they often maintained power through divide-and-conquer tactics that favoured one ethnic group over another, thereby exacerbating tensions between them.

But while it is true that colonialism often aggravated ethnic tensions, anti-colonial partisans were mistaken in believing that self-rule would quickly produce national unity. On the contrary, in countries such as

---

box 8.3   ethnic conflict in rwanda and burundi

In pre-colonial Burundi and Rwanda, for example, the Hutus (primarily poor farmers) and the Tutsis (generally more affluent cattle herders) shared the same language and customs, lived amongst each other, and often intermarried. But their Belgian colonisers (and the German rulers who preceded them), impressed by the Tutsis' higher social status, greater height, and thinner body frames, favoured them and erroneously saw the two groups as distinct tribes. 'The Europeans were quite smitten with the Tutsi, whom they considered too fine to be "negroes"' (Prunier 1995: 6). Over time, these colonial attitudes influenced the native population's thinking, 'inflating the Tutsi cultural ego inordinately and crushing Hutu feelings until they coalesced into an aggressively resentful inferiority complex' (Prunier 1995: 9). That psychological legacy, fanned by intense competition for land in a highly overpopulated region, helped set in motion events that culminated 32 years after independence (in 1994) with Hutu extremists directing an unimaginable massacre of their Tutsi neighbours.

India, Pakistan, Congo and Angola, independence was followed by spasms of ethnically-related bloodshed. Two factors contributed to these conflicts. First, independence transferred state control over resources for roads, schools, hospitals and the like from colonial bureaucrats into the political arena where rival groups now had to compete for them. Second, many of the region's new political leaders used ethnic identity – frequently embellished by mythology and invented history – as a means of mobilising support. Not infrequently, then, ethnic conflict is the result of elite manipulation (Williams 2003: 185–9). Further evidence of this contention comes from the collapse of communist rule in Central Europe and the disintegration of Yugoslavia and illustrates how unscrupulous political leaders can stir up ethnic hatreds as a means of gaining or maintaining power. Looking for a new basis of political legitimacy in Serbia, former communist leader, Slobodan Milosevic, promoted hostility toward neighboring Croats and Bosnian Muslims (Williams 2003: 185–9; Gilberg 1998). Serbs and Muslims – who had lived together relatively amicably for many years and had frequently intermarried – were persuaded that they had long-standing enmities. In a process of 'enforced ethnicity', Hutus and Tutsis in Burundi and Rwanda were similarly manipulated by their leaders (Weinstein 1972: 27).

Just as national independence often proved no panacea for ethnic tensions, neither did economic and social modernisation. (For a discussion of the interaction of religion and modernisation, see chapter 7.) Since so much recent ethnic violence has taken place in the world's least developed countries, many analysts have assumed that 'tribalism' (that is, ethnic chauvinism) is a primitive phenomenon likely to disappear under the enlightening influences of urbanisation, education and economic development. But, although these transformations may improve ethnic relationships in the long run, in the short-to-medium term, the forces of modernisation may intensify tensions. The massive rural-to-urban migration that has caused African and Asian cities to grow at phenomenal rates often brings different ethnic groups into close proximity for the first time, where they compete for employment, government programmes and other economic resources. The expansion of government activities in newly independent, multilingual countries such as Sri Lanka created desirable public-sector jobs, but also provoked heated disputes over what language or languages would be used in the civil-service exams. At the same time, urbanisation, rising educational levels, and the spread of mass communications have often served to politicise previously unmobilised sectors of the population. Because so many people identify with their own race, religion, nationality or tribe, their newly acquired political awareness has often brought them into conflict with other ethnic groups. Indeed, even the spread of higher education, rather than generating mutual understanding, may produce a class of chauvinistic intellectuals who become the ideologists of ethnic hostilities. In sum, processes of modernisation, including rural–urban population movements, have often helped to exacerbate ethnic competition and conflicts, especially in Asia and Africa.

types of ethnic identities and conflicts

In various parts of the developing world, ethnic identity tends to be based on one of the following characteristics:

- race;
- nationality;
- religion;
- tribe; or
- caste.

Since caste distinctions are significant only in a small number of countries (India, Nepal and a few African nations), we will confine our discussion to the other four categories.

race

Race is the most geographically extensive type of ethnic identification and usually the most visible. For example, an outside observer can normally distinguish easily between Asians, blacks and whites living in countries such as Jamaica and South Africa. In some instances, however, a person's race is determined as much by custom and dress as by physical attributes. For example, an indigenous couple living in the rural highlands of Peru are perceived as American Indians, not so much by their skin colour or other physical features as by their distinct clothing, their occupation (farming), and their communication in the Quechua language. So, should their son later attain a secondary or university degree, speak primarily in Spanish, dress in modern slacks and sports shirts, and move to the city, he would no longer be considered an Amerindian, but rather a *mestizo* (a person representing a *cultural* mix of Indian and white).

Surprisingly, race had no political significance until the age of Western imperialism (starting in the 15th century) brought people of different races into contact with each other and subjected blacks, Asians and native Americans to white domination (Anderson, C. et al. 1974). Only then did people of a particular race begin to perceive themselves as having common customs, traditions and political interests that bind them, supersede other cleavages within their ranks, and distinguish them from other races. Today, for example, a successful black entrepreneur, attorney or teacher in South Africa or Britain may in several ways share more political interests and beliefs with poor blacks than with white businessmen, attorneys or teachers.

Of course, racial animosities and violence are not confined to less developed countries. Both Britain and the United States, for example, have seen their share of urban race riots. But, during the past half century, South Africa probably has endured the most intense racial hostilities anywhere in the world. From its colonisation by the British in 1806 until its transition to majority rule in 1994, that country was ruled by a white minority currently constituting a mere 15 per cent of the population.

In the 1960s South Africa came under mounting domestic and international pressure to end white domination. The massacre of demonstrators in Sharpeville (1960) began a cycle of widening black protest and government repression later accelerated by massive black resistance in the Johannesburg township of Soweto in 1976. Soon, the country became a diplomatically and culturally isolated pariah. An international boycott restricted trade, travel and investment. Though initially slow to take effect, economic sanctions, particularly restrictions on investment, eventually limited the country's growth. Heightening unrest in the black townships coupled with South Africa's international isolation and a worldwide trend toward democracy intensified the pressures for change (Baker 1990; Shubane 1992). Finally, a growing number of powerful voices within the white business, legal and intellectual communities also began pressing for racial reform.

box 8.4   ethnicity and politics in south africa

Following World War II, political power, by then in the hands of white South Africans, shifted from people of British origin to the more conservative Afrikaner population (descendants of Dutch and French Protestant settlers) (Horowitz 1991: 47). Blacks, though constituting about 70 per cent of the nation's population, were denied fundamental political and economic rights, including the right to vote or hold public office. Apartheid – the all-encompassing and highly repressive system of racial separation introduced in 1948 – imposed a four-part racial hierarchy that defied international ethical standards and often fell victim to its own internal contradictions. *Blacks*, by far the largest group, were subjected to the greatest level of discrimination. Both *coloureds* (people of mixed racial origin, constituting less than 10 per cent of the country's population) and *Asians* (mostly East Indians, representing about 3 per cent of the population) had more legal rights than blacks, but still ranked considerably below whites. Finally, the *white* minority held virtually all political and economic power. Today, a decade after the demise of apartheid and the advent of majority rule, South Africa remains one of the world's most economically unequal nations, with white incomes still averaging about ten times higher than blacks' (Chazan et al. 1999: 485).

By 1990, the government of President F. W. De Klerk, recognising that apartheid was no longer viable, began repealing segregation laws. At the same time, it legalised the African National Congress (ANC) and two less influential black opposition groups after decades of banishment. The ANC's now-legendary leader, Nelson Mandela, undoubtedly the world's most renowned political prisoner, was released from jail – after 26 years of confinement and isolation – together with hundreds of other political prisoners. These changes, coupled with the ANC's suspension of its armed struggle, opened the door to a new constitution enfranchising the black majority and ending white rule. In May 1994 Mandela was elected president of the new, now majority-ruled, South Africa.

Nearly a decade later, however, major hurdles still hinder progress toward a stable, multiracial democracy. Blacks have discovered that even though majority rule has brought them greater social justice and human dignity, it has not appreciably improved their living standards. The governments of Nelson Mandela and his successor, Thabo Mbeki, have pursued moderate economic policies, which sidestep redistributive programmes in order to reassure the white business community. But, with a national unemployment rate of 30–40 per cent, most blacks have seen little economic progress other than sizeable government housing and electrification programmes for the urban poor. Not surprisingly, many of them have become frustrated. At the same time, even though whites were generally very well disposed toward President Mandela, many are now concerned that Mbeki or his successor, in an effort to maintain the support of black voters, may resort to racially divisive redistributive measures – such as the seizure of large white-owned farms – similar to that of neighbouring Zimbabwe (Mattes 2002; du Toit 2003).

nationality

Although the term 'nation' in common parlance is synonymous with 'country' or 'sovereign state' – as in the United Nations – it has a more specialised meaning in discussions of ethnicity. Like some of the other ethnic categories, it refers to a population with its own language, cultural traditions, history and aspirations. But, unlike racial identifications (which stretch across international borders) or tribal boundaries (which are usually smaller), nations either control their own sovereign state (Danes or Costa Ricans, for example) or aspire to do so (Kurds and Chechyns; van den Berghe 1987: 61; A. D. Smith 1992). That is to say, nations normally either have or claim to have sovereignty over a specific geographic area. Thus, Rupert Emerson (1967: 95–6) defines the nation as 'the largest community, which when the chips are down, effectively commands men's loyalty, overriding the claims of both lesser communities within it and those which cut across it [such as race] or potentially enfold it within a still greater society'.

Conflicts arise when proposed *national* and *state* boundaries do not coincide. In some cases, independent countries such as Pakistan, Russia, Spain and Sri Lanka include two or more distinct *nationalities* (cultural identities), at least one of which seeks greater autonomy or wishes to secede. In recent decades, secessionist struggles by Chechens in Russia, Bengalis in Pakistan, Eritreans in Ethiopia, and Tamils in Sri Lanka have led to violence or even civil war. In other instances, a nationality may spill over into several states – the Chinese in Vietnam, Singapore, Malaysia and Indonesia, or the Kurds in Iraq, Iran, Syria and Turkey.

If immigrants adopt their new country's language and customs as their own, their prior national identities are rarely cause for ethnic tension. For example, descendants of Italian emigrants to Argentina or of Polish emigrants to Australia often maintain some of their forefathers' cultural identity, but most have also thoroughly integrated themselves into their new national culture and language. On the other hand, when French Canadians, Turkish Kurds, or Malaysian Chinese continue to speak primarily in their ancestral languages, their original national identity remains politically salient and can become divisive. How divisive it is depends on the broader political and economic context. For example, even though Spain's Basques have maintained their distinct language and customs over the years, by the early 20th century they were integrating into Spanish society. During the 1970s, however, new political and economic developments reversed this trend, producing demands for self-rule and a pro-independence, terrorist movement. First, the death of long-time dictator Francisco Franco and the subsequent democratisation of Spanish politics raised Basque hopes for greater autonomy and allowed legitimate (non-violent) nationalist parties to campaign openly. Second, the decline in the region's industrial economy turned some young Basques against the government in Madrid (D. Brown 2000: 70–88).

the problematic case of the kurds

The Middle East's Kurds – some 20 to 25 million people (McDowall 2000: 3–18) – are currently the world's largest nationality without their own sovereign state. Living primarily in a mountainous region that stretches from south-east Turkey, through northern Iraq, to north-western Iran, over the years they have often been persecuted by each of those governments. As ethnic nationalism grew throughout the world in the late 19th century, Kurdish movements emerged seeking either greater autonomy or an independent country called Kurdistan (Land of the Kurds). Turkey, with its population of 12 million Kurds, has been the centre of Kurdish nationalism. Although the Kurdish people are scattered throughout the country and many of them have assimilated fully into Turkish society, they have traditionally been concentrated in the south-east, one of Turkey's poorest regions. Because ethnic minorities were treated fairly equally under the Ottoman empire, which governed most of the Middle East from the 17th to the early 20th centuries, Kurdish nationalism did not bloom until the empire collapsed following World War I. At that time, several victorious nations – Britain, France and Italy – signed a short-lived treaty calling for the birth of an autonomous or independent Kurdistan (Fuller 1999: 225). But those hopes were soon dashed by the rise of General Mustafa Kemal Ataturk, the father of modern Turkey, who rejected the treaty. Since that time, Turkish policy has made individual Kurds fully equal to any other Turkish citizen as long as they abandon their Kurdish national identity. In the words of Ataturk's prime minister, Ismet Inonu, '[o]nly the Turkish nation is entitled to claim ethnic and national rights in this country' (quoted in Entessar 1992: 81). To be sure, assimilated Kurds have suffered little discrimination and are able to reach the highest level of Turkish society. At the same time, however, the government has refused to recognise any shred of Kurdish ethnic identity. 'For decades the Kurds were officially [called] *mountain Turks*, and [even] the use of [the words] *Kurds, Kurdish and Kurdistan* as well as [the use of] the Kurdish language were prohibited' (Gürbey 1996:

13). Occasional Kurdish uprisings early in the twentieth century were crushed by the armed forces.

It was in this context that the PKK (the Kurdistan Workers' Party) emerged in the 1980s as the militant voice of Kurdish nationalism. Dominated by its charismatic founder Abdullah (Apo) Ocalan, the party combined Kurdish nationalism, Marxist-Leninist ideology, and a cult of personality surrounding Apo. In 1984 the PKK unleashed a guerrilla insurgency in south-east Turkey. By the end of the 20th century the two warring sides had killed a total of 30,000–35,000 people, mostly innocent civilians (White 2000: x; McDowall 2000: 442). More than 2,000 villages in the region were evacuated or destroyed by the Turkish military and thousands of Kurds were relocated elsewhere in the country, either voluntarily or involuntarily.

In the early 1990s, both sides temporarily softened their position. The Turkish government came under increasing pressure from international human rights groups and the European Union (which Turkey has hoped to join) to eliminate its brutal military tactics and its repression of free speech regarding Kurdish issues. At the same time, the influx of more than 500,000 Kurdish refugees from Iraq during the 1991 Gulf War swelled the Kurdish population and focused greater international attention on their plight. Turkish president Turgot Ozal, after revealing that he himself was partly Kurdish, lifted the ban on public discussion of Kurdish issues and ended some of the restrictions on the use of the Kurdish language in the press, public speech and public songs. For the first time, some of the country's media discussed the Kurdish question. But, even though the veil of silence previously imposed upon this issue has been lifted, journalists must remain cautious about what they write and say, since they still risk fines or imprisonment for spreading 'separatist propaganda' if they offend the authorities (Fuller 1999: 230). Meanwhile, the PKK's own brutal tactics were alienating many Kurds, though most of them still supported the party. More important, the rebels were clearly losing the armed struggle against the powerful Turkish military. Consequently, in 1993, the party dropped its call for Kurdish independence, declared an indefinite cease-fire, and narrowed its demands to greater cultural freedom, the right to broadcast in Kurdish, and an end to government repression in the south-east. (McDowall 2000: 437). Unfortunately, shortly thereafter President Ozal died, bringing his more conciliatory policies to an end. His successors gave the armed forces a free hand to repress the Kurds – allowing mass relocations, rape, torture and assassinations. At the same time, the PKK expanded its terrorist activities, including kidnapping foreign tourists and attacking Turkish diplomats and diplomatic buildings in Europe.

In 1999, the PKK's legendary founder, Abdullah Ocalan, was abducted from abroad, brought to trial in Turkey, and sentenced to death. In an apparent attempt to avert execution, Ocalan renounced his party's armed struggle, calling on it to work within the Turkish political system. Still, the government has continued its military campaign and has subdued the Kurdish separatist movement, at least for now. But the issue of Kurdish cultural expression and political autonomy will not go away either in Turkey or in its neighbours. In Iraq, where the government of Saddam Hussein had executed thousands of captured guerrillas and used chemical weapons in 1988 to kill some 6,000 Kurdish civilians (Ciment 1996: 62–3), the United States and Britain established an autonomous Kurdish 'no-fly zone' following the Gulf War of 1990–91. Following Saddam's overthrow in 2003, the United States has supported a greatly expanded Kurdish authority in northern Iraq, presenting Turkey with a large Kurdish autonomous region across its frontier. At the same time, many Turkish political leaders realise that their country will never be admitted into the European Union until they have reached an accommodation with the Kurdish minority. Moreover, it appears likely that because the Kurds already constitute 23 per cent of Turkey's population and have a birth rate twice as high as that in the rest of the country, the government can hardly ignore their demands indefinitely.

religion

Religious values are usually among society's most profoundly felt beliefs. Not surprisingly, then, religious differences have often generated intense violence. Of course, religious conflict is not unique to the developing world. In recent years, Europe has experienced warfare between Catholics and Protestants in Northern Ireland and between Orthodox Christians, Muslims and Catholics in the former Yugoslavia. For the most part, however, religious strife has subsided in the West because socio-economic modernisation has gradually secularised politics (D. Smith 1974: 4; Cox 1966). By contrast, in the Middle East, as well as parts of Latin America and Asia, dominant religions, such as Islam and Catholicism, are in some cases officially linked to the state, contributing to the politicisation of religion. The probability of religious strife rises further when one religious community is economically and politically dominant (as are Hindus in Kashmir) or when a religious group insists that it is the one true faith and disdains other religions (Shi'a Muslims in Iran). (I will confine myself largely to comments about religio-political issues in the context of India–Pakistan relations in this chapter. See chapter 7 for a wider treatment.)

muslims and hindus in india

Clashes between Muslims and Hindus in the Indian subcontinent present a striking example of the destructive potential of religious hostilities (Varshney 2003). India and Pakistan were born in a convulsion of communal violence and both have been torn by ethnic violence ever since. Mohandas 'Mahatma' Gandhi, Jawaharlal Nehru, and the other authors of Indian independence had tried to create a secular state to govern the nation's Hindu majority and considerable Muslim and Sikh minorities. But during independence negotiations with the British, the powerful Muslim League insisted on the establishment of a separate Muslim nation. League leader Mohammed Ali Jinnah declared: 'We are a nation with our own distinctive culture and civilization, language and literature . . . customs . . . history and tradition' (quoted in Wallbank 1958: 196). As independence approached, mounting tensions – fanned by Hindu and Muslim zealots – touched off rioting that left thousands dead. Faced with the prospect of unending communal violence, Britain reluctantly divided its most important colony into two new countries: India, with a population at that time of roughly 300 million Hindus and 40 million Muslims and Pakistan, with approximately 60 million Muslims and 20 million Hindus.

No sooner had independence been declared (15 August 1947), than blood began to flow in both countries. Whole villages were destroyed, 10–12 million refugees of both faiths fled across the border, more than 75,000 women were abducted and raped, and upwards of 500,000 people were killed in one of the 20th century's most horrendous ethnic conflagrations (B. Brown 1990: 479–80). Virtually all of the Hindus and Sikhs living in Pakistan fled to India, but India maintained a large Muslim minority, which today exceeds 100 million people.

But partition failed to end hostilities between the two bordering states or to stop communal violence within India. As recently as 2002, Hindu rioters killed some 1,000 Muslims in the state of Gujarat (Mohandas Gandhi's birthplace). In 2003, Islamic militants detonated car bombs in Bombay that killed dozens. For decades, conflict over the status of north-western India's valley of Kashmir (bordering on Pakistan) has kept the neighbouring countries on the brink of war. With its Muslim majority, this previously princely state logically should have belonged to Pakistan, as most of its inhabitants undoubtedly desired. But its ruler at the time of partition, Maharaja Hari Singh, a Hindu supported by the principality's Hindu elite, chose to join India. Pakistan, left with control of only one-third of the state, has never accepted that outcome and has long demanded that India honour its promise to allow Kashmiris to vote on their status (Rahman 1996; Schofield 2000). Since independence, the two nations have twice gone to war over the region (1947–8 and 1965) and have come perilously close several other times, most recently in 2002–3.

Ironically, although India and Pakistan have crossed swords over the region, violence between Hindus and Muslims *within* Kashmir remained relatively limited for years. As a new generation of more politicised Kashmiris emerged, however, their resentment toward Indian rule mounted (Ganguly 1997: 91–3). Since 1989, a series of Islamic separatist movements – seeking either union with Pakistan or full independence – have waged an *intifada,* a religious war, against the Indian government and the state's Hindu minority. Since then, more than 34,000 people have been killed and several hundred thousand refugees (mostly Hindu) have fled the area (Amnesty International 2001; Ganguly 1997: 2; Schofield 2000: 151–2). Both separatist guerrillas and Indian security forces have been guilty of serious human rights abuses. Recently, the conflict has been further inflamed by the intervention of several hundred foreign *mujahadeen* – Islamic fundamentalist warriors, from Afghanistan, Iran, Pakistan and the Arab world (Malik 2002: 299). Although India and Pakistan (both armed with nuclear weapons) pulled back from the brink of war in early 2003, a stable resolution of that conflict remains extremely elusive.

tribe

The term 'tribe' refers to *sub*national groups in Africa, Asia, the Middle East or the Americas that share a collective identity and language while believing themselves to hold a common lineage. Unlike nationalities, however, tribes generally make no claim to a sovereign state. It is important to note that many experts on African culture object to the use of the label 'tribe', especially when applied to ethnicities (their preferred term) such as Nigeria's Yoruba and Ibo, each of which has millions of members. Furthermore, they argue that the term is too often used pejoratively and that it sometimes erroneously lumps together heterogeneous groups (Southall 1970). In this chapter, however, I still speak of tribes in Africa not only because the term will be familiar to many readers and but also for the reason that it has long been used by a number of respected scholars who have studied that continent.

Because European colonialism created countries with multiple tribal communities, independence sometimes unleashed fierce ethnic competition for political and economic power. Indeed, Chazan et al. (1999: 112–18) argue that it is largely in the 20th century that Africans began to identify strongly with their ethnicity (tribe) as they were absorbed first into colonial administrative systems and later into independent nations. Thus, in Africa, tribe is 'a political and not a cultural phenomenon, and it operates within contemporary political contexts and is not an archaic survival arrangement' as many Westerners have suggested (Cohen 1969: 190).

Several factors produced a seemingly unending series of ethnic civil wars since a wave of independence swept the continent in the 1960s and 1970s:

- first, the proliferation of multi-ethnic countries;
- second, mounting competition for scarce, government-controlled resources at a time of increasing mass political mobilization, often along tribal lines;
- third, the inability of Africa's weak states (governments) to peacefully resolve tribal conflicts and reduce ethnic tensions;
- finally, the existence of many unscrupulous political leaders willing to inflame tribal differences for personal gain. Recently deposed Liberian president Charles Taylor, who helped foment indescribable atrocities in his own country and in bordering Sierra Leone and Côte d'Ivoire, is a clear example of such irresponsibility (Adebajo 2002).

Consequently, at one time or another, ethnic violence has afflicted more than half the countries of sub-Saharan Africa. Angola, the Democratic Republic of Congo, Ethiopia, Liberia, Nigeria, Sierra Leone, Uganda and Zimbabwe, among others, have been torn apart by civil wars that were at least partially tribally related. It is estimated that in the Congo alone, ethnic violence during the past decade has led to the deaths of perhaps three million people, mostly from starvation. Previously, millions more had died across Ethiopia, Nigeria, Angola, Mozambique, Rwanda and Burundi. Ethnic violence continues today in Liberia, Congo and elsewhere.

ethnic conflict in burundi

A series of ethnic massacres in the small, Central African nation of Burundi and the 1994 genocide in neighbouring Rwanda demonstrate both the questionable use of tribal labels and the deadly consequences of ethnic hostilities. In both countries the population is divided primarily into two ethnic groups, the Tutsi minority – including its privileged elite, favoured by the Belgian colonisers – and the Hutu majority, relegated to a lower status under the Belgians and, to some extent, prior to colonialism as well. As we noted earlier, though the two ethnic groups differed in social status and physical appearance, they shared a common language and common customs, lived amongst each other, and often intermarried, leading many experts to question the Western media's practice of calling them distinct tribes.

Yet, as these Belgian colonies moved toward independence, both faced a rising tide of ethnic belligerence. In 1959, three years before independence, a Hutu uprising in Rwanda forced 130,000 Tutsis to flee the country, largely to adjacent Uganda, which later became the centre of organised Tutsi opposition to Rwanda's Hutu-led dictatorship. Meanwhile in Burundi, the Rwandan violence convinced the Tutsi-dominated armed forces to tighten their grip on power and ruthlessly repress a series of Hutu uprisings during the succeeding decades (Prunier 1995: 50–1). Indeed, over the years, events in one country repeatedly precipitated backlashes in the other and sometimes spilled ethnic warfare into other bordering nations as well. The Hutu-controlled government's repression of Tutsis in Rwanda was matched by a cycle of Tutsi persecution of Hutus in Burundi. In 1972 alone, Burundi's armed forces massacred some 150,000 Hutus, with many more victims fleeing to Rwanda. Years later, Tutsi refugees from Rwanda helped overthrow the governments of Uganda and the Democratic Republic of Congo, and went on to play prominent roles in their new regimes.

In 1993, following some three decades of Tutsi dictatorship, Burundi's first democratic election produced the country's first Hutu president, Melchior Ndadaye. Only five months later, however, Tutsi paratroopers kidnapped and murdered Ndadaye, setting off a new round of tribal warfare in which roughly 30,000 Tutsis and 20,000 Hutus were killed, while some 300,000 Hutus (out of a national population of less than seven million) fled the country, primarily to Rwanda (Prunier 1995: 199). Burundi's parliament soon elected another Hutu, Cyprien Ntaryamira, as the new president. Next door in Rwanda, Hutu president General Juvénal Habyarimana faced growing international pressure to end his 21-year dictatorship. But on 6 April 1994, as the plane carrying Presidents Ntaryamira and Habyarimana from a regional peace conference in Tanzania was about to land near the Rwandan capital, it was hit by shoulder-fired missiles, killing all on board. Although the identity and backing of the people who shot down the plane remains unknown, Hutu extremists in the Rwandan government used the assassinations as a pretext to launch a horrendous assault against the Tutsis and, to a far lesser extent, against Hutu moderates. Within weeks approximately 800,000 people – almost all Tutsi – were hacked or beaten to death by local Hutu militia and villagers, producing a daily rate of killing roughly five times higher than in the Nazi concentration camps (Prunier 1995: 261–5). Subsequently, however, a disciplined Tutsi revolutionary army, based in neighbouring Uganda, gained control of the country and jailed thousands of Hutus. Several hundred thousand others fled to nearby Congo, where many were later starved or massacred by the anti-Hutu regime of then-president Laurent Kabila. Currently, while Rwandan president Paul Kagame (a Tutsi) has done much to heal ethnic tensions in his country, nearly 100,000 Hutus still languish in jail, generally under wretched conditions, awaiting trial for participation in the 1994 genocide. Across the border, the death of Burundi's president in the 1994 plane crash and the subsequent Rwandan massacre sparked a continuing civil war between the Tutsi-led armed forces and Hutu rebels. In 2001, South Africa's Nelson Mandela brokered a power-sharing agreement and the following year a cease-fire was signed bringing 900 South African troops to Burundi as peace keepers. In spite of these developments, however, the fighting continued, including a substantial battle within the nation's capital in July 2003.

prospects for ethnic relations in the 21st century

Many analysts, noting the spread of 'Third World' ethnic conflict as well as the break-up of several ex-communist European countries, have anticipated growing ethnic unrest and national disintegration in the years to come. A widely cited book by Daniel Patrick Moynihan (1993), for example, predicted that the number of independent states worldwide would increase from approximately two hundred currently to some three hundred by the middle of the 21st century as countries broke apart under the strains of ethnic hostilities. More recently, other analysts have argued that globalisation – especially the spread of capitalism and democracy – simultaneously advantages economically skilled minority groups (such as the Chinese in Indonesia, East Indians in East Africa, and the Ibos in Nigeria) while politically activating the ethnic majorities who resent them – a deadly combination (Chua 2003).

Ethnic civil wars have indeed replaced war between nations and class-based revolutions as the developing world's most common form of mass violence. It would be a mistake, however, to see ethnic conflict as an insoluble problem bound to undermine multicultural nations. For example, in sub-Saharan Africa, although the toll of ethnic warfare has been staggering, most countries in the region have achieved some kind of peaceful accommodation between tribal groups. Elsewhere, multicultural countries as diverse as Singapore, Malaysia, and South Africa have also reached ethnic accords. The most fortunate countries are those such as Trinidad and Tobago where the political elite has maintained relative ethnic harmony since independence so that bitter antagonisms have never developed. Once tensions have burst into violence, however, restoring cooperation between warring factions is much more difficult.

---

box 8.5   resolving ethnic conflict through political frameworks

Analysis of 'success stories', where bitter ethnic conflict has been averted or contained, reveals several potential political frameworks for reducing tensions. One approach has been constitutionally-based power-sharing, which divides political control among major ethnic groups. In federal systems such as Nigeria's, many government functions are devolved to the states, which often house particular ethnic groups. Another form of power-sharing is consociational democracy, which guarantees minorities a share of power (including the right to veto policies that they believe would negatively affect them), in order to protect them against the ethnic majority. In Lebanon, for example, consociationalism divided government positions between the different Christian and Muslim communities roughly in proportion to each group's population (Lijphart 1977: 25–40).

Unfortunately, power-sharing has rarely worked over a protracted period of time. Sometimes, in cases such as Nigeria and Lebanon, it breaks down and produces a period of intense violence until new consociational arrangements can be devised. And when such political settlements cannot be reached, one possible outcome is secession, a breakaway by an ethnic group to form a new country. As one author has noted, 'secession, like divorce, is an ultimate act of alienation' (Premdas 1990: 12). But it offers a potential way out of a 'failed marriage' between a country's ethnic groups. Many ethnic groups have tried to secede – the Kurds in Turkey, Ibos in Nigeria, Muslims in Kashmir, and Tamils in Sri Lanka among others – but few have succeeded since national governments are invariably determined to stop secessions at all costs, a sentiment generally backed by the international community. The few secessions that have taken place – including Eritrea's break from Ethiopia and Bangladesh's secession from Pakistan – were only achieved at an enormous cost in human life. Indeed, contrary to the predictions of many analysts, the number of active secessionist struggles in the world has actually been declining since the start of the 1990s, as a number of them have been resolved peacefully without a break-up of the country. From 1991 to 1999 16 secessionist wars were settled and 11 others were limited by cease-fires or continuing negotiations. Particularly in Africa, successful peace negotiations in one country have encouraged parallel efforts in other nations. Thus, as the 21st century began, only 18 secessionist wars continued throughout the world, fewer than at any time since 1970 (Gurr 2000: 276).

When warring ethnic factions are unable to resolve their differences, one possible outcome is outside intervention. The long civil war between Lebanon's religious communities was finally ended when Syrian troops intervened and when Israel created a protected zone for Christians in the South. India's intervention allowed Eastern Pakistan (now Bangladesh) to secede. More recently, multilateral intervention by West African and United Nations forces in Liberia and Congo have at least temporarily restricted tribal violence. On the whole, most outside actors – be they western countries, developing nations, or international organisations – have been reluctant to intervene in ethnic civil wars unless invited to do so by the affected country's government. To do so would violate the doctrine of national sovereignty. Recently, however, African governments have softened their prior antipathy toward outside intervention and accepted the necessity of intervening in failed states. At the same time, the United Nations has sent peacekeeping troops to help enforce ethnic settlements in countries such as Bosnia and Congo. But unless all combatants are ready for a settlement and accept outside military intervention, external actors are likely to fail, as the United States did in Somalia. India's intervention in Sri Lanka not only failed to bring peace to that country, but led Tamil extremists within India to assassinate that country's prime minister. Israel's intervention in Lebanon (including its condoning of a Christian massacre of Palestinian refugees) helped give rise to today's Palestinian extremist groups such as Hamas.

Ultimately, when all forms of constitutional compromise, political negotiations, secession, or outside intervention have failed, ethnic conflicts eventually end for two reasons – either the insurgency is crushed or both sides reach an agreement because they are exhausted from the carnage. The defeat of the Ibo effort to secede from Nigeria in 1967 (to form a new nation called Biafra) falls in the first category and the possible end to fighting in Liberia and Sri Lanka (early 2000s) may fall into the second.

conclusion

The surge in ethnic bloodshed during the 1970s and 1980s, and the international attention focused on tragic conflicts in countries such as Rwanda, Sudan, India, Indonesia and Afghanistan, led many observers to believe that ethnic hostilities would only continue to grow. Contrary to that prediction, however, the level of ethnic protests and rebellion in the world has actually diminished since the start of the 1990s, after rising steadily during the previous fifty years (Gurr 2000). While ethnic warfare will unfortunately remain part of the political landscape for years to come, hopefully more mature political leadership, stronger national political institutions, and enhanced mechanisms for international peacekeeping through the United Nations and other multinational organisations will maintain or accelerate the recent trend toward reduced hostilities.

note

Some of the material in this chapter previously appeared in Handelman (2003).

9

the natural environment

pauline eadie and lloyd pettiford

introduction

In his inauguration speech in 1949 President Truman first coined the phrase 'underdeveloped'. This became a catch-all category for those areas known, during the Cold War, as the 'Third World'. Subsequently a *de facto* understanding emerged that the relationship between economic activity and states, societies and indeed natural environments could be categorised in terms of their levels of 'development'. States might be more or less developed, but the underlying rationale was that everyone was bound to the market-orientated path of progress and development. The inevitability of this path was said to lie in the ideas of founding father of liberal economics Adam Smith and the belief that prosperity would 'trickle down' and bring wealth to all peoples and nations.

As an alternative to this liberal-based optimism it is useful to cite Karl Polanyi (1944: 73), who claimed in 1944 that 'nature would be reduced to its elements, neighbourhoods and landscapes defiled, rivers polluted, military safety jeopardized [and] the power to produce food and raw materials destroyed' if market mechanisms were allowed to be the sole director of the fate of natural environments. Unfortunately it appears that Polanyi's prescient warnings, reflecting accurately the situation in many areas of the global South today, were ignored.

Liberal approaches to development have meant that the natural environment has been viewed essentially as an economic commodity valuable not for itself but for what it offers 'us'. Any intrinsic value of the environment and its integral role in the long-term maintenance of human and non-human societies is consequently sidelined. The natural environment has become subsumed within the globalised logic of supply and demand. Natural environments have always provided the resource base from which humans have found the sustenance to survive; the difference now is that global patterns of over-consumption of resources and over-population have combined to threaten the carrying capacity of the planet.

This chapter focuses on the effect of 'development' on the natural environment of the peripheral countries of the global political economy. Here it is perhaps useful to categorise areas in terms of social and economic viability rather than geographic location, a point to which we shall return. It should also be noted that market mechanisms are social constructions and, because of this, it is not markets which impact upon environments but the nature of social and thus economic (dis)organisation. Wolfgang Sachs (1993: 12) notes for example that man's relationship with nature has evolved into a 'full-scale attack [and that] since time immemorial humanity defended itself against nature, now nature must defend against humanity'. Intrinsic to such attacks are ideas of social, economic and environmental injustice. It shall be argued here that this inequality, which can be seen also as a lack of freedom (see Sen 1999b) is a central cause of environmental degradation.

The chapter begins by examining the relationship between environmental degradation and development through three broad theoretical schools of thought: the neo-liberal economic, the reformist/ interventionist and the radical. This tripartite approach offers a comparative framework through which to understand international and domestic socio-political forces which impact upon the natural environment. We also explore two specific issue areas: (1) biodiversity and (2) the impact of industrialised agriculture. After that, we look at the relationship between development and global warming, specifically the way that symptoms of global warming tend to manifest themselves in developing countries, while its causes tend to be found elsewhere.

The Earth can be viewed as an organic whole in terms of both the causes and effects of environmental degradation. (Images sent back from Apollo 11's mission to the moon in 1969 contributed significantly to the idea of the Earth as a vibrant and 'blue' planet; for the first time the earth could be viewed in its entirety. This led, amongst other understandings, to the development of James Lovelock's Gaia theory.) Critically however, politically the planet is organised into discrete sovereign territories (countries or nation-states) operating in an unregulated international space. Tensions have occurred between the interests of these domestic political structures of control (very often motivated by short-term economic and political considerations) and the wider interests of humanity in environmental problems (with international and long-term aspects). Economic globalisation has particularly impacted upon less politically and financially robust countries in ways which have compromised their ability to protect their natural resource base. In countries as diverse as the Philippines, India, Indonesia, Malaysia, Chile and Brazil short-term economic imperatives have frequently held sway over longer-term environmental arguments. We show how local effects of a global economy can influence approaches to environmental conservation. A complicated picture includes the form and function of democratic control, geographic and biological endowments and the nature of the relationship between population pressure, economic growth and environmental degradation.

Despite the importance of state responses to environmental problems, they are undoubtedly influenced (or even controlled) by a number of external influences. A range of international political and economic actors has the ability essentially to dictate how 'development' will be pursued by the developing countries. At the macro-level, despite the noble rhetoric of 'sustainable development' (WCED 1987) when choices have to be made between profit and preservation, profit has invariably come first.

Meaningful political solutions to environmental problems in the global South remain elusive as poorer states lack the economic/political apparatus to protect the natural resource base. The incongruence between sovereign states, as discrete political entities, the structure of the global economy and increasingly trans-boundary environmental problems poses fundamental problems for devising political strategies to protect the environment across states that differ in wealth, power and priorities. Attempts have been made to counter this at local and international levels through the development of international regimes. An international regime is 'the collective response of two or more states to a problematical situation in the form of institutionalised co-operation' (List and Ritberger 1992: 87). Such regimes may be based on treaties, protocols and conventions which give them a legal basis. There is, however, a difference between states signing up to a regime and actually complying and implementing the regulations to which they have agreed. Such conventions include the Basel Convention on the Control of Transboundary Movements of Hazardous Waste (1992) which is designed to stop states dumping their waste in countries poorly equipped to resist the short-term economic benefits of this practice. In this chapter we also address the question of whether developing countries enjoy any level of environmental protection from international regimes and whether they are active in their formation or merely passive signatories.

Various non-governmental organisations (NGOs) have attempted to challenge apparent trajectories of humanity in the context of state sovereignty and global economic pressures. Around the world, growth in their numbers has been rapid, covering a wide spectrum: from small-scale 'NIMBY' (Not In My Back Yard) organisations to global-scale pressure groups with considerable clout. We shall explore their role in implementing development initiatives and highlighting environmental abuses.

We shall conclude by noting that forces of self-interest fundamentally undermine development, defined as progress and improvement. Arguably all of global society can be located somewhere on the path to development which liberals argue will lead ultimately to social and environmental utopia. However instead of development leading to a convergence of global economic and social standards of well-being, the reverse has been true. Political colonial structures of exploitation have simply been replaced by economic ones; in many countries, the result has been social disruption and environmental devastation. The world's rich advocate development in a manner that ensures that they stay rich, while the poor stay poor. Put another way, far from being underdeveloped many peripheral states have gone straight to being 'overdeveloped' (that is, over-exploited), never having reached any measure of prosperity and often at the cost of their natural resource base.

development and the environment: theoretical approaches

Environmental theory, especially in relation to economic growth or development, offers a range of alternatives ranging from *laissez faire* models of economic activity through to calls for the overthrow of the capitalist system in favour of a society based on ecological principles. Located between these two extremes are various remedial frameworks that are said to allow economic activity to be adapted to accommodate conservation of the natural resource base. Although debate is most properly characterised as a wide-ranging spectrum of opinion (Hayward 1995), here we simplify by breaking the thinking down into three broad schools of thought:

- free-market/neo-liberal;
- reformist and interventionist; and
- radical.

While others opt for a simplified dichotomy characterised by divisions such as shallow and deep or anthropocentric and eco-centric (Steans and Pettiford 2001), we hope our modified analysis allows for more complexity without being confusing. This theoretical overview will inform comparisons between the rhetoric and reality of developmental approaches to conservation of the natural environment.

neo-liberal/ free market approaches

Proponents of the free market believe that trade is not the cause of environmental degradation and that capitalism encourages the rational use of resources under conditions of free-market competition and the specialisation of production through comparative advantage (Ricardo 1973). For free-marketers economic globalisation is an opportunity to rationalise the use of resources. Restrictions on trade would merely lead to economic decline, which could in turn devastate environments and societies. Economic stagnation would mean that populations would be forced to into non-sustainable strategies regarding their environment just to meet their immediate needs. Importantly free-marketers see trade and environmental conservation as a win-win situation in the guise of ecological modernisation (Gouldson and Murphy 1997); as profit is generated this can be channelled into environmental conservation if need be. Similarly free-marketers see economic growth as essential for social well-being. While they do accept that gains may not be equally distributed, overall – they argue – everyone will gain *to some extent*. This is the thinking behind the notion of 'trickle down'. Free-marketers recognise the need for 'perfect information' as consumers can only make environmentally informed choices if the facts are open to them. Armed with this information consumers can then demand that businesses produce goods in an environmentally sustainable way and, through the logic of supply and demand, productive behaviour will be altered.

The idea of replacing natural capital with other types of capital that can be measured in monetary terms has also led to attempts to allocate prices to natural resources. Market economics assumes the establishment of clear and private property rights, so that natural resources, such as the high seas or the atmosphere, which are held in common, are effectively worthless in market terms. According to Hardin (1968) this leads to over-exploitation of the common resource and ultimately its collapse. This had led to techniques such as 'ecological footprinting', which converts different types of consumptive behaviour into a single type of resource (land), so that it can be estimated whether we are breaching the carrying

---

box 9.1   free market approaches and the brundtland report

Free market approaches to environmental conservation broadly coincide with 'weak' versions of sustainable development, along the lines of those advocated in the 1987 Brundtland Report (WCED 1987). (The Report became commonly known as the Brundtland Report because the Commission's Chair was a former prime minister of Norway, Gro Harlem Brundtland.) Weak sustainability 'means that any form of natural capital can be run down, provided that proceeds are reinvested in other forms of capital, for example, man-made capital. Strong sustainability, however, requires that the stock of natural capital should not decline' (Bretschger and Hannes 2001: 185; for a critique of the weak/strong dichotomy see Holland, 1997). The Report was widely accepted as a way to reconcile economic development and environmental conservation. However this may have less to do with the wisdom contained therein and more to do with the answer it suggested; this being simply that more economic growth was needed. As such, Brundtland can be seen as a charter for business interests. The Report famously advocated 'development that meets the needs of the present without compromising the ability of future generations to meet their own needs' (WCED 1987: 43). This beguilingly simple phrase is difficult to disagree with, and appears to pay more than lip service to the importance of inter-generational equity; however, how we are supposed to specify the idea of 'needs' was left notoriously vague (see Bartelmus 1994, Ekins 1993; Finger 1993).

---

capacity of the single planet that we have at our disposal (or indeed of the individual country in which we live). The land that we live on, the food and water that we consume, the raw materials for our buildings, belongings and infrastructure and the energy used to generate these materials are all factored into an ecological footprint (Wackernagel and Rees 1996). Energy is the most problematic to quantify as different forms of energy (fossil, solar and so on) may be more or less sustainable. To give an example, it is estimated that the population of London has a total footprint of 32 million hectares of land (see www.ecocouncil.ac.cr). This is the land needed to provide what Londoners currently consume; yet London is only 0.16 million hectares in area and so is using the resources/space of others in order to meet its own needs.

'Contingent valuation' has also been set up as a survey technique to gauge consumers' so-called *Willingness to Pay (WTP)*, and *Willingness to Accept (WTA)*. WTP is the amount of money a person would pay in order to secure an environmental benefit which did not necessarily impact directly on that person and WTA is the amount of money a person would accept in exchange for the loss of an environmental commodity (Burgess 2003: 266–85). WTP effectively puts an economic value, albeit one arrived at subjectively, on an aspect of environmental conservation, such as a panda or the preservation of an area of land. This is matched against the respondent's social profile and income so the importance of the environment in their priorities becomes clearer.

Proponents of the neo-liberal approach do not necessarily see a conflict between economic growth through trade, and natural resource conservation. (For a discussion on the relationship between trade and development, see O'Hearn 2003.) However, they do highlight the importance of private property rights and it seems that environmental resources are more easily dealt with when a monetary value is allocated to them. This is what is meant by commodification. However, problems have been noted with WTP and WTA surveys as respondents have sometimes made economically irrational choices – that is, they would be prepared to pay £50 to save one panda but only £25 to save ten, meaning perhaps that they are too far removed from the problem to really understand it! That is, some respondents appear to see the figures they come up with as indicators of the extent of their charitableness, rather than the extent of the actual issue they are being asked to address. The WTP/WTA analysis also fails to acknowledge that it may be how effectively money is spent on environmental problems, rather than how much of it there is, that will make a real difference.

reformist and interventionist approaches

These two approaches can be conflated for our purposes as adaptations of free market behaviour. Simply put, reformist approaches provide incentives or penalties for consumers and producers to move towards environmentally friendly economic behaviour. This may be in the form of financial instruments such as subsidies (reward) or taxation (punishment). Interventionist approaches, on the other hand, wish to legislate for change. Whereas taxes and subsidies can be used to alter economic behaviour by manipulating markets, interventionism is a stricter form of control involving legal penalties for 'dirty' producers.

Both approaches have their drawbacks. Under reformist approaches consumers may simply be willing to bear the higher cost for the goods they desire (higher fuel costs and tax bands do not appear to have got everyone into 1 litre Daewoos for instance). Under interventionism it becomes difficult to enforce environmental penalties at an international level and in order to alter behaviour the financial penalties imposed must be larger than any savings made through polluting or degrading business activities. If a firm saves $3 million dollars by dumping toxic waste in the oceans, a fine of $2 million will not necessarily act as an incentive for it to change its behaviour.

Environmental issues first hit the international and public consciousnesses in the 1970s. The civil environmental movement grew out of the activism that found its voice protesting against the Vietnam War and subsequently gave rise to NGOs such as Greenpeace and Friends

---

box 9.2   company environmental behaviour and adverse publicity

Rather than financial punishments, the detrimental impact of adverse publicity about its activities seem more likely to alter a company's behaviour. For instance, in 1995 Shell was seen to be complicit with the Nigerian government over the hanging of the Ogoni Nigerian activist Ken Saro-Wiwa, who had challenged the degradation caused by Shell on Ogoni tribal lands. Saro-Wiwa was jailed by the Nigerian authorities for his protests about the way that Ogoni concerns were politically marginalised by the Nigerian authorities (this reflected a situation where both domestic and international structures interacted not only to silence the collective voice of the Ogoni people but also to help to degrade the environment). However Saro-Wiwa was successful in bringing international attention to the problem and Amnesty International and Greenpeace, amongst other NGOs, orchestrated the blockading of Shell petrol stations in order to bring attention to the Ogoni cause.

In short, while international economic forces caused a great deal of the Ogoni problems, transnational social forces helped to focus attention on their cause in a way that was not possible at the domestic level. However, despite international and transnational protests Saro-Wiwa's death sentence was carried out. Since then evidence has emerged that Shell has provided some financial compensation to the Ogoni people and that the company is now seeking to introduce better environmental standards of production in the region. However, neither reformists nor interventionists challenge the underlying logic of consumption which lies at the heart of capitalism.

---

of the Earth. Amidst a series of oil spills, nuclear and chemical accidents and fears over imminent resource scarcity, various doom-laden scenarios were put forward. Analogies were offered to try and show the development path on which the earth is heading. Variously, the earth was a car with an oil leak, an oil tanker heading towards the cliffs, or a plane popping rivets every now and again. Reformists and interventionists alike would accept that with human behaviour unchanged these were all relevant and disturbing pictures to paint. However, an oil leak can be fixed and the car can continue as before, oil tankers can be turned, if slowly, and rivets can be reapplied providing we don't fly past the point of no return. However what needs also to be highlighted here is that it is not necessarily over-exploitation of environmental resources that is the problem, it is unequal access to environmental resources. Inequality not scarcity needs to be addressed and market mechanisms – underpinned by the logic of mass consumption – are poorly equipped to address this.

radical approaches

Radical approaches to the relationship between economic development and the natural environment differ fundamentally from our two previous approaches. The labels you might come across to describe various radical approaches include 'deep green', 'eco-centric' and 'deep ecology'. Such radical perspectives can be said to suggest that western consumption patterns are environmentally unsustainable *and* undesirable.

Driven by capitalism's imperative for continuously expanding demand rather than any relation to meeting human needs, 'consumptive growth does not make people happier [....] people would actually be better off, Greens argue, if they consumed less and concentrated more on genuine well-being: on personal development, on relationships with others and social belonging' (Jacobs 1997: 50).

Radicals call into question the entire logic of capitalist consumption. It is argued that the capitalist market, as a mode of production, must undergo fundamental reform for moral *and* practical reasons; and that technological 'fixes' (mending the oil leak) not only fail to address some fundamental questions about life under capitalism but do not have the capacity to redress economically-driven degradation.

---

box 9.3   cleavages in radical environmental approaches

A cleavage within radical thinking can be identified between anthropocentric ecological perspectives and non-anthropocentric ecological perspectives. Although technically speaking it is impossible for a human being to be anything other than human-centred, some theoretical approaches treat humans as distinct from the rest of the environment and seek to reconcile human emancipation with environmental objectives, thus privileging the human animal in its analysis of the natural environment. Meanwhile others adopt an eco-centric approach that endeavours to make no distinction between human and other species; to this view the environment is valued for its intrinsic worth rather than its use-value to humans (see, for example, Eckersley 1992).

It is useful for our purposes here to note that some radicals link forms of economic production and resource use with social ill/well-being. This echoes Polanyi (1944: 71) who wrote that 'labor and land are no other than the human beings themselves of which every society consists and the natural surroundings in which it exists. To include them in the market mechanism means to subordinate the substance of society itself to the laws of the market'. For Polanyi (1944: 73) this ultimately results in the 'demolition of society'. If we consider this in terms of an international society then it can be argued that economic development is responsible for both social and environmental destruction, an argument that will expanded throughout this chapter.

the nature of the issues

biodiversity

The developing countries are home to the greater part of the globe's remaining biological resources. This biodiversity, measured in terms of genetic material, species and habitat diversity, forms a rich ecological resource which in modern times has been exploited at increasing rates, resulting in accelerated rates of extinction. Biodiversity formation has always been a dynamic process rather than static condition, with species naturally evolving and becoming extinct; this is known as the *background rate* of extinction. However in modern times, development has increased habitat loss and rates of extinction have exceeded by many times the background rate. As well as the extinctions we know about, many other species are becoming critically endangered and it is highly probable that yet-to-be identified species have become extinct before we even knew of them. Such mass extinctions can cause the collapse of food webs and further habitat disruption. As more and more 'keystone species' are affected (those species which hold together their particular eco-system and whose removal is crucial) effects are multiplied on the overall level of biodiversity.

---

box 9.4   science and biodiversity

Scientific techniques informing biodiversity are similarly evolving. In early 2004 it was reported that a new research programme is under way at Oxford University in the UK which will adopt a long-term approach to biodiversity monitoring using sediment cores and radio-carbon dating methods which will indicate biodiversity levels of periods of thousands of years. This will indicate long-term time scales over which levels of biodiversity can be compared allowing trends or events to be identified and how environments have regenerated. This could prove more meaningful in terms of environmental understanding than current research which only draws on data going back perhaps 50 years. Countries such as Mexico, Congo, South Africa and Mongolia have been identified as biodiversity 'hotspots' and will be the focus of this research. (*Guardian* 2004).

---

genetically engineered crops

Habitats can be lost through processes such as deforestation but they can also be disrupted by shifts from traditional to industrialised forms of farming. Similarly the introduction of cereal types based on genetically engineered 'terminator technology', by conglomerates such as Cargill and Monsanto threatens the loss of seed variations that have been harvested by indigenous farmers for thousands of years (see Shiva 1999). Local farmers are scarcely able to resist these new seed types as credit, transport and infrastructure also tend to be controlled by the seed manufacturers. This sort of exploitative relationship, for environments and workers in developing countries, can also be seen in the closely related pesticide industry.

Pesticides are widely used in developing countries that are either banned or restricted in the developed North. The results of this are that local environments are polluted by run-off containing pesticides and workers suffer from increased levels of skin complaints and cancers, and their children suffer birth defects. For instance in the banana industry in Central America it has been found that women working in packing plants 'suffer double the average rate of leukaemia and birth defects. And 20 per cent of male banana workers … have been left sterile' (Smith 2002: 40). During the course of their work they may ingest up to 4kg of pesticides annually, that is eight times the global average.

The argument of agricultural conglomerates is that genetically engineered crops supply higher yields and are the answer to food insecurity suffered by many people in developing countries. What this argument fails to highlight is that there is no food shortage globally, only unequal access to the food which is produced. While free-marketers advocate economic development through increased trade as a route to prosperity, they fail to acknowledge that with issues such as loss of biodiversity or human health there is nothing that can replace this capital; once it is lost it is lost forever. Given the now global nature of trade, many consumers are physically far removed from the consequences of their habits of consumption and are thus poorly equipped to understand the impact, or *environmental shadow,* of their actions. In addition, the cost of goods often fails to reflect the environmental *externalities* of production; that is the consumer does not pay for any degrading side effects of production. Indeed if such costs *were* factored into the price of goods, under World Trade Organisation rules these may be seen as non-tariff barriers to trade and therefore illegal. Consequently 'the objectives of trade liberalization and of environmental protection frequently do not march so happily hand in hand' (Brack 1995: 498).

Indigenous forms of farming traditionally utilised small-scale plots where many crops were planted in sympathy with one another in the same area. This meant a natural balance occurred between pests and predators and there was no need for pesticides. These areas also provided habitats for many species to thrive. However under conditions of industrial farming, monocultures occur where the same crop is planted for areas miles across; these monocultures invariably require high levels of pesticides and irrigation both of which are detrimental to the long-term fertility of the land and biodiversity. Though credit may be available, and 'hard-sell' used to boost pesticide sales, with time larger and more potent 'cocktails' of pesticide are needed to do the same job, as insects begin to gain immunity. The leaders in developing states are poorly able to resist this trend given the desire to develop and also the need to raise export earnings to manage high levels of debt. Ultimately however rural communities and southern environments feel the direct impacts of such practices. What should normatively happen is that global society should shoulder their wider and longer-term effects.

global warming

'Global warming does not exist'. So proclaim a large number of scientists in the United States whose funding – incidentally – comes from a big business community whose continued use of resources and fuelling of domestic consumption may be seen as reliant on such a conclusion. Despite claims of impartiality, it is amazing what funding can do to scientific rigour. It is easy to be sceptical. In the early 1970s there were warnings of a new ice age; during World War II official statistics indicated global warming – although it seems likely that this was due to those doing the measuring (of sea temperature) taking their buckets indoors first because of blackout regulations. The point is that natural variations are part of what makes our planet so special and mysterious – would we not be foolish to change everything without really solid evidence?

---

box 9.5   global warming and science

Global warming is a serious threat. So say British scientists who are funded by the UK government. On the other hand, big business continues to fund research which says global warming does not exist – not least it needs to continue to justify their environmentally unhelpful actions. However, would a government, such as that of Britain, continue to plough public money into proving that something does not exist? This is very unlikely. There is not for instance a programme of investigation to confirm on an ongoing basis the impossibility of alchemy. So, scientists whose funding depends on the existence of global warming are finding that it does indeed exist. This tale of two groups of scientists tells us something important about the caution we should maintain in dealing with those who call themselves scientists.

Away from scientific investigation and statistics what is the situation like? We might notice hotter summers, milder winters. Weather patterns and ocean currents appear to have changed. Species extinctions have accelerated to a level comparable with the time before dinosaurs became extinct. So-called 'natural' disasters have increased dramatically. But might this not all be happening naturally? Why get rid of the good things in life – cars, foreign holidays, manufactured goods – because of something that might not even have anything to do with these things?

The answer of course is precaution. Smoking may not kill you but that is hardly an argument for smoking. Thus, with evidence that human activity is contributing to a 'greenhouse effect', through the production of certain gases and the destruction of forests which have acted as 'sinks' to absorb these gases, it would be prudent to modify our behaviour and to reduce our production of these gases even if that means fewer cars, more public transport, less foreign travel and so on.

Alas, selfish arguments prevail. Neo-liberal economic logic fails to see the need for socially motivated and funded public transport schemes, people enjoy their cars and holidays and – at least in Britain – people are prepared to 'put up with' milder winters and hotter summers. However, for several small-island developing states the failure to act and to address this problem means the actual threat of complete disappearance. Generally speaking, temperature rises and incidences of hurricanes and so on are going to have most impact in those areas of the globe already suffering from the highest levels of poverty and environmental degradation.

domestic factors shaping environmental policy and politics

Majid Rahenema is highly critical of the relationship between local elites and international actors. She suggests that aspects of this relationship have caused development to be a 'deceitful mirage' and that it 'mainly served to strengthen new alliances that were going to unite the interests of the post-colonial foreign expansionists with those of the local leaders in need of them for the consolidation of their own positions' (1997: x). This follows what we identified above when discussing the activities of Shell in Nigeria. The inference here is that development, in terms of economic growth, has been set up to favour the already powerful as opposed to it leading to any qualitative social change or conservation of the natural environment. In the next two sections, we will look at how both internal and external factors serve to marginalise conservation of the natural environment, if such conservation hinders quantitative economic development.

disparities in economic and political power within the state – and beyond

Democracy is no guarantee of political morality in governance. While corrupt activity may be present under conditions of authoritarianism because of lack of accountability, corruption can also easily emerge as a by-product of the market economy. We again get insight from Polanyi (1944: 249) who critiques the market economy 'not because it is based on economics – in a sense, every and any society must be based on it

– but that its economy is based on self-interest.' This self-interest may be served by the legitimate creation of profit but it can also be done through corruption. Polanyi's point here is that markets, and therefore liberal approaches to development, are not free but manipulated by various actors, including governments, in order to secure the greatest spoils of capitalism for themselves. Unfortunately in some developing countries the natural environment has become a casualty of corrupt and self-seeking forms of governance. (See chapters 2, 3 and 4 for further discussions of the relationships between political power and authority in the developing world.)

deforestation

The formation of an effective international regime on deforestation, which could have acted against what occurred in Indonesia in the 1990s (see Box 9.6), has proved enduringly problematic since the Rio Conference in 1992. This is partly because deforestation presents a contentious issue in terms of the identity of forests as either a global resource, a carbon sink or a sovereign resource to be disposed of as a country sees fit. To date, no forests regime has been negotiated, despite the signing of Conventions on Climate Change and Biodiversity and associated high hopes among some constituencies in the North. The governments in the South saw such a regime as a device of the North to wield control over its southern sovereign resources. All that was eventually agreed on was a Non-Legally

---

box 9.6   deforestation in indonesia

In the rural context disparities in economic and political power tend to manifest themselves in disputes over land use. Deforestation is a major example of corrupt officials either turning a blind eye or actively encouraging economic behaviour which is detrimental to the environment. In Indonesia in 1997 and 1998 millions of hectares of forest were destroyed by fires deliberately set by logging companies. The fires 'produced greenhouse gases equivalent to the annual emissions from all the cars in Europe. They spread poisonous smoke over six countries, affecting more than 70 million people and costing billions of dollars in health, transport, trade and environmental damage.' (EIA 1998: 39). This is to say nothing of the massive loss of biodiversity.

Burning as a means of land clearance was banned in 1995 but unscrupulous landowners still use the practice as a means to swiftly clear forested areas for other types of land use, such as plantation farming. In 1997 the Indonesian government named and shamed 176 companies accused of deliberately setting fires. On the list were companies owned by relatives and close associates of ex-President Suharto, including his own daughter. The fires in Indonesia happened because those in positions of political power had corporate interests that stood to benefit from it and the Indonesian state was unwilling or unable to challenge this logic. It would seem also that the international community were poorly placed to bring the Indonesian government to account.

Binding Authoritative Statement of Principles for a Global Consensus on the Management, Conservation and Sustainable Development of All Types of Forest, the so-called forests principles, and Agenda 21 (of which Chapter 11 was entitled 'Combating Deforestation').

In the mid-1990s a series of negotiations on deforestation were conducted under the auspices of the Intergovernmental Panel on Forests. This UN organ was created in 1995 and reported to the UN Commission on Sustainable Development in 1997. The UN General Assembly Special Session then created a new Intergovernmental Forum on Forests and some southern countries favoured a convention as a possible means of attracting aid. By now however some countries in the North did not want a convention, notably the United States under President Clinton (1992–2000), whose business community was complaining that increasing environmental agreements was making it uncompetitive. The result of this was that a convention was still not agreed upon.

Here we can see that southern states had some level of power in that they were able to block a UNCED Convention that they saw as potentially detrimental to their interests. However as the issue evolved, and countries such as Malaysia became more amenable to this idea, the North cooled on the forests issue. It is important to note though that the economy rather than the environment may motivate behaviour over the forests issue, and that unless a clear and present danger (usually to the North) is identified, then regimes can be highly problematic to initiate. It seems in this case also that the South feared that a regime would compromise their autonomy, although subsequently this could have been negotiated if there was financial gain to be had. Here again, as in the case of Nigeria, we can note a complex interplay of domestic and international political and economic forces which undermine both social justice and effective environmental conservation.

sanitation in the city

Similar problems occur in the urban context in developing countries. A growing number of cities in the South are now regarded as 'mega-cities' and are indicative of a global trend towards urbanisation. In 1950 only London and New York had populations of more than eight million but by 2000 29 cities had populations this large, 23 of which were in the developing world. In poorer countries the size of these cities has led to conflicts over urban space between the mass of often-impoverished humanity and the needs of the economic aspirations of the state. The need for living space conflicts with the desire of governments to set up infrastructure such as roads and business parks in order to attract inward investment. The result of this is often that the poor are forced to live in crowded, unsafe and unsanitary conditions.

sanitation problems in payatas

Payatas, an area of Manila in the Philippines, is a dramatic, yet unfortunately not unique, example of how corrupt forces can contribute to environmental degradation. Payatas is a vast rubbish dump where at least 6,000 tons of refuse, which is produced by Manila's 12-million-strong population, is brought daily. Scavengers make a living from sifting through the rubbish. This they either sell for recycling, or make use of themselves. This earns them 60 to 70 pesos (approximately £1) a day, in a country where the minimum wage is set at 250 pesos per day. Payatas' families average six to eight children. Such large families are deemed necessary for economic security, as welfare provision is non-existent. The children are often ill because of ailments associated with living in such an environment, and the average age of death is 40 years because of toxic fumes rising from the decomposing rubbish.

The community is made up of shanty houses located immediately around the dump where other members of the urban poor, owing to the lack of affordable housing and land in Manila, also live. A 1998 Presidential Commission report stated that 37 per cent of Manila's population lived in informal housing, characterised by overcrowding and lack of basic services. Most blue-collar, and some white-collar workers, cannot afford proper housing; this leads to squatter communities emerging on every available piece of land. Verges at the side of roads, railway cuttings and Payatas are all appropriated as informal settlements. These communities frequently live under the threat of demolition and forced eviction, especially when the government wants the land for building the infrastructure to attract foreign investment.

On taking office in 1998, President Estrada ordered Payatas shut. He also designated a 'Task Force for the Development of Payatas', but the rubbish kept coming and the Task Force never materialised. Then in July 2000 a landslide of rubbish, precipitated by heavy monsoon rains, buried more than 200 people. Estrada ordered the dump shut, but this left Manila with nowhere to put its rubbish. The residents of the neighbouring San Mateo dump successfully petitioned through the courts to block the reopening of this site. Plans to ship Manila's rubbish to Semirara, 372 miles away in the Visayan islands, were blocked by a court order, despite efforts to fast-track the necessary legislation by the government. Semirara is close to the World Heritage Site of Tubbataha Reef Marine Park and also Boracay. Meanwhile rubbish was piling up on the streets of Manila in

30°C heat. So, four months later Payatas re-opened, despite warnings by the UNDP that if Asia did not address its garbage crisis then such tragedies would become more frequent. The environment at Payatas is not only of concern for those living in the immediate vicinity however. The rubbish is located a mere 2 kilometres from La Mesa Reservoir, which is the main water supply for Quezon City's 1.4 million population, meaning that the run-off from the dump is leaching into the water supply.

But the origins of this problem are not just a simple equation of too many people equals too much rubbish. Wider forces and corrupt local politics cause and perpetuate this situation. After the Payatas landslide, the Integrated Ecological Solid Waste Management Act of 2000 was given governmental attention after previously being sidelined. And in January 2001 the Solid Waste Management Act was signed by the new President Gloria Macapagal Arroyo. This advocates the use of modern technology and recycling as well as making the illegal dumping of rubbish a criminal offence. However the suggestion of an incinerator plant immediately fell foul of the Clean Air Act, passed in 2000.

The Clean Air Act made swift progress through Congress by virtue of being supported by politicians who had a vested interest in the continuation of open site dumping. Every load that comes into Payatas must be paid for by those dumping, and these payments may make their way into the back pockets of officials working in a political environment which is endemically corrupt. These same officials also control the granting of government contracts for refuse collection. On the issue of the illegal dumping of rubbish, squatter communities in Manila have no rubbish collection facilities, just as they may have no sanitation and no legal electricity supply, so they have no choice but to drop rubbish where they can. So every stream and waterway throughout the city, as well as areas of Manila Bay, are clogged with rubbish.

In conclusion, the cases of both Indonesia and the Philippines suggest that a combination of neo-liberal development strategies and corrupt governance had devastating environmental impacts. Many international institutions such as the World Bank and the Asian Development Bank now advocate the devolution of governance as a way of enhancing the capabilities of the poor and transparency of governance. However in some cases it seems that the opposite happens: instead of encouraging transparency, devolution just opens up the possibility of increased corrupt interventions at many levels of the state economy – illicit kickbacks rather than judgements of best value. Efficiency or environmental conservation may prove a greater influence over how contracts are awarded for sanitation and utilities. In terms of implementing environmental policy developing countries may pay little more than lip service to environmental conservation because quite simply there is money to be made, or saved, in environmentally degrading activity. This is especially the case where no clear system of property rights exist. De Soto (2000) explains how the weak legal system in many developing countries results in the poor staying poor while the rich get richer. Powerful state actors can follow the neo-liberal line while simultaneously lining their own pockets often at the expense of weaker members of society and the natural environment.

population pressures

As we have already noted through our discussion on urbanisation, sheer volume of human numbers in developing countries cause specific pressures on the state in terms of environmental impact. No discussion on population growth is complete without reference to Thomas Malthus and his 1798 text *An Essay on the Principle of Population*. Malthus questioned the idea that science and technology would be sufficient means to achieve prosperity. The core problem he identified was that while population grows exponentially, agricultural production can only grow arithmetically so that population will eventually outstrip the capacity of the land to feed it. In order for prosperity to be achieved population had to be checked. Checks could take the form of 'positive' checks – 'starvation, sickness, war, infanticide, reduced longevity' – and preventative checks – 'delay of marriage, restraint of sexual passion'. Malthus' ideas are still cited by *neo-Malthusian pessimists* who question the *carrying capacity* of the Earth in relation to population size. Malthus' ideas would for instance explain why the Green Revolution in India did not result in an increase in food resources for the population. From the 1960s India massively increased the volume of its rice yield. However, population growth outstripped this increase such that there was no quantitative increase in food supply per capita, a situation complicated by questions of distribution.

There is clearly a correlation between population levels and resource availability in terms of a state's ability to feed its population, but other variables impact upon this relationship. This can be illustrated by the I=PAT equation:

Environmental Impact = Population (P) x Affluence (A) x Technology (T)

The affluence part of this equation applies to consumption per capita as the environmental impact of population size varies depending on levels of consumption. Similarly the more a population consumes the more waste it produces. Even though the global South accounts for perhaps

80 per cent of the global population it only consumes 20 per cent of the globe's resources. For the North these figures are reversed, so it is not population size that matters, of itself, but more particularly overall levels of consumption. Similarly access to technology may alleviate environmental problems, but for the developing countries access to this technology may be problematic.

Disparities between levels of population and consumption between the North and the South have meant that international agreements have tended to be characterised by a North/South split between those who blame either overpopulation or over-consumption for environmental degradation. This was true of the UNCED conference in Rio in 1992. However, it is important to note that both affluence and poverty result in environmental degradation, the former through desire and the latter through necessity.

Large families tend to be the norm in developing countries because they provide more hands for manual work and also someone to care for parents in their old age when welfare provision from the state may be non-existent. Large families may also be the result of the desire for sons in patriarchal societies. As daughters tend to go to the families of their husbands in some cultures, it is essential for parents to produce a son to ensure the security of the family. The average number of children born to each woman in a reproductive lifetime is call the *total fertility rate* or TFR; this has declined in many developing countries but not as quickly as mortality rates. The change from high mortality and high fertility to low mortality and low fertility is called *demographic transition*. Mortality generally declines earlier or faster than fertility in a state as it reaches a certain level of development and health and welfare provision improves. Therefore as deaths decline and fertility remains high, a period of rapid population growth results. In general, demographic transition is associated with development, but not always. The oil-rich Middle Eastern countries still have high levels of fertility, despite their wealth, while countries such as Sri Lanka and Bangladesh have witnessed declining fertility. However because of the long gap between birth and reaching reproductive age these processes are delayed. A state may then have a *population momentum* built into its demographic structure, as the children from a period of population boom store up a future boom. This means that countries which have recently reached certain levels of development, with a corresponding decline in fertility rates, will still continue population growth for decades because of this inbuilt momentum. This is true of Indonesia, Malaysia and South Korea amongst others.

conclusion

Looking at the environment and development in what has previously been termed the 'Third World' reveals a truly complex and fascinating picture. While it is true that the pressures such states face from the global economy and institutions such as the IMF/World Bank is huge, it also reveals that the depression of various neo-Marxist theories, which would argue that such states have no space for agency, is also misplaced.

Thus in international debates over the environment it is, on the one hand, quite right that many developing states are in effect victims left with no choice but to despoil their environment in a desperate bid to win a game whose rules have been determined by someone else. On the other hand, the pertinence of local factors, such as population policy and corruption, have important effects which can either ameliorate or exacerbate the situation. The future also looks to be a fascinating arena to study; as the effects of increasing resource use on a finite planet 'boomerang' back on humanity ever more, those states currently without political power may be seen to hold environmental trump cards. Efforts to wrest these trump cards away or prevent them being played will undoubtedly be made. Ultimately however, 'triumphal capitalism' may have to accept that its historical externalising of the environment is its Achilles' heel and this may necessitate greater strategies of reform and intervention, and ultimately possibly even radical solutions. If this happens it seems that radical solutions are more likely to come through necessity (due to harsh environmental conditions) than through the planned creation of a better society. It is not a reassuring scenario.

10
human rights in an unequal world
james chiriyankandath

introduction

Since the end of the ideological stand-off of the Cold War human rights has emerged as one of the chief themes of international discourse. Yet this has not resulted in great advances in the realisation of rights, certainly in the developing world. Why? Principally because human rights remain contested and the terrain on which they have to be realised is extremely uneven. The language of rights continues to be used by states more to justify their practices than determine their actions. For instance, powerful western states often use human rights as a stick with which to beat non-western states regarded as hostile while soft pedalling abuses by friendly or client states. On the other hand, in the 1990s the governments of some East Asian states promoted the notion of distinctive 'Asian values' to discredit criticism of their record on human rights and political freedom.

Many non-westerners such as the Sudanese Muslim scholar Abdullahia An-Na'im (2001) accept human rights as 'rights that are due to all human beings by virtue of their humanity, without distinction on such grounds as race, sex (gender), religion, language, or national origin'. Yet the notion lends itself to controversy because there is so much disagreement on how to define rights, the relative importance of particular kinds of rights and about whether they are universal or specific to cultures. The dominance of the universalistic and individualistic western discourse of human rights has posed many problems for states with very different historical, cultural, religious, political and economic experiences. In poorer countries the situation is especially complicated by the greater limitations placed on the state's capacity to provide for and protect basic human rights. This makes ideas of human rights that have been developed through philosophical discourse and legal debate very difficult to put into effect.

Drawing development and human rights together is essential to get to grips with the problems and dilemmas posed by the challenge of successfully articulating and protecting human rights in developing countries. For many years thinkers and activists in the fields of human rights and development tended to focus on the one to the neglect of the other. Those concerned with development were mainly interested in issues such as capitalism and dependency, class and community, and later, the environment and sustainability, gender and development, and appropriate technology and indigenous peoples. Human rights did not figure overtly as a central theme in their discourse, though it was necessarily implicit in many of their concerns. Similarly, the primary focus of those working on human rights, especially within the western tradition, was on civil and political, rather than economic and social, rights. In relation to the developing world this mainly took the form of anti-colonialism and anti-racism. The end of the Cold War, and the rise of globalisation, made this tenuous boundary between development and human rights even more unsustainable. As the United Nations' Development Programme's annual *Human Development Report* (UNDD 2000: 2) put it, 'Human development is essential for realizing human rights, and human rights are essential for full human development'.

The chapter begins by briefly reviewing the evolution of the modern western conception of human rights in an era of capitalism, colonialism and imperialism. It then considers the spread, through the United Nations system, of a global conception of human rights covering the newly independent developing countries. Subsequent sections focus on the problems of cultural relativism and the right to development in an era of globalisation. The chapter concludes by considering the rise of humanitarian interventionism in the post-Cold War era and the scope for the incremental strengthening of human rights in the developing world via national non-governmental organisations and state and regional institutions.

the modern idea of human rights

The contemporary discourse of human rights has been shaped primarily by the evolution of the idea of such rights through the western Enlightenment with its emphasis on reason and the individual rather than ethics derived from religious tradition. The writings of men like John Locke (1632–1704), Jean-Jacques Rousseau (1712–78) and Tom Paine

(1737–1809) in the era of the English Revolution of 1688, the American War of Independence (1776–83) and the French Revolution of 1789 left a seminal imprint on what came to be regarded as human rights. So did proclamations such as the French Declaration of the Rights of Man and the Citizen (1789) and the Bill of Rights appended to the constitution of the new United States of America (1791).

From its birth, the translation of the modern conception of rights into action was infected with disturbing ambiguities. The English utilitarian philosopher Jeremy Bentham (1748–1832) famously dismissed the very idea of 'natural rights' as 'rhetorical nonsense – nonsense upon stilts', holding that rights could only be endowed by real laws and not imaginary laws of nature (1843: 491). Moreover, its universal claims were contradicted by the effective exclusion of the majority of humankind from its effective purview. For instance, John Locke's *First Treatise of Government* (1977: 157–8) focused on the biblical first man (Adam) as the exemplary right-holder and his *Second Treatise* makes clear that only propertied males could be Adam's successors – not women, wage labourers or slaves. In the USA African-Americans remained enslaved for more than seventy years after the passing of the Bill of Rights and were denied equal voting rights for a century after the abolition of slavery. Similarly, women had to wait until the first half of the twentieth century (as late as 1944 in France) to be granted equal voting rights. Legislation to eliminate discrimination based on sex in Western Europe and the USA only followed the rise of the women's liberation movement in the 1960s. Even then it was not always successful – though the US Congress passed the Equal Rights Amendment in 1972, it failed to win ratification by the necessary two-thirds of the 50 states.

The most glaring contradiction between the universal tones in which the idea of rights was expressed and the realisation of those rights was seen in the relationship between Europe and much of the rest of the world. During the nineteenth and early twentieth centuries, the language of reason, and in particular the pseudo-science of race, were often found strangely twinned with the civilising missionary purpose of the Christian West in justifying the European colonisation of the Americas, Australia and much of Asia and Africa (Viswanathan 1989: 45–67; Rich 1986). Even in an instance like the cooperation of European powers led by Britain in the suppression of the slave trade it was not commonly-held equal human rights that formed the justification for action as much as the notion of a civilising mission and Christian duty. The legacy of the paradox of the development of the discourse of rights in the West just when European empires were extending their dominion over hundreds of millions of non-Europeans is one that still inhibits the acceptance of the idea of universal human rights. Nevertheless, the paradox also ensured that undeniable human rights became an important part both of the rhetoric of anti-colonial nationalism and the constitutions and the legal and political discourse in post-colonial states.

---

box 10.1   indian nationalism and human rights

In British India the 60-year campaign for self-government and, ultimately, independence drew heavily from the western discourse. Surendranath Banerjea (1999: 101), one of those who had founded the Indian National Congress in 1885, declared in his presidential address to it in 1895: 'English history has taught us those principles of freedom which we cherish with our lifeblood. We have been fed upon the strong food of English constitutional freedom'.

A quarter of a century later, at the 1931 Karachi session of the Congress, Jawaharlal Nehru drafted a resolution on fundamental rights. Five years later he also played a central role in the formation of the first Indian human rights group, the Civil Liberties Union. Following independence, with Nehru at the helm as India's first prime minister, the constitution of the new republic came into force in 1950. In many respects its provisions relating to 'Fundamental Rights' and 'The Directive Principles of State Policy' (Parts III and IV) resembled the 1948 Universal Declaration of Human Rights (UDHR). Many constitutions in other post-colonial states across Asia and Africa that won independence in the 1950s and 1960s were directly inspired by the UDHR. Since 1989, most states in Eastern Europe and the former Soviet Union, as well as post-apartheid South Africa, have incorporated its articles in their constitutions (UNDP 2000: 4).

The shared lineage of human rights in western and post-colonial countries is only to be expected because the contemporary conception of human rights evolved in response to two central developments, both of which had become globalised in the course of four centuries of European imperialism:

- the rise of the powerful modern state; and
- the spread of capitalism.

Human rights emerged to fill the gap left by the gradual disappearance of the hierarchically determined and socially circumscribed safeguards that had existed in medieval pre-capitalist Europe. As the new Europe extended its dominion across the world so did this new language of rights with its rational and universal claims.

However, unlike in Britain, human rights in much of the developing world had initially served only as a convenient subtext to the anti-colonial movement. In most cases decolonisation left a post-colonial state only superficially, if at all, marked by human rights struggle and a society in which there were few manifestations of an active rights movement. (Even

---

box 10.2   september 11 and human rights

After the aerial attacks on New York and Washington on 11 September 2001 and the subsequent onset of the United States-led 'war on terror' with the invasion of Afghanistan, the British human rights lawyer Conor Gearty (2001) recalled this background of resistance to state power in warning:

Our liberal, tolerant, diverse society does not exist because it has been carefully nurtured by a benign state ... The society we have now has been constructed in the teeth of the opposition of such bodies [as the police, the Army and the intelligence services], which are historically the antagonists of pluralism and human rights ... The most dangerous opponents of our open society may not be those hiding in the caves of Afghanistan.

---

in India with its comparatively substantial pre-independence record of political and social mobilisation, the nascent Civil Liberties Union soon became moribund.)

towards a global human rights regime

The role of the state in the denial of human rights has been strikingly highlighted by a calculation of those killed by governments in the twentieth century – put at 169,202,000 (Freeman 2002: 2). The Universal Declaration of Human Rights was pre-eminently a response to one of the worse single instances of such killing – the Holocaust perpetrated by Nazi Germany during World War II. The UDHR took shape in the infancy of the United Nations when it was dominated by European states and states governed by European settlers (in Latin America, South Africa, Australia and New Zealand). Although there were others, these amounted to barely a third of the membership. This context is important because it helps explain some of the controversy that has characterised the notion of universal human rights in relation to developing countries, most of whom were still under colonial rule in 1948.

If the UDHR was primarily informed by the traumatic experience that Europeans had just gone through, it was, from the outset, also perceived as a potential weapon in the ideological struggle between the capitalist western liberal democracies and the emerging communist bloc led by the Soviet Union (Gearty 2001). The latter saw the UDHR as reflecting liberal-democratic concerns and so when the United Nations General Assembly voted on it in December 1948, six communist countries abstained, along with white-supremacist South Africa and the Muslim kingdom of Saudi Arabia (Rehman 2003: 54). This presaged the Cold War stand-off that dominated UN deliberations for the next four decades. It ensured, for example, that plans for a permanent International Criminal Court with jurisdiction over grave crimes such as those had been dealt with the post-war war crimes tribunals in Nuremberg and Tokyo were shelved (Weller 2002: 695).

---

box 10.3   the udhr and the western human rights tradition

The 30 articles of the UDHR bore the unmistakable imprint of the western human rights tradition, with the first 21 enshrining a wide range of civil and political rights. Also included were rights to social security, work, equal pay, paid holidays, an adequate standard of living, education and participation in cultural life. These latter provisions represented an important departure from the focus on the right to life, liberty and property that had been espoused by Locke and other natural-rights theorists. Partly a response to the Marxist historicist critique of natural rights as an expression of bourgeois class interest, these new rights were subsequently elaborated in the International Covenant on Economic, Social and Cultural Rights (ICESCR). Passed, together with the International Covenant on Civil and Political Rights (ICCPR), by the UN General Assembly in 1966, both Covenants came into force in 1976.

However, in the light of the cultural relativist critique of the UDHR we will be discussing later, it is noteworthy that the 48 states that voted for it included predominantly Hindu India, the Buddhist kingdom of Thailand, largely Buddhist Burma and eight mainly Muslim states. Others were China with its Confucian, Taoist and Buddhist heritage (though the US-backed Nationalist Chinese President Chiang Kai-shek was a convert to Christianity). When the Saudi Arabian representative, Jamil Baroody, objected to the freedom to change one's religion (Article 18), the Pakistani delegate, Zafarullah Khan, responded by quoting a passage from the Koran: 'Let him who chooses to believe, believe, and him who chooses to disbelieve, disbelieve' (Glendon 2002). (Ironically, Baroody was a Lebanese Christian married to an American while Khan, representing a state whose very *raison d'être* was religious identity, belonged to the Ahmadi sect rejected as non-Muslims by Sunni Muslim purists.)

In addition to the UDHR and the two covenants mentioned in Box 10.3, the UN has passed five other global human rights conventions that taken together constitute the main basis for global international human rights law. The five relate to:

- prevention and punishment of genocide (1948);
- elimination of racial discrimination (1965);
- discrimination against women (1979);
- torture and other cruel, inhuman or degrading treatment (1984);
- protection of the rights of children (1989).

However, the most widely ratified of these has been the Convention on the Rights of the Child (191 states by 2002) and the one with the fewest ratifications has been the Convention against Torture (128 by 2002) (Rehman 2003: 476). When it comes to the optional protocols that seek to make states more accountable for their obligations under these treaties, none but the First Optional Protocol to the ICCPR has been ratified by a majority of the state parties.

This reflects the unwillingness of most governments to circumscribe, as they see it, their sovereign rights and be held to more than formal acceptance of these human-rights norms. In 1967 the UN's Economic and Social Council gave its Commission on Human Rights, established in 1946, the right to discuss human-rights violations in particular countries (Resolution 1235) and in 1970 granted it powers to review complaints from individuals in secret (Resolution 1503). These were initially little used (Rehman 2003: 35–45; Donnelly 1999a: 75–6). Set up in the wake of the wave of decolonisation and anti-racism, the new measures were primarily meant to deal with the situation in the remaining isolated racist pariahs – apartheid South Africa, the white-minority regime in Rhodesia and the Portuguese African colonies. While the Commission also addressed human-rights complaints relating to other widely unpopular regimes, such as those of General Pinochet after the 1973 coup in Chile, the Greek colonels' (1967–74) and in the territories occupied by Israel after the 1967 Arab–Israeli War, its activity in the 1970s and after was very selective. It overlooked the worst instances of human-rights violation in the developing world, such as the massacres by the Pakistani military in East Pakistan in 1971, in Uganda under the tyrant Idi Amin in the 1970s, by the communist Khmer Rouge in Cambodia in the 1970s, and the Indonesian army in East Timor in the late 1990s. It also failed to address the deaths of perhaps over three million people in the anti-communist war waged by the US in Indochina until 1973 involving aerial carpet bombing and the widespread use of chemical and biological weapons (Smith 1997: 60; Lindqvist 2001: 346; Blum 2001: 105–7).

From the 1980s the Commission broadened its scope. It set up working groups on Enforced and Involuntary Disappearances (1980) and Arbitrary Detention (1991) and appointed some 27 special rapporteurs with particular thematic mandates, beginning with one on Extra-Judicial, Summary and Arbitrary Execution in 1982 (since 1998 the Pakistani human-rights activist Asma Jahangir) (http://www.unhchr.ch/html/menu2/7/b/tm.htm). It also nominated independent experts with country mandates (Rehman 2003: 39–40), starting in 1979 with the tiny West African state of Equatorial Guinea (its ruthless dictator Francisco Macias

Nguema was overthrown and executed for crimes against humanity in the same year). Three more countries were specified in the 1980s – Guatemala in Central America (1982) and Afghanistan and Iran (1984) – and all but one of the 13 country mandates issued after the end of the Cold War also related to developing countries (the sole exception was the former Yugoslavia in 1992). By 2003 these included a total of eight in Africa, three in the Middle East (Iraq and the Israeli-occupied Palestinian territories joined Iran), three in Asia (Burma and Cambodia joined Afghanistan) and two in Latin America and the Caribbean (Haiti joined Guatemala). Despite the cumbersome and secretive nature of many of the Commission's procedures and the lack of effective sanctions, they have become increasingly utilised. By 2000 the Commission was receiving around 50,000 complaints annually under Resolution 1503 (Sklair 2002: 307), and since its creation the Working Group on Disappearances has considered 50,000 cases from over 70 countries (Rehman 2003: 39).

In addition to the Commission, a separate Human Rights Committee was established under the ICCPR to which state parties had to submit reports. It also dealt with an optional inter-state complaint procedure and, if the relevant state had signed the First Optional Protocol to the ICCPR, with individual complaints. Although like the Commission, its rulings are not binding and it cannot impose sanctions, a majority of developing countries including China, India, Indonesia, Brazil and Nigeria have (like the USA, the UK and Japan), yet to sign the protocol.

The reality is that the UN human-rights bodies have tended to focus their attention either on collapsed states or others ravaged by civil war, like Afghanistan, the former Yugoslavia, Haiti, the Democratic Republic of Congo, Rwanda or Somalia. Post-Cold War international pariahs such as Saddam Hussein's Iraq, isolated regimes such as that in Myanmar (Burma) and others regarded as hostile by the West like Iran and Sudan have also regularly come under scrutiny. However, powerful and influential states have largely ensured that they avoid censure. For instance, India, along with Russia the only country to serve continuously on the Human Rights Commission since its inception, never faced examination over the possible culpability of state officials in occurrences such as the massacre of Sikhs in Delhi in 1984 or of Muslims in Gujarat in 2002. It was also able to defeat an attempt by Pakistan in 1995 to raise the repression of the insurgency in Kashmir. China has faced greater difficulty but has also managed to block a debate of its record.

The proceedings of the 59th session of the Human Rights Commission in 2003 (ECOSOC 2003) reflected these *realpolitik* realities. Apart from Israel, a perennial target of the Arab states and their allies in the old non-aligned bloc of developing countries, it was relatively small and internationally isolated states that again attracted censure. Five motions critical of Israel were passed. Other states reproved were Myanmar, Burundi, Iraq, North Korea, the ex-Soviet republics of Belarus and Turkmenistan, Cuba, Cambodia and Colombia. A draft resolution on the conflict in the Russian region of Chechnya was rejected.

---

box 10.4   human rights and ethnic cleansing

Following the end of the Cold War in the late 1980s, the UN went through its most active phase in setting up institutions to punish the gross abuse of human rights. Shamed by its failure to act to prevent ethnic cleansing in the civil wars in the former Yugoslavia and the genocide in Rwanda, the Security Council passed resolutions establishing International Criminal Tribunals for the former Yugoslavia (in May 1993) and Rwanda (November 1994). Costing over $400 million a year to run (2002/3 figures), the courts based in The Hague and Arusha (Tanzania) had, by the end of 2003, convicted 20 and 12 persons respectively (http://www.un.org/icty/glance/index.htm and http://www.ictr.org/default.htm).

Those convicted include a former Rwandan prime minister and the trial of Slobodan Milosevic, the ex-president of Serbia, began in 2002. Under a Security Council resolution, in January 2002 the UN also agreed with the government of Sierra Leone on the establishment of a Special Court to try those bearing 'greatest responsibility' for serious violations of international humanitarian and local law committed in the course of the country's civil war (http://www.sierra-leone.org/specialcourtagreement.html). By the end of 2003 this court had indicted 13 persons including the former Liberian president, Charles Taylor, in exile in Nigeria after his forced resignation in August 2003.

Ad hoc actions on ex-Yugoslavia, Rwanda and Sierra Leone, discussed in Box 10.4, had all been taken under the mandate of the Security Council as the principal UN organ dealing with peace and security. In July 2002 a new permanent body came into being with jurisdiction over crimes against humanity, war crimes and genocide. The proposal for an International Criminal Court (ICC), long stymied by the Cold War, was finally approved at a UN conference in Rome in 1998 by a vote of 120–7. Although only the US, unhappy about exposing its nationals to any international jurisdiction, together with Israel, China and four Arab states are believed to have voted against, another 21 countries abstained in the secret vote and it was four years before it achieved the necessary ratification by 60 states (Weller 2002: 697). The jurisdiction of the court only applies if the state on whose territory a situation being investigated has taken place, or one whose nationality is possessed by the person being investigated, is a party to the Rome Statute or has accepted the ICC's competence. Cases can be referred by any state that is party to the Statute, the UN Security Council or by the Chief Prosecutor on the authority of the court (http://www.icc-cpi.int/php/show.php?id=jurisdiction).

Though its judges and chief officers were appointed in 2003, and it is potentially an innovation in international human-rights law of immense significance, there is a danger that the ICC could prove stillborn if major states persist in their opposition. It is not only the US, the post-Cold War world hyperpower, which has not ratified it but also Russia, China, India and Japan. While more than 50 African, Asian, Latin American and Caribbean states, including Brazil, Nigeria and South Africa, were among the 92 that had done so by the end of 2003, the majority of developing countries still had not. Across the Middle East and South and South East Asia, the only two countries to have done so were ones that had witnessed some of the worse human rights abuses of the past quarter of a century – Cambodia and Afghanistan (http://untreaty.unorg/ENGLISH/bible/englishinternetbible/partI/chapterXVIII/treaty10.asp). Nevertheless, considering the attitude of many powerful states and the record of gross human rights abuse since World War II, the probability is that the ICC's main activity will be in relation to developing countries.

Though the efficacy of the developing UN human-rights regime might still be doubtful, it has helped promote global awareness of human rights. This is reflected in:

- the spread of regional human rights systems (considered later in the chapter); and
- the growth in non-governmental human rights organisations. Paralleling the worldwide growth in non-governmental organisations (NGOs) – their number almost doubled in the 1990s to 44,000 (UNDP 2000: 8) – by 1993 there were 168 international human-rights NGOs and 1,500 attended the UN World Conference on Human Rights in Vienna that year (Freeman 2002: 143). In 2003 over 200 NGOs had consultative status at the UN Human Rights Commission (ECOSOC 2003: 478–80).

Given this growing global awareness of human rights, is it possible to come up with a credible measure of the observance of rights that is applicable across developing countries? In the early 1990s the UN Development Programme sought to develop a human and political freedom index to supplement the annual Human Development Index (HDI) that it launched in 1990. The attempt was abandoned because it was felt that such an index would necessarily be based on 'qualitative judgements, not quantifiable empirical data' and therefore could not serve as a viable tool for policy advocacy (UNDP 2000: 91).

box 10.5   freedom house and measuring human rights

Misgivings about possibly crude subjective analysis have not prevented other organisations from producing measurements. The most comprehensive effort is the annual global survey of political rights and civil liberties carried out by Freedom House (FH). Partly funded by the US government, FH came into being at the onset of the Cold War as 'an outspoken advocate of the Marshall Plan and NATO' (http://www.freedom house.org/aboutfh/index.htm). In 2003 a former director of the US Central Intelligence Agency (James Woolsey) chaired its Board of Trustees. Using a checklist derived in large measure from the UDHR, its *Freedom in the World* survey assesses states, categorising them as Free, Partly Free and Not Free. Its conclusions have been used to inform surveys of human rights in the developing world (e.g. Haynes 2002: 165–82, UNDP 2003: 28), and the results of the 2003 survey for states in the different regions of the developing world (http://www.freedomhouse.org/research/survey2004.htm) are tabulated in Table 10.1.

Table 10.1   'Freedom' in developing countries – the Freedom House perspective, 2003

Region	Free	Partly free	Not free	Total
Latin America and the Caribbean	21	10	2	33
Asia Pacific (excluding Japan, Australia and New Zealand)	14	11	11	36
Sub-Saharan Africa	11	20	17	48
The Middle East and North Africa (including Turkey)	1	6	12	19
Total	47	47	42	136

Source: http://www.freedomhouse.org/research/survey2004.htm. Note: The survey gives the USA, as well as 22 West European states, Canada, Australia and New Zealand, the top rating (1.0) (Japan gets 1.5).

cultural relativism

The FH survey reflects the mainstream of the international human rights tradition in focusing on the rights of the individual and particularly his or her civil and political rights. This western emphasis on the individual as the right-holder was highlighted in Thomas Jefferson's original rough draft of the American Declaration of Independence (1776): 'We hold these truths to be sacred and undeniable; that all men are created equal and *independent*, that from that equal creation they derive rights inherent and inalienable, among which are the preservation of life, and liberty, and the pursuit of happiness' (Jefferson, 1950). More than two hundred years later the Declaration and Programme of Action adopted by the 1993 Vienna Conference (http://www.unhchr.ch/tbs/doc.nsf/view40?SearchView) echoed Jefferson's words in: 'recognizing and affirming that all human rights derive from the dignity and worth inherent in the human person, and that human person is the central subject of human rights and fundamental freedoms ...'

Yet the Conference itself was marked by intense controversy over whether human rights should start from individual rights, a debate centring on the notion of cultural relativism. The cultural relativists rejected the idea that there could be a universally applicable standard of human rights based on some universally held sense of moral rules. Instead they argued that moral claims, even if they shared common sensibilities, derived from and gained their validity in particular cultural contexts. For that reason, the concept of universal human rights evolved through the western tradition was itself the product of a particular culture.

---

box 10.6   johan galtung and human rights

Johan Galtung (1998: 219) has described the debate between postmodern and cultural relativist perspectives as the dialectic between 'I-cultures' and 'we-culture'. 'I-cultures' begin with the freedom of the individual to make choices without being coerced while 'we-cultures' see individuals as both enmeshed in and the product of a dense web of social relations. Galtung goes on to identify 'I-cultures' primarily with the affluent West and 'we-cultures' with the 'Third World'. While this may be oversimplifying the distinction by glossing over aspects of both types of cultures found in Western and developing societies, it is the way many proponents of the relativist viewpoint perceive it. As a 1991 Singapore government White Paper put it, 'Nation before community and society before self' (quoted in Hurrell 1999: 295).

The idea of western human rights being based on unattached modern individuals alien to the tradition-bound societies of the developing world is a misrepresentation. It relies on conflating the 'modern' with the 'western', as well as holding tradition in non-western societies to be immutable. To deal with the first point, while the focus on the individual, both as a claimant and violator of rights, has been traced back to the Judaeo-Christian notion of sin (Evans 1998: 16), the salience of human rights was a response to political, social and economic change. As Amartya Sen (1997) has pointed out, we don't find the idea of individual liberty in ancient Europe. Besides, the pre-20th-century interpretation of 'universal' human rights in the West fell, as previously noted, considerably short of being genuinely universal. When it comes to tradition, Jack Donnelly has shown why, cultural traditions being no more than socially-created legacies, traditional practices should not simply be assumed to possess continuing relevance in modern conditions (1999b: 81, 87). For instance, in South Asia, in spite – and partly because – of the rise of

Hindu nationalism as a modern political force, '*dharmic* India increasingly belongs to the past' (Chiriyankandath 1993: 259).

---

box 10.7   the 1981 banjul african charter of human and peoples' rights

The 1981 Banjul African Charter of Human and Peoples' Rights, with 53 state parties the most subscribed regional human-rights treaty, has been seen as embodying the 'we' rather than the 'I' approach to the recognition of rights. Following the UDHR in referring to individual rights it also features: 'solidarity within the group, the symbiosis between the individual and society and between the basic community (family, ethnic group, village) and the wider society, including the state' (Mbaya 1996: 73).

In doing so the Banjul Charter was not only reflecting what were seen as characteristics of the African social personality. At a time when most African states had been independent for barely twenty years and apartheid persisted in southern Africa, there was also a continuing political concern with both nation-building and the right of peoples to self-determination.

The cultural relativist argument remains influential across the developing world. But it is in Muslim countries and in East Asia that the cultural relativist argument has possessed greatest currency. The FH (2004: 5,7) survey identifies only two 'Free' countries with Muslim majorities, both West African – Mali and Senegal – and holds up Israel (excluding the territories occupied by Israel after 1967) as the only 'Free' country in the Middle East. Unsurprisingly, such a damning evaluation of the Muslim world scarcely accords with the self-perceptions of proponents of a distinctively Muslim polity and society. Abu'l Ala' Mawdudi (1903–79), the founder of the Jama'at-i Islami movement in South Asia, saw the rights conferred by God in the Koran as incomparably superior to the UDHR: 'The charter and the proclamations and the resolutions of the United Nations cannot be compared with the rights sanctioned by God; because the former is not applicable to anybody while the latter is applicable to every believer' (Mawdudi 1980).

The crux of the problem lies in the clash between the Muslim understanding of human rights, especially as held by dogmatists like Mawdudi, and the UDHR. Let us take three areas of controversy – freedom of expression, women's rights and freedom of conscience. On the first, while Mawdudi sees the right to freedom of expression 'for the sake of propagating virtue and righteousness' as not just a right but an Islamic obligation, he also denies that it gives anyone the right to use abusive or offensive language or propagate 'evil and wickedness'. On the second, the only specific right Mawdudi sees Islam as giving a woman is respect for her chastity. The 1990 Cairo Declaration on Human Rights in Islam issued by a conference of foreign ministers from member states of the

Islamic Conference Organisation, contradicted Article 16 of the UDHR as it omitted any religious bar – while rejecting restrictions on the right to marry (Article 5 of the Cairo Declaration) (Mayer 1999: 204). Third, while Article 18 of the UDHR gives everyone the right to 'change his religion or belief', conservative Muslims regards apostasy as unacceptable and punishable, even by death. In 1985 Mahmud Muhammad Taha, the 76-year-old leader of the liberal Republican Brotherhood movement in Sudan, was hanged as an apostate by the Ja'far Numeiri regime (Mayer 1999: 170–1).

Liberal and rationalist currents in Islam, represented by men such as the Iranian scholar Abdolkarim Sorush and the Sudanese Abdullahi A. An-Na'im, a one-time Republican Brother, reflect a different perspective from what has been considered here (Mayer 1999: 44; An-Na'im 2001). However, they remain on the periphery of what is regarded as mainstream Islamic discourse by both governments and the officially recognised religious establishment in most Muslim countries. The Cairo Declaration qualifies all the rights and freedoms it stipulates by holding them subject to the Islamic Shari'ah. Similarly, the constitution of the Islamic Republic drafted after the 1979 revolution in Iran made all rights enjoyed by citizens subject to Islamic criteria (Mayer 1999: 70). The secular international human-rights discourse therefore continues to pose a challenge to the conception of human rights in many Muslim societies. To cite just one instance, Article 37 of the 1993 Vienna Declaration calls for 'the eradication of any conflicts which may arise between the rights of women and the harmful effects of certain traditional or customary practices, cultural prejudices and religious extremism'.

If Islam posed one kind of challenge to the idea of universal human rights, another that attracted considerable attention, until its abrupt eclipse after the 1997 East Asian economic crisis, was the 'Asian values' argument. In the run-up to the 1993 Vienna Conference, an Asian intergovernmental meeting in Thailand adopted the Bangkok Declaration (http://www.thinkcentre.org/article.cfm?ArticleID=830). Though, unlike the Cairo Declaration, it reaffirmed the UN Charter and the UDHR, Article 8 of the Declaration set out the case for cultural relativism:

> while human rights are universal in nature they must be considered in the context of a dynamic and evolving process of international norm-setting, bearing in mind the significance of national and regional particularities and various historical, cultural and religious backgrounds.

The Declaration upheld the principles of non-interference in the internal affairs of states and the right of countries to determine their own political systems, and rejected the politicization of human rights and the linking of development assistance to human rights. In affirming the interdependence, indivisibility and equality of all categories of rights, it was noticeable that it mentioned economic, social and cultural rights before civil and political ones, reversing the order in the UDHR.

---

box 10.8   'asian values' and human rights

Favoured by many East Asian governments, the leading proponents of Asian values were Mahathir Mohamad, prime minister of Malaysia from 1981 to 2003, and Lee Kuan Yew, premier of neighbouring Singapore from 1959 to 1990. As two of the central figures credited with managing the East Asian economic miracle, their stance could be portrayed as intellectual window-dressing for economically successful authoritarian government. While their idea of Asian values depended on being assertively anti-western for a great deal of its popular appeal it could, ironically, itself be criticised as Eurocentric (Tatsuo 1999: 30, Sen 1997) and its advocates have even been termed 'reverse Orientalists' (Thompson 2003).

Even if the official Asian-values discourse may have become discredited, there is still a problem to be addressed. The homomorphic equivalents of human rights in the main cultural traditions of Asia, those of India and China, appear antithetical to any notion of uniformly applicable, commonly held rights. In Brahmanic Hinduism, a person's *dharma* (Sanskrit: duty related to sustaining the moral universe) was determined by his or her position in a hierarchical network of relationships (Chiriyankandath 1993: 247). Traditional Chinese society emphasised an analogous pursuit of harmony at all levels through hierarchically ordered social interaction (Donnelly 1999b: 79); again a notion seemingly incompatible with the egalitarian individualism of the modern human-rights discourse. On the other hand, India and China are two of the world's fastest-growing major economies at the beginning of the 21st century and both societies are undergoing rapid social and economic change. If it is accepted that the rise of human rights in the West was primarily the outcome of such change rather than a cultural artefact, than it should follow that human rights need not be all that different in modernising Asia.

Amartya Sen suggests that the West *v*. East debate is a sterile one and it is more fruitful is to identify the constituents in different cultures of the compound idea that is freedom (1997). Recognising that societies may undergo similar processes of change differently, these constituents can then be utilised to indigenise the modern human-rights discourse – even

Donnelly admits the need for 'weak cultural relativism' (1999b: 83). Another argument for adapting rather than simply adopting universal human rights is that a uniformly secular conception of human rights may not be capable of inspiring the commitment of religious believers, who still constitute the great majority of people in the developing world (An-Na'im 2001).

In sum, the case for the relevance of the UDHR is a strong one. If we disregard the government apologists, cultural relativists have valid points to make but some are blinkered by their obsession with anti-imperialism. As Michael Freeman pithily puts it, their problem is that they seem 'to oppose the universalization of freedom in the name of a universal right to freedom' (2002: 108). It could be argued that universal human rights are an especially necessary safeguard for small and vulnerable developing countries in a post-Cold War era where many are apprehensive of western dominance and, particularly, of the unilateral exercise of power by the United States. Article 5 of the Vienna Declaration sought to strike such a necessary balance between cultural relativism and universal rights:

> While the significance of national and regional particularities and various historical, cultural and religious backgrounds must be borne in mind, it is the duty of States, regardless of their political, economic and cultural systems, to promote and protect all human rights and fundamental freedoms. (http://www.uhhchr.ch/huridocda/huridoca. nsf/(Symbol)/A.CONF.157.23.En?OpenDocument)

globalisation and the right to development

It is only relatively recently that development has been seen as covering much more than economic growth. One milestone was the UN's adoption in 1986 of the Declaration on the Right to Development. Another was the launch of the Human Development Index in 1990. The Vienna Declaration also addressed the issue of reconciling human rights with development. While admitting that 'democracy, development and respect for human rights and fundamental freedoms are interdependent and mutually reinforcing', it asserted that 'the lack of development may not be invoked to justify the abridgement of internationally recognised human rights' (Section I, points 8 and 10).

A significant trend in Western liberal thought has been to associate the free market and economic development with human rights. This is reflected in, for instance, the FH survey. It notes that while 'states that are most successful in producing wealth are almost uniformly free', the

---

box 10.9   various kinds of rights

Human rights theorists have long sought to distinguish between various kinds of rights. One of the most important of these distinctions has been that drawn between negative rights, which require the state and its citizens to refrain from doing anything that erodes the freedom of others, and positive rights, which citizens can claim from the state. Economic and social rights belonged to the second category and it was argued that it was unreasonable to put such costly rights on the same footing as relatively cost free negative rights (Cranston 1973). However, in the real world such a distinction is hard to maintain. The securing of certain basic rights (life, security and subsistence), which may be seen as positive is indispensable if people are to be able to effectively lay claim to, ostensibly negative, civil and political rights (Shue 1996). This goes to the heart of the symbiotic relationship between human development and human rights. Donnelly is right to say human rights cannot be reduced to a guarantee of mere survival (1999b: 75) but survival is the necessary beginning for the exercise of rights.

---

level of freedom is significantly lower in the poorest countries – only three out of the 29 with a gross national per capita income of under \$300 are judged to be 'Free' (2004: 10).

So what is the connection between a country's economic record and freedom? Sen (1999a: 91) finds no evidence of a causal relationship between economic performance and the existence of political rights in a country. However, he goes on to note that economic development involves much more than merely growth in gross national product. It is in this connection, referring to economic and subsistence security, that he makes his famous claim 'that no substantial famine has ever occurred in any country with a democratic form of government and a relatively free press' (1999a: 92). India, where there has been no major famine since independence, provides the best example and Sen contrasts this both with the regular famines that occurred under British rule (2–3 million died in the last of these in his native Bengal in 1943) and the Chinese experience. Following Chairman Mao's disastrous Great Leap Forward up to 30 million people died in China between 1958 and 1961 (Dreze and Sen 1995: 75). The famines in Ethiopia and Sudan in the mid-1980s and in Somalia in the early 1990s further corroborate Sen's thesis. Democratic and civil rights allow both for early warning of dire need and incentives for corrective measures. Beyond this political rights also afford a society the freedom to define what its economic needs are (Sen 1999a: 96).

Another problem, as Malaysia's Mahathir Mohamad put it with characteristic hyperbole, is that 'markets corrupt, and absolute markets corrupt absolutely' (quoted in Ghai 1998: 262). The reduction of a swollen state sector through cutbacks and privatisations, whether in the developing world or in post-communist states, often just replaced one source of corruption with other, often more predatory, forms. In a poorly regulated market environment, this often left people belonging to the more vulnerable sectors of society even less able to survive. Yet as increasing numbers of people from the developing world fleeing from war or escaping poverty seek to enter Western Europe, North America and Australia they find the barriers constantly being raised. Western governments have sought to interpret the right to asylum enshrined in Article 14 of the UDHR and the 1951 Convention on the Status of Refugees in ever-narrower terms in order to shut out those who have strikingly been termed the 'vagabonds' of globalisation (Bauman 1998: 93).

Modern human rights came into being to address the twin challenges of the state and the market economy. In facing a third, globalisation, it finds itself caught between the two. Especially in the straitened context of developing countries, the shrinkage in the state's capacity and preparedness to enhance human rights by providing social goods has left a vacuum. If the market does not see it as its job to protect human rights and the state finds itself imprisoned by the global logic of the market, to whom can people look to secure their economic and social rights? One response has been the privatisation of human rights (Galtung 1998: 215), with the exponential growth in human-rights and other NGOs referred to previously. However, this helps to illuminate the problem more than provide a solution. NGOs operate unevenly through the developing world, in part reflecting the differential development of organised civil society (Haynes 1997: 6,18). They are stronger in Latin America, parts of Asia (India, the Philippines) and sub-Saharan Africa (for example, South

---

box 10.10   globalisation and human rights

Globalisation is often said to be diminishing the scope for states in the developing world to intervene effectively to support the struggle of their citizens to claim basic economic and social rights effectively (see chapter 13 for a discussion of globalisation on developing countries). The architecture of the international human rights system has been built on the basis of the Westphalian state system but that system itself is now, arguably, being eroded by economic globalisation (Falk 1999: 190). In the 1980s and 1990s the International Monetary Fund (IMF) and the World Bank pressed structural adjustment programmes (SAPs) upon highly indebted poor countries as a condition for new loans – no less than 42 in Africa alone (Monshipouri 2001: 42). These SAPs embodied the Washington Consensus (so called with reference to three powerful institutions based in Washington – the IMF, the World Bank and the US government). It reflected the neo-liberal economic perspective that governments should cut back their social expenditure and subsidies for the poor and concentrate on instituting policies geared to the global marketplace and attracting foreign investment. Social and economic rights received short shrift in such a climate and, as one study noted, 'compared to the start of the SAP era, many Africans are both poorer and less healthy' (Monshipouri 2001: 42).

Africa) than in the communist states in East Asia, the greater part of Africa and the Middle East. In addition, the international human rights network tends to be dominated by organisations headquartered in the West, such as Amnesty International (UK) and Human Rights Watch (US). Such bodies are liable to be labelled as paternalist and even imperialist by their critics in the developing world, not least governments.

In many ways an outcome of globalisation, as a response to it the contemporary expression of universal human rights remains woefully inadequate. The most important reason for this is the dominance of capital in the contemporary international system. Multinational companies and international financial institutions (IFIs) like the IMF and the World Bank exercise far greater power and influence than the great majority of developing countries. The IFIs can be seen as supporting an international structure of economic dominance that helps limit the spread of effective social and economic rights across the developing world (Thomas 1998: 182). They are also scarcely democratic with, for instance, the Group of Seven (G7) leading industrialised countries accounting for 45 per cent of the vote at the IMF (http://www.imf.org/external/np/sec/memdir/members.htm) and between 43 and 52 per cent in the main constituents of the World Bank (http://www.worldbank.org/). Though the World Trade Organisation (WTO) operates on the basis of consensus, many poorer countries are handicapped by being unable to even fund permanent delegations to the WTO. On the other hand, delegations from the rich states routinely include – or cooperate closely with – business representatives, and the top officials of IFIs often come from – or subsequently move to – international private corporations and banks (Evans 2001: 98–9; Stiglitz 2002: 19). Given such a decision-making environment, it would be surprising if the IFIs were to prioritise issues such as human rights in their process.

The striking contrast between the perspectives and debates at the annual World Economic and Social Forums highlight the difficulties in constructing an effective dialogue on rights between those who demand them and those with much of the power to grant them. The overwhelming concern for the first, which has brought together world political and business leaders at the Swiss Alpine resort of Davos since 1970, is sustaining economic growth and the expansion of the global market. For the radical activists and NGOs from across the developing and developed worlds who meet at the much newer parallel World Social Forum, held in Porto Alegre in Brazil for three years before it moved to the Indian city of Mumbai in 2004, the priorities are rather different. According to one of those attending the Mumbai Forum, the Indian writer and activist Arundhati Roy (2001:

215) 'the only thing worth globalizing is dissent'. Opposed to what they see as the neo-liberal globalisation favoured by the giant multinational corporations and their allies in the governments of the wealthy global North, they seek a more economically and socially just global order. (For more on this topic, see chapter 12 in this volume.)

The UN has sought to bridge the gap. At Davos in 1999 Secretary-General Kofi Annan proposed a Global Compact under which businesses would pledge to support human rights (including labour rights and the abolition of child labour) and be environmentally responsible (http:// www.unglobalcompact.org/un/gc/unweb.nsf/content/thenine.htm). But at the 2004 Social Forum the Iranian human-rights lawyer and Nobel Peace laureate Shirin Ebadi struck a more radical note. Describing extreme poverty as the violation of human rights, she called for reform of the UN, the WTO and IFIs, and for economic and social rights to be made a matter of international justice (http://www.fidh.org/article.php3?id_article=452).

humanitarian intervention and institutionalising human rights

In 1899 Rudyard Kipling, Britain's leading poet of empire, wrote 'The White Man's Burden' to celebrate the US occupation of the Philippines. A century later – and barely half a century after the Philippines and other colonies across Asia, Africa and the Caribbean began emerging as independent countries – it seemed as if human rights might form an important part of the rationale for a new era of 'benign' Western imperialism in the developing world (Ferguson 2001). In the 1990s and early 2000s Western armies again engaged in missions, at least partly justified on the basis of humanitarianism, in almost a dozen countries.

The UN became much more active in armed peacekeeping after the end of the Cold War. A total of 41 missions were approved between 1988 and 2003, compared to just 13 in the previous 40 years (http://www. un.org/Depts/dpko/dpko/home.shtml). Four-fifths of these missions (the main exceptions were in former Yugoslavia) were in developing countries, most arising out of some form of civil war. In the past 15 years the UN has deployed forces in 15 sub-Saharan African countries – some of the poorest countries in the most impoverished region in the developing world. This is scarcely coincidental. It underscores the political repercussions and human-rights consequences of being at the bottom of a hierarchical international state system and a lopsided global economy.

This leads us on to an uncomfortable aspect of modern human rights. Having initially arisen as a feature of the European response to modernity, it is not surprising that implicit in documents such as the International Human Rights Covenants is a 'hegemonic political model something very much like the liberal democratic welfare state of Western Europe' (Donnelly 1999a: 84). Not just intervention to avert a humanitarian disaster but also the intention to introduce such a model could therefore perhaps be presented by powerful Western states as the corollary of their commitment to human rights and political freedom. However, in rejecting the US administration's effort to defend the primarily Anglo-US invasion and occupation of Iraq in 2003 on humanitarian grounds (that is, it had resulted in the overthrow of a ruthless dictator accused of large-scale human right abuses and made democracy possible), the international NGO Human Rights Watch (HRW) made an important qualification. Its 2004 report asserted that such intervention can only be justified in the event of 'ongoing or imminent genocide, or comparable mass slaughter or loss of life' (http://hrw.org/wr2k4/3.htm). In calling for the UN in particular to establish such clear criteria, HRW recognised the dangers of the principle of humanitarian intervention becoming discredited through its expedient use by powerful states to serve their own national interest.

---

box 10.11   external interventions and human rights

Whether in Africa, the Middle East, South East Asia, the Balkans or the Caribbean, the cause of human rights has been repeatedly invoked in support of military interventions. The US sent forces to Somalia (1992), Haiti (1994) and Liberia (2003) on humanitarian grounds. Similar actions were carried out by Britain in Sierra Leone (2000), France in Côte d'Ivoire (2003) and the Democratic Republic of Congo (leading a European Union force in 2003), Australia in East Timor (1999) and the North Atlantic Treaty Organisation in Bosnia (1995) and Kosovo (1999). Humanitarian concerns were also highlighted to reinforce the case for military actions primarily taken on other grounds. This was the case with the expulsion of Iraqi forces from Kuwait by the US-led international coalition (1991), the invasion to oust the al-Qaeda terrorist threat from Taliban-ruled Afghanistan (2001) and the invasion of Iraq to overthrow Saddam Hussein with his alleged weapons of mass destruction (2003).

This is especially so following the September 2001 terrorist attacks and the subsequent 'war on terror' proclaimed by the Bush administration in the US. The international focus shifted to security rather than human rights and development. The detention since January 2002 of hundreds of unidentified Muslims deemed 'enemy combatants' (about 660 from 44 countries in January 2004) at the US base in Guantanamo Bay in Cuba has come to symbolise the way in which human-rights standards have been devalued (LCHR 2003: chapter 4; Dyer 2004). The prisoners, although mainly Afghans, Pakistanis, Saudis and Yemenis, include nationals of another 40 countries taken to Cuba from places as far afield as Afghanistan, Bosnia and Gambia. Not publicly identified, they have been denied access to any legal process (in apparent contravention of Articles 7, 9 and 10 of the UDHR). Their treatment, as well as other anti-terrorist actions adopted by the US, has given the cue to governments across the world, including many in developing countries, also to seize the opportunity to introduce Draconian security measures, using the global threat of terrorism as a pretext (LCHR 2003: chapter 5).

Returning to the theme of humanitarian military intervention, the fact is that even when it can be justified, it cannot serve as anything more than the equivalent of famine or disaster relief. One sign of this has been the growing reluctance of the UN since the mid-1990s to initiate peacekeeping missions. Chastened by the relative failures of three of its biggest operations in Somalia (1992–95), former Yugoslavia (1992–95) and Angola (1988–99), it has also been prompted by the need to scale back escalating expenditure. Only three missions were launched in the four years from 2000 (this included one in East Timor that represented the extension of an existing commitment).

Since the end of the Cold War the majority of western military interventions have been undertaken under a UN Security Council mandate but not under UN command (for example, the NATO forces occupying Kosovo after 1999 and as part of the International Security Assistance Force in Afghanistan since 2002). Others have not even had UN authorisation (the attacks on Kosovo in 1999 and Iraq in 2003). Unlike these, the UN peacekeeping missions typically involve military forces from many developing countries – at the end of 2003 they included the ten largest contributors, accounting for more than three-fifths of the 45,815 blue helmets deployed on 13 missions around the world (http://www.un.org?depts/dpko/dpko/contributors/December2003Countrysu mmary.pdf). Even though they still have to rely on the major western contributors to the UN system for the greater part of their funding, they are therefore not seen as primarily western undertakings.

This is not the case with the UN human-rights agencies headquartered in western capitals. In 2003 developing countries on the Human Rights Commission succeeded in passing a resolution expressing concern that 60 per cent of the staff of the UN High Commission for Human Rights were West European (ECOSOC 2003: 271–3). The bias in personnel and, from a critical perspective, outlook is also evident in international human-rights NGOs. In making this point Sklair (2002: 316–17) suggests that, while efforts at change may now be under way, historically, in order to make an impact within capitalist societies such elitism and acceptance of the liberal emphasis on civil and political rights was probably necessary.

Yet many of the most widespread abuses of human rights in poor societies do not arise from an arbitrary state's deliberate effort to deny rights to its citizens. For instance, at the beginning of 2004 violence perpetrated by lawless armed groups, whether political, ethnic or criminal, disfigured public life across the developing world, from Columbia to Liberia, Congo, Afghanistan and Indonesia. Such violence featured in most countries that witnessed forceful international humanitarian intervention and seems likely to loom large in the work of the new ICC. In 2003 the Chief Prosecutor, Luis Moreno-Ocampo selected the mass killings by ethnic militias in the Ituri region of the strife-torn Democratic Republic of Congo, a party to the ICC, as the first situation to monitor closely (http://www.icc-cpi.int/otp1030909_prosecutor_speech.pdf). In December 2003 neighbouring Uganda became the first ICC member to request an investigation. In 17 years of fighting in the north of the country, the rebel Lord's Resistance Army had been accused of summary executions and ritual killings, and the widespread use of torture and mass rape. Thousands of abducted children were said to have been used as soldiers, forced labour and sex slaves (http://www.un.org/News/Press/docs/2004/afr821.doc.htm).

More commonly human rights abuses arise from a context of mass poverty, ineffectual state institutions, and the unregulated or poorly regulated activities of business corporations, often multinationals. Oppressive and discriminative culturally- or religiously-sanctioned practices such as the caste system in India, male and female circumcision in the Middle East and Africa and discrimination against women in a variety of cultures can also be blamed. This is in part why increasing emphasis is being put on building up effective regional and national human rights institutions and infrastructure across the developing world.

Over the past 40 years several regions have followed the example set by the 1950 European Convention for the Protection of Human Rights and Fundamental Freedoms and the establishment of a European Commission (1954–98) and Court of Human Rights (1959). An Inter-American Commission was established in 1959 and the African Charter adopted in 1981. However, neither the American or African systems are as well established as their European precursor (Donnelly 1998: 72–8). It was only in January 2004, 23 years after the signing of the Charter, that an African Court on Human and People's Rights came into being (http://www.fidh.org/article.php3?id_article=450).

Nevertheless, this is in advance of the Middle East and Asia and the Pacific where there are still no such bodies. A Commission established by the Arab League in 1968 has done little, although an NGO initiative started in 1983 and now based in Egypt, the Arab Organization for Human Rights, has been more active. In South and South East Asia greater headway has been made in setting up national human rights commissions. Such bodies came into being in India and Indonesia in 1993, Malaysia (1999) and Thailand (2001) (one had already been established in the Philippines with the constitution passed in 1987 after the overthrow of the dictator Ferdinand Marcos) (Mohamad 2002: 238–9). Primarily a response to the new international salience of issues of human rights and good governance after the Cold War, the purpose was unambiguously stated by a spokesman for the then-ruling Congress (I) Party in India in 1993. He said the country's National Human Rights Commission (NHRC) provided 'an effective answer to the politically motivated international criticism' (Chiriyankandath 1993: 260). It is worth noting, however, that while the impact of the NHRC so far is limited, not least by India's notoriously overburdened legal system, it does afford a legal route for turning 'abstract rights into economic and social realities' (Sklair 2002: 310). In addition, the various truth-and-reconciliation commissions established in states that emerged from authoritarian rule in the 1980s and 1990s, most notably in post-apartheid South Africa in 1995, also provide proof of how some developing countries now seek to break new ground in addressing human rights (13 are listed in UNDP 2000: 72). Overall, however, the main burden of asserting human rights in the developing world will continue to fall upon the human-rights activists, political and legal campaigners, the media, NGOs and other manifestations of civil society that provide it with its indispensable foot soldiers.

conclusion

The globalisation of the modern human rights discourse that intensified after the Cold War threw up huge challenges for the developing world. Some, as we saw in the debate surrounding cultural relativism, arise out of the exploitation of ideological conflicts, between human rights as the modern 'good' and religious and cultural values. Others from the international political and economic inequality of states that put formidable obstacles in the path of the poor majority in so-called developing countries actually being able to claim the right to development. Humanitarian intervention can be seen as an extreme solution to both sets of problems but poses others of *realpolitik* and self-interest, and the potential for the denial of justice and freedom. On the other hand, with the autonomy of the poorer and weaker states in the international system shrinking as a consequence of globalisation, the capacity to safeguard the broad range of human rights through domestic action is limited.

It seems clear that the neo-liberal idea that human rights can be produced simply by introducing democratic politics and the free market is seriously flawed (Freeman 2002: 176). The empirical evidence suggests that the reverse may be the case: emancipative values that help determine how effective democracy is (Welzel et al. 2003: 366). However, it seems difficult to avoid the conclusion that human rights are only meaningful provided that individuals have access to what can be described as 'the ways and means of civil society' (O'Byrne 2003: 386). Awareness of the symbiosis of different kinds of rights – civil, political, economic, social and cultural – is necessary to create the essential synergy for the world's poor to have the prospect of realising such rights (UNDP 2000: 73).

While there is an inescapable contradiction in the simultaneous promotion of economic liberalisation, democracy and human rights in developing countries, the freedom to make choices is arguably fundamental to the exercise of any kinds of rights. When it comes to the great majority of people living in the developing world, their rights are restricted by the limits on their capacity and freedom to choose. This is why enhancing capability is seen as crucial to the right to human development (Fukuda-Parr 2003).

In the context of globalisation such enhancement cannot take place domestically in developing countries without fundamental changes in the international system. It requires integrating notions of care and responsibility with that of rights (Robinson 1998: 75). At a global level Galtung (1998: 227) argues that the erosion of national sovereignty and statehood, particularly pronounced in the weaker states in the developing world, necessitates a concept of global citizenship. This idea found an echo in the UNDP's annual *Human Development Report* focusing on human rights. It included a recommendation for a global commission on human rights in global governance to consider, among other things, 'human rights safeguards in global economic agreements and secure a fair global economic system' (UNDP 2000: 13).

In short, at the start of the 21st century, the prospects for significant progress in such a direction appear bleak. For much of the developing world realising the universal character of human rights remains a distant hope, if not quite a chimera.

11
gender and development
shirin m. rai

This chapter outlines the various feminist interventions in the debates on development over time.[1] It suggests that: (1) these debates broadened our understanding of the practical and strategic needs of women and men in different contexts; and (2) the feminist engagements with theoretical debates and development policy-making structures secured a valuable and critical space for women within development projects. I suggest, however, that these interventions were and largely continue to work within the liberal framework, and that this makes certain strategies of empowerment of women feasible, while at the same time closing off other alternative spaces. The conclusion is that a focus on power relations within any socio-economic system would need to address not only issues of empowerment for women but also the power relations within which both men and women work and live.

introduction

After World War II, the first decade of development saw an emphasis on two sets of initiatives by the United Nations and developed ('First World') countries. The first was foreign aid, tied to the expansion of markets and support of export-oriented economic projects within the poor countries. International market rationality was at the heart of aid projects in this context. Technical training, capital-intensive investments, mechanisation of agriculture, and the building of communications infrastructures formed the list of priorities. The impact of these policies would be, the story went, the 'trickle down' effect of development. But see Toth (1980: 127–47) for an analysis of the way in which cotton-based monocultural economic development was encouraged in Egypt by both US and Soviet aid, and despite some land reforms and state help to farmers, led to increased dependence of the country on both the western and eastern blocs.

The second set of initiatives resulted from a welfare agenda in the context of crises – aid to tide over 'Third World' countries coping with natural disasters, famine or wars. The overall aim was to ameliorate the worst of the hunger and disease that made 'Third World' countries poor participants in the international economy (Burnell 1997).

In sum, during the first UN Decade of Development, the major international institutions of development took shape within the liberal capitalist framework. Further, these institutions worked within the context of diffusion politics – in effect, the task was to tie in the developing countries into international capitalist trade regimes. The promise was that via the 'trickle down effect', sustained growth in the western developed economies would be duplicated in the 'developing world'. Aid became an important means for this process of integration. However, as Bayart (1993: 79–81) points out, in Africa aid fuelled the corruption within the state and its elites. Considerable amounts of aid were channelled through private interests, and state-imposed duties even on humanitarian aid were used to increase the revenue of the state. The one exception to such corruption was Tanzania under President Nyerere.

Other planks of this modernisation model of development included the building of economic infrastructure in developing countries, as well as direct capitalist investment.

women in development

In the debates about development in the first Development Decade, women became visible as a group only in specific contexts. This was evident in the ways in which the growing body of United Nations (UN) Conventions focused on the liberal welfare conception of women's rights (see chapter 10 for a wider discussion on human rights). The UN Conventions of particular concern to women during this period were:

- the 1949 Convention for the Suppression of Traffic in Persons and the Exploitation of Prostitution of Others;
- the 1951 Equal Remuneration for Men and Women Workers for Work of Equal Value;
- the 1952 Convention on the Political Rights of Women (Wallace with March 1991: 1).

As far as development strategies were concerned, women appeared most prominently in debates on population control. Women were the 'targets' of most population-control programmes sponsored by national and international agencies. Their education also became an issue in this context, as did their health needs. In most other respects, women, like other marginalised groups, were aggregated into 'the people' of the 'Third World'. Their visibility in some contexts was not accidental – constructed gender relations framed them; they were primary workers in the reproduction of labour, and as such important to the ways in which they fitted in with the nationalist and international agendas for population control (Davin 1992). However, there was on most questions an assumption of sameness between men and women that rendered the latter invisible in the political discourses of the time. The meta-narratives of the nation and nationalism articulated through political elites rested upon normalising the aspirations of the dominant classes and elites. We can identify several reasons for the absence of women's agendas at this stage of national development and international policy making. They were:

- women were living in an age of hope;
- this hope was based upon the expectation of some immediate benefits accruing to women, in the shape of political citizenship;
- growing disquiet among females about the place they occupied in the 'world system', as citizens of post-colonial nations.

First, women were living in an age of hope. Nationalist successes, after the processes of decolonisation, demanded their forbearance. The defeat of imperialism and regaining of sovereignty conjured up vistas of 'progress', but also realistic assessments of the developmental tasks ahead. Most developing countries inherited huge problems of economic and political chaos, and in some countries there was, in addition, infrastructural devastation. Thus reconstruction was the primary task at hand, and the hopes of most marginalised groups were tied to this overarching project. More generally, the language of development encompassed men and women alike. Constraints on national economies were painfully evident – illiteracy, traditional cultural practices, mass poverty in most cases, and economic 'underdevelopment'. To bring down the entire edifice at one time could lead to political instability.

Second, in most developing countries, this hope was based upon some immediate benefits accruing to women, in the shape of political citizenship. To be enfranchised – and therefore able to participate in the reshaping of a country's political system and future agendas – was enormously empowering. However, political citizenship did not necessarily mean that civic and social citizenship rights accrued to women and men equally. Neither did it focus attention on women's labour – in the home and in the workplace. However, while the language of rights was not employed in similar fashion by all post-colonial states, political rights could form the basis of real claims upon the state. In countries where women had been active and visible during the national movements political citizenship became a starting point for waging other struggles, despite the fact that they too were faced by the dilemmas posed by the politics of prioritisation. In countries where the process of decolonisation had been dominantly either a male, or elite affair, women's political rights reflected their marginalised position. Ali (2000:43–4) discusses the position of women in the development of Pakistan's legal system. She points out that the 'Islamisation' of the law in Pakistan posed a dilemma for the state. As the Sharia law gives the right to property to Muslim women, this was 'contrary to the interests of the landlord-dominated [legislative] assembly which ventured to delay its adoption'.Women were able to invoke Islam in this debate, while the state struggled with maintaining the dominant property relations in the region of Punjab. This standpoint was recently endorsed by Amartya Sen in his work on gender and poverty (Dreze and Sen 1989: 56–61; and Sen 1996b).

---

box 11.1   women in china

In state socialist countries, such as China, there was a focus on redistribution of economic resources, on the one hand, and on opportunities of employment for both men and women, on the other. While political rights were not emphasised for either men or women, state planning and control of resources meant real changes in the ways women were situated within social and economic spheres. For example, land redistribution in China has meant that women were allocated land in their own right for the first time.

A third reason why women continued to give their assent in the formation of overarching national agendas was their growing disquiet about the place they occupied in the 'world system', as citizens of post-colonial nations. While the nationalist movements of many 'Third World' states had created an optimism based on the discourse of equality, and these states sought to join the community of nation states as equal members, the language of development and modernisation ensured that they were constantly characterised as 'underdeveloped', 'undeveloped', and essentially a 'problem' that needed addressing and managing. This language built upon and fed the cultural constructions of the colonial world analysed in the work of Edward Said (1978) as 'Orientalism'. Women occupied a central though particular place within this discourse

(Enloe 1989; Mohanty et al. 1991; Spivak 1988, Liddle and Rai 1998).
They were the victims of barbaric cultures, as well as their markers. The
social relations that enmeshed them were barbaric, and therefore

---

box 11.2   ester boserup and women in development

The work of the Danish economist Ester Boserup was an important liberal feminist challenge to the
early patterns of modernisation as development, since it was a combined argument for equality and
efficiency and therefore a powerful political statement in the interests of women. Boserup argued that
women's status varies with the nature of productive activity and their involvement in it. She argued
that women are marginalised in the economy because they gain less than men in their roles as wage-
workers, farmers and traders. Focusing on rural production, Boserup contended that mechanisation of
agriculture, generally equated with economic development, had resulted in the separation of women's
labour from what is characterised as agricultural labour, which in turn undermined their social status. She
pointed to shifting agriculture and irrigated agriculture as economic regimes where women's participation
in production as well as their social status was high. Tinker (1976) reinforced Boserup's analysis by
suggesting that because western aid agencies exported gender stereotypes, then modernisation of
agriculture led to the widening of the gap between men and women, both economically and socially.
Whyte and Whyte (1982) reached similar conclusions, while at the same time citing the 'cultural' as
mitigating factors. So, for example, while a system of irrigated agriculture in Thailand could mean an
improved status for women, the presence of Islam mediated this form of agriculture in Bangladesh to
give women a low social status. However, the key to women's social status remained their participation in
agricultural production, which is largely calculated through empirical data. Rogers, writing a decade after
Boserup, made a similar analysis of women's work and social status, but also emphasised the importance
of women to the development process itself; it was not only women who would benefit from expansion
of opportunity, but the development process itself would better achieve its targets. This was an appeal to
efficiency as much as to a better deal for women. This analysis became the basis upon which the women
in development (WID) agenda was crafted. The project was to ensure that the benefits of modernisation
accrued to women as well as men in the 'Third World'.

   WID's focus on access — in line with its liberal theoretical approach — led to an under-emphasis on the
social and political structures within which women were located and acted.

   As Beneria and Sen (1997: 279) have argued, Boserup presumed that 'modernisation is both beneficial and inevitable in the specific form it has taken in most Third World countries...[S]he tends to ignore
processes of capital accumulation set in motion during the colonial period, and...does not systematically
analyse the different effects of capital accumulation on women of different classes'. As such, Boserup not
only did not take into account the stratification of women along the lines of class, but also could not build
into her analysis the negative impact of capitalist accumulation regimes on women as well as men. Thus,
Boserup's analysis could not hold in tension the subversive aspects of capitalist modernisation as it broke
down traditional social relations, and the new forms of subordination created by it.

   What Boserup and other WID scholars offered in terms of policy insights were the oft-repeated
prescriptions regarding improving women's standards of education and skills so that they might compete
more vigorously with men in the labour market. The individual rather than social categories were the
focus of such analysis; the privileging of the male productive norm led to a 'truncated understanding of
their lives' (Kabeer 1994: 30).

threatening to the civilised world. For 'Third World' women this posed significant problems of identity and struggles. On the one hand, they were faced with making difficult choices within the national boundaries in terms of pressing their claims upon the national states. On the other, they did not want to be seen to be participating in any validation of the Orientalist and racist discourses that were part of the development policies and regimes.

The declaration of the First Development Decade did not mention women specifically. However in 1962 the UN General Assembly asked the Commission on Women's Status to prepare a report on the role of women in development. It was only in 1974 that Esther Boserup's (1970) pathbreaking study, *Women's Role in Economic Development*, was 'discovered'. This occurred when the Society for International Development's Women in Development (WID) group put together the first bibliography on WID (Tinker 1997: 34).

By 1980, feminist scholars were already criticising the access-based framework. For example, in Britain, the Subordination of Women collective argued for a comparative approach to issues of gender relations, rather than the assumption of 'women's interests'. It also questioned the eliding of gender issues with the practice of development agencies (Jackson and Pearson 1998: 2).

Despite such problems, however, the work of the WID theorists made an important correlation between work and status, which had thus far been ignored by the development agencies and governments in the West. This analysis also resonated with the attempts of liberal nation-states like India to address the persistent gender gap in their societies by focusing on issues of access and equal opportunities as means of improving women's social status. However, a Jackson and Pearson (1998: 8) question was important: How do we conceptualise 'gendered identities and subjectivities in a manner that avoids both essentialism and the unproblematic assumption of the self-determining individual'? Recovering a female subject risks essentialism; 'refusing a female subject risks erasing gender difference'. This was the conundrum that feminist development theorists and practitioners set out to address in a shift from the WID to the gender and development (GAD) framework.

from women to gender – feminist analyses of development

By the 1980s, not only had the 'women in development' framework been critiqued by feminist scholars and activists, but this critique had led to a shift in focus from women to gender relations as the major concern. While some saw, and continue to see, this shift as depoliticising and de-centring the claims of women, the GAD theorists argued that a focus on the relationships that position women within society must be at the heart of political activity (see Young 1997: 51–4). The major differences among and WID and GAD theorists and activists are sketched out in Table 11.1.

Table 11.1 Comparing WID and GAD

	WID	GAD
The approach	Views the absence of women in development plans and policies as the problem	Views unequal social relations between men and women and their 'naturalisation' as the major problem
The focus	Women	Socially constructed, endorsed, and maintained relations between women and men, with special focus on the subordination of women
The problem	The exclusion of women from the development process – an efficiency approach that focuses on the loss of half of developmental resources as a consequence of this exclusion	Unequal power relations, which prevent equitable development and women's full participation
The goal	More efficient, effective development that includes women	Equitable development with both women and men as full participants in decision-making
The solution	Integrate women into the existing development process	Empower the disadvantaged and women and transform unequal relations
The strategies	• Focus on women's projects, on women's components of projects, and on integrated projects; • Increase women's productivity and income; • Increase women' ability to look after the household.	• Reconceptualise the development process, taking gender and global inequalities into account; • Identify and address practical needs, as determined by women and men, to improve their conditions; at the same time, address women's strategic interests; • Address strategic interests of the poor through people-centred development.

Source: Based on Parpart et al. 2000: 141.

A focus on the gender division of labour within the home and in waged work, access to and control over resources and benefits, material and social position of women and men in different contexts, all form part of the GAD perspective on development. Cynthia Enloe's (1989: 1) work, for example, is a comprehensive exposition of the ways in which a whole series of international political economy (IPE) issues, from debt servicing to the development of the tourist industry, are based upon particular positionings of women and men within patriarchal societies. She shows, for example, how national governments, international organisations, and many INGOs and NGOs are implicated in supporting these relations which means that it is rarely acknowledged that 'Gender Makes the World Go Round'. As Enloe (1989: 185), notes:

> The politics of international debt is not simply something that has an *impact* on women in indebted countries. The politics of international debt won't work in their current form *unless* mothers and wives are willing to behave in ways that enable nervous regimes to adopt cost-cutting measures without forfeiting their political legitimacy.

Enloe concludes (1989: 11, 13) that 'making women invisible hides the workings of both femininity and masculinity in international politics'. Making men and women visible does not necessarily mean essentialising them. On the contrary, such visibility prompts an examination of the politics of femininity and masculinity between countries and within ethnicities of the same countries. In short, operationalising gender in policy analysis is critical to the GAD approach and discourse.

There is also an important focus in gender debates on what are distinguished as practical, more immediate, and strategic or long-term and transformative needs of women in their specific social and political contexts. Assessment of these needs is important to the spaces women have for negotiating for an enhancement of their social status, and in their capabilities (Molyneux 1998; Moser 1993). Increasingly, this concern with interests was also reflected in the debates about empowerment (Moser 1993; Rowlands 1997; Parpart et al. 2001). While the GAD framework has become predominant in the feminist development debates, this is not the case in development planning and in the work of many development agencies. Moser (1993: 4) argues, for example, in the context of development planning, that:

> Because it is a less 'threatening' approach, planning for Women in Development is far more popular...Gender planning, with its fundamental goal of emancipation is by definition a more 'confrontational' approach. Based on the premise that the major issue is one of subordination and inequality, its purpose is that women through empowerment achieve equality and equity with men in society.

It is possible to argue, however, that while this challenge of 'gender and development' remains *potentially* a powerful one, in practical policy terms it has too often been used interchangeably with 'women and development'. While the GAD approach is theoretically a clearly 'feminist' approach, and therefore more challenging to existing social relations, we have only to see the way in which the major national and international development agencies have embraced the terminology of GAD to be aware of the dangers of co-option and the limits of its challenge. It is worth noting that the World Bank and the IMF have taken on the GAD terminology. In the 'Gender Dimension of Development' in the Operational Manual of the World Bank, the Bank 'aims to integrate gender considerations in its country assistance program'. There is an increasing network of national machineries for women to address issues of empowerment of women (see Rai 2001), as there is an exponential growth in gender-focused NGOs (Stienstra 2000) and a gender focus in the work of major INGOs.

Institutionalisation of gender, as integration of women before it, poses critical practical and political questions for feminist activists and theorists (Baden and Goetz, 1997: 10). Perhaps the issue at heart is the question of power relations – among women and men, but also between women occupying different socio-economic spaces. Another 'motherhood' term acceptable to all development agencies, and even private business, is empowerment (see World Bank 2001, Part III: Empowerment). For a critical reflection on this term and the way it is being used within the GAD framework see Parpart et al. (2001). One might argue that the challenge before GAD is to take into account issues of relations of production and accumulation, as well as of patriarchal relations – if the disjuncture between GAD aspirations and its co-optation is to be adequately addressed.

ecofeminism

What are known as 'ecofeminist' critiques have been wide ranging, focusing generally upon the gender context of environmental degradation and destruction. (See chapter 9 for a discussion about the relationship between development and the natural environment.) Ecofeminist critiques have challenged the policies of modernisation as well as the paradigm of modernism. They have also incorporated the sustainable-development argument, while pushing it further to incorporate the relations between social and biological life, on the one hand, and the relations of power that structure these, on the other.

In addition, ecofeminism's anti-modernism provides a radical edge to its critique of growth. The alternative model of development that ecofeminists espouse is anti-patriarchal, decentralised, interdependent

box 11.3   ecofeminism and environmentalism

Ecofeminism has an egalitarian basis that it shares with the ecology movement. It reasserts the 'age-old association' between women and nature (Merchant 1980). 'The new developments in biotechnology... have made women acutely conscious of the gender bias of patriarchal, anti-nature and colonial and aims to dispossess women of their generative capacity as it does the productive capacities of nature' (Shiva and Mies 1993: 16). The approach also questions the trajectory of modern science and technology by making a strong link between patriarchy and arrogation of knowledge to Science. 'It focuses on the costs of progress, the limits to growth, the deficiencies of technological decision making and the urgency of conservation...' (Merchant 1980: xix). Vandana Shiva, in particular, has made direct links between colonialism and the degradation of the environment and of women's lives themselves in her work on the Chipko movement in India. She has argued that when science was harnessed to technology of war and trained against the societies that did not own such technology, science waged war against nature. 'Whenever women acted against ecological destruction or/and the threat of atomic annihilation, they immediately became aware of the connection between patriarchal violence against women, other people and nature....' (Mies and Shiva 1993: 16). Thus 'the "corporate and military warriors" aggression against the environment was perceived almost physically as an aggression against our female body' (ibid.).

and sustainable (see Braidotti et al. 1994). However, some feminist scholars have also expressed a growing unease with the 'women, environment and development' (WED) articulation. Jackson and Pearson (1998: 9) argue that:

> it is the very separation of women from the context of economic, social and political reproduction rather than their insertion into a notion of a sustainable future that differentiates a socially grounded feminist analysis from a free floating 'naturalistic' perspective which equates women's realities with natural futures.

deconstruction and representation: women and the politics of post-development

Building on the WID/GAD debates, but extending them in different directions, the post-modernist feminist critique of development emerged in the 1980s and extended in the 1990s. Post-modern critics argued that 'Development has been the primary mechanism through which the Third World has been imagined and imagined itself, thus marginalizing or precluding other ways of seeing and doing' (Escobar 1995: 212). As such, development shares this framing characteristic with Orientalism. For feminists engaged in debates on development and participating in this critique of development opened up new spaces. The emphasis on 'difference' is what attracts many feminists to postmodernism, without giving up on the GAD framework. Feminists have long claimed that they have been constructed as the social 'other' in male-dominant worlds of philosophy and science. They have been denied their subjecthood within the traditional structures of knowledge/power. They have also, as noted above, struggled between the essentialising focus of WID and the potentially pluralistic understanding of gendered social relations. As Marchand and Parpart (1995: 7) comment in their excellent summary of feminist debates on postmodernism, it is unsurprising that the feminist focus on difference and attraction to postmodernism coincided with the critique of middle-class, white western feminism by women who did not recognise themselves and their experiences in these early articulations of feminism.

The displacement of Feminism by various feminisms was a starting point for a self-examination for many feminists, creating a space within which their subject positions came under scrutiny as did those of others. For some 'Third World' feminists this new space was one within which they could critique not only western feminisms, but also where they could begin to examine the vexed issues of identity-based politics, which the nationalist discourses had either obscured or co-opted. The link between modernity, development and Orientalism that was made by post-development theorists has resonated with many feminists. The link with Orientalism in particular allowed feminists to open up the issue of differences among women in the developing world. Although this had been done within the Marxist framework of class, the intellectual complicity of modernising elites was brought into focus by post-development feminists, as was the hierarchical relationship between donors and recipients of aid, the NGO worker and the 'clients' of the developing world. Above, we noted the critique of science articulated by ecofeminists. In addition, other post-development feminists point to the empowering element of their approach, that is, where women of the developing world find space to articulate their own needs and agendas (Marchand and Parpart 1995).

Various analysts – including Moghissi (1999), Harstock (1990), Walby (1990), Nzomo (1995), Udayagiri (1995) and Rai (1997, 2002) – have recently raised questions about the nature of the postmodern critique, as well as, more generally, the issue of women and 'post-development'. First, such questions focus on the issue of agency. That is, if there is no structure, as the postmodern critique contends, if all power is diffuse and all hierarchies redundant, how are we to approach the question of political activism? The focus on difference rather than on the structural framing of men and women makes mobilisation of opposition difficult. The question of organisation – political, social and economic – also becomes unanswerable as the question of achievable goals is brought into question. Perhaps most pressing in this context is the relative value placed upon different standpoints (see Moghissi 1999: 50–1). Is there nothing to choose between right-wing mobilisations of women claiming a 'motherhood' persona for women and those struggling to find a public space for women to articulate their interests as individuals, or members of groups? Does not a postmodern perspective thus lead to political nihilism? Is it a 'stranded' standpoint?

Harstock (1990: 167) points to the postmodern view of power as one 'in which passivity or refusal represent the only possible choices. Resistance rather than transformation dominates...thinking and consequently limits...politics'. Walby (1990: 2), on the other hand, argues that 'postmodernism in social theory has led to the fragmentation of the concepts of sex, race and class and to the denial of the pertinence of overarching theories of patriarchy, racism and capitalism'. Moghissi (1999: 52), discussing changing gender relations in Iran, notes postmodernism's 'well-advertised but fictitious radicalism, which rapidly dissolves into a celebration of cultural difference, its privileging of the "local"...and in consequence, its curious affinity with the most reactionary ideas of Islamic fundamentalism'.

In her analysis of democratisation struggles in Africa, Nzomo (1995: 131) asks, 'What relevance...[has] postmodernist discourse?'. Nzomo also points out (1995: 141) that the postmodernist critique 'Would indeed dismiss the current strategies and visions of African women whose struggles for gender-sensitive democratisation hinge upon universalist feminist ideals'. From another standpoint Udayagiri (1995: 171, 172) notes the 'curious silence about the political changes wrought by earlier resistance to modernization, in counter discourses such as dependency theory'. In this silence, she contends, lies the privileging of the postmodernist discourse of its own position. Further, it also raises the important question, 'has the relationship of policy to the scholarship on women in the South been a complete failure?' In sum, for many critics, the question of feminist engagements with nation-states remains critically unanswered within the context of postmodernist critiques (see Rai 1997 and 2002).

marxist and neo-marxist feminist interventions

Many commentators would agree that Marxist and socialist feminists have made a major contribution to the structuralist debate on gender and development. Writing of women as 'the last colony', a group of German socialist feminists, including Mies et al. (1988) and Kabeer (1994), have argued that primitive accumulation remains essential to capitalist growth, and that both international and national capital and state systems exploit both the developing world, and women more generally, in its pursuit of profit. They identify several commonalties between 'women and the colonies':

> First, both are...placed within – or more accurately demoted to – the 'realm of nature', because prior to capitalism the idea of a supposedly 'backward' nature did not exist....[Further], they are treated as if they were means of production or 'natural resources' such as water, air, and land...the relationship between them is one of *appropriation*
>
> (Mies et al. 1988: 4–5)

Such critiques argue that capitalist exploitation of wage labour was based upon the male monopoly of violence in a modified form; that patriarchal violence at home and in the public space was intrinsic to the lives of women and to their exploitation. They also suggested that this patriarchal dominance was maintained through the agencies of the state which institutionalised the 'housewifization' of women's labour via marriage and work legislation (Mies et al. 1988). However, it was not in their suggestion of the super-exploitation of 'Third World' labour that they differed from Marxist interpretations, but in their conceptualisation of the work of the housewife: 'in Marxian schema of accumulation these milieux and classes had no place' (Mies et al. 1988: 6). As an alternative, Mies argued for a society based on 'a feminist conception of labour, involving direct and sensual interaction with nature, unmediated by technology...autonomy for women over their lives and bodies, and rejection of any state or male control over their reproductive capacity; and finally men's participation in subsistence and nurturing work...' (Kabeer 1994: 66). Again, while many commentators agreed that this was a powerful critique of existing social relations, and its focus on the gendered nature of capitalist accumulation provided a critical development of structural analysis, there was much acceptance that their utopian radicalism remained politically 'essentialising' of women, while the rejection of any engagement with the state made it difficult to translate this critique into practical development policy agendas.

pragmatic feminism?

An increasingly influential group of feminists have taken on the challenge of 'transforming practice'. They drew early inspiration from Marxist critiques of capitalist development, but have been widely eclectic in theoretical approach. This group of what have been called 'pragmatic feminists', including Elson (1994) have participated in the debates on modernisation and development, arguing not only against the 'male bias in the development process', but also for initiating an engagement with institutions on the 'inside' of the policy processes – at both national and global levels (Elson 1994). The focus of this body of literature was the differential positions of women and men in the development processes, seen as being integral to the fashioning of modern capitalist economies and technologies. Two key areas have been at the core of this critique of development:

- the issue of women's work; and
- the gendered nature of structural adjustment policies (SAPs), especially since the 1980s.

In sum, the debates discussed above influenced policies of both international agencies and particular countries both directly and indirectly. The alternative vision of measuring 'quality of life' rather than simple economic growth rates and per capital income adopted by the United Nations Development Programme (UNDP) reflects the strength of the arguments. The disaggregation of economic data by gender now found in many national statistical data, and the Human Development

---

box 11.4   gender and structural adjustment programmes (saps)

An important feminist critique insists upon opening up the area of work to economic analysis. It has posed difficult issues for both the development economists and what might be called 'the development establishment'. Such critiques have built upon Sen's critique of the altruistic family, to show how not only the life chances of women are affected by the gender relations obtaining within the family, but also how their contributions to family income are being appropriated without acknowledgement within the 'family income' (Sen and Grown 1988). In disaggregating the impact of SAPs on the family, and focusing on the disproportionate burden of the privatisation of social welfare that women are being forced to carry, this powerful critique has resulted in some important shifts within the economic discourse of international institutions. These critiques have as much built upon the Marxist understanding of the bases of gender inequality, as they have on the liberal concepts of equality and equal opportunity. They have also further developed the interventions of 'Third World' feminist and development groups, such as DAWN ('Development Alternatives with Women for a New Era') that advocate a strategic engagement with the policy community, and with state and international economic institutions in order to challenge the assumptions of neutral goals of development (Sen and Grown 1988). Because the focus of this group of feminists was on 'the achievable', and because it engaged actively with the policy machineries especially at the international level, both its influence in the field of Development Studies and on interventions in the debates on development grew considerably in the 1990s.

and the World Development Reports shows the impact of WID/GAD theorising and research. The various world conferences on women, from Mexico to Beijing in the 1990s, organised by the UN allowed gender-and-development agendas to be articulated, reassessed, critiqued, and pushed forward. Bi- and multi-lateral aid, and various programmes of assistance have been affected by these wider debates on development though major issues of gender-blindness, and power relations among the donors and recipient countries remain (Staudt 2001). Finally, it is also useful to note that until the 1990s the debates on development took place largely in the context of the nation-state. In the concluding section, I will reflect upon how globalisation has influenced GAD agendas and where we need to go from there.

gender and development: the challenges of globalisation

It is, of course, interesting (perhaps predictable?) that feminist scholars figure hardly at all in the traditional international relations and IPE accounts of globalisation. However, feminists are now engaging with and as a result extending the debates on globalisation from different perspectives (Sen and Grown 1988; Chang and Ling 2000). Faced with new challenges, feminists have also sought to examine and theorise how globalisation is changing political activism at both grassroots level and at the level of global institutions (Stienstra 2000). In terms of political activism, feminist scholars have built on and stretched further the ideas of 'borders' and a 'borderless world' through studies of women's migration (Pellerin and Overbeek 2001; Kofman 2000), world communities such as those based on religion (Moghissi 1999), and by examining the growing density of women's networking through informal and formal organisational structures (Stienstra 2000).

While some feminist scholars have focused on communicative expansion that has been brought about by globalisation (Eisenstein 1997), others have been concerned about global economic regimes. In particular, global production and structural adjustment policies that affect women's lives directly and indirectly, reshaping gender relations within the home and in the workplace (Elson 1994; Jackson and Pearson 1998) have been the focus of attention, as have issues of security and insecurity, and of well-being (Elson 1994). In general, however, most such approaches focus on the global political economy, seen as the interaction of reproductive, productive and virtual economies. Within such a view, we can also note further issues, including:

- the nature of the 'reproductive economy' and 'intergenerational, social/cultural/ institutional reproduction';
- continuity and change in power relations within and outside the family; and, finally
- non-waged labour/informal sector activities.

Such a perspective on the 'productive' economy of globalisation allows us to map the gendered nature of production (which includes a critique of the traditional economic and political divisions between the public and the private spheres) and to stretch the boundaries of what is considered the appropriate domain of the 'global'. In sum, postmodern, as well as institutionalist feminists, have examined the changing understanding of borders – in relation to the changing forms of masculinities and femininities, as well as the consequences for local communities and politics as national borders become more porous and regional boundaries more secure (Parpart et al. 2000; Marchand and Parpart 1995; Staudt 2001). Overall, various feminist scholars have examined the changing form and nature of the nation-state in the context of globalisation (Rai 2002) and made a political and normative case on the environmental damage being done in the name of free markets.

Bakker (1994) identifies five paradoxes that affect women's lives under global restructuring:

1. The changing nature of the state, which is at the same time minimising its remit in the area of economy, and becoming more invasive in the area of regulation of reproduction. For women this has meant increased awareness of the power of the state at a time when the state is in retreat from its earlier social roles. The repressiveness of some population programmes, as well as their differential impact upon women of various groups is causing women to organise, and at the same time confront differences among themselves.
2. The paradox of austerity and consumerism. Austerity measures are resulting in increased insecurity, convergence of male/female employment patterns with decreasing male wages, casualisation of labour, at a time when consumer-led economic recovery is being touted as a way out for 'Third World' economies. In India, for example, this paradox has had tragic results with a sharp increase in dowry-murders in areas hitherto less influenced by the dowry culture.
3. The paradox of the privileging of women as producers as well as reproducers in the context of the withdrawal of state provision of welfare. Women are being increasingly mobilised into work, as

austerity and insecurity means that the male income is no longer secure. However, with the withdrawal of health and education provision by the state, and the privatisation of these facilities, women's lives are being further stretched to cover the expanded time/ space within which they have to operate. As carers, and increasingly as providers, women's labour is being considered infinitely elastic, leading many (Elson 1994) to suggest that this will result in the breakdown of women's health and reproductive capacity. At the same time, the displacement of male labour by a feminised workforce is leading to increased levels of violence against women, and not everywhere do women experience an enhanced social status for being the 'bread-winner' (see Stitcher and Parpart 1990).

4.   The paradox of sustainable development and the consumerist model of development, at odds with each other on counts of environmental degradation, and the impact of consumerism on the rights of marginalised populations of today and of the future. Thus, both in Andhra Pradesh in India and Chiapas in Mexico, peasant movements have originated from the commercialisation of agriculture under the new World Trade Organisation initiatives in the agrarian sector.

5.   Finally, Bakker (1994) points to the paradox of the home being constructed at the same time as a haven, and as a worksite with the flexibilisation of work.

According to a survey by the Womens' Environment and Development Organization (WEDO) , for example, 'Women...pay a disproportionate share of the costs of economic globalization while being excluded from its benefits' (www.wedo.org/). The indicators used by WEDO for an assessment of the gender impact of macroeconomic policies under globalisation are women's rights and access to land, property and credit, employment, the environment, education, health and housing (www. wedo.org/). Elson and Moser (1989: 69) have used four criteria to assess the impact of SAPs on women's lives – changes in incomes, in prices, in levels and composition of public expenditure and in working conditions. They make the point that intra-household distribution of resources will vary from inter-household distribution, and that we need a class-differentiated analysis of SAPs based on empirical research on the 20 per cent richest and 20 per cent poorest households. Moser (1989) makes a similar point when 'she claims that low-income women have different capacities to cope with SAPs, according to whether they are 'coping', 'burnt out' or 'hanging on'. While both points are important, I am not aware of the second insight having resulted in any systematic gender and class-based data-gathering on the consequences of SAPs that limits the analysis and also the policy recommendations of scholars.

Evidence in all categories is mixed depending upon the sectors, geographical areas, and the depth of SAPs implementation. However, Elson (1989: 79) points out that there is sufficient evidence to suggest that women's labour is being stretched unbearably to accommodate the cuts in public social spending and the expansion of women's work outside the home. Moser points out that more poor women in SAPs-affected areas are working for longer hours than before. Cerrutti (2000: 889) points out that 'in relative terms, more women now are compelled to work than ever before but they are also more frequently unemployed and with intermittent labour force trajectories'. It is now well established that women form the majority of the workforce in the sites of globalised production – the Export Processing Zones (EPZs). For example, women are 85 per cent of the EPZ labour force in Taiwan, 87 per cent in the Philippines, 88 per cent in Sri Lanka, 71 per cent in South Korea, 80 per cent in Mexico, and 83 per cent in Malaysia. However, as Truong (1999) points out, in Taiwan, women's representation in the administration in this sector is only 2 per cent of the total employees. Safa (1995), however, in her research on the effects of export-led industrialisation in Puerto Rico and the Dominican Republic, found that although women seem to be enjoying greater autonomy with the expansion of work, the levels of insecurity are also high due to the increased dependence of these countries on US capital as a result of which there has been a considerable weakening of the workers' bargaining power in the phase of 'feminisation of labour'. This suggests that the trend towards the expansion and casualisation of work of women, while contributing towards strategies of survival, is not conducive to a 'sustained growth and development both on a personal and national level' (Elson 1989: 72).

Finally, women's identities – as consumers and producers, as femininities and masculinities – have also a key focus of feminist theorising on globalisation. Theorising changing femininities and masculinities under a converging globalisation, Ling (1997) evokes the concept of hypermasculinity as the glorification of aggression, competition, accumulation and power, to explain the developmentalism of the East Asian states. Ling suggests that in these states the nationalist elites replay the relationship of hypermasculinity's dominance over a feminised society through enmeshing it in public patriarchy and political authoritarianism. 'Women in the [East Asian societies] as the most feminized or feminized subjects, suffer the most extensive exploitation and silencing' (Ling 1997: 10; also Ling 2000). She also argues that 'globalisation serves as a venue

---

box 11.5   women and migration in a globalising world

Another area of women's economic and social place in a globalising world is that of migration. Between two and three million people migrate each year. This accounts for about 2.3 per cent of the world population (World Bank 2001: 37–8). It has also been noted that migratory flows are increasingly feminised (Castells 1996). Such gendered and high levels of migration are also testing the limits of globalisation. As Sassen (1995: 59) notes, 'when it comes to immigrants and refugees...the national state claims all its old splendor in asserting its sovereign right to control its borders', despite their denationalised economies. Where migration is concerned the vulnerability scales for women are also very high – most migration that takes place for both men and women is 'distress migration' across either rural–urban boundaries, or regional and national boundaries. In many cases, where migration is difficult and women resort to 'illegal' means for gaining access to other countries, this vulnerability is further increased in the face of the wrath of the 'host' nation state and the often racialised hostility of the 'local' populations. For example, as Truong and del Rosario (1994) have shown in the case of Filippina sex workers in the Netherlands, it is the sex worker who pays the price for seeking to bypass the gendered regimes of immigration law, through deportation, and not the procurer of her services.

---

for the mutual reconstruction of both global and local forces, precisely because identity is open, organic, and unpredictable'; and that it allows for 'the convergence of global and local patriarchies that underpin East Asia's oft-cited "economic miracle".'

In terms of feminist politics, Ling (1997: 9) asserts, the analysis of global and local convergence of masculinities means avoiding a 'flattening' of the identity of women in the developing world, by pointing to the participation of the national elites of East Asian countries in the privileging of masculinist regimes of discursive and political power. In terms of the debate on globalisation, the convergence of patriarchal control may best be studied across cultural, spatial, and systemic divides (Chang and Ling 2000). The converging media plays a significant part in this construction, and legitimisation of a masculinised consensus, as do varied access of men and women to the various 'scapes' – techno-, finan-, ethno- (Appadurai 1990). The representations of femininity find clear reflection in the recruitment of female labour into the labour markets, the differential wage systems, the denial of property rights, and through structural-adjustment-inspired cutbacks in public provision, and the increased burden of women's work within the family.

Taking Karl Polanyi's concept of embeddedness and expanding it to cover 'non-market relations which surround and structure all markets' (Bakker 1994: 4), feminist economists have argued that 'market goods and services are allocated through the political structure and social relations of markets, which may promote dominance and subordinacy between parties to an exchange' (ibid.). Further, that although markets do enable those previously excluded to access the economy, they are also 'likely to reflect and reify existing resource allocations and socially constructed gender divisions of labour that influence endowments' (ibid.). This is the clear challenge that feminists pose to the neoclassical conceptions of perfect competition guiding markets. It is argued that gender relations based on unequal terms of exchange between men and women lead to resource misallocations that can be viewed as a tax on women and lead to systematic 'market distortions' of a so-called neutral field, which are not recognised as such, and therefore continue to be obscured in the market-competition/efficiency rhetoric. Folbre (1992), in the context of Latin America, and Gordon (1990) in her study of OECD countries, take up this analysis in the context of citizenship-deficit that women experience as a result of this structural, unacknowledged tax. The argument is that market-based inequalities reinforce a masculinised economic and political citizenship, which does not recognise the unequal division of unpaid work, and consequently the unequal time allocations that men and women can make between the private and public worlds. The limitation of welfare states, the restructuring of state expenditure on public provision, the delegitimisation of Keynesian interventions, however contested and partial, in the market economy, all reinforce this growing gap between men and women in the exercise of their citizenship rights.

conclusion

Feminist movements as social movements have achieved a great deal in politicising gender not only within the nation-state but also within the international system. That has been the success of the women's and feminist movements. In the new millennium, it is important to view this achievement with justifiable pride. When the World Bank begins to view gender as an important issue, when 'Women's Eyes on the Bank' make the Bank uncomfortable and wanting to engage in the gender debate, feminist movements can take heart. When gender inequality becomes one important issue for assessing human development then women's social movements can be seen to have succeeded. However, such engagements should also come with health warnings attached – changes in project funding and even perhaps some new policy initiatives, while important, do not make for the paradigmatical shifts in neo-liberal economic thinking that feminist economists have been demanding. Hoskyns and Rai (1998: 362) argue that:

> [f]or both strategic as well as practical reasons women have had to organize separately as women....[However, the] feminist challenge is

limited by a current lack of focus on the importance of redistributive policies that are rooted in the structural inequalities of capitalist production and exchange.

In conclusion, it is necessary to emphasise that 'the next phase of women's struggles needs to take on board more centrally the issue of redistribution of resources if power relations in society are to be refashioned' (Hoskyns and Rai 1998: 363).

note

1. This chapter is derived from my book, *Gender and the Political Economy of Development*, Cambridge: Polity Press, 2002.

part 3

development and globalisation

12

the global political economy

timothy m. shaw

introduction

The global political economy has evolved dramatically since World War II in terms of structures and relations, notably global governance via international financial institutions, multinational corporations, and the World Economic Forum (WEF). Together, these actors facilitate and legitimate just-in-time production and distribution involving global supply chains using airfreight and containers all linked via computer networks. Meanwhile, the early optimism of the nationalist era in the South – the 1950s and 1960s – had later yielded – in the 1970s and 1980s – to considerable scepticism given the mixed legacy of a quarter-century of neo-liberal hegemony from 'Asian miracle' to 'African renaissance'.[1]

In the 1990s, the formal end of state socialism in the East and South (although the jury may still be out on China and Cuba), as well as the contemporaneous rise of 'anti-globalisation' movements and a series of economic crises – from East Asia to Latin America (see chapter 5 for a discussion of these events), collectively indicate that the first decade of the 21st century is characterised by debate over future mixes of state and capital in development trajectories. For example, new 'partnerships' are now emerging around ethical trade initiatives and corporate codes of conduct (for example, the 'tobacco framework' and 'cocoa initiative') encouraged by the WEF and a plethora of think-tanks. In addition to the rise of global finance and high-tech sectors, and the continuing resilience of energy and mineral 'enclaves', other legal and illegal global industries are currently expanding, such as sports and drugs.

Meanwhile, global inequalities have intensified, particularly in 'post-welfare state' Central Europe/Asia as well as in Africa and the Americas, indicating that the so-called 'world' economy does not actually include all countries and communities, classes or regions. Of today's nearly 200 states, a significant minority have weak regimes where strong mafias and militias operate. This has led recently to the emergence of analyses of the political economy of conflict or resource wars, while development debates and policies (state and non-state) increasingly reflect these and other novel challenges. But much (international) political economy remains rather traditional in assumption and orientation, overlooking profound changes in the nature of contemporary capitalisms.

While the focus of this chapter is on the global political economy as it affects the developing world, key examples and illustrative points come mainly from sub-Saharan Africa. Africa, virtually all analysts would agree, is marginal in the contemporary global political economy. While other issues could have provided the focus – for example, the remarkable rise of China, a key post-Cold War economic success story, a country that has been able to exploit recent global opportunities, I have chosen Africa. This is because since the end of the Cold War, the economic and developmental plight of Africa has been at the top of the international developmental agenda. In the context of the development of the post-Cold War global political economy, this chapter elucidates what the region has been doing for itself to try to resolve its developmental quandaries. However, for comparative purposes, the chapter also draws on various case studies and illustrations – including North Africa and the Middle East – to illustrate both the heterogeneity and the inequality of today's global political economy.

development dilemmas:
sub-saharan africa in comparative perspective

Sub-Saharan Africa – referred to in this chapter as 'Africa' – constitutes an especially challenging case study for a focus on analytic and policy directions in relation to the global political economy – not least because it is frequently overlooked because of its apparent economic marginality. However, given its history of structural adjustment programmes (SAPs) and Highly-Indebted Poor Country (HIPC) conditionalities, Africa is actually a prime site for governance partnerships, informal and illegal sectors, and supply chains. As Pliny remarked in an earlier age: *Semper aliquid novi Africa affert* ('Out of Africa there is always something new').

The year 2001 was one of marked changes in the world economy and in Africa itself…Africa remains the only region in the world where poverty is rising, with 70% of the poor living in rural areas…the majority of

African countries are unlikely to meet the Millennium Development Goals of reducing poverty in half by the year 2015.   (ADB 2002a: i)

In 2001, the global economy experienced the worst economic conditions in over a decade....In marked contrast to the experience during most earlier global recessions, Africa actually outperformed all regions of the world – with the exception of Asian developing countries.

(ADB 2002a: 4–5)

African *countries* lag behind other developing country regions in terms of attracting FDI inflows.   (UNCTAD 1999: 52)

This chapter traces the development of the global political economy from the aftermath of World War II to the early 21st century. We can note several distinct stages in this 60-year period:

- *post-colonial modernisation* – as Africa and Asia achieved formal 'independence' in the 1950s and 1960s;
- *dependencia* in the 1960s and 1970s;
- *neo-liberalism and globalisation(s)* in the 1980s and 1990s (Parpart and Shaw 2002);
- *'market fundamentalism'* (Soros 2002) of the early 2000s.

With the sudden demise of state socialism in Eastern Europe in the late 1980s, not only was bipolar competition no longer a challenge for the 'West', but also the hegemony of the market seemed assured. Yet the excessive triumphalism – perhaps overconfidence would be better – of neo-liberalism was itself seemingly shattered by the 'battle of Seattle' at century's end (Broad 2002). While the 'anti-globalisation' movement (focused upon in the first section below) is quite heterogeneous and does not constitute a cohesive alternative to contemporary capitalism, it does significantly challenge many assumptions about the character of the contemporary global political economy. While the 'anti-globalisation' movement was pushed off-balance by the terrorist attack on the World Trade Center on 11 September 2001, it subsequently managed to incorporate some of the alienation symbolised by al-Qaeda into its activism. As Marlies Glasius and Mary Kaldor (2002: 3) assert:

On 10 September 2001...the phenomenon that we call 'global civil society' was flourishing...street demonstrations in Gothenburg, Quebec and Genoa were becoming part of our daily news. Above all, the period was characterized by the growing importance attached to global norms and values – human rights, the environment, social justice – which were beginning to displace the geo-political discourse of international affairs...Indeed, global civil society seemed to be on the verge of a new dialogue with the representatives of global political institutions and global corporations...On one reading, [September 11] can be interpreted as an attempt to close down civil society...But there is another reading of September 11...the moment when global civil society comes of age...

The events of '9/11' and its aftermath symbolise how the global political economy has become much more unequal over the 60 years since 1945 (www.wider.unu.edu), especially over the last decade. During this time, the balance between state and non-state actors – in particular, private business companies and civil societies – has moved away from any notion of a 'welfare state', towards ubiquitous 'competition states' (Cerny 2003). The global system has also evolved from a world of less than a hundred states to one approaching 200. Yet a growing proportion of states actually control very little – in contrast to the assorted mafias and militias that many now host (discussed below). Furthermore, given new technologies, capital and products are highly mobile – whereas labour is much less so.

Aside from the disparate shocks of Seattle and 9/11, the world economy has also suffered a series of recent crises focused in the South – from those in Asia in 1997–98, to those that followed in Argentina, Mexico and Russia (also see chapter 5 on this topic). These events helped stimulate a series of questions about the sustainability of the world economic system. The issue has attracted critiques both from within and outside the 'global establishment', notably from George Soros (2002), Joseph Stiglitz (2002) and the *Financial Times*, which suggested in mid-2003 that 'the Washington consensus fades into history' (Ramachandran 2003).

It is appropriate at this stage to define and discuss some of the key terms used in this chapter.

1. I perceive *globalisation(s)* to refer to ideology and policy as well as to technology and practice. It presents both opportunities and constraints everywhere at the start of the 21st century, especially in the developing world or 'global south'. Nevertheless, as suggested below, niches do now exist for competitive countries, companies, communities and sectors after their five years of crises.
2. While 'capitalism' can be treated as a singular system, as it has become more global so distinct variations can be identified. The dominant

type remains the most 'liberal' and market-driven – Anglo-American
– but it can be contrasted with the more 'corporatist' European version
and emergent (East, South and South East) Asian 'developmental'
varieties. And if we recognise that there may be an 'African' variant
of capitalism too, then we can include informal and illegal as well as
formal and legal trade. Certainly inclusion of unrecorded informal
trade and familial investment would boost the numbers of capitalisms
in the South.

3. If we analyse the 'real' economy of regions in conflict like Central
   Africa/Asia/Europe, then the global political economy consists of a
   much more interesting and varied picture. This is especially so if we
   also include a 'political economy of conflict' perspective; that is, at
   least some civil wars in Africa and Asia are about economic survival
   and gain (Duffield 2001; Reno 1998), which in turn impact on the
   terms and contents of trade in these regions.

4. The global supply-chain of coltan and cell-phones is symptomatic
   of the interconnections between the informal and formal, illegal
   and legal economies. As Marysse (2003) indicates, familiar brands of
   cell-phones, including Ericsson, Motorola and Nokia, all have their
   roots in informal mining of coltan in eastern Congo, a trade that
   is inseparable from the continuing conflicts involving neighbours'
   armies, assorted militias, and global arms traders.

5. We can note estimates of the value of some 'conflict goods', that is,
   those that emanate from zones of conflict: for example, diamonds
   from Sierra Leone (US$30–125 million a year) and rebel-held territory
   in Angola ($4.1 billion between 1992 and 2000), and timber from
   Cambodia ($150 million annually) and Liberia ($187 million annually).
   (See sections below on supply chains and emerging coalitions to
   regulate and legitimate such goods.)

---

box 12.1   developmental states and globalisation

It is sometimes argued that Asia's 'developmental states' (see chapters 3 and 5) may now be succeeded
by 'African democratic developmental states' (Mkandawire 2001), such as, Botswana and Mauritius.
In addition, many 'new' IT industries – for example, micro-computers and mobile telephones – are
now often manufactured in various Export-Processing Zones (EPZs) in the South. Further, new labour-
intensive sectors are also growing there – such as tourism and fresh fruits, flowers and vegetables. And,
moreover, the world of brands and franchises includes logos from South Africa as well as from the North
Atlantic and Japan. Consequently, any 'real' international political economy (IPE) for the 21st century
should recognise informal as well as formal trade, illegal as well as legal markets, along with the roles of
diasporas and mafias (Shaw 2004).

Next, I provide an overview of: (1) the formal structures of the global economy, and (2) current debates about globalisation and anti-globalisation, including emerging notions of partnerships.

from human development indices to millennium development goals

Aside from private corporate and financial headquarters and centres like Frankfurt, London, New York and Tokyo, there is a trio of cities which host global organisations that are central in the management of today's global economy. First, inter-state negotiations to advance free trade in the global economy have been focused in the General Agreement on Tariffs and Trade/World Trade Organisation (GATT/WTO) in Geneva, reinforced by more informal discussions in the WEF in nearby Davos. Second, conditionalities over structural adjustment programmes (SAPs) come from the International Financial Institutions (IFIs) in Washington. And, third, United Nations (UN) attempts to advance human development recently through its HDIs (human development indices) and now through agreed Millennium Development Goals (MDGs) (UNDP 2003). (However, the degree to which these are compatible is problematic, as different analytic perspectives would rank their roles and impacts differently.)

- Emergence of the WTO from GATT is symbolic of the currently unassailable dominance of global market forces. Moreover, particularly after China's admission, increasing numbers of 'Third World' states now seek to join. It is worth noting that the WTO's procedures do allow governments that offend its rules of free trade to be subject to judicial proceedings and financial penalties.
- Mixed results of 'cookie-cutter' SAPs by the early 1990s led to their replacement by the IFIs of somewhat more flexible HIPC arrangements, ostensibly reflective of national Poverty Reduction Strategy Programmes (PRSPs). The first, Ugandan, case is one of the better known and certainly involved an active role for the Uganda Debt Network (www.udn.org.ug) in negotiating PRSPs.
- Despite the claims of some pro-globalisation interests, the elusiveness of development in many countries and communities, as recorded by declines in HDIs, has led the UN to design a set of MDGs (see below). However, the extent to which the WTO and HIPC can advance MDGs is debatable; consequently, there is continued pressure from 'global civil society' in the shape of the 'anti-globalisation' 'movement', even though these concepts are

somewhat problematic analytically (Laxer and Halperin 2003). But, as we shall see below, persistent pressure from the margins (Grant and Short 2003), including from Africa, has begun to affect state and corporate responses.

the power of anti-globalisation: pre-emptive responses from multinational corporations

The backlash to economic globalization may not be powerful enough yet to win all the time or to become the prevailing view...Nor is the backlash going to disappear in the wake of the terrorism of 11 September 2001...The citizen backlash is no longer a 'fringe' movement that governments, international institutions and private corporations can ignore...It has the IBRD [the World Bank], the IMF and the WTO on the defensive; so too with pharmaceutical, apparel, biotech and other transnational firms (Broad 2002: 9).

Given the apparently unassailable hegemony of neo-liberalism, rather naïve assumptions prevailed around the WTO in the 1990s, a time when in the aftermath of the Cold War, many western governments seemed in a triumphalist mood. In this climate, the anti-globalisation 'battle of Seattle' was quite unanticipated as was, in a different way, 9/11. The subsequent relaunch of free-trade talks at Doha in November 2001 did serve to kick-start new negotiations, but in very different circumstances and contexts. Later meetings included the so-called 'Doha Round' – that is, the Doha Development Agenda – with gatherings in September 2003 at Cancun following a Montreal inter-ministerial meeting in late July 2003.

Symptomatic of the changing times, under pressure from a variety of actors and strategies, from consumers to shareholders and pension funds, many companies in the South as well as the North began to adopt a range of corporate codes of conduct and strategies to emphasise their corporate social responsibility. In some cases, these led to various Ethical Trade and Fair Trade Initiatives (Broad 2002; Oliviero and Simmons 2002). At the current time (2004), the range of such codes and guidelines – which vary in terms of degrees of accountability and enforcement – include WEF Guidelines for Global Corporate Citizenship (www.weforum.org), OECD Principles of Corporate Governance (www.oecd.org), the UN's Global Compact (www.unglobalcompact.org), and the Global Reporting Initiative (www.globalreporting.org). These measures collectively suggest that, 'corporations pay attention to their role as corporate citizens largely in response to the pressures from, and resulting partnerships with, civil society' (Oliviero and Simons 2002: 82).

A more general point is that antagonism between non-governmental organisations (NGOs) and multinational corporations (MNCs) may moderate enthusiasm for such 'partnerships' – yet the latter may amount to a foretaste of the future, as indicated by their proliferation in the North (www.copenhagencentre.org), and symbolised by the UN's Global Compact. Indeed, MNCs' partnerships constitute something of a growth industry as major global companies seek to polish their image and protect their reputations, reflecting the proliferation of corporate codes of conduct, social responsibility, and best practice. Further, in 'vulnerable' sectors, corporations rush for the cover afforded by coalitions like the Framework Convention on Tobacco Control (www.who.org) and International Cocoa Initiative (www.ilo.org) (see below for further discussion).

In sum, the proliferation of such codes, many of which were developed in and for the continent of Africa, has led to myriad schemes for monitoring, sometimes by NGOs (www.corpwatch.org), leading in turn to many lists of best (global/regional/ national/sectoral) companies and practices.

africa's economy at the start of the new millennium: how marginal?

Africa has become an interesting and challenging continent in terms of international political economy because of two key developments:

- the achievement of majority rule in South Africa in 1994;
- attempts by a trio of current leaders (Presidents Mbeki (South Africa), Obasanjo (Nigeria) and Wade (Senegal)) both to define and advocate the New Partnership for Africa's Development (NEPAD), launched in mid-2001 around the replacement for the Organisation of African Unity, the new African Union (AU) (AU Directory 2002).

The first development has led in less than a decade to a dramatic push of South African companies and franchises into the rest of the continent. The second constitutes the latest attempt by leading African states and presidents to articulate an indigenous direction for the continent, at a time when neo-liberalism's global 'over-confidence' began to be followed by a somewhat less triumphalist version of 'development' (Taylor 2003; also see chapter 13). The overall point is that there may now be a little more space for novel ideas for the analysis and practice of development/ political economy – even in hitherto 'marginalised' Africa.

At the end of the last century, Africa already had a distinctive – albeit marginal – place in a world of globalisation(s). This was reinforced by the intense impacts of 9/11 and the war in and on Iraq from 2003. To be sure, multicultural relations become more problematic in as well as around the continent. But at the same time Africa's oil and gas reserves – as well as UN votes – become ever more valuable. In a world of nearly 200 states, Africa's 50-plus collectively have some credibility, even if they now constitute a smaller proportion of the total in the early 2000s (25 per cent) than in 1990 (33 per cent). While some African states are gradually increasing their economic significance, most are insignificant global economic players: sub-Saharan Africa produces just 0.4 per cent of the world's manufactured exports or just under 2 per cent of those from developing countries. This falls to 0.5 per cent if South Africa's significant contribution is excluded.

While the African continent includes some 'Fourth World' 'countries' – 'collapsed states' is probably a better term – which control very little (for example, Liberia, Somalia), it also contains some aspiring 'Second World' economies which are not (yet?) in the privileged minority of the western industrial countries.

For the first time, in early 2003 the annual 'Globalization Index' from the US journal, *Foreign Policy* included some African states. This index ranks countries according to a mix of economic, personal, political and technological dimensions, such as trade/foreign direct investment (FDI), travel/telephone calls, numbers of memberships in international organisations/embassies and information technology (IT). The top eight African countries in 2003 were: Botswana (#33), Uganda (#36), Nigeria (#37), South Africa (#38), Tunisia (#39), Senegal (#41), Kenya (#43) and Egypt (# 46) ('Measuring globalization: who's up, who's down?' 2003).

In addition, while Africa faces daunting development challenges in the new century – from street children to HIV/AIDS – the rise of civil society, especially in the 1990s, gave pause for some hope. The proliferation of NGOs along with other civic groups and social movements, from ecological and feminist to governance and peacekeeping, served to a degree to balance oppressive regimes and rapacious MNCs. In particular, the proliferation of focused campaigns against particular companies, such as Shell, along with the popularisation of anti-corporate and anti-government demands from the HIV/AIDS lobby in South Africa (www. tac.org.za) may help inform future policies and prospects of states and companies alike (Seckinelgin 2002) (www.oneworldtrust.org).

---

box 12.2   african development: from third world to second world?

Aspiring 'Second World' economies in Africa include Botswana, Mauritius and South Africa. This trio, along with Senegal, are the only African states below the Sahara with 'sovereign' – that is, good – credit ratings. A further group comprises a large number of relatively impoverished – but not hopeless – political economies (for example, Kenya, Morocco and Senegal), as well as a few that may yet become 'democratic developmental states' (for example, Ghana and Uganda). In addition, the region can also 'boast' a few regimes which have excelled in replicating Mobutu-style avarice (for example, Angola). And, as some of Africa's established economies declined at the start of the century (for example, Côte d'Ivoire and Zimbabwe), others rose phoenix-like (for example, Ghana and Tanzania). In sum, such diversity on the continent means that inter- as well as extra-continental trade now has significant possibilities – as long as 'competition states' (Cerny 2003), entrepreneurial companies and labour are sufficiently agile and ready to take risks (Shaw 2004).

In short, the popular, stereotypical image of Africa as concentrated anarchy or chaos is overdrawn. The point is that there are actually several 'Africas', from would-be developmental states to 'basket cases'. To be sure, inequalities between and within the countries of the continent are growing – perhaps unsurprisingly given the uneven impacts of 'globalisations' as indicated below in the context of NEPAD, whose aim is to seek to moderate such divergencies (see chapter 13). However such inequalities are likely to be exacerbated in the future rather than moderated as global conflicts over scarce resources – including energy and water – seem set to intensify (Klare 2002). Seven points follow that sum up Africa's mixed bag of development potentialities in the context of the global political economy.

1. By the 1990s, some African regimes had already achieved a greater degree of ownership of their political economies – as SAPs yielded to the HIPC initiative, whereby macroeconomic policy was a function of nationally-agreed Poverty Reduction Strategy Programmes or Papers (PRSPs). The latter were generated through distinctive national discussions and negotiations, typically involving major elements from civil society and the private sector. Such 'triangular' talks led to enhanced debt reduction and official development assistance (ODA) provision, the former encouraged by global campaigns such as Jubilee 2000, the latter by the growing aid budgets of some western countries, although not the USA.

2. Following the HIPC experiment after the end of the post-bipolar 'honeymoon' of the 1990s and in recognition of the continent's continuing conflicts and development deficit, the Group of Eight

leading industrial countries (G8) became increasingly concerned at Africa's development predicament and, as a result, invited leading African presidents to its Genoa summit in mid-2001. This novel dialogue led to NEPAD and the G8's response in mid-2002 at Kananaskis in Canada (de Waal 2002; www.nepad.org). Given the particular commitment of G8 leaders like Tony Blair and Jean Chretien, new programming for the continent was provided by at least some G8 countries, notably Britain, Canada and France. In addition, the Global Coalition for Africa (GCA) – 'An Intergovernmental Forum for African Development' – organises among states and NGOs on and off the continent, and is primarily concerned with corruption, governance, private sector development, and security issues (www. gca-cma.org). In addition, the World Economic Forum continues to draw attention to Africa at both the annual Davos discourses and also via regular conferences in and on the region.

3. The US African Growth and Opportunity Act (AGOA), announced by the Clinton Administration in the late 1990s, provided significant opportunities for new manufacturing in Africa for countries which met its criteria. From some US$1 billion in investment by the early 2000s, there were around US$3 billion annual exports to the US from Africa in 2001 (www.agoa.gov). So far, the primary sources of and beneficiaries from such exports have been Lesotho, Nigeria, Kenya, South Africa, Swaziland and Uganda (Mattro et al. 2003).

4. Reaching out post-apartheid, some larger South African companies are increasing their extra- as well as intra-African investments. For example, SAB Miller is now the second largest global beer corporation with activities concentrated in emerging markets in Eastern Europe and China as well as in Africa and now the USA. In addition, de Beers is active in new diamond mines and explorations in Canada, while other South African companies – including Digidata, Investec and Old Mutual as well as AAC and de Beers – are now both UK- and South African-based.

5. Conversely, major global MNCs are increasingly active on the continent, especially in its higher-growth countries and regions. For example, Bata (Canada) operates its shoe business in eight African states in the Southern African Development Community (Botswana, Congo, Malawi, South Africa, Zambia and Zimbabwe) (see chapter 14 in this volume), as well as Kenya and Uganda (www.bata.com). Parmalat (Italy) has a major presence in Southern Africa with milk/ yoghurt outlets also in Botswana, Mozambique, Swaziland and Zambia and many in South Africa (www.parmalat.co.za). The French

company Danone manufactures and sells food products in southern Africa and North Africa. In addition, after fifty years, Volkswagen (VW) in Uitenhage now produces one in five of the cars sold in South Africa and by 2001 had exported 100,000 units, mainly Golfs (www. vw.co.za). (Also note VW's major presence in Puebla, Mexico where it produces the new Beetle for the world.) Similarly, having advanced from the assembly of Completely Knocked-Down (CKD) imported parts to full manufacture, BMW invested a billion rand in the mid-1990s and now exports 60,000 units a year, with another 2 billion rand investment in its plant in Gauteng – Rosslyn – expected before 2010 (www.bmw.co.za). Indeed, South Africa's automotive sector has grown – in terms of values of exports – from 20 billion to 40 billion rand since 2000, partly because Volkswagen, BMW and Daimler-Benz began integrating South African operations into their global supply chains in 1996.

6. Regional organisations have been one familiar means by which African states and others in the South have sought to achieve growth (Grant and Soderbaum 2003). (On southern regionalism in general, see chapter 14 in this volume.) But, at least at a formal level, such arrangements have rarely realised their targets, even if more informal regionalisms – ecological, ethnic, social and so on – have often proved more creative and resilient (Taylor 2003). Whilst the East African Community has risen phoenix-like from the ashes, the Economic Community of West African States (ECOWAS) is still largely moribund and the SADC has arguably over-stretched by admitting further members, notably the (non- or multi-state?) Democratic Republic of Congo; that is, SADC has expanded from a meso- to a macro-level grouping. In addition, various other regional groupings now compete with SADC (Soderbaum and Taylor 2003).

7. Finally, despite endless reassuring noises about good governance and the erstwhile 'African Peer Review Mechanism' (APRM), doubts remain about how stringent and effective such criteria/processes will be, given African governments' reluctance to speak out against human rights and constitutional abuses in Zimbabwe ('Africa' 2003). Yet, in mid-2003, ahead of the G8 summit in France, the first set of eminent Africans was selected to implement the process – Adebayo Adedeji (Nigeria), Bethuel Kiplagat (Kenya), Graca Machel (Mozambique), Dorothy Njeuma, Marie Angelique Savane (Senegal) and Chris Stahls (South Africa) – a continental response to endless pressures about accountability and transparency.

ipe of conflict: economies without states

The illegal trade in drugs, arms, intellectual property, people and money is booming. Like the war on terrorism, the fight to control these illicit markets pits governments against agile, stateless and resourceful networks empowered by globalization (Naim 2003: 29).

Like much of the 'new' Central Europe/Asia, Africa is not marginal in terms of its role in illegal networks. Neither is it marginal in relation to the numbers of conflicts that have their roots in the political economy of human insecurity, itself a commentary on global inequalities. Whilst it is recognised that some of the continent's contemporary wars are functions of 'national security' imperatives, most have causes in the deficiencies of human development/security. Moreover, the continent has to deal with related threats such as endangered species, toxic waste and trade in human organs, all of which are informal or illegal niche markets. However, the human, economic and ecological costs of such regional conflicts are incalculable, posing a fundamental challenge to the claims and ideals of NEPAD (MacLean et al. 2002).

There is a growing minority of states in Africa – as in Central Asia and Central Europe – whose governments control little even in the capital city: that is, economies without states (note emerging banking and cellphone as well as traditional drug (qat) networks in the Horn of Africa). In turn, piracy along the long coast of Somalia, in particular Puntland, has prompted shipping companies to dramatically increase their insurance costs or refuse to provide any cover.

---

box 12.3   duffield on security and development

In response to the context of growing insecurity in some developing countries, including in Africa, a new genre of analysis has begun to emerge from scholars and development agencies on the economic causes of conflict on the continent, characterised by Mark Duffield (2001) as the 'merging of development and security'. Duffield argues that this is a function of new insecurities associated with growing inequalities in the global political economy, along with changes in the character of war itself. War now often involves intra- rather than inter-state conflict and a range of actors not just states. As Duffield (2001: 7) notes, 'The focus of the new security concerns is not the threat of traditional interstate wars but the fear of underdevelopment as a source of conflict, criminalized activity and international instability'.

Interestingly, such a perspective has been articulated by both conservative and radical political economists. The former includes classical macroeconomists from the World Bank, while the latter features scholars like William Reno (1998) as well as Duffield and a range of NGOs, especially Partnership Africa Canada (Smillie et al. 2000).

The political economy of war and conflict is also not unrelated to the significance of African diasporas (Sassen 2002), both as a conduit for trade and source of remittances as well as transnational expressions of national identity. This is despite the extent to which they remain marginal to debates about development and Africa's role in the global political economy. Despite difficulties in estimating total flows, for societies like Cape Verde, Eritrea, Sudan and Uganda, remittances account for around 10–25 percent of the GDP of each country. In addition, Ghanaians in the USA sent home between US$ 250 and $350 million per annum throughout the 1990s, more than Ghana gained in FDI.

Finally, looking beyond the short term, a set of longer-term resource wars within and around the continent can be anticipated. These may involve a range of factors and actors – such as, oil/gas, fresh water/river valleys (for example, around the Nile or Zambezi), and biodiversity/DNA/ oxygen (Klare 2002). The point is that conflicts in Africa and elsewhere in the developing world are unlikely to disappear, just to change (RAND Corporation 2003).

partnerships for millennium development goals?

Africa, like other regions in the South, now hosts a range of think-tanks and networks, as well as companies and mafias. As suggested below, these affect development debates and prospects (Parpart and Shaw 2002). The optimistic aura of the turn of the century, something of a companion to HIPC, led to the articulation at the UN General Assembly of the Millennium Development Goals (MDGs). This was a set of basic human-development targets that would be of particular relevance to the poorest countries and communities; those left behind. These have been espoused in NEPAD, which seeks 7 per cent growth through which to achieve them. Given the elusiveness of many if not most MDGs for the continent, notwithstanding a new initiative, the Millennium Development Compact, we turn next to four very visible IPE issues which bring together state (national and international) and non-state actors in forms of limited yet targeted 'global governance'. They are the HIV/ AIDS epidemic; global anti-tobacco campaigns; the International Cocoa Initiative; and the novel Extractive Industries Transparency Initiative.

First, the HIV/AIDS epidemic poses major economic and developmental challenges throughout the continent with global implications (Seckinelgin 2002). The infection rate is still rising in Southern Africa even if it has peaked further north, especially in Uganda (Barnett and Whiteside 2002). The post-apartheid South African state has been the most reluctant to prescribe anti-retrovirals despite some four million HIV-positive citizens. But such reluctance incited an activist NGO Treatment Action Campaign (www.tac.org.za) campaign in the late-1990s, reminiscent of the anti-apartheid movement. Meanwhile, mining companies like Anglo American and de Beers are actively pursuing HIV/AIDS campaigns, including access to anti-retrovirals and are central to national and global corporate efforts (www.businessfightsaids.org). Furthermore, encouraged by the support of Bill Gates' Foundation financed by Microsoft and George Bush's administration, novel and generous partnerships have also developed around the Global Fund to Fight AIDS, TB and Malaria.

Second, global anti-tobacco campaigns versus ubiquitous MNCs like Altria (*aka* Philip Morris) (www.altria.com) and British American Tobacco (BAT) (www.bat.co.uk) have potentially profound implications for African producers and consumers, let alone tax-collectors. This is because manufacturers have begun to target the South rather than the litigious North as growing markets. Such stand-offs led to a WHO Framework Convention on Tobacco Control agreed amongst states and non-states in early 2003. It was cautiously welcomed by the industry, with its important African connections: historical production of tobacco leaf in Southern Africa and growth of sales and production in other southern markets like China. This appears to be a distinctive form of South–South exchange. Tobacco is the biggest non-food agricultural crop and BAT is the largest tobacco company on the continent, especially in Côte d'Ivoire, Kenya and South Africa (www.bat.co.uk). As part of the International Tobacco Growers Association (ITGA), which includes Nigeria, South Africa, Tanzania, Zambia and Zimbabwe, it claims to welcome the WHO process and Convention, but there are significant legal and health dimensions with which to contend (www.who.org).

Third, a parallel International Cocoa Initiative (ICI) is intended to head off any allegations about negative fall-out from 'child slavery' in the global chocolate industry. Like the Kimberley Process and Tobacco Framework, this is another example of a mixed-actor 'governance' initiative involving consumers, inter-state organisations like the ILO, labour, MNCs and NGOs, to pre-empt any boycott campaign like that which Nestle endured over baby food (Klein 2001) (www.cocoafederation.com, www.ilo.org).

Finally, in part a reflection of the integration of the formal and informal, legal and illegal, the novel Extractive Industries Transparency Initiative (EITI) (www.publishwhatyoupay.org) is drawing attention to corruption around mining minerals and pumping oil and gas. Some 130 NGOs, lead by the Open Society Institute and Global Witness, are beginning to expose

---

box 12.4   academic and think-tank initiatives in relation to africa

It is appropriate to highlight a trio of academic and think-tank initiatives within and around Africa which affect the intellectual and theoretical context of IPE on the continent as they do elsewhere. First, the African Economic Research Consortium (AERC) is a novel graduate and research programme supported by western bilateral and foundation donors which has advanced 15 years of graduate training and research (www.aercafrica.org). Second, the IBRD and OECD donor-financed African Capacity Building Foundation (ACBF) has established a series of networks of research and advocacy institutions throughout the continent for development, economy, ecology and otherwise (www.acbf-pact.org). It has thereby helped to finance major think-tanks in several African capitals (48, with more than one in a few major states), for example, the Botswana Institute of Development Policy Analysis and Economic Policy Research Centre (Uganda). And finally, there is the IBRD-initiated Global Development Network (GDN) with a considerable African as well as Asian presence. Its networks and conferences are increasingly separated from those of the international financial institutions (IFIs), such as the IMF and the World Bank; yet, critics contend, its orientation remains overly economistic and positive as well as positivist (www.gdn.org). Together, such think-tanks help to determine state and non-state responses to globalisation.

---

massive forms of corruption by major mining and energy companies, notably in the South (www.globalwitness.org).

Various South African think-tanks are increasingly dominant in continental policy circles, as are South African companies, franchises and networks. It is to this issue we turn next.

ipe of the 'new' south africa in africa

At the current time (2005) there is more foreign direct investment (FDI) in the rest of the African continent from South Africa than elsewhere: states and companies north of the Limpopo now have a choice not only between 'old' European or American capital or new capital like Japan and the rest of Asia; in addition, there is now also South Africa with its relative proximity as well as relative relevance and familiarity.

Symptomatic of the possibilities of 'leap-frogging' is the explosion of cell-phones throughout the continent at the beginning of the 21st century, from Somaliland to Botswana. Currently, there are twice as many cell-phones on the continent as fixed lines, which are concentrated in both North and Southern Africa. And in 2001 alone, cell-phone usage on continent was up by 50 per cent, especially in the latest (and very challenging) market, Nigeria.

South African franchises have 'invaded' the continent. I turn here from retail chains to the service sector. First, in terms of food, clothing and related sectors, for example, by the early 21st century, Shoprite had become the continent's largest retailer with 92 supermarkets in 13 countries from the Cape to Cairo in addition to South Africa, leading to exports from the latter of over R400 million per annum. For the emerging upper-middle classes, Woolworth franchises are now found in Botswana (nearly a dozen), Kenya, Lesotho, Mauritius, Namibia, Swaziland, Tanzania, Uganda, Zambia and Zimbabwe. Interestingly, with the exception of Tanzania and Zambia, all these fall well within the 2002 Human Development Report medium human development category, suggesting that not unlike the 'Big Mac index', Woolworths stores may be suggestive of the size and presence of a middle class!

Second, meanwhile, in the service sectors, from finance to communications, Stanbic Bank operates in Botswana, Congo, Ghana, Tanzania, Uganda, Zambia and Zimbabwe (not to mention Moscow!) and is contemplating opening in Angola and Kenya. Two South African-originated financial companies are becoming both continental and global: Investec operates in SADC, especially Botswana, Mozambique and Namibia, along with UK and USA, plus Australia, Ireland and Israel, while Old Mutual is already in Kenya, Namibia and Zimbabwe as well as the UK. Two major South African-based hotel companies are increasingly active in SADC and COMESA: Protea prides itself on being the largest hotel company in the continent: in a dozen African states from Egypt to South Africa, including a half-dozen in Tanzania; and Sun International occupies a more exclusive segment around casinos and golf in SADC. MTN has mobile phone licences in Cameroon, Rwanda, Swaziland and Uganda as well as Nigeria. And MNet/DStv operate satellite TV facilities throughout the continent via a series of concentric circles from RSA hub, franchises and joint ventures in SADC and the Commonwealth, and then agents in the francophone/Sahelian states plus Congo; almost all of sub-Saharan Africa including the islands: some 850,000 subscribers!

In sum, South Africa's growing economic and technological hegemony in the African region is symptomatic of its new political economy. This presents lessons for regions other than Africa: what will be the character of political economy in the new century by contrast to earlier ones – especially the 19th and 20th? It is for this reason that I have concentrated on Africa in this chapter.

what futures for ipe?

This chapter has presented challenges to a set of interrelated approaches, disciplines and debates which comprise established IPE, with relevance beyond the global South. In particular, I have suggested that lingering state-centrism, along with an over-emphasis on formal and legal sectors, is now misplaced in terms of both analysis and prescription: 'success stories' among 'competition states' in the new century require flexible, innovative coalitions or partnerships involving a range of non-state actors (Lewis 2002). Furthermore, this perspective challenges established notions in a set of social science disciplines around the state and market. Even more than before, successful, sustainable governance of IPE in the new century requires creative networking amongst a range of actors as found in some flexible production and outsourcing arrangements, franchise agreements and supply chains. Globalisations necessitate continuous adaptation at regional, national and local levels everywhere.

Contemporary policy responses entail transcending orthodox assumptions still prevalent in established disciplines and even interdisciplinary fields such as development or security studies. Likewise, policy responses from state and non-state actors at all levels need to be creative in a world of nearly 200 states and competing companies, regions and sectors, as indicated in the myriad national and regional competitive indices, 'globalisation tables' and Human Development Reports. IPE needs to begin to notice and incorporate corporate codes, innovative partnerships, economic causes of conflict, informal and illegal sectors etc. Despite its marginality, then, insights from Africa can point the way.

note

1. Because of the large number of websites and acronyms noted and used in this chapter, interested readers will find a list of each at the end of the chapter (following this note).

websites

www.agoa.gov   US Growth and Opportunity Act
www.ashantigold.com   Ashanti Gold Company (Ghana)
www.attac.org   anti-globalization network
www.bat.co.uk   British-American Tobacco
www.businessday.co.za   RSA daily business paper
www.copenhagencentre.org   Danish partnership organization
www.debeers.com   De Beers (diamond) Company (South Africa and United Kingdom)
www.ethicaltrade.org   ethical trade site
www.ifg.org   International Forum on Globalization
www.foreignpolicy.com   US journal
www.gdn.org   Global Development Network
www.globalreporting.org   CERES's Global Reporting Initiative (on corporate codes)

www.globalsullivanprinciples.org   Global Sullivan Principles (on corporate codes)
www.humansecurity-chs.org   Canadian (NGO) Consortium on Human Security
www.humansecuritynetwork.org   Canadian (inter-state) Network on Human Security
www.nepad.org   New Partnership for Africa's Development
www.nologo.org   anti-globalization site
www.oneworld.org   pro-development site
www.oneworldtrust.org   UK parliamentary think tank
www.polity.co.uk/global   site to read Held, McGrew et al
www.publishwhatyoupay.org   Extractive Industries Transparency Initiative
www.tac.org.za   HIV/AIDS Treatment Action Campaign (RSA)
www.tni.org   Transnational Institute anti-globalization site
www.undp.org   UN Development Program
www.unglobalcompact.org   UN's partnership initiative
www.weforum.org   World Economic Forum pro-globalization site
www.wider.unu.edu   UNU World Institute on Economic Development (Finland)
www.worlddiamondcouncil.org   seqway into the Kimberley Process
www.wto.org   World Trade Organization
www.zadek.net   site of leading advocate/analyst of partnerships

list of acronyms

GATT   General Agreement on Tariffs and Trade
HIPC   Highly Indebted Poor Country Initiative
IBRD   World Bank
IFIs   international financial institutions
MDGs   Millennium Development Goals
MNCs   multinational corporations
NEPAD   New Partnership for Africa's Development
NGOs   non-governmental organisations
OECD   Organization for Economic Cooperation and Development
PRSPs   Poverty Reduction Strategy Programmes
SADC   Southern African Development Community
SAPs   Structural Adjustment Programmes
UN   United Nations
WEF   World Economic Forum
WHO   World Health Organization
WTO   World Trade Organization

13
globalisation and development
ian taylor

introduction

Development and other terms such as 'North–South', 'First World–Third World', 'developed world–developing world', and so on can be endlessly unpacked and debated. In this chapter, 'development' refers to 'the increasing capacity to make rational use of natural and human resources for social ends' (Mittelman and Pasha 1997: 25). The term 'the North', refers to the western industrialised states, for example, the United States, Western Europe, Japan, and so on. The 'South', on the other hand, refers to the developing/industrialising countries, primarily located in the ex-colonial states of Africa, Asia and Latin America. Such states – in general – have faced immense development challenges and at the turn of the 21st century and in the current neo-liberal epoch this appears to be continuing. Indeed, under the catch-all rubric of 'globalisation' topics such as trade, investment, aid, capital flows and economic integration; as well as migration from the South to the North; narcotics smuggling (invariably in the same direction); and environmental issues – often the (illicit) shipping of toxic waste from the North to the South – are firmly on the developmental agenda. However, the recently emerged reformist discourse that seeks to ameliorate neo-liberal globalisation with various ill-defined 'developmental' ingredients has now become perhaps the dominant elite position on the potentiality of development in the new millennium. The inherent limitations, constraints and contradictions of this agenda and how current features associated with globalisation undermine development is a key theme of this chapter.

In the context of globalisation, of major importance is the scenario whereby 'mono-economics', that is, the belief that there exists a universal set of economic laws that apply across the board (Hirschman 1981), has

---

box 13.1   the vexed relationship between globalisation and development

Globalisation itself is a term open to debate, and it is vital to be specific as to what we mean, rather than talk in fairly meaningless terms of 'space' and 'time' (Rosenberg 2000). Capitalism has always striven to be global and Marx's comments that the bourgeoisie 'compels all nations, on pain of extinction, to adopt the bourgeois mode of production; it compels them to introduce what it calls civilisation into their midst, that is, to become bourgeois themselves', remain arguably as true today as when Marx wrote them (Marx and Engels 1971). Indeed, the type, context and the essential impetus of the current process of capitalism associated with globalisation represents the universalisation of capitalist social relations (Wood 2002). Today, globalisation implies the making global of a host of social and economic factors which in aggregate further undermine distinctions between the international and domestic. Integral to this process – and something which profoundly impacts upon the potentiality of development – is the continuing – but now challenged – hegemony of neo-liberalism. It is against this 'standard' that all countries are judged; and 'development' itself must square with the familiar neo-liberal package if it is to receive the stamp of approval from important powers-that-be within the global economy. Neo-liberalism has, in the view of many, 'become the predominant ideology legitimating the privatisation of the state-controlled economy and the substitution of the market for the social provision of basic welfare' (Overbeek and Van der Pijl 1993: 1). How this might increase capacity to make rational use of one's natural and human resources for social ends is of course a moot and controversial point. Indeed, the privatisation of everyday life is increasingly problematic, not least in the realm of welfare provision, public goods or, even, security (Muthien and Taylor 2002).

---

emerged as a means of informing and shaping development practice. This is however highly dubious if not dangerous if we are to advance a developmental agenda. Primarily, this is because, as Gray points out (1998: 3), the dominant discourse surrounding globalisation

> represents as inevitable what is, in fact, a highly unlikely outcome of the current drive to create a free market…[conflating]…the end-state favoured by the project with the actual development of economic globalisation…[They] represent…an historical transformation that has no end-state and which is subverting American capitalism as well as its rivals, as a process leading to a universal acceptance of American free markets.

Critics contend that if the development model – informed by 'American capitalism' – is so blissfully ignorant of all other experiences while projecting 'hyper-liberalism' as a universal, then development must certainly be under serious attack. That is, if development is about the ability to make sensible use of resources in the service of society then we are all in trouble. As Cox (2002: 180) remarks:

In America, which is the model for globalisation, a thriving economy has in recent years generated both a high level of employment, much of in low-paid and precarious jobs, and a growing polarisation of incomes. There are signs that rampant individualism may have passed a point at which it serves as a dynamic of economic competition to become a threat to social cohesion.

It can be argued that this scenario hardly amounts to a rational developmental plan for American – much less global – long-term growth and empowerment. Intimately linked to the above is the dynamic of social relations and the reconfiguration and intensification of social and/or class struggles. The point is that to many critics 'globalisation' appears to be primarily about: *reconfiguration of power on a global scale with a profound influence over epoch-making changes* vis-à-vis *economic, social, gender, financial and political relations.*

In sum, these shifts, generated by the impulses associated with the global-wide diffusion of the power of capital arguably serve to make discussions of development inherently problematic. This is can be illustrated by examining the last half-century or so – that is, since the end of World War II – of the history of 'development' in the context of globalisation. Consequently, this chapter focuses on globalisation over time, and posits that that the currently underdeveloped status of many Southern countries is closely linked to its trajectory.

locating development in the context of globalisation

Modern debates regarding development emerged from the trauma of World War II. It was in the post-war period that the developing world began to 'fit' into the wider international political economy in a way that had not been readily apparent in the pre-Cold War era, that is, before the war. The developing world was rapidly configured in a series of often overlapping layers of spheres of economic and political influence, which were continuations or developments from the colonial period. Many commentators note that this development was intimately linked to the Cold War: during this time, Latin America remained under *de facto* United States tutelage, as American-based transnational capital continued to dominate the economic life of the continent. The presumption of US foreign policy was that this was a state of affairs that required defending at all costs, particularly in the post-Castroist era – hence the USA's 'Alliance for Progress' in the 1960s. In addition, both East and South East Asia, following the injection of massive amounts of American capital that was poured into the region in the aftermath of the Korean War (1950–53), were largely under the 'direction' of a revived Japanese capitalist class. Arguably, this class was in effect acting as a proxy for Washington, during a time when the US sought to reconfigure the region as a site of investment and a particular form of state-led growth.

---

box 13.2   the south and the bretton woods institutions

After 1945, the broader milieu within which to locate southern development was that provided by the post-war economic-political settlement, the 'embedded liberalism' of the Bretton Woods institutions and its sister groups, namely the World Bank, the International Monetary Fund (IMF), and the General Agreement on Tariffs and Trade (GATT) – now the World Trade Organisation (WTO) (Helleiner 1994). Some see this period as a post-war 'Golden Age', a compromise between capital and labour via various Keynesian welfare nationalist schemes. Under the aegis of the Bretton Woods institutions, 'mixed economies' and a liberalising international economy became central to this arrangement. This settlement stimulated the development of what are often perceived as 'economic-political agents': externally-oriented transnational corporations, national (inwardly-looking) monopolistic/oligopolistic corporations, and state administrations (Van der Pijl 1984). Some contend that these agents created in both the North and, to a lesser degree the South, 'triple alliances' which to a large degree overlooked the economic and political evolution of both.

The concurrent rise of the 'Asian Tigers' – Hong Kong, Singapore, South Korea and Taiwan – complemented this process and indeed, in many cases appeared to be driven by the demand to bolster a capitalist-orientated – that is, anti-communist – barrier to the further spread of socialism. The desire to protect this scheme of things was one of the fundamental reasons for Washington's (ultimately disastrous) involvement in Indochina (Vietnam, Cambodia, Laos) in the 1960s and early 1970s. Finally, Africa was more or less left to the metropolitan powers and their transnational (or in 'semi-peripheral' states, such as Portugal, national) corporations to continue 'business as usual'. There was, however, some realisation that eventually a re-thinking of Euro-African relations was both imminent and long overdue (see chapter 12).

It is important to understand that this development occurred at an important juncture: the 1960s, a time when many newly-independent nations, especially in Asia and Africa, were, so as to speak, 'flexing their muscles'. Moreover, there was an accompanying heady optimism regarding the manoeuvrability of the developing world in relation to the western developed countries. Indeed, some writers, asserting that dependent relations constructed during the colonial period precluded development within the wider world economy, advocated an autocentric 'de-linking' from the capitalist world economy (Amin 1985). However, contrary to what some have suggested, this did not actually imply an autarchic utopia, but rather a development strategy that emphasised domestic requirements over excessive reliance on external demand. While, over time, such impulses declined in significance they did not quite die, but retained an attraction for a number of scholars disillusioned with the marginalising processes at work alongside what has been called 'deepening globalisation' (see, for example, Carmen 1996 and Mengisteab 1996).

The overall point is that the South's development after 1945 was in essence a micro-process within a broader macro-process.

globalisation and the historic retreat of the south

The South's efforts to put forward a New International Economic Order (NIEO) in the 1970s was not to last long and this initiative has virtually disappeared in the contemporary 'globalised' world. What many commentators see as the reassertion over the South of northern politico-economic dominance came at a particular period – the 1980s – when the financial indebtedness of large numbers of developing countries acted drastically to undermine – if not entirely remove – the sovereignty and manoeuvrability of many of them. Although now formally independent, most developing countries, because of their dependent relationship with the western developed countries, have continued to borrow from the industrialised world in order to seek to develop their economies.

During the 1980s, many leaders of developing countries were increasingly drawn into the continuing economic restructuring process promoted by neo-liberalism. Indeed, the call for such liberalisation – strongly informing the accompanying rhetoric about economic 'realities' – is said to have provided space for conservative figures within the governments of many developing countries – people who in most

---

box 13.3   recycling petro-dollars and international indebtedness

The recycling of petro-dollars made borrowing an easy option in the 1970s and early 1980s, and many developing countries indulged in massive borrowing – which meant that their external indebtedness expanded rapidly. Lending practices of western bankers contributed both to this process and its outcome. Such a practice was clearly unsustainable for long. This is because massive indebtedness created immense problems for the South – creating a Catch-22 situation whereby many funds to finance development were actually diverted to service debts. In addition, the necessity to secure foreign currencies to service the debt led to a quick depreciation of many southern currencies and eventually significant price inflation. Paradoxically, oil prices, which had initially stimulated the lending/borrowing spree, exacerbated the problem.

cases had long been reluctant to commit themselves fully to the NIEO. It was convenient in many cases for them to seize upon the growing globalisation discourse to help explain away unpopular policies to cope with the debt crises, a policy that reflected at best minimal commitment to any major restructuring of the global economy (except, perhaps, where it benefited such figures personally). This, combined with an ever-increasing – and increasingly dominant – consensus among such elites over the liberalisation of economic policies, led to the virtual redundancy of 'alternative' visions regarding the international political economy. As a result, what might be termed 'confrontationist' expressions, stances that were common in much of the South's rhetoric in the 1960s and 1970s, appeared increasingly incongruous from 1980s. This was a period where it was often suggested that in fact there was 'no clear alternative' to neo-liberal policies and programmes. In short, impulses generated by the insights of dependency theory in the 1960s and 1970s gradually gave way to what was essentially a return to the certainties of modernisation theory, via the imposition of Structural Adjustment Programmes (SAPs) (Lensink 1996).

During the 1980s, as the debt crisis worsened in many parts of the South, growth stagnated, employment declined, monetary arrangements collapsed and financial agreements between creditors and debtors were increasingly undermined by mass bankruptcies. Later, with the demise of the Cold War (a process, many argue, that began in the mid-1980s with President Gorbachev's decision to curtail Soviet foreign adventurism), options emanating from the Soviet 'East' appeared to evaporate. The consequence was that in such a climate room for manoeuvre for southern leaders became ever more constricted (Little et al. 1994). The means to overcome what had become a crisis in development thinking linked to globalisation was a resort to borrowing from two older theoretical approaches: neoclassical economics, and modernisation theory (Mengisteab and Logan 1995). As already noted, this combination was part and parcel of the SAPs that reconfigured whole swathes of the developing world in the 1980s and 1990s. The core of SAPs was an implicit echoing of the modernisers' argument that the 'fundamentals' had to be in place to assure economic development. Failure to do this, particularly by African states, was blamed for the common failure of SAPs (Harvey 1996).

It was in this context and at this juncture that southern-dominated development-oriented bodies such as the United Nations Commission on Trade and Development (UNCTAD) and the Non-Aligned Movement

(NAM) sought to re-package and re-present their organisations. However, while the logic of neo-liberalism was often broadly accepted, globalisation's negative effects were widely felt. Consequently, ameliorating policies to cope with the perceived malign impacts of globalisation emerged as defining principles for both organisations and informed how 'development' might be re-thought in the context of globalisation. This process gathered pace following the end of the Cold War and formed a key focus of a leading organisation of the developing countries: the Non-Aligned Movement (see Box 13.4).

---

box 13.4   the non-aligned movement and globalisation

At the ninth summit of the NAM in Belgrade in 1989, Yugoslavia 'pleaded for the modernisation of the Movement [thus] discarding the NAM's attitude of assertiveness *vis-à-vis* the two power blocs. Instead, the NAM [adopted] a more tolerant and flexible position with emphasis on co-operation and dialogue' (Syatauw 1993: 129). The next summit in Indonesia in 1992 produced the Jakarta Declaration, which many commentators saw as 'the first major reaction of the NAM to the emerging world order' (Sesay1998). Post-Jakarta the NAM changed its approach and orientation from one that was often viewed as confrontational to one that was conciliatory and cooperative. This process was also exhibited at UNCTAD VIII in Cartagena, Colombia, in 1992 where the 'Spirit of Cartagena' recognised the central roles of private enterprise and the market for growth, and recognised the 'shared responsibility and partnership for development'.

This 'Spirit' reflected in essence an acceptance of neo-liberalism, with the abandonment in the final communiqué of any confrontational posturing. Instead, there was talk of the need to overcome confrontation and to foster a climate of genuine cooperation and solidarity in order to facilitate development. The Cartagena summit of the NAM, held in October 1995, continued the broad trajectory that Jakarta had exemplified. In sum, the 'Call from Cartagena', although containing with many of the old familiar non-aligned themes such as sovereignty, disarmament and anti-colonialism, also contained within it a commitment to 'sound macro-economic management' and growth as necessary precursor to development.

As with the NAM, Mittelman and Pasha (1997: 53) contend that in the current globalisation era many international organisations reflect changes in global production and politics:

They disseminate values and norms that contribute toward redesigning the global political economy. From the height of the Cold War to the more recent concerns of globalisation, international institutions have absorbed the realities of global political economy and its contradictions. Imbued with neo-liberal doctrines, the current remedy for all ills is the market.

That this was broadly so with the NAM was shown by Cartagena's demand for better working relationships with the World Bank, IMF and the WTO. This wish to further increase the dialogue between the key institutions of neo-liberalism and the NAM was to remain a feature of both the NAM's and UNCTAD's position over the next few years. This reflected a playing out of the increasing integration of the world's markets and the desire by local southern-based elites to benefit from this process wherever possible. Combative posturing against the structural inequalities of the capitalist system, characteristic of the *dependencia* (dependency theory) position, were seen to be of little use in facing up to globalisation, particularly when – as many have noted – numerous southern leaders appeared to 'sign up' to the theory and practices of neo-liberalism. Even those that did not fully accede to this 'New World Order' were painfully aware of the continuing marginalisation that many developing countries continued to endure. It was in this context that, with the exception of Cuba and North Korea, no governments of developing countries *openly* rejected the ideology of neo-liberalism as the 'correct' path to development.

development and democracy: the missing link under globalisation

The discussion above has sought to highlight the main reasons for the neo-liberal turn in development thinking manifested during the 1980s and 1990s, a process widely seen as part and parcel of contemporary globalisation as it affected most developing countries. However, we must try to try to avoid what would be a teleological leap: from the NIEO and the global structural inequalities that mark out the international political economy – to the inculcation of norms surrounding what is widely regarded as a neo-liberal hegemony. The point is that we must not forget the role of *agency* in a focus upon the *structural conditionalities* that have facilitated the embedding of the dominance of neo-liberal economic policies and programmes. The discourse of 'democratic development' was particularly crucial in crafting the neo-liberal agenda.

William Robinson (1996) has presented a powerful thesis concerning the promotion of liberal democracy in the developing world by Washington and various international agencies ('the Washington Consensus'). Robinson provides evidence for his argument by examining the promotion of a particular form of 'low level' 'democracy' in the Philippines, Chile, Nicaragua and Haiti. This policy, he suggests, had significant social and economic implications for the chances of development in these countries.

Until perhaps the end of the Cold War, authoritarian and dictatorial styles of government were often seen as prerequisites for rapid economic growth and development in the South. Western governments often seemed happy to advance funds and support to undemocratic regimes throughout the developing world, often with minimal if any reference to democracy. For example, there were substantial funds advanced to Taiwan and South Korea as they industrialised, while other friendly leaders – such as Marcos (the Philippines), Mobutu (Zaïre, now the Democratic Republic of Congo) and Pinochet (Chile) – received funds often unsuccessfully earmarked for development purposes. However, since the latter part of the 1980s and particularly after 1989, there has been what is known as the 'third wave of democracy' (Huntington 1991). Most analyses have taken for granted a particular understanding of democracy and its role in the rhetoric surrounding development. This common sense conceptualisation takes western models of liberal democracy as the normative standard by which democratisation processes can be measured and evaluated. Indeed, there exists today a sort of nascent industry within democratic studies of practitioners embarking upon various forms of 'democratic audits' and such like. What such views share is a starting point that assumes the very formal and procedural models of democracy at face value. Critics contend however that such an approach is flawed – not least because of a common failure to find out whether there have actually been any substantive developmental gains achieved for ordinary citizens during, or as a result of, democratisation processes. Furthermore, some analysts also argue that the democratisation waves were based on calls for liberal democracy *per se* – whereas in many cases they might instead be seen as expressions of frustration and resentment against austerities and life-threatening strictures enforced upon the South by structural adjustment during the 'lost decade' of the 1980s and beyond. (See chapter 4 for an alternative interpretation of democratisation and its consequences in developing countries.)

Critics have noted that preoccupation with procedural forms of democracy in the context of globalisation fitted well with the agenda advanced by various international financial institutions (IFIs) – including the IMF and the World Bank – as well as aid donors and lending agencies. The political repertoire of such agents often seemed, critics contended, to be dominated by references to democracy and good governance as the foundation of development. Later, in the 1990s, these discourses

box 13.5   globalisation and the preoccupation with democracy

Rita Abrahamsen (2000) argues that preoccupations with democratic norms – 'the rediscovery of rights', as it were – emerged when the Cold War was coming to an end – and as, contemporaneously, the impact of globalisation was becoming more and more profound. As a result, oppressive dictators could no longer be maintained and supported by references to the supposed threat from the USSR. However, critics have suggested that this good governance agenda actually comprises only very hollow democratic institutional forms, crafted to advance a specific type of democracy harmonious with further promotion of SAPs, very often in the teeth of popular opposition. In short, it can be suggested that the type of democracy advanced by the IFIs and donors entails a vital strategy to deal with such opposition: the demobilisation of popular energy post-elections and the diversion of political activity into party politics and matters pertaining to parliamentary participation (Taylor 2002).

The consequence of the demand for democratisation was that governments in the developing world were virtually hostage to a Janus-faced dilemma. On the one hand, they were now supposedly beholden to their (increasingly dissatisfied) domestic constituencies while, on the other, they were accountable to unelected external creditors and donors (Abrahamsen 2000). This often resulted in the creation of highly fragile 'democracies', which remained unable to satisfy the demands and aspirations of their populations, especially their poor majorities. At the same time, socio-economic improvements and development played second fiddle to the increasingly strident requirements of the IFIs and donors, with everything wrapped up in the 'no alternative' thesis associated with specific readings of globalisation (see Taylor and Vale 2000).

became part of wider conditionalities attached to granting of foreign developmental assistance.

The foregoing analysis suggests that 'development' is a historically contingent form of knowledge, closely tied to dominant structures and global power relations. That is, 'development' does not appear to be an ahistorical set of universally applicable goals as many modernisation theorists, including the American economic historian Walt Rostow (1960), claimed. However, it appears that the type of neo-liberal precepts that underpin the contemporary development discourse associated with good governance and particular notions of democracy have arguably contributed to what has been seen as a continuation of a profoundly undemocratic world order, despite the claims made by its promoters. The question remains how this is legitimised by the good governance discourse, which takes as common sense the notion that democracy is only relevant within states and cannot be applied outside to the IFIs or more broadly to issues of global good governance.

William Robinson (1995: 647) focuses on this point in suggesting that 'struggles for popular democracy around the world are profound threats to the privileges of US-led Northern elites and their junior counterparts in the South'. He goes on to say that 'the USA, in the age of globalisation, [is] not acting on behalf of a U.S. elite, but...[plays] a leadership role on behalf of a transnational hegemonic configuration representing transnational capital' (ibid.). It is possible to suggest that popular opposition to various non-democratic (and by extension, anti-development) regimes during the 1980s and 1990s – such as the 'anti-globalisation' movement – was often linked at grassroots level to the goal of forms of democracy that would appear a threat to the continuing dominance of capitalism. As a result of such aspirations, critics such as Robinson suggest that it was imperative for those interested in maintaining the status quo to find means by which such struggles could be undermined and the interests of the privileged defended.

In sum, under current conditions, critics suggest that where globalisation continues its push for greater integration and inter-penetration of economies across formal state boundaries, the promotion of liberal democracy in the South has developed as a structural feature of the globalised 'new world order'. The 1970s and 1980s saw the rise of numerous popular movements that generally organised against repressive governments and their exploitative, non-democratic rule. Very often, such opposition was simultaneously attempting to construct alternative grassroots forms of popular democracy. As Robinson (1996: 16) points out, while dictatorships began to crumble and 'a general crisis of elite rule began to develop in the South...the "elective affinity" between authoritarianism and [capitalist] domination unravelled [and] "democracy promotion" substituted "national security"' in the language of the West and its relations with the South. This process was no doubt exacerbated by the decline of the state-socialist economies, which meant that direct coercive intervention to stem the 'communist threat' of popular action could no longer be mobilised by the West in an attempt to restore or maintain the status quo.

With the decline in utility of sheer coercion (though the 'armour of coercion' – force – is always of course in reserve as the ultimate guarantor of the status quo), authoritarian regimes were no longer 'acceptable' to western governments and society and, consequently, could no longer be openly propped up as they had been in the past. In the context of neo-liberalism whereby the state is said to be 'rolled back', traditional forms of social control had to be reinvented and consent secured, alongside coercion. Some suggest that this consensual mechanism of social control was part and parcel of the globalising neo-liberal economic project, adding crucial legitimacy via liberal democratic political systems to a specific economic (though not necessarily developmental) model that could not be achieved under authoritarian regimes. Hence, 'formal democratic structures are...seen as more disposed to diffusing the sharpest social tensions and to incorporating sufficient social bases with which to sustain more stable environments under the conflict-ridden and fluid conditions of emergent global society' (Robinson 1995: 642).

For Graf (1996: 41): 'Democratisation nowadays has become...a hegemonic discourse allowing the North to define the South in its own image'. In support, Hyden (1997: 236) avers that 'support for [democratisation] efforts in Africa is part of a global strategy to promote "Western" values and institutionalise political regimes that are likely to be non-belligerent and generally positive towards the realisation of the liberal paradigm'. This is also conducive to advancing the supposed seamless utopia of the 'global village' based on essentially western capitalist values and strictures. Naomi Klein clearly captures what this village means for many in respect of development and empowerment:

> This is a village where some multinationals, far from levelling the global playing field with jobs and technology for all, are in the process of mining the planet's poorest back country for unimaginable profits ...IBM claims that its technology spans the globe, and so it does, but often its international presence takes the form of cheap Third World labour producing the computer chips and power sources that drive our machines. On the outskirts of Manila, for instance, I met a seventeen-year-old girl who assembles CD-ROM drives for IBM. I told her I was impressed that someone so young could do such high-tech work. "We make computers", she told me, "but we don't know how to operate computers". Ours, it would seem, is not such a small planet after all.
> (http://www.mindspring.com/altaflo/globalization.html)

However, some warn that it is important to avoid the reductionist tendency to see globalisation as simply a manufactured conspiracy emanating from the North. Instead, it might be argued, the globalisation process perhaps more accurately represents a 'complex convergence of interests among an increasingly cohesive transnational elite headed by a US-led Northern bloc' but also 'incorporating elite constituencies in the South' (Robinson 1995: 643). This process, it is suggested, is designed explicitly to thwart the developmental demands and aspirations of the mass of ordinary people at a time when open coercion is no longer either acceptable or economical (though, as already noted, the use of force can never be completely ruled out). Indeed, as Neufeld (1999) points out: 'The framing and circumscribing of democratic thought and discourse in terms of the precepts of polyarchy can be understood as an effort by core state elites to solidify and stabilise the hegemony which safeguards their positions of power and privilege' within the global economy. By doing so the current politico-economic arrangements appear to be legitimised, as suffrage has been increasingly universalised and hence, at least potentially, grievances are now remedied via the ballot box, not by mass action or community groups' self-development. As Graf (1996: 44) notes:

> The combination of economic and political liberalism [in polyarchy] is...not democracy per se...but that is not the point; the point is that the dominant discourse has determined that it is. And of course economic liberalism is but another term for capitalism, so that capitalism appears as the economic face of democracy, thus downplaying the negative associations, in the South, between capitalism and imperialism and collapsing the elite ideological construct into [an] amorphous but demagogically effective concept of democracy.

In sum, critics contend that the globalisation process acts to bolster the structural position of pre-existing southern political and economic elites already enjoying both status and trappings of power. Consequently, their activities shift from active democratic intercourse with the mass of ordinary people – towards increased identification and solidarity with power holders in the North.

globalisation and development: a free and fair international system?

It is suggested that the scenario sketched above marks the current period, that is, where neo-liberalism appears as the hegemonic economic ideology. Having said that, however, we need to note the emergence of a nascent call for another (possible) NIEO, albeit drastically limited in scope. This is still very much at an embryonic stage as yet and needs further clarification, but it seems that there is what might be gathering momentum for *some* reformist impulses within what still remains a globalised and neo-liberal era. This development:

- is in essence a synthesis of modernisation theory-inspired precepts – associated with neo-liberal SAPs and with what constitutes 'good governance';

- draws on the assertion that the world order is currently heavily weighted in favour of the North and needs redressing;
- appears to link up with the insights of dependency theory – although many of its advocates might not admit it.

Indeed, concern has increasingly been expressed that what amounts to a historic bargain undertaken by the South – to drop its confrontational posture in return for benefiting from globalisation – has been a largely one-sided affair as development has stagnated in large parts of the globe, not least in much of Africa (see chapter 5 for an alternative view). Critics contend that how the developmental remit of organisations such as UNCTAD relates to the World Trade Organisation (WTO) is now a source of concern for many developing countries. This is particularly so as the North has opposed any reference to the implementation of 'specific WTO agreements, especially if developing countries suggested that their developed counterparts were not honouring their obligations' (Carim 1996: 3). The overall point is that while the South has accepted a less overtly hostile attitude to various international financial institutions and dominant global players, and has actively facilitated forums where business can be involved in economic matters, reform of various facets of the world economy has also been put onto the agenda.

In this emerging perspective, the WTO is seen as strengthening the rules-based trading system, while furthering liberalising and opening up opportunities for sustainable development and growth. To some degree, confrontation with the North has now given way to 'dialogue'. As the (former) South African Foreign Minister, Alfred Nzo (1997:3) puts it: 'the previously confrontational and sterile style of the world-wide debate on North–South issues has made way for a vigorous and healthy debate on core issues. This too mirrors our own change in which matters previously caused division and dissension are now open to wide discussion'. Yet, as this 'toned down' message from the South emerges, it is also apparent that with the acceptance of the hegemonic norms of trade liberalisation and the implicit acceptance of the modernisation project of the SAPs, goes recognition of the uneven process of globalisation. This is translated into a *partial* counter-hegemonic position that has called for a lessening of the worst aspects of this process (see Mkandawire and Soludo 1999). This position 'has largely taken on board the "realities" of the liberalising globalised world order, although [it] adopt[s] a more holistic and questioning approach [raising] issues of particular concern to the developing world' (African NGO Declaration to UNCTAD IX, 1996). Such impulses have informed the evolution of Africa's latest development

box 13.6   the new economic partnership for africa's development (nepad)

It is suggested that a sense of urgency to expose what many see as the hypocrisy of the North in its calculated push for free trade in the South – while keeping various of its own markets closed to southern competition – has led some developing countries to engage with the North, through such initiatives as the NEPAD, rather than confront them. Generally speaking, many southern leaders now seem to accept the call for neo-liberal restructuring, but nevertheless try to turn this rhetoric around and urge the North to engage in *real* free trade, rather than the 'actually existing free trade' situation that currently characterises international commerce and frustrates many developmental ambitions. This urge for a critical engagement with the North tends to be characterised as 'partnership' – also exemplified by the NEPAD – which attempts to deal with both the positive and negative aspects of the ongoing globalising process. Such 'pragmatic' policies have increasingly been transposed to specifically continental institutions, such as the African Union (which replaced the Organisation of African Unity [OAU] in 2003).

At the OAU Heads of State meeting in Algiers in July 1999, it emerged that there was some movement towards a shift in the overall approach of the body towards a more engaging and 'constructive' dialogue with the North (*Business Day* [Johannesburg], July 14, 1999). President Thabo Mbeki of South Africa was quite explicit in this regard at the same OAU Heads of State meeting. Mbeki (1999) argued that past 'negative' rhetoric had to be ditched in order for the Organisation to move on:

> The Draft Algiers Declaration contains a paragraph on globalisation which I believe is, in many respects, fundamentally flawed and should be changed. it reads: '...Ushered in with promises of progress and prosperity for all, (globalisation) has today aroused fears, in that it poses serious threats to our sovereignty, cultural and historical identities as well as gravely undermining our development prospects. We believe that globalisation should be placed within the framework of a democratically conceived dynamics, and implemented collectively to make it an institution capable of fulfilling the hope for a concerted developmental of mankind [sic] and prosperity shared by all people'. I am certain that in our discussions today we will help one another, among other things, to understand better the objective process of globalisation and its positive and negative features.

Such notions have broadly underpinned the NEPAD initiative—as well as South African foreign policy in general (see Taylor 2001a). This being said, such impulses should not be caricatured as being an abject surrender by the South before the North. Though at a basic level many leaders of developing countries have embraced neo-liberalism, with all its implications for development, many do seem aware of the negative downside and pressures concurrent with globalisation. Thus some such figures promote a reformist agenda aiming to 'improve' the global system while promoting a more rules-based international regime (Taylor 2001b). According to South Africa's Minister of Trade and Industry, Pretoria is a 'very strong supporter...in the WTO as a rules-based system...Correctly administered and managed it prevents the abuse of "might is right"' (Erwin 1998: 63). Here, and in other multilateral fora, southern engagement with what is perceived as the unstoppable juggernaut of globalisation strives to match the rhetoric of liberalisation with its universal application. Thus recent calls for 'partnership' between North and South are predicated upon this free trade framework. It aims to move towards some form of workable relationship with the North in order to lessen the more negative aspects encountered by some developing countries – especially in Africa – as they seeks to engage with the 'objective process' of globalisation.

plan, the New Economic Partnership for Africa's Development (NEPAD), although the fundamentally neo-liberal (or at least post-Washington Consensus) underpinnings are quite clear (see Taylor and Nel, 2002). (Also see chapter 12.)

The viability of the call for a new world order – which explicitly aims to promote development within the context of a globalising world market – remains open to question. Indeed, while the history of North–South relations, with its concomitant struggle between the precepts of modernisation theory and dependency theory, may well now be turning, whether this new turn in development thinking is sustainable is unclear. The question might be posed in this way:

- Is it actually possible to deregulate markets and roll back the state, allowing a free rein for international capital and, at the same time promote equity and mutual development in both North and South?

It might be the case that those advocating such a policy need first to focus upon three prior and fundamental questions:

- Is it intrinsic to the capitalist system that the generation of wealth is predicated upon poverty-producing principles and must there always be a *dominant* sector and a *dominated* sector in society – in international terms, a North and a South?
- Is the call for a new development partnership a chimera or attainable?
- Can this development actually be seen to exemplify how dominant neo-liberal ideas have become, with key figures in the South now clamouring to sign up to economic prescriptions that, many argue, have actually helped to immiserate many in the developing world?

It seems clear that engagement and calls for partnership seem far more likely to gain a hearing in London or Washington than would the rhetoric of anti-imperialism and appeals for special treatment. Yet it is this very acceptability and 'fit' that carries within it the danger that the message of this group will serve to legitimise (perhaps unwittingly?) existing global power relations rather than try to restructure them to the benefit of the developing countries. In short, being able to sell the message in the corridors of power in the North is all very well, but how does that relate to the very real developmental challenges facing the South? Asserting that the developing world must basically 'get with the programme', without questioning too loudly the global structural situation – and come up with concrete proposals on how to restructure them – is, in the long run, highly problematic. Furthermore, the reformist agenda that seems to be advancing holds within it seeds for a further marginalisation of the majority of the developing world's peoples while granting a highly privileged strata of southern elites the potential to benefit from the ongoing globalisation process. Indeed, a main criticism of the initiatives being advanced is that they serve the interests of externally-oriented individuals and groups within key (comparatively developed) developing countries while leaving other, weaker, southern states to work out alone how they might pursue development within the context of globalisation.

Of equal importance is whether or not the positive receptivity shown towards initiatives such as the NEPAD by the North is genuine or not. Certainly, widespread political unease at the social cost of liberalisation and economic restructuring, as well as growing protests against 'globalisation' in all its myriad forms by massed ranks of protestors at every transnational meeting point, means that global power-holders must now contend with a number of major issues related to development. Post-Seattle and Genoa – the loci of recent 'anti-globalisation' protests – the issues surrounding the continued thrust and direction of globalisation need to be taken seriously in global power centres. Having said that, the inherent limitations within such a debate is important if we are to understand the potentiality (or lack of it) for advancing broad-based development. Such criticism starts with the southern elites themselves, who have been promoting an eclectic agenda of and for themselves. It has been suggested that many of the objections raised by delegations from the developing world at Seattle were a *pot pourri* of often contradictory agendas which rarely touched upon key structural issues relating to transformation of the global economy. Most delegations pressed for increased access to the world market for developing-country exporters rather than seeking to amend or even 'stop' globalisation. Indeed, the reformist message as a whole is premised on greater integration into the global capitalist order, but with some renegotiated terms favouring certain actors. However, it would appear that the actual neo-liberal underpinnings of the global market are sacrosanct. This position reflects the fact that in most cases, the South power-holders are, in the main, just as interested in maintaining the global system as their colleagues in the North and that genuine development – that is, development for the mass of ordinary people – is less high on the agenda.

As if to prove this point, reforms currently being advocated are increasingly cast as sensible strategic choices in order to defend worldwide neo-liberalism from some sort of populist reaction against globalisation. The United Nations Secretary-General, Kofi Annan, has made this quite explicit, stating that:

> the unequal distribution of benefits and the imbalance of global rule making which characterises globalisation today inevitably will produce backlash and protectionism. And that in turn, threatens to undermine and ultimately unravel the open world economy that has been so painstakingly constructed over the past half-century.
>
> (quoted in *Business Day* [Johannesburg] 16 February 2001)

Nevertheless, 'there is [a] quite obvious tension between on the one hand supporting global free trade, and on the other committing oneself to changing the rules of the system to ensure greater equity' and development (Thompson and Leysens 1996: 8).

The opportunities afforded to those in the South with the vision and ability to 'ride the globalisation wave' implies that those pushing integration and/or accommodation with global capitalism have had their positions emboldened in clear ways. Such a position undermines the potency of the reformist message. It also suggests that such calls are crafted by *and for* externally-oriented interests. Such people, along with their transnational allies in the North, recognise that with the increasing questioning of globalisation, some sort of cosmetic changes may be required if the whole house of cards is not to collapse in on itself. But, the fundamental foundations of such a position leave the issue of 'development' for the global capitalist system to decide upon – a sort of global 'trickle down'. It could be argued that what is emerging is not a 'partnership' between state and capital in the developing world in the service of the public good. Instead, it is a a deal between the political elite and transnational capital – supported by the Group of 8 (G8) developed countries and the international financial institutions – further to advance liberalisation, albeit discursively dressed up as a development project. In doing so, the pay-off is predicated on the belief that 'development' will inexorably follow growth. However, this discourse falls short in providing an alternative to the hegemonic market logic of neo-liberalism. In accepting this neo-liberal ideology the reformist impulse currently being observed from certain quarters in the South treads a particular path – that is, it may well end up becoming the disciplining spokesman of global economic forces, a 'transmission belt' for economic globalisation, rather than a mediating influence seeking to craft beneficial partnerships that promote *real* – that is, beneficial to all, especially the poor – development (see Söderbaum and Taylor 2001).

In this light, calls for limited global reform might be cast as a defensive measure to protect the positions of key southern elites in the face of often withering domestic criticism at the paths they have chosen to take for their countries. But, although a great deal of emphasis is placed on the phenomenon of 'globalisation', the absence of any sustained structural analysis of global interaction is also evident in another way. It is in the failure to interrogate the structural effects that globalisation, driven by the liberalisation of the markets for goods, ideas and capital, has had on the very nature of the state and, indeed, development itself. The agenda for change being pursued is clearly a restricted, *reformist* agenda and not one aimed at *transforming* global relations, which would appear a precondition for real long-term development.

Only long-term and indirect instruments are asked for (through, for example, the NEPAD) as a means to promote development. But most of these have been tried in the past (via SAPs) and have demonstrably failed. Reformist initiatives such as NEPAD in this sense represent a frustrated dead-end of worn initiatives, reflecting the paucity of alternative ideas *vis-à-vis* development and, at the same time, the apparent hegemony of neo-liberalism:

> African officials are so conditioned by the neo-liberal 'development' paradigm, or, alternatively, they are so conditioned by their own class interests, that…[alternatives cannot be envisioned] without pressure from below. At the end of the day, it is the people, especially the working people in mines, factories, farms, and the service sector, that have must take upon themselves the responsibility to protect their own jobs, income, family welfare, the environment and national patrimony.
>
> (Tandon, n/d)

conclusion

Any alternative vision regarding global development might have been expected to fundamentally interrogate the inequitable global trading system and re-think aspects of its rules-based regime so as to benefit the least developed countries and the poorest people. It is clear that a thorough overhaul of the international financial system is a necessary prerequisite if the South as a whole is even to begin to pursue and achieve development. After all, in a world characterised by 'footloose' capital, it is nigh on impossible to acquire any capacity to make rational long-term use of one's resources for developmental ends. Furthermore, the high levels of subsidies for agricultural producers in the North would need to be addressed as such structures effectively close off the North's markets to African and other developing countries' exports, and hence clearly obstruct rural-poverty-alleviation strategies. Indeed, the whole debate on market access currently misses the essential point. Of course, tariffs and quotas are important for already active traders and investors but the issue of subsidies is actually far more important. After all, what kind of global system is it that permits a cow in Europe to receive nearly $2.50 a day while over half of Africans have to live on less? Any development plans that even pretend to want to support agriculture in the South and help alleviate rural poverty have to target directly the subsidies in the West.

This chapter has contended that the reformist and essentially neo-liberal line inherent in the reformist message emanating from the South, part and parcel of the current globalisation discourse, is deficient as it neglects major structural issues in the global economy. As a result, it is very likely to be counter-productive. It is simply not good enough to predicate such calls around 'growth' and hope that development will somehow occur. In this light, the reformism that stakes out much of the South's intercourse with the North is likely to fail to address developmental aspirations as it fails to advance any concrete agenda regarding the asymmetric power relations between the North and the South. It is this inequality that is a main cause of *maldevelopment* and a huge hurdle for any developmental project to get off the ground. In this sense, globalisation – understood here as the political and economic reconfiguration of power on a global scale – is clearly having a profound impact upon the developmental opportunities of the South. As long as southern elites remain beholden to the overarching influence of hegemonic neo-liberalism and the globalisation discourse of 'no alternative', the paucity of new ideas regarding development and global transformation remain wedded to an inherently limited and short-termist vision of reform. This is unlikely to question fundamentally – something which is urgently required – the current economic and political relations that characterise our grossly unequal world and, as a result, is likely to perpetuate the crisis of development under conditions of neo-liberal globalisation.

14
regionalism and regionalisation
kato lambrechts and chris alden

Regionalism and *regionalisation* are the terms used to describe, respectively, the political project of building a community of states, and the regional expression of global processes of integration and changing structures of production and power in a given geographic area. Historically, these processes have exercised enormous influence over the strategies adopted by developing countries to extricate themselves from their relative weakness in the international trade, political and production system and from the cycle of poverty that formed their post-colonial inheritance. This chapter will focus on both these processes.

To contextualise the domestic, regional and global factors that have influenced these twin processes, this chapter maps out key theories of regionalism and regionalisation and their impact on developing countries' policies. These serve as analytical tools to understand the motives for region-building among developing countries and the difficulties they face in achieving closer co-operation. It will do so by examining:

- the most prominent theories of regionalism in the dominant paradigms of the international relations discipline, namely neo-realism, neo-liberal institutionalism and structuralism;
- their impact upon the shaping of regional projects within the developing world, and the experience of regionalism; and
- empirical examples of regionalisation in the developing world.

We derive this schema from Hout (1998) with some modifications.

introduction: regions, regionalism and regionalisation

Although regions cannot exist without a physical reality, they are neither naturally constituted geographical units nor 'common sense' expressions of shared identity. On the contrary, they are the outcome of a complex interaction between the structures of the international system, the political and ideological struggle among states and social actors, as well as their conscious strategies in response to global changes. In this sense, they are above all 'imagined communities', like the nations of Benedict Anderson (1991). Their boundaries are therefore not fixed, and who is 'inside' and 'outside' are both a matter of political negotiation and the configuration of structural forces in the world system.

Many commentators have noted that regionalism can be understood as a state-led project intended to reshape social, political and economic space in a particular geographic region, or between two distinct geographic regions. *Regional cooperation* and *regional integration* are the terms often used to depict different forms of 'regionalist' strategies. *Regional cooperation* refers to a range of situations in which individual countries will act together for mutual benefit because of a shared interest in an issue, whether a single issue, field of activity, or a particular sector. Cooperation agreements are born of special circumstances to address particular problems, and would include situations where countries make available their resources, technologies or expertise to one another. They can collaborate in joint projects or act jointly in their external economic relations. However, cooperation does not necessarily imply a relationship of equality among partners.

The notion of *regional integration* is often associated with community-building. It takes into account 'the collective nature of the process of building a common space in a conscious, negotiated and irreversible manner by partners who have chosen to share a common destiny in a politico-institutional framework, which is pre-established through negotiation and based on a strategic vision of a common future' (Bourenane 1997). It can also be understood as a process in which the economies or markets of individual states are merged into a distinct entity by eliminating any existing discriminatory barriers between them that would serve to restrict the movement of people, goods and services. This process can be gradual or immediate, but its end purpose is always to establish a single economic space. Regional integration is voluntary, collectively undertaken, and geographically defined, and regional cooperation is part of the process towards regional integration. This process also includes the regional coordination or harmonisation of policies, strategies and regulations in areas that are seen to be of mutual benefit to all the regional partners.

theory and practice:
regionalism in action in the developing world

The appeal of regionalism is primarily as a route to enhanced and speedier development. Linked to the European Union's (EU) own positive experience of cooperation, it has provided the necessary foundation for drives towards greater economic and political co-operation across the developing world. We can note two discrete 'waves' of regionalism over time:

- The first wave, characterised as 'closed regionalism', attempted to address development concerns in the 1960s and 1970s with recourse to a hybrid form of collective reliance and aspects of customs unionism.
- The failure of the first wave and the concurrent rise of globalisation led to a second wave of regionalism, often characterised as 'open regionalism'. From the 1980s and especially the 1990s, it actively sought to integrate developing economies into the global economy, in line with the ideological, institutional and material parameters shaped by the dominant neo-liberal world order. (See chapter 13 for discussion of this topic.)

the 'first wave' of regionalism

The dependency theory or *dependencia* school was the intellectual basis inspiring the political movement that sought to establish a new international economic order (NIEO). In the 1970s, many governments of developing countries contended that the major impediment to their development was the unequal balance of global economic and political power. The desire for a NIEO was primarily manifested in the formation of a number of political forums such as the Group of 77, the Afro-Asian Solidarity Organisation, and the Non-Aligned Movement in the decades after World War II. In May 1974, the United Nations General Assembly, which had recently adopted the Charter of the Economic Rights and

---

box 14.1   dependency theory and regionalism

A focus on dependency theory and the doctrine of collective self-reliance encouraged many governments of developing countries to form regional groupings in the 1960s and 1970s. Such decisions were also motivated by the demonstration effect of the 'success' of the EU. To achieve such goals, the new regional organisations used several techniques, including: import-substitution industrialisation, autocentric or 'self-reliant' development, and various models of economic development. Politically, they also sought to build the kind of institutions that characterised the EU. Results, however, were often disappointing, for various reasons discussed in the next section.

Duties of States, approved a resolution calling for a NIEO. In addition to promoting a more equitable economic order, as well as specific measures to realise structural change and improvements in North–South trade relations, the NIEO's Programme of Action also called for cooperation amongst developing countries in order to try to achieve 'collective self-reliance' (Oteiza and Sercovich 1976).

Collective self-reliance implied:

- severance of existing links of dependence operated through the international system by the dominant countries;
- full mobilisation of domestic capabilities and resources;
- strengthening of collaboration between developing countries; and
- reorientation of development efforts in order to meet popular social needs.

In short, collective self-reliance represented a coordinated stance among developing countries in their negotiations with industrial countries on a NIEO. Cooperating with one another, it was believed and hoped that developing countries could achieve three main goals:

- improve their collective bargaining power *vis-à-vis* the industrial countries;
- mobilise countervailing pressure; and
- generally acquire more global leverage.

'South–South cooperation' was another facet of collective self-reliance . The aim was intensification of South–South trade and other linkages between developing countries. This would be achieved, first, through increasing cooperation among groups of countries at the regional or sub-regional level, and second, through more extensive collaboration among developing countries. Over time, it was hoped, collective self-reliance would replace the dependent and assymetrical relations between developing and industrialised countries by establishing integrated autonomous regional production and trading systems among developing countries. This, however, would necessitate the integration of their technological, services, and communications and information infrastructure, with the primary purpose of meeting the developmental and social needs of the poorest members of society.

During the first wave of regionalism, groups of developing countries often attempted to follow a 'positive' integration strategy, an approach

box 14.2   from 'old' regionalism to 'new' regionalism: the case of sadc

The Southern African Development Community (SADC) is an offspring of the political association of 'frontline' states that united against the apartheid regime in South Africa by forming the Southern African Development Cooperation Conference (SADCC) in 1980. The main objective of SADCC was to bring an end to the apartheid regime in South Africa, partly through international campaigning, and partly through isolating its economy from the region. Historically, the Southern African economy (which includes the 14 member countries of today's SADC) has always centred on the industrial hub of South Africa, from where British companies spread to other parts of the region. Today, three-quarters of the region's gross domestic product (including oil production in Angola and mining in the Democratic Republic of Congo) is produced in South Africa. SADCC aimed to develop an intra-regional transport and communications network and set up joint mega-industrial projects, such as energy and hydropower, to allow the region to become 'independent' from South Africa. However, apart from the successful construction of a few trans-regional transport corridors, SADCC was never really successful in 'delinking' the region from South Africa.

In 1992, following a new 'post-apartheid' government in South Africa, which was admitted to SADCC, the organisation changed direction and became the South African Development Community (SADC). As before, the new grouping aspired to a form of 'developmental regionalism', which in practice meant that countries would cooperate to identify, raise funding for, and implement joint projects and programmes in areas considered to be of mutual interest. These included: development of a regional electricity grid and telecommunications infrastructure, harmonised financial policies, joint management of regional water resources, and pooling resources for agricultural research and early warnings of crop failures. Each member country was allocated a portfolio of projects to manage on behalf of the region. A small Secretariat managed regional meetings, donor relations and policy development. In 2000, however, after a few years of deliberations, all portfolios were centralised to a more powerful and larger central secretariat to try to improve the projects' efficiency.

In the early 1990s, SADC members became interested in negotiating a regional free trade area. Low-income and landlocked members wanted to expand their small national markets in the hope that this would encourage domestic and foreign investment, especially from South Africa. The South African government and corporate sector viewed the Southern African market as a 'hinterland' for South African business expansion. SADC joint infrastructure projects also offered many opportunities for state-owned or newly-commercialised South African enterprises to buy into public–private partnership in hydropower, electricity, telecommunications, and energy projects across the region.

Critics argue that the South African government used its political and economic weight to reinforce a core-periphery (or 'hub-and-spoke') model of regional integration, whereby all commercial transactions and investments occur between South African and other member countries, but not between SADC members without South African involvement. For its part, the South African government argued that South African investment in infrastructure projects and industries in the region, facilitated by SADC programmes and projects, was contributing to the economic and social development of the region, paving the way for direct investment from industrial countries.

In sum, the evolution from SADCC to SADC is a clear example of the shift from old regionalism, based on the philosophy of 'collective self-reliance', to new or open regionalism. This is where regional market integration is seen as a first step towards inclusion of developing countries into the global economy.

also known as 'developmental regionalism'. That is, instead of focusing only on removing tariffs, regionalism was also perceived as a means to develop the industrial bases of their economies. It was hoped that this could be achieved mainly through a regional industrialisation strategy of import-substitution, exploiting economies of scale in joint ventures and integrated production structures, and jointly developing transportation and communications infrastructures across regional groupings. This approach necessarily implied some form of 'centralised' industrial planning at a regional level, particularly to determine the scope and direction of trade and the location and concentration of joint industries and development projects, and also to formulate joint policies towards multinational corporations. As a result, regionalism was often seen as an 'alternative' development strategy compared to nationally-orientated strategies. It was believed that it could widely assist countries in overcoming the economic disadvantages of small resource bases, low per capita incomes, small populations, and a disproportionate dependency on fluctuating international commodity markets.

failures of closed regionalism

Many commentators would agree not only that most regional groupings of developing countries have 'failed', but also on reasons for their failure. They can be grouped into four broad categories:

- weak states;
- continuing relations of dependency with Western industrialised countries;
- economic structures of many developing countries; and
- the fallacy of transposition of the EU's model of integration.

weak states

Although seeking to respond to real or perceived threats by centralising political power, many developing states nevertheless remained weak relative to internal groups competing for power and economic resources in fractured, widely divergent societies (Mahwood 1989). The point is that regionalism demands that states cede authority to a regional decision-making body in certain functional areas of cooperation such as trade policy, transport policies, some areas of education, and so on. However, as a consequence of the economic weaknesses of developing states, what traditionally was perceived as 'low politics', came to be seen as 'high politics' for such states. The result was that they were often reluctant to cede any authority in such areas. In addition, 'mutual suspicion and differences of political outlook arising from heterogenous cultures and varied colonial heritage, fear of being dominated by others and an insular view imposed by ultra-nationalism', also led to the failure of regional groupings (Adedeji 1977).

continuing relations of dependency with western industrialised countries

National development plans and annual budgets of most developing states tended to perpetuate – or even accentuate – their dependency, largely through an over-reliance on foreign resources. Economies of weak states were often dominated by foreign capital in terms of investment, aid, and loans. This was inclined to undermine their long-term development planning and thus impede coordinated development planning at a regional level, widely agreed to be a long-term exercise.

developing countries' economic structures

Many developing economies suffered from structural economic features which impeded the achievement of regional goals. These included a lack of complementary production structures; narrow economic bases, lack of the necessary infrastructure to facilitate intra-regional trade and production; and the production of similar or near-similar commodities. The latter meant that these economies were not only competing for external markets, but also had very little to trade with one another. A lack of sufficient skilled labour also prevented the internalisation of the development process and hence self-sustaining development. Not only did the nature of their non-complementary labour-surplus economies discourage the free mobility of labour in regional groupings; it also perpetuated dependence on foreign technicians and managers.

the fallacy of transposition of the eu's model of integration

The EU's model of linear regional integration, which would supposedly lead to political union, was often not well suited to developing countries' socio-political, economic, cultural and/or spatial circumstances. The result of transposing this model to their own strategies was that regional integration came to be identified primarily with both technical and bureaucratic modalities and institutional mechanisms for enhancing economic cooperation among developing countries. The problem was that not only historical experiences but also specific regime characteristics, forms of private enterprise, and other civil society actors were ignored in the conceptualisation of these regional schemes, as were potentials for conflict in trying to achieve various countries' differing socio-economic objectives. Critics contend that these factors should have determined the modalities, time frames, sequencing, approaches and institutions of regional groupings. Instead, most groupings emphasised the creation of a free trade area and a customs union, rather than more pragmatic and strategic production and political cooperation. It is suggested that a more flexible, gradual and pragmatic approach, with a greater emphasis on the roles and responsibilities of states, might have resulted in more successful developmental regionalism.

the 'second wave' of regionalism

The political ascendancy of conservative governments in the United States, Canada, the United Kingdom and West Germany in the 1980s provided a fertile environment for the neoclassical 'counter-revolution' in economic theory and policy. As opposed to the demand-side and systemic focus of the *dependencia* theorists, this school of thought emphasised the implementation of supply-side measures to achieve optimal development, and called for:

- dismantling or significant reduction of public ownership;
- disavowal of statist planning; and
- diminution of government regulation of economic activities in developing countries.

Many of the political proponents of this school obtained controlling votes on the boards of international financial institutions such as the World Bank and the International Monetary Fund (IMF). They argued that underdevelopment resulted from both poor resource allocation due to incorrect pricing policies and to too much state intervention in economic management, especially in most developing countries. To stimulate economic efficiency and growth, they argued, several steps should be adopted. These included:

- elimination of trade barriers;
- privatisation of state-owned enterprises;
- expansion of export industries;
- creation of an enabling environment for private investment; and
- elimination of government regulations and price distortions in factor, product and financial markets.

The predominance of this school of thought coalesced with the economic policy-reform conditionalities imposed by the IMF and the World Bank during the 1980s and 1990s on countries applying for loans from them. The aim of such reforms was to assist the clients of these international financial institutions (IFIs) to balance their import payments with export earnings and to continue paying the rising interest on their high debt stocks. For many developing countries, their debt burden started to assume 'crisis' levels during the 1980s in the wake of a world-wide economic recession. This was characterised by falling international market shares for the commodity exports of developing countries, hyper-inflation and the general contraction of industrial markets. Regional trade in the developing world also suffered a steep decline as countries sought to reduce their imports in an effort to meet balance-of-payments crises. The economic reforms prescribed by the IMF and World Bank were similar for all client states, despite the different economic structures of Latin American, African and Asian countries. The consequence was that, throughout the developing world, governments abandoned import-substitution industrialisation and 'delinking' as a development strategy, and instead opened up their economies to external capital.

During this period there were also other changes that affected perceptions of the desirability of regionalism among developing countries. Not only was there the consolidation of liberal ideology among the leading industrial nations, but also revolutionary developments in information and communication technology associated with contemporary globalisation. Together these factors facilitated a new international division of labour, which had its origins in three fundamental changes in global production conditions from the 1970s and 1980s:

- The 'reserve army' of comparatively cheap labour in developing countries both grew in size and became more visible.
- It became technically possible to split up the production process/ chain into many constituent parts (in a radical departure from the Fordist model), many of which could be carried out by unskilled or quickly trained and semi-skilled workforces.
- The development of cheaper global transport and communications systems reduced the significance of geographical distance and location for production costs. As a result, multinational companies could now reduce their total production costs by relocating certain parts of their production to low-income, developing countries. This was particularly the case for the electronics and textile industries, which benefited both from extremely cheap, female and non-

unionised labour and from improved transport and communications technology.

In addition, stricter environmental legislation and growing wage levels in the western industrialised countries in the 1980s encouraged multinationals to relocate to developing countries. Where they chose to locate depended on factors such as the national legal framework, the 'discipline' and quality of the workforce, and the comparative incentive structure offered by countries in the developing world.

How can we best account for the revival of regionalism from the 1980s and 1990s? It is important to note that this trend coincided not only with the abandonment of import-substitution industrialisation and collective self-reliance approaches to development, but also with the shift from the post-Fordist production modes of the 1970s to global production methods. Whereas the 1970s were characterised by the relocation of certain production processes of multinational corporations to other countries, the 1980s and 1990s were characterised by a new production process commensurate with globalisation. The rapid growth of global financial markets from the late 1970s, facilitated by national deregulation of financial transactions in Organisation for Economic Development (OECD) countries and new information technologies favoured the emergence of *trans*national or mega-corporations, companies that organised their entire production and sales processes with the aim of operating globally in what amounted to a profound reorganisation of manufacturing, trade and services (Oman 1994). From the 1990s, these new global production processes were further facilitated by the gradual multilateral elimination of both tariff and non-tariff trade barriers under the Uruguay Round obligations of the GATT (General Agreement on Tariffs and Trade).

This development, coupled with the disintegration of the Soviet Union at the end of the 1980s, led to the ascendance of a neo-liberal world order, with an emphasis on economic deregulation, low inflation, reduced public intervention in social and economic services, and cuts in government expenditure. It has also led to a political effort, especially by 'neo-classical economists and financial capital' to establish international rules and institutions that would promote the policies desired by firms and capital owners, a development termed 'neo-institutionalism' (Gill 1997).

According to the IFIs, structural adjustment programmes (SAPs) were compatible with regionalism, which they define as the initial liberalisation of trade among developing countries, a stepping-stone towards the gradual integration of their markets into the world economy (World Bank 1989a).

It is the case that SAPs led to a greater convergence among economies of some developing countries, a precondition of regional trade. It is also true that the correction of macroeconomic imbalances and distortions in the form of overvalued exchange rates, protected and inefficient industries, and price controls could theoretically create an enabling environment for trade, competition and factor mobility within a region, all of which would assist regional integration (Daddieh 1995, 260–1). For example, an across-the-board liberalisation of trade could reduce the administrative and tariff barriers to trade, including bans, quotas, import licences and duties, and taxes. It could also stimulate new specialisations, since the transfer of investment decisions to the private sector often leads to different industrial choices than those previously made by the governments of developing countries, thus leading production structures to become more complementary than competing. In addition, the process of streamlining over-valued national currencies and establishing realistic exchange rates and minimum convertibility could facilitate the functioning of clearing houses and other payment systems in regional groupings, as well as the development of private banking services across national borders (Boidin 1988: 67–8).

However, in practice four aspects of SAPs in particular served to undermine developmental regionalism:

- SAPs focused exclusively on reforms in individual countries, and not at the regional level. This discouraged countries either to harmonise their economic policies or to improve the efficiency of certain elements of SAPs at regional level. Moreover, the design and implementation of short-term orthodox structural adjustment and stabilisation programmes ignored the long-term objectives of the transformation of production structures and infrastructure through regional co-operation and integration, thus undermining regionalism as a means to development (Onitri 1997: 412–13). Commitment to trade liberalisation on the part of structural adjustment proponents led to what many critics saw as unwarranted opposition to price discrimination of any kind. This was despite evidence showing that reciprocal preferential tariffs or the selective raising of non-tariff barriers had actually benefited industrial and agricultural development in some African regional groupings. In practice adjustment policies reduced the size of existing preferential margins among member states of some regional groupings, thus exacerbating the asymmetrical access of member states to one another's markets, in favour of the development of trade outside the region (Boidin 1988: 70).

- SAPs also tended to reinforce and reproduce, rather than transcend, the historical role of developing countries in the international division of labour, namely supplying industrial markets with cheap agricultural products and minerals. This is because the World Bank policy prescriptions insisted on export-oriented industrialisation, or extraction and production for external markets. This outcome was a far cry from the original goals of developmental regionalism.

- Budget cuts prescribed by SAPs, and attendant social consequences, may have been at least partly responsible for increased xenophobic outbursts directed against citizens of neighbouring countries. For example, there was the expulsion of non-nationals in parts of West Africa in countries undergoing SAPs, as well as violence against minorities in South East Asia in the wake of dire

---

box 14.3   open regionalism in latin america: the case of mercosur

The Treaty of Asuncion, signed in 1991 by Argentina, Brazil, Uruguay and Paraguay, established the Common Market of the South, or MERCOSUR. During the five-year transition period, MERCOSUR states pursed their aim of building a common market through the lowering of tariff and non-tariff barriers to intra-regional trade with the goal of achieving full integration of external tariffs by 2006. To this end, average external tariffs – excluding automotive products – fell from 41 per cent to less than 12 per cent between 1991 and 1996, while intra-regional trade grew from US$3.6bn to US$20.4bn between 1991 and 1998 (Bartholomew 2001: 239, 253). However, difficulties emerged in the competitive national automotive industry, which had strong trade-union links in Argentina and was threatened by Brazilian imports. The unilateral devaluation of the Brazilian currency, which had a considerable impact upon the cost of regionally traded goods, was greeted with dismay in Buenos Aires and was credited (along with the Asian crisis of 1997–98) with causing intra-regional trade to fall to US$15.3bn in 1999. In addition, the onset of the financial crisis in Argentina in 2001 resulted in economic hardship and political instability in that country, a factor that deleteriously affected trade as well as dampening immediate expectations of further regional integration via MERCOSUR.

Presiding over the dominant economy in Latin America, Brazil's government appears to regard MERCOSUR in a largely instrumentalist way. That is, it sees it primarily as part of a wider national strategy aimed at increasing international bargaining power towards other proposed trading agreements and attracting foreign investment, rather than as an end in itself. Interestingly, increased levels of regional interaction have not resulted in higher levels of regional institutionalisation (the 'spill over' effect) or in notable cooperation in other areas. The enhancement of dispute-settlement mechanisms in 1994, for example, did not replace presidential diplomacy as a key source for resolution of trade-based disputes within MERCOSUR. Despite these internal dynamics and conflicts, many observers regard this example of 'open regionalism' in Latin America as at least a qualified success in orienting the region towards meeting the challenges of globalisation – if not offering a solution to all of the accompanying problems.

economic circumstances that accompanied the imposition of IMF conditionalities in some regional countries. Finally, prolonged freezing of public spending created strong incentives to reduce national contributions to the budgets of regional organisations or regional development programmes and projects, especially if they had to be paid in scarce foreign exchange.

We can locate the emergence of new regionalism from the 1980s in the context of growing southern discontent with the form and content of structural adjustment policies. In Latin America, for example, the emergence of MERCOSUR (see Box 14.3) was guided by a view of regionalism as complementary to individual regional countries' development strategies.

More generally, the gradual but spectacular shift from state intervention in economic management and import-substitution industrialisation strategies, to the privatisation of economic activity and export-oriented industrialisation strategies, combined with the emergence of a neo-liberal disciplinary world order, created a suitable environment for what has been called *open regionalism* (Hettne et al. 1999: 6–9). New regionalist strategies have moved away from the principles of collective self-reliance, partly in response to an increase in the growth of trade and investment within South–South and North–South regional groupings. Such 'regionalisation' of production is a counterpart of globalisation, only on a different spatial scale (Higgot 1997: 280).

These processes of change at both global and regional levels, which partly determined the opportunities and parameters for state policy, gave rise to state strategies that viewed regionalism as an effective form of regional governance in the face of economic globalisation and their concomitant marginalisation. In effect, the hyper-mobility of capital compelled many developing countries to yield some of their sovereignty to a system of corporate hegemony, in which transnational corporations, often backed by their home states, formulated the 'rules of the game'. In this context, developing states started to view regionalism as a way to strengthen the competitive position of their national economies within the global process of economic restructuring, a development that had reduced their bargaining power in relation to transnational corporations. The hope was that regionalism, and the attendant process of regional policy coordination and harmonisation, might serve to strengthen the effectiveness and the credibility of developing states (Oman 1994: 99).

States were encouraged to extend their policies to supply-side intervention, for example, by promoting industrial productivity to

---

box 14.4   the 'regional governance' approach in latin america

The 'regional governance' approach was informed to a large extent by what was known as the 'neo-structuralist school', the growth of whose ideas was a response to the patterns of slow growth and social exclusion among Latin American states that had been practising import-substitution industrialisation. While retaining the original emphasis on the need to promote domestic industry associated with the ideas of the development economist Raoul Prebisch, as well as the need for endogenous and structural conditions for economic growth, the neo-structuralists moved away from focusing on the state's central role in demand creation and investment planning. They acknowledged that the domestic markets of developing countries were often too small to sustain extensive industrialisation processes, and consequently emphasised the importance of supporting the promotion and formation of an efficient indigenous entrepreneurial class able to compete in the global market.

---

enable exports to become more competitive. This promotion of export-oriented strategies, as well as an emphasis of the role of the state as a facilitator rather than an agent of economic transformation, set the neo-structuralists apart from the earlier *dependencia* school. Middle-income developing states, according to the neo-structuralists, were forced by globalisation to become 'competition' or 'entrepreneurial' states. Such states view regionalism as a strategy through which to attract foreign investment to their markets, seen as an important stimulant of economic growth, and to improve the market position of companies with production sites within their geographical boundaries (White 1996: 111–28). As a result, the private sector is assigned a key role in regionalist projects, a radical departure from previous attempts at regional integration among developing countries which were built around state-led initiatives. The problem was that states increasingly realised that without the involvement of private enterprise in regional schemes, their collective attempts to build more competitive and productive industrial bases would remain merely political rhetoric and hopeful intention (Rwegasira 1998: 18–19).

The wider point is that in the new era of integrated global production, the South is no longer a homogenous bloc of underdeveloped countries. Rather it is a mass of differentiated groupings where the more advanced states, or the 'semi-periphery', that is those with an already-established industrial base, are aiming to adapt to the 'new rules of the game' (Hettne et al. 1999). It is suggested that one possible way to make the necessary transition is to adopt new forms of regional networks, which might also include industrial countries. In so doing, they are trying both to

- attract foreign direct investment to a large and secure market; and

- 'lock-in' their economic policy reforms by underwriting them through regional cooperation, free trade and other agreements. Such policy credibility is considered a dynamic effect of the new regionalism (Fine and Yeo 1997: 438–9).

Western developed states, on the other hand, tend to view their 'peripheries' or 'satellites' as 'captive' markets once they are locked into a regional agreement, not only for the exports of the industrialised country, but also for the provision of energy and labour for the various production chains of their transnational corporations. While this may seem like a continuation of the traditional dependency or neo-colonial relationship between developing and industrial countries, neo-structuralist theories would view the developing state as an active agent pursuing regionalism to enhance its capability to influence the outcomes of its domestic production, finance, and trade policies. Combined with the 'positive assistance' given by the more advanced members of the regional grouping, which often include structural adjustment assistance, such regional schemes potentially offer a 'structural historic opportunity' for developing countries to expand and deepen their commercial-industrial base (Marshall 1998: 677).

According to this interpretation of regionalism, the world system is not static, or characterised solely by subordination and marginalisation of developing countries. Instead, the core-periphery structure is fluid and open to historical and human contingencies. Within the cycles of world economic fluctuations, geographic shifts and core-hegemony relations, a few countries may be presented with a unique structural opportunity to ascend in the world system. In sum, however, many critics contend that the economic reform conditionalities imposed upon the least developed members of new regional groupings have seriously undermined the goals of developmental regionalism.

why and how do developing countries and regions cooperate?

These theories of regionalism and regionalisation help to construct a picture of the actors involved, their motives, the nature of the regional cooperative process and its prospects. Four basic approaches from the academic literature on regionalism provide differing accounts of the sources, processes and potential viability of regional cooperation among developing countries. They are:

- classical economic theory;
- neo-realism;
- liberal institutionalism; and
- structuralist approaches.

In this section we look at each in turn to highlight what they have to say about regionalisation and regionalism in the South.

classical economic theory

Most mainstream economic literature on regionalism in the developing world examines it as an issue of trade theory, in particular customs-union theory. The main debate among economists is whether welfare and production efficiency will be maximised through the multilateral trading system, through 'protectionist' and preferential regional trading systems, or through both. Most analysts would now agree that, while regionalism and multilateralism are competing sets of ideas, they are not necessarily mutually exclusive principles and processes that underpin processes of global economic integration.

The literature contends that customs unions are likely to be most successful among countries with competitive, yet potentially complementary, industrial and production structures. However, very few regional groupings among developing countries fulfil these conditions. This is because most developing countries suffer from structural disequilibria and the lack of well-developed manufacturing sectors. Moreover, not only are their production costs similar, but they are also often countries that do most of their trade with the developed countries (that is, trade represents a high percentage of gross national product). At the same time, trade among the developing countries themselves is either very low (below 10 per cent of total trade) or non-existent. Such countries also tend to produce similar kinds of goods (mostly minerals and agricultural commodities), and have similar industrial structures, that is, light manufacturing and textiles. This has led Ahmed (1994: 37) to conclude that 'reallocation gains are therefore not expected to accrue from these unbalanced patterns of production and foreign trade'. According to him, integration along this model may at best be neutral, and hence useless for increasing trade among developing countries. When neither country produces a certain commodity, the removal of tariffs on trade between trading states would cause no change in the pattern of trade in this commodity – each country will continue to import it from the cheapest source outside the regional group.

Using the concepts of 'trade creation' and 'trade diversion', Jacob Viner has challenged the proposition that customs unions are a move in the direction of worldwide free trade. According to Viner's pioneering study, the formation of a customs union would lead to increased trade between the union members. However, the desirability of this from the point of view of the union member would depend on the balance between trade creation and trade diversion. *Trade creation* refers to a situation where the production of some goods is shifted from a less efficient source of supply within the union (that is, previously protected domestic producers) to a more efficient source within the union. *Trade diversion* refers to a situation where the production of some goods is shifted from a non-member efficient producer or source of supply (the most competitive suppliers as long as the importing country's tariffs remained the same regardless of the origin of goods) to a less efficient member, which becomes a supplier only because the duty on its imports is abolished in the context of the customs union (Viner 1950: 43–55).

Influenced by the European integration experience, many developing country regional groupings adopted a linear approach to regional integration, irrespective of their objective political, economic, and/or operational capacity to sustain it. Typically, such a staged approach would chronologically comprise:

1. **Free trade area**   Member states remove all trade barriers amongst themselves, but retain their freedom to determine their own trade policies *vis-a-vis* the outside world, and continue to levy customs duties on imports from 'third country' trading partners.
2. **Customs union**   In addition to removing trade barriers amongthemselves, members of a customs union also pursue a common external trade policy. For instance, they must adopt common external tariffs on imports from non-member countries.
3. **Common market**   This is a customs union which also allows for the free mobility of factors of production – capital, labour, technology and enterprises – across the national borders of member countries.
4. **Economic union**   A common market where member countries not only adopt common monetary and fiscal policies and establish central monetary and fiscal authorities, but also harmonise their policies in other areas relevant for economic integration, such as administration systems, taxation, social welfare, and infrastructural planning.
5. **Political union**   Members establish common supranational political institutions, including a parliament, judiciary, and executive body, to legislate on and implement common policies (Balassa 1961).

Critics contend however that regional groupings in Asia, Africa and Latin America, in seeking to emulate the above model, did not take sufficiently into account that the institutional choices made by the EU linked to: high regional growth rates; low income differentials among member states; considerable local managerial and technological capabilities, high levels of intra-regional trade; governmental structures with a high degree of legitimacy; and, finally, access to massive external support through the Marshall Plan after World War II. In short, this model, like the process theories of the neo-liberal institutionalists (see below), appeared to be divorced from the socio-historical realities of the developing countries.

neo-realism

According to Kenneth Waltz (1979), a key theorist of neo-realism, relations among states determine their mutual behaviour. In his view, the distribution of power is the main determinant of the behaviour of states in any political system. Thus, the relative capabilities of one state *vis-à-vis* another will determine the nature of their relationship: states will always try to prevent other states from becoming too powerful or resist threats from these states, be it in an international or a regional system. In a given region, states will form alliances to maintain the 'balance of power', or, in other words, to prevent those states with more military capacity, and larger economies and populations, from dominating the region. According to Waltz, balance-of-power relationships are exclusive by nature and only last for as long as a state poses a threat to others, although collective defence and security alliances tend to be longer term.

William Zartman has adapted the balance-of-power theory to try to explain inter-state cooperation among developing countries. In his view, the major reasons for the failure of regionalism in the developing world include: weakness of post-independence developing countries; the priority most give to internal affairs; the struggle to put into place a framework for inter-state co-operation; and power that is borrowed from an external environment. In light of these problems, the balance-of-power model, according to him, shows the most potential for deeper regional cooperation, although it would necessitate much political will to move from a balance-of-power situation to that of regional cooperation (Zartman 1993: 31).

The theory of *hegemonic stability* was first developed by Kindleberger (1973) to explain that an open world economy requires the existence of a hegemonic or dominant power. Keohane, Gilpin and others later modified his hypothesis, maintaining that the existence of a dominant

box 14.5   the euro-mediterranean (euromed) agreement and 'north-south' open regionalism

The Euro-Mediterranean (EuroMed) Agreement, signed in Barcelona in 1995, is an example of the new or 'open' regionalism. It is an agreement between a core entity (the European Union [EU]) and its semi-periphery (and various Southern Mediterranean states including those in the Maghreb and Middle East). The agreement has three objectives: to establish a Mediterranean area of peace and stability, to establish by 2010 a free trade area comprising 40 countries and an estimated 800 million people, and to promote human development in the Mediterranean.

The Agreement forms part of the EU's new Mediterranean policy, which has two axes: negotiation of free trade area agreements with Southern Mediterranean countries, and cooperation between European civil societies and their counterparts in the Southern Mediterranean area. The policy stemmed from a new realisation of the strategic and economic importance of the Southern Mediterranean countries, and was partly based on an expanded understanding of the security 'threat' posed by these countries; hence, the approach acknowledged the need for political, social, economic and human development. It followed a shift in the EU's approach to developing countries away from development cooperation – based on financial aid and trade concessions – to a partnership based on reciprocal trade and a multi-dimensional approach to cooperation, including human security, human rights and democracy.

The EuroMed Agreement is also an extension of the EU's trade policy, which is to gain access to emerging markets both through multilateral negotiations in the World Trade Organisation and via bilateral negotiation of free trade areas (FTAs) with developing countries and/or regions. Other bilateral FTAs include those with Mercosur, South Africa and Mexico and various regional groupings or individual countries among the African Caribbean and Pacific (ACP) group of countries which until now have benefited from preferential access to EU markets without having to open up their own markets to EU exports. In the context of the EuroMed Agreement, the EU has already negotiated bilateral FTAs with Morocco, Tunisia, Israel and Algeria.

A number of motivations have driven Maghreb states to negotiate free trade areas with the EU, despite the cost to their industries (and the associated loss of employment and potential for a rise in poverty) that compete with European imports. First, they are hoping that a free trade area with the EU would be an incentive to EU companies to relocate to Maghreb countries, where labour and other costs are much cheaper. This hope is based on evidence from the North American Free Trade Agreement (NAFTA), whereby many US companies have relocated to Mexico, as well as from the 'flying geese' model in Asia. In the latter case, Japanese investment in lower-cost developing countries has helped such countries to adapt to new technological developments and diversify production through the creation of 'upstream' and 'downstream' industries. (In relation to oil, for example, the upstream oil industry finds and produces crude oil and natural gas, while the downstream industry includes oil refineries.) Second, Maghreb governments believe that a FTA with the EU will 'lock in' economic policy reforms they were already planning to implement, such as trade liberalisation and privatisation, against the challenges of vested interest groups. The EU would act as a regional 'policy anchor', assisting them in their reform paths, partly through giving them financial assistance to implement reforms. This would, they hope, impact positively on the way international capital markets would view their reforms. Third, for the semi-peripheral Maghreb states, a free trade area with Europe offers the best hope of inclusion in the international economy, increasingly regionalised around three (or four) main industrial poles – the United States, Japan, Europe and, in future, China. The Maghreb countries would now be able to compete on a more equal footing with Eastern Europe and southern EU members for European investment. Finally, Magreb regimes are hoping to legitimise their increasingly contested hold over power by internal opposition forces and the international community, and to deflect external critique of their dismal human rights records by entering into FTAs with the EU.

In sum, the new wave of regionalism is predicated on the emergence of a new form of 'competition' or 'entrepreneurial' state in the South, which wants to enhance its capability to influence production, finance, trade and migration policy outcomes by entering into regional agreements with western countries. However, these states are not necessarily ceding power or externalising key decision-making by negotiating North–South free trade area agreements, as some critics would argue. Instead, it appears that they are trying to deepen and expand their industrial-commercial base through a process of open regionalism.

state or hegemon was a prerequisite for states to cooperate. A world power structure dominated by a single country, according to Keohane (1984), is most conducive to the development of strong international regimes whose rules are relatively precise and well obeyed. Such leadership is based on a general belief in the legitimacy of the dominant power, as well as its prestige and status in the international political system (Gilpin 1987: 72–3).

In the case of regional groupings, the theory of hegemonic leadership implies that regionalism would develop 'more fully in those areas of the world in which there is a local hegemon able to create and maintain regional economic institutions' and will not progress 'in those areas where hegemonic leadership is less visible' (Grieco 1997: 173). The dominant state(s) will either be able to impose cooperation or bear a disproportionate part of the burden of the regional arrangement. In regional groupings among developing countries potential hegemonic states do not yet have the power to initiate regional cooperation, since all their resources and capacity are directed towards internal objectives, with external initiatives mostly 'drowned' by internal problems. Neither do these states want to carry the burden of regional leadership, which means that they would have to offer more resources to pursue this goal than other states.

In this situation, smaller member states, many of which are both fragile and unstable, may view their reliance on a hegemon as a sign of dependency. This fear is particularly apparent when the dominant power in a region, as is often the case, does not share integration benefits equally. This led Zartman to conclude that in developing regions, a regional hegemon may be counter-productive and may even force regional partner states to seek protection elsewhere, for example by joining other regional groupings. This would therefore lead to the disintegration of a regional grouping, the initial aim of the hegemon (Zartman 1993: 36).

Karl Deutsch (1966) has made a substantial contribution to the theory of regionalism in his work on the relationship between communication and the integration of political and security communities. According to him, the flow of communication within such a unit, as well as between the unit and the outside world, exercises a crucial influence over the formation and sustainability of regional groupings. He distinguished three prerequisites for the formation of what he called 'pluralistic security' or political communities: (1) the compatibility of values among decision-makers; (2) mutual predictability of behaviour among decision-makers; and (3) mutual and non-violent rapid responsiveness to the actions and communications of other governments. In short, community-building is not a linear process, as background conditions at any time could influence the sequence of communications and their coding.

Deutsch (1966) also identified conditions that would lead to the disintegration of a political or security community. These included: extended military commitments of any member government; an increase in political participation in the community on the part of a previously passive group; growing ethnic or linguistic differentiation; prolonged economic decline or stagnation in any of the community members; relative 'closure' of political elites to outside influences; excessive delay in social, political and economic reforms; and the failure of a formerly privileged group to adjust to its loss of dominance.

Building upon Deutsch's work, Barry Buzan and Ole Waever (2003), have introduced a constructivist dimension into the debate with their conception of regional security complexes. They claim that, in the post-Cold War period, the regional level is most salient as a site for political action, as it serves as the interface between statist concerns and those of the international system. Traditional and non-traditional security issues are said to be both articulated and framed through a political process by actors (primarily states) at this regional level. The impact of the material environment is seen to be a key factor, especially the territorial boundaries of the region, as is the distribution of power in the social construction of regions. The world is accordingly divided up between regional security complexes, insulator states and global actors where it is only the latter that has the capacity to 'penetrate' at all levels.

liberal institutionalism

This paradigm departs from neo-realism in its conception of the nature of the world system. In the view of neo-liberal institutionalists, relations among states are not primarily determined by their relative power, but by the 'complex interdependence' of the international political economy. The power of states therefore varies according to the issue area involved and cooperation is the rule rather than the exception, especially in areas where policy coordination is necessary to secure public goods such as stable monetary relations, free trade, and sustainable development (Keohane and Nye 1977).

Neo-liberal institutionalists also assume that regimes, or the 'sets of implicit or explicit principles, norms, rules, and decision-making procedures around which actors' expectations converge in a given area of international relations', influence substantially the policies of national governments (Krasner 1983). The creation of such regimes does not depend on the existence of a hegemon, as neo-realists would argue, but on the existence of shared interests. The creation of regimes also offers possibilities for states from the periphery and the semi-periphery to influence the outcome of international political and economic relations. As such (semi)-peripheral states will try to minimise the working of the market allocation mechanism preferred by core countries, in certain areas, and replace it with allocation through international regimes (Krasner 1985).

Neo-liberal institutionalists view regional schemes as regimes through which the allocation of certain public goods can be established. Many neo-liberal institutionalist theories were based on the integration experience of Western Europe since the late 1950s, and their focus has been on processes whereby states and elites cooperate and the preconditions for such cooperation. However, critics contend that such a view neglects to examine the world structure within which cooperation takes place, as well as the agency of cooperation, namely states, elites and non-state actors.

According to the 'functionalist' approach, technical and functional cooperation would reorient international activity away from national competition, war and conflict towards peace. This assumption is based on the hypothesis that national loyalties can be diffused and redirected to a framework for international cooperation. Ernest Haas has suggested that technical cooperation would lead to new forms of political action, instead of bypassing it. In turn, functionally specific international programmes would give rise to organisations whose 'power and competencies gradually grow in line with the expansion of the conscious task, or in proportion to the development of unintended consequences arising from earlier task conceptions' (Haas 1964: 48). The most effective 'carrier agents' of regional integration are likely to be the expert managers of functionally specific bureaucracies from different states joined together to meet specific needs, rather than a combination of system elites and ruling elites (Haas 1958: 49). Thus, central to neo-functionalist integration theory is the gradual politicisation of actors' tasks and purposes, which were initially regarded as 'technical' or 'non-controversial' (Haas and Schmitter 1964: 707). To some extent the Association of South East Asian Nations (ASEAN) can be seen as an example of neo-functionalist regional integration (see Box 14.6).

structuralist approaches

By the 1970s, the neoclassical-economics approach to regionalism embodied by modernisation theory and the structural change model were themselves subject to criticism by an emerging radical movement. Proponents of the *dependencia* school – including Raul Prebisch, Hans Singer and Gunnar Myrdal – argued that the structural disequilibria

---

box 14.6   asean and regionalism in south east asia: towards a regional security complex

The establishment of the Association of South East Asian Nations (ASEAN) in 1967 came at a time of intensive regional political turmoil, external intervention and a host of developmental challenges to the states of the region. The leaders of Indonesia, Thailand, Malaysia, Singapore and the Philippines committed themselves to a broad agenda of cooperation that included the economic, diplomatic and security spheres. In its first decade, ASEAN made notably little progress in furthering cooperation in any of these areas and it was only the withdrawal of American forces from Vietnam that brought about a recommitment of the organisation to strengthening cooperation at the Bali summit in 1976. The establishment of a Secretariat in Jakarta, followed by a period of intensive diplomacy aimed at resolving Vietnam's occupation of Cambodia, culminated in a peace settlement in 1991. The subsequent expansion of ASEAN membership to include Cambodia, Laos, Vietnam and, in 1997, Myanmar (Burma) brought with it the dilemmas of integrating substantively weaker economies into regional practice as well as highlighting shortcomings in human rights and democracy within ASEAN.

Throughout its history, ASEAN has proved to be adept at managing political dialogue with extra-regional actors such as the United States, Japan and China. Indeed, some analysts believe that ASEAN's success can be measured less in terms of its limited achievements in fostering greater economic integration and more by its politico-diplomatic functions as a mediator between global and local security interests (Buzan and Waever 2003: 154–5).

In ASEAN, intra-regional trade only took off after 1991 with the creation of a free trade area, 'growth triangles' and a tariff reduction programme. By 2002, intra-regional trade had increased to US$86 million, although this represented only a small percentage of the region's global exports of US$381 billion (www.aseansec.org.15067.htm). The Asian financial crisis, which was driven by currency speculation aimed at major trading states like Thailand, Indonesia and Malaysia in 1997, resulted in serious economic and political fall-out across the region. Despite these economic difficulties, ASEAN continues to function as a regional hub for security issues as is witnessed by its engagement with China and North Asia through the Asian Regional Forum and its role in managing the East Timorese transition from Indonesian province to independent state.

of developing economies was the outcome of the nature of their incorporation into the global capitalist division of labour, mostly through colonialism. The economies of the South had been restructured during colonialism to supply the colonial powers with inexpensive labour, raw materials and primary commodities. This led to the historical evolution of a highly unequal international capitalist system, divided between a powerful centre and a powerless periphery. This unequal power relationship scuppered the attempts of poor states to become self-reliant and independent. Theories of dualistic development underlined this view, by maintaining that the coexistence of rich and poor states was embedded, not merely transitional, and that the gap between them was likely to increase (Todaro 1994a).

Building upon the work of Immanuel Wallerstein, André Gunder Frank (1970) argued that this imperialist–satellite relationship of dependency permeated the entire global system in a chain-like fashion. According to him, capitalism in the wealthier core countries *actively* underdeveloped poorer or peripheral countries, mainly through 'surplus extraction' via the market, or in other words, unequal conditions of trade. The gradual deterioration of the terms of trade of developing countries meant that capital was continually being transferred from the periphery to the core. This exploitative relationship was facilitated in the post-colonial period by a group known as the 'comprador bourgeoisie', who assisted the agents of the capitalist system, notably transnational corporations. Under these conditions, the possibilities for development in peripheral countries was said to be minimal – unless they were able to leave the capitalist system.

An Egyptian economist, Samir Amin (1985), developed a model of self-reliance that is said to have inspired movement towards regional 'collective self-reliance' in African and Latin American regional groupings. According to Amin, an 'autocentric economy' is characterised by the manufacturing of the means of production, as well as goods for mass consumption. In such an economy, these two sectors, along with the industrial and agricultural sectors are interlinked, so that they each support growth in the other. Thus, such an economy would be self-reliant because intra-societal linkages between the main sectors of production would predominate over and shape the economy.

conclusion

We have seen that regionalism – as a demonstrably successful strategy for promoting economic development and political independence amongst countries of the South – often remains in many respects an elusive goal. Examining the record over time, we can conclude that it may be that attainment of the kind of development aims characterising regionalism are fundamentally compromised by (if not incompatible with) the exigencies of the political aspects of the project. Indeed, with the onset of rapid globalisation and the concurrent adoption of the tenets of neo-liberalism as a world standard by international institutions, bilateral and multilateral donors and most developing countries, the nationalist impulse underlying many regional projects has been subsumed within the framework of variants on open regionalism. Furthermore, developing countries have experienced tremendous socio-economic change in the decades since independence and this in itself has resulted in an unprecedented diversification of development amongst what was, at least roughly, a relatively homogeneous grouping. A re-positioning and reassessment of the costs and benefits of cooperation both with other developing countries and across the North–South divide is arguably a rational response by states as they confront the challenges posed by globalisation.

Clearly the closed regionalism of the 1970s and 1980s has failed both as an economic development strategy and as a device to reduce the dependence of southern states on their former colonial powers. New or open regionalism, premised on the emergence of the 'entrepreneurial' state trying to position itself in a world of globalised production, may nevertheless lead to increased opportunities for economic and social development. However, experiences from NAFTA, SADC and the EuroMed agreement may only show that – so far – the winners in North–South trade agreements have been primarily corporate business. The jury is still out on the long-term social, political and economic development consequences for developing countries.

15
conclusion

jeffrey haynes

The most basic assumption underlying development studies – both in theory and practice – is that development implies, if anything, poverty reduction and, by extension, accretions in well-being for the mass of ordinary people over time. Certainly, this was the underpinning assumption behind the emergence of Development Studies after World War II, when the concept of development first appeared on the international agenda. We noted that, in the 1950s, there was a growing realisation that, in fact, development was a complex concept that became more complicated following the emergence of large numbers of post-colonial countries. By the 1970s, there was also a growing realisation of a developmentally polarised world. In the 1980s, to attempt to deal with developmental imbalances, the international community, including both state and non-state actors, sought to 'roll back the state', working on the presumption that states in the developing world often 'tried to do too much', spending too much money and time in the process but often achieving little.

By the 1990s, it became apparent that development depended on more than injections of capital from external sources while reducing what the state did and spent. This highlighted the fallacy that all efforts towards improving development outcomes must emanate from the state. On the other hand, it was also widely accepted that development goals are much more likely to be achieved when state and society work in tandem rather than in different directions. Not least in importance was the realisation – expressed in the notion of the 'third wave of democracy' – that governments are more likely to propose, put into effect and implement pro-development policies and programmes when they are encouraged to do by popular pressure – most obviously via the ballot box. Put another way, while across-the-board improvements in health and education are fundamental to improvements in the development position of millions of people in the developing countries, such outcomes do not occur as a matter of course. Often, indeed, such policies are strongly resisted by incumbent elites who see the issue of development as a zero-sum game: gains for anyone other than themselves, their families, friends, kin and allies are to be resisted. In short, analysis of development and its shortfalls necessarily starts from an understanding that developmental policies *always* have major resource implications and, as a result: (1) they are always highly *political* decisions; and (2) elites will normally try to prevent them if they can.

Development is of course not only a domestic issue. It is also an international concern, and perceived development failures over the last six decades have led to periodic conceptual re-thinks in this regard. Following perceived developmental 'failures' in the 1960s, the international focus shifted in the 1970s to concern with 'basic needs' strategies, whereby development would be catalysed through ensuring that all people had the necessary 'basics': clean water, basic health care, primary education, and so on. This strategy generally failed, however, for two main reasons: first, the developmental issue became subsumed into the wider Cold War ideological division, with development funds not necessarily going to the most 'deserving' cases but to allies of the key aid-providing countries; and, second, because of the unwillingness of ruling elites and their supporters to allow the fundamental transfer of resources upon which the basic needs strategy depended. There was another directional shift in the 1980s: the perceived 'panacea' of structural adjustment programmes (SAPs), ubiquitously introduced and consolidated in dozens of developing countries. The key belief, articulated by the then World Bank president, Barber Conable in 1994, was that 'market forces and economic efficiency were the best way to achieve the kind of growth which is the best antidote to poverty' (quoted in Thomas and Reader 2001: 79).

Conable's statement reflected the intellectual dominance in the 1980s and early 1990s of neo-liberalism, an economic and political philosophy that ideologically underpinned the pro-market and monetarist ideas of influential governments, such as those of Britain's Margaret Thatcher (1979–90) and, in the USA, the administrations of Ronald Reagan (1980–88) and George Bush, Snr (1988–92). The core belief of neo-liberalism was that to achieve development, government's role must be diminished, with private capitalists 'set free' from state control. Under pressure from western governments and IFIs, many regimes in developing countries sought to put in place neo-liberal policies, albeit with variable – usually disappointing – effects.

The ideological power of neo-liberalism was at its zenith in 1989–91 when the Cold War came to an end and the Eastern European communist bloc collapsed. These developments not only appeared to offer spectacular evidence of the superior power of liberal democracy and capitalism over communism, but also provided pro-market forces with momentum. The dominant neo-liberal development strategy – the 'Washington consensus' – reflected the pre-eminence of such ideas among key, Washington DC-based, opinion leaders: 'the IMF and the World Bank, independent think-tanks, the US government policy community, investment bankers, and so on' (Thomas and Reader 2001: 79). However, as the (growing numbers of) critics of the Washington Consensus model subsequently pointed out, its studiously pro-market view appeared to overlook the fact that only governments have the power to alter prevailing socio-economic realities through the application of appropriate policies and programmes. In other words, the market is not very good at allocating resources fairly; only governments can do that. And whether they do or not is strongly linked to the varying amounts of pressure put on governments by competing societal interests.

What is now clear is that, at the start of the third millennium, Washington Consensus policies are not the answer to developmental shortfalls in the developing world. After 60 years of 'development' policies and programmes and a quarter-century of neo-liberal economic policies, over a billion people still live on less than one US dollar a day, more than two billion – one third of the global population – do not have access to potable clean water, while hundreds of millions of humans, especially women and the poor, do not have access to anything like adequate health care or basic educational opportunities. Overall, at the end of six decades' pro-development policies the global developmental picture is characterised by rising global poverty and polarising inequality. Reflecting such a concern, the international community has now set itself the challenge of a new 'onslaught' in the developing world on poverty and human deprivation. The deadline to achieve the United Nations' Millennium Development Goals (MDG), declared in September 2000, is 2015 – a decade from now.

The MDG reflect the fact that development thinking has undergone two important revisions since the late 1990s. First, it is now widely accepted – by western governments and development agencies alike – that to achieve beneficial developmental changes things cannot be left entirely to the market. Second, there is much agreement that early development successes, such as that of Britain, did not come about quickly or by chance. Instead, they were the outcome of specific governmental decisions to:

- reduce the power of business interests;
- adopt relatively high levels of taxation to fund growth of welfare states;
- pursue policies for full employment; and
- redistribute wealth from rich to poor via progressive taxation policies.

In the early 2000s, the World Bank admitted the need for a changed emphasis to achieve development goals. The Bank noted in its *World Development Report 2000/2001* that adjustments would be necessary at both global and national levels to record widespread developmental gains. Nationally, goals of promoting opportunity were inherently linked to increases in overall economic growth, as were patterns and quality of growth. While market reforms could be central in expanding opportunities for poor people, reforms needed to reflect local institutional and structural conditions. And this, the Bank admitted, was difficult to achieve – not least because it would necessitate a significant shift in power between groups, an outcome that would likely be fought against by those currently enjoying disproportionate shares of wealth and power.

Shifting focus on how to facilitate popular capacities, the Bank (2001: 7) stated that the 'choice and implementation of public actions that are responsive to the needs of poor people *depend on the interaction of political, social, and other institutional processes*' (my emphasis). But to facilitate the abilities of ordinary citizens not only depends on 'active collaboration among poor people, the middle class [sic], and other groups in society', but is also linked to wider changes in governance style and outcomes. These would be necessary in order to make public administration, legal institutions and public-service delivery both more efficient and accountable to all citizens – rather than only serving the interests of a privileged few. In short, the Bank accepted that to deliver enhanced participation in development required the inclusion of both poor and middle-class people in decision-making structures and processes.

In order to enhance security in various ways, the Bank noted that effective national actions were necessary to manage the risk of economy-wide shocks – as well as to build effective mechanisms to reduce the risks faced by poor people, including health- and weather-related risks. In respect of the national aspects necessary to lead to more and better development, the Bank explicitly referred to and discussed not only the necessity of *collective, political* actions to try to achieve development gains – but also the fact that national governments must necessarily interact with processes of globalisation in order to get what they can from it. In sum, the Bank noted the significance of both domestic and global factors in relation to development outcomes in the developing world.

In sum, the 2001 *Report* was cautiously optimistic, with a basic presumption that, for millions of impoverished people in the developing countries, major reductions in dimensions of poverty were now theoretically possible; it was also notable for the adoption of some of the critical alternative approach's concerns. Whereas the World Bank's chief concern in the 1980s and early 1990s was to roll back the role of the state in development and leave it to the market, the 2001 Report emphasised the possibility that stated development goals might be achieved by a three-way collective effort, involving domestic markets, state institutions and civil society. However, the Report also accepted that to attain these 'international development goals will require actions to spur economic growth and reduce income inequality, but even equitable growth will not be enough to achieve the goals for health and education' (World Bank 2001: 6). However, it remained to be seen whether relevant actors could actually work together to 'harness' globalisation, via economic integration and technological changes, so as to better serve the developmental interests and goals of poor people and facilitate an increase in their share of society's prosperity,

The most recent *World Bank Development Report* (2004) – subtitled, 'Making services work for poor people' – basically restates the same kind of themes and concerns as those referred to in the 2001 *Report*. It notes that to improve service delivery, institutional changes are necessary to strengthen relationships of accountability – between policy-makers, providers and citizens. The current president of the World Bank, James Wolfensohn, proclaims in his foreword that

We enter the new millennium with great hopes. For the first time in human history, we have the possibility of eradicating global poverty in our lifetime. One hundred and eighty heads of state signed the Millennium Declaration in October 2000, pledging the world to meeting the Millennium Development Goals by 2015. In Monterrey, Mexico, in the spring of 2002, the world's nations established a partnership for increasing external assistance, expanding world trade, and deepening policy and institutional reforms to reach these goals. Foreign aid, which declined during the 1990s, has begun to increase again. ...

These changes will not come overnight. Solutions must be tailored not to some imaginary 'best practice' but to the realities of the country or the town or the village. One size will not fit all. But I am convinced that this new way of thinking about service delivery, and indeed about development effectiveness, will bear fruit, particularly when matched with adequate resources and a desire to assess what works and what does not, and to decide what must be scaled up and, indeed, what must be scaled down.   (Wolfensohn 2004)

Although relatively optimistic in tone, the 2004 *Report* also acknowledges that the current time is characterised by highly significant developmental challenges, including HIV/AIDS and other diseases, as well as illiteracy, unclean water, conflict within and between states, and widespread examples of misused foreign developmental assistance in many developing countries.

The stated aim of the 2004 *World Development Report*, the 26th in the World Bank's 'flagship' series, is to 're-ignite and reinforce' development hopes by setting out ways to confront and deal with extant development challenges. However, the 2004 *Report* also acknowledges that to achieve the Millennium Development Goals by 2015 will require more than 'simply' finding the necessary sums of money – difficult though that in itself will be. While the requisite levels of funding are of course crucial, the 2004 Report also claims that what may be of even more significance in achieving the 2015 goals are the efforts of 'ordinary' people. In a focus reminiscent of the 'basic needs' approach to development first adopted in the 1970s, the 2004 *Report* stresses how important for development outcomes are the provision of basic services – particularly health, education, water and sanitation – for all citizens.

But the *Report* also notes that services often fail poor people, and that while these failures may be less spectacular than financial crises, their effects are just as – if not more – profound. But the *Report* also provides examples of what happens when services *do* work for poor people. The point is that services can work when people believe that they have a stake in their success, for example, 'when girls are encouraged to go to school, when pupils and parents participate in the schooling process, when communities take charge of their own sanitation'. Services are also likely to function better when corruption is curtailed, particularly when it affects provision of basic health services, which of course poor people need greatly. Instead, development needs to be viewed comprehensively by recognising, for example, 'that a mother's education will help her baby's health, while building a road or a bridge will enable children to go to school' (econ.worldbank.org/wdr/wdr2004/).

In sum, the 2004 *Report* emphasises that to bring about broad improvements in human welfare it is necessary that poor people receive wider access to affordable, better-quality services in health, education, water, sanitation and electricity. If such improvements are not forthcoming then 'freedom from illness' and 'freedom from illiteracy' – two of the most important ways poor people can escape poverty – will remain for many elusive. Finally, the strategies and objectives stated in the 2004 *World Development Report* are clearly central to the World Bank's two-pronged strategy for development: (1) investing in and empowering people, and (2) improving the climate for investment.

The focus on 'ordinary people' in the 2004 *World Development Report* is welcome, not least in that it serves to emphasise that development outcomes, ultimately can only be measured in the extent to which they affect people's quality of life. However, while it is important to note that the clout of bottom-up movements in relation to development outcomes is a crucial issue, it is not the whole story. In particular, there is the question of the role of globalisation in relation to development outcomes in developing countries. The chapters of this book have collectively emphasised that, until recently, there was a perceived lack of ideological alternatives to the apparently omnipotent global market. Several contributors have also identified and described how, during the Cold War, there were three main alternative development models – western-style liberal democracy/capitalism, Soviet-style communism, and state-led, often 'single party' or military-dominated, strategies that were pursued in many developing countries. However, the end of the Cold War in 1989 led to the pre-eminence during much of the 1990s of one model – the Washington Consensus, a *modus operandi* championed by the most influential international actors: western governments, IFIs and big business.

Recently, and recognising the importance of globalisation, development strategies have undergone significant changes. In relation to the development of the 2015 Millennium Development Goals, two objectives were proclaimed at an important international get-together in London in February 2001: (1) generally to increase economic well-being; and (2) to bring the swathe of poor countries and people into the development mainstream. The background to the meeting was that, despite some clear successes, overall the share of the poorest countries in world trade had halved in 20 years: from 0.8 per cent in 1980 to 0.4 per cent in the early 2000s. Reflecting this unfortunate development, Clare Short, then Britain's Minister for International Development, claimed that 'marginalisation rather than globalisation poses the greatest threat to the economies of impoverished countries' (Elliott 2001). In an attempt to reverse this trend, Short, in tandem with the then director-general of the World Trade Organization (WTO), Mike Moore, put forward a three-pronged argument:

- debt relief on its own is insufficient to put the poorest countries on the road to sustained prosperity;
- further trade liberalisation is needed to help boost export growth and overall economic performance; and
- enhanced global economic integration – via free trade – is a key approach to reducing global poverty and hunger.

Through application of this strategy, Moore and Short expected to achieve the greatest possible global economic growth that, in turn, was expected to result in the greatest possible contribution to enhanced global economic welfare and development. Critics argued, however, that there was a key problem inherent in the Moore/Short formulation: it did not contain a clear strategy to secure a necessary and equitable distribution of the expected benefits.

Overall, the main goal of the Moore/Short plan – to bring the poorest countries and people into the development mainstream – reflected the growing importance of the bottom-up, critical alternative approach to development. It is likely that high-profile 'anti-globalisation' protests – the first was at Seattle in 1998 at the WTO's millennium conference – helped to focus the attention of Moore/Short on the bottom-up development approach. As we noted above, compared to a decade earlier, there was certainly a changed emphasis in the *World Development Report 2000/2001*. The Report built on earlier strategies in the light of the cumulative evidence and experiences of the 1990s – not least the impact of globalisation and its perceived developmental impacts in many poor countries and regions, especially sub-Saharan Africa. To deal with the malign effects of globalisation, the *Report* proposed a strategy to attack poverty in three ways: to promote opportunity, to facilitate empowerment, and to enhance security.

The contributors to this book no doubt have different views as to how development can be delivered in the poor countries of the world. Most however would probably agree that, in the developing world, successes and failures in relation to attempts to build democracy, develop successful economies, protect natural environments, and address shortfalls in human and women's rights – all key development goals – are linked primarily, although not exclusively, to a range of domestic factors. It may be that in relation to development, unhelpful structural factors can be overcome by the determination of individual political leaders and governments, encouraged by civil society organisations. This helps explain why – when there are apparently similar forces at work in different countries – there may be quite different political, economic, societal and developmental results. However, to identify and explain a theoretically significant pattern can logically only take place after detailed empirical research over time in a large number of developing countries; so far, this has not been done. What does seem clear, however, is that we should not assume that all societies are destined to arrive sooner or later at similar developmental destinations, or, indeed, that they should be expected to do so.

an agenda for future thought and problems in relation to development

In the early years of the third millennium it is increasingly clear that approaches to development, as well as development outcomes in the regions of the developing world, are increasingly polarised. On the one hand, in relation to *theorising* about development, there are both 'radical' and 'reformist' interpretations of what needs to be done to ameliorate development outcomes in developmentally under-achieving countries in the developing world. Radical approaches – such as those adopted in this book by Rai (on gender and development) and Taylor (on globalisation) – argue that they are necessary in order to resolve fundamental development impasses. Critics contend, on the other hand, that many such radical approaches are excessively concerned with often purely theoretical criticisms of the status quo. The perceived problem is that this does not allow sufficient attention to the actual experiences and developments on which such theories and theoretical perspectives are focused: the conditions in which, for example, women or the poor live and work, and the actual effects of greater (and lesser) degrees of involvement with global markets and forces on national economies and sectors. It might be that future insights on development are likely to be provided by an amalgamation of both theory and practice, so that the various subject matters that collectively comprise the issue area of 'development studies' benefit from clear and robust theorising underpinned by various forms of empirical evidence from a number of sources.

The field of development studies more generally currently features an unresolved – perhaps unresolvable tension – between radicalism and reformism, for example between those who view 'liberal' democracy as hopelessly formal and manipulative and who dismiss calls (by the World Bank, the United Nations Economic Commission for Latin America, and others) for the reform of neo-liberal schemes as merely cosmetic and window-dressing. As editor of this book I have attempted to deal with tension in this respect – evident in different approaches adopted towards various subject matters in the book's chapters – by encouraging contributors to present both their own views and alternative ones.

It may be however that evident divergences between radical and reformist solutions to developmental quandaries are but the tip of the iceberg. What I am referring to is the general manner in which many of the problems and issues identified in the book – such as the state, gender, poverty, religion, armed force, human rights and regions – are examined. Such issues are not of course unfamiliar more generally in social science. This might in turn suggest that what we examined as 'development studies' is not actually a distinct discipline, or set of disciplines. Instead, its subject matter is not especially distinctive – as it is actually at the heart of social science issues anyway, and has been since the time of Adam Smith.

On the other hand, all the contributors would probably agree that, in the developing world, developmental successes and failures in relation to attempts to democratise and then consolidate democracy, develop and sustain successful economies, protect natural environments, and pay more attention to human and women's rights, are best explained by allusion to both domestic and external factors – different mixes depending on context and a host of other factors – probably in most cases with the main emphasis on the domestic. Overall, the book's chapters have emphasised that various unhelpful structural factors can be overcome by the determination of individual political leaders, encouraged by civil society organisations and more generally bottom-up pressure on rulers. The key example provided in the pages of the book was the developmental successes of the NICs of East Asia that achieved their enviable results in just such a way.

This helps explain why, when there are apparently similar forces at work in different developing countries, there may actually be contrasting political, economic and societal results. However, identifying and explaining a theoretically significant pattern can only take place after detailed empirical research in a large number of developing countries; so far, this has not been done. What does seem clear, however, is that we should not assume that all societies are destined to arrive sooner or later at similar political, economic and societal destinations, or, indeed, that they should be expected to do so.

No doubt, multifaceted change will follow a variety of paths in Asia, Africa, Latin America and the Caribbean, and the Middle East. In some cases, people will be led in circles, only later to find themselves essentially back where they began. However, it is equally sure that the pressures to open up political systems will almost certainly not abate – and if civil and political society develop in ways conducive to democratisation and democracy then issues of accountability and performance will continue to be top of developmental agendas in the future. Yet it is important to note that despite widespread movement from authoritarian to elected governments, many developing countries are unfortunately still characterised by regular encroachments upon the dignity of individuals and by often egregious denial of civil, political and human rights. However, an optimist might agree that this book provides some evidence that, at least in some developing countries, there is growing, albeit gradual, focus both on the rights of the individual and on collective development outcomes. This is not only in respect of the right to be free of arbitrary abuse at the hands of the state but also to enjoy an array of political rights, civil liberties and economic benefits: in sum, development. A pessimist, on the other hand, might claim that such evidence is not only absent but also, ultimately, irrelevant. The time has not yet arrived, he or she might remark, when developing-country governments must take seriously popular demands for greater human, civil and political rights or be concerned about economic justice.

bibliography

Abrahamsen, R. (2000) *Disciplining Democracy: Development Discourse and Good Governance in Africa*, London: Zed.

Adebajo, A. (2002) *Liberia's Civil War: Nigeria, ECOMOG, and Regional Security in West Africa*, Boulder, CO: Lynne Rienner.

Adedeji, A. (1977) 'The need for concrete action', *Regional Co-operation in Africa: Problems and Prospects*, Addis Ababa: African Association for Public Administration and Management.

'Africa' (2003) *IISS Strategic Survey 2002/3*, Oxford: Oxford University Press, May: 291–342.

'African NGO Declaration to UNCTAD IX' (1996) Parallel NGO conference to UNCTAD IX, April 24–28, Johannesburg. Available at: http://aidc.org.za/archives/unctad-91.html

ADB (African Development Bank) (2001) *African Development Report 2001: Fostering Good Governance in Africa*, Oxford: Oxford University Press for ADB.

ADB (African Development Bank) (2002a) *African Development Report 2002: Rural Development for Poverty Reduction in Africa*, Oxford: Oxford University Press for ADB.

ADB (African Development Bank) (2002b) 'Did East-Asian developing economies lose export competitiveness in the pre-crisis 1990s?', ADB Institute Research Paper 34, Tokyo: ADB Institute.

AU (African Union Directory) (2002) 'First heads of state summit', Port Louis, Mauritius: Millennium Publications.

Agarwal, B. (1997) 'Editorial: re-sounding the alert – gender, resources and community action', *World Development*, 25, 19: 1373–80.

Aghion, P. (2001) 'A corporate balance-sheet approach to currency crisis', Working Paper Number 01.05, Gerzensee: Study Centre Gerzensee and the Swiss National Bank.

Aguero, F. and Stark, J. (eds) (1998) *Fault Lines of Democratization in Post-Transition Latin America*, Miami: North-South Center Press.

Ahmed, A. (1994) *Economic Cooperation in Africa: In Search of Direction*, Boulder, CO: Lynne Rienner.

Ahrens, J. (1997) 'Prospects of institutional and policy reform in India: toward a model of the development state?' *Asian Development Review*, 15, 1: 111–146.

Ali, S. S. (2000) 'Law, Islam and the women's movement in Pakistan', in S. Rai (ed.), *International Perspectives on Gender and Development*, New York: St. Martin's/Palgrave: 41–63.

Allen, T. (1991) 'Understanding Alice: Uganda's Holy Spirit movement in context', *Africa*, 61, 3: 370–99.

Almond, G. A. and Coleman, J. S. (1960) *The Politics of the Developing Areas*, Princeton: Princeton University Press.

Amin, S. (1985) *Delinking: Towards a Polycentric World* London: Zed Books.

Amnesty International (2001) Available online at: http://www.amnestyusa.org/news/2001/india12112001.html

Amsden, A. (1989) *Asia's Next Giant: South Korea and Late Industralization*, New York: Oxford University Press.

Anderson, B. (1991) *Imagined Communities: Reflections on the Origin and Spread of Nationalism*, London: Verso.

Anderson, C. von der Mehden, F. and Young, C. (1974) *Issues of Political Development*, 2nd ed., Upper Saddle River, NJ: Prentice Hall.

An-Na'im, A. (2001) 'The synergy and interdependence of human rights, religion and secularism', *Polylog: Forum for Intercultural Philosophy*, 2: 1–43.

Appadurai, A. (1990) 'Disjuncture and difference in the global cultural economy', in M. Featherstone (ed.), *Global Culture: Nationalism, Globalisation and Modernity*, London: Sage: 295–310.

Argenti-Pillen, A. (2003) *Masking Terror: How Women Contain Violence in Southern Sri Lanka*, Philadelphia: University of Pennsylvania Press.

Asante, S. K. B. (1986) *The Political Economy of Regionalism in Africa: A Decade of ECOWAS*, New York: Praeger.

Austin, G. (1999) *Working a Democratic Constitution. The Indian Experience*, New Delhi: Oxford University Press.

Ayub Khan, A. (1967) *Friends, Not Masters*, Oxford, Oxford University Press.

Baden, S. and Goetz, A. M. (1997), 'Who needs [sex] when you can have [gender]? Conflicting discourses of gender at Beijing', *Feminist Review*, No. 56, Summer: 3–25.

Baker, P. (1990) 'South Africa on the move', *Current History*, 89, 5: 197–200, 232–233.

Bakker, I. (ed.) (1994) *The Strategic Silence. Gender and Economic Policy*, London: Zed Books.

Balassa, B. (1961) 'Towards a theory of economic integration', *Kyklos*, 14, 1: 1–17.

Balassa, B. (1971) 'Trade policies in developing countries', *American Economic Review*, 61, 2: 188–94.

Baloyra, E. A. (ed.) (1987) *Comparing New Democracies: Transitions and Consolidation in Mediterranean Europe and the Southern Cone*, Boulder, CO: Westview.

Banerjea, S. (1999) 'Faith in England', in S. Hay (ed.), *Sources of Indian Tradition*, Volume 2, *Modern India and Pakistan*, New Delhi: Penguin Books: 100–1 (first published c.1927 in *The Speeches and Writings of Hon. Surendranath Banerjea*, Madras).

Banerjee, S. (2003) 'Human rights in India in the global context', *Economic and Political Weekly*, 38, 5: 424–5.

Bardhan, P. (1993) 'Economics of development and the development of economics', *Journal of Economic Perspectives*, 7, 2: 129–42.

Bardhan, P. (2000) 'Understanding underdevelopment: challenge of institutional economics from the poor country perspective', Villa Borsig Workshop Series 2000.

Barnett, T. and Whiteside, A. (2002) *AIDS in the Twenty-first Century*, London: Palgrave.

Barro, R. and Sala-i-Martin, X. (1999) *Economic Growth*, 2nd ed., Cambridge, MA: MIT Press.

Barro, R (2001) 'Economic growth in Asia before and after the financial crisis', NBER Working Paper No. 8330.

Bartelmus, P. (1994) *Environment, Growth and Development: The Concepts and Strategies of Sustainability*, London and New York: Routledge.

Bartholomew, A. (2001) 'MERCOSUR and the rest of the world', in V. Bulmer-Thomas (ed.), *Regional Integration in Latin America and the Caribbean: The Political Economy of Open Regionalism*, London: Institute of Latin American Studies, University of London: 237–59.

Bauman, Z. (1998) *Globalization. The Human Consequences*, Cambridge: Polity Press.

Bayart, J.-F. (1993) *The State in Africa: The Politics of the Belly*, London: Longman.

Beck, U. (1997) *The Reinvention of Politics: Rethinking Modernity in the Global Social Order*, Cambridge: Polity Press.

Bell, C. (1998) 'Development economics', in J. Eatwell, M. Milgate and P. Newman (eds), *The New Palgrave Dictionary of Economics, Volume 1 A–D*, London: Macmillan: 818–85.

Bell, D. (1973) *The Coming of Post-industrial Society*, London: Heinemann.

Bellin, E. (2002) *Stalled Democracy: Capital, Labor, and the Paradox of State-Sponsored Development*, Ithaca, NY: Cornell University Press.

Beneria, L. and Sen, G. (1997) 'Accumulation, reproduction and women's role in economic development: Boserup revisited', in N. Visvanathan, L. Duggan, L. Nisonoff and N. Wiegersma (eds), *The Women, Gender and Development Reader*, London: Zed Books: 279–98.

Bentham, J. (1962) 'Anarchical fallacies', in J. Bowring (ed), *The Works of Jeremy Bentham, Vol. 2*, New York: Russell and Russell (first published 1843): 489–534.

Berryman, P. (1994) 'The coming of age of evangelical Protestantism', *NACLA Report on the Americas*, 27, 6 (May/June): 6–10.

Birand, M. A. (1987) *The Generals' Coup in Turkey: an Inside Story of September 12, 1980*, London: Brassey.

Blum, W. (2001) *Rogue State. A Guide to the World's Only Superpower*, London: Zed.

Boidin, J.-C. (1988) 'Regional co-operation in the face of structural adjustment', *The Courier*, No. 112: 67–70.

Bond, P. (ed.) (2002) *Fanon's Warning: A Civil Society Reader on the NEPAD*, Trenton: Africa World Press.

Boserup, E. (1970) *Women's Role in Economic Development*, New York: St. Martin's.

Boserup, E. (1989) *Women's Role in Economic Development*, 2nd ed., London: Earthscan.

Bourenane, N. (1997) 'Theoretical and strategic approaches', in R. Lavergne (ed.), *Regional Co-operation and Integration in West Africa*, NJ: Africa World Press: 48–59.

Brack, D. (1995) 'Balancing trade and the environment', *International Affairs*, 71, 3: 497–514.

Braidotti, R., Charkiewicz, E., Hausler, S. and Wieringa, S. (1994) *Women, the Environment and Sustainable Development: Towards a Theoretical Synthesis*, London: Zed.

Bratton, M. and van de Walle, N. (1997) *Democratic Experiments in Africa*, Cambridge: Cambridge University Press.

Bretschger, L. and Hannes, E. (2001) 'Sustainable growth in open economies', in G. Schulze and H. Ursprung (eds), *International Environmental Economics: A Survey of the Issues*, Oxford: Oxford University Press: 183–208.

Broad, R. (ed.) (2002) *Global Backlash: Citizen Initiatives for a Just World Economy*, Lanham, MA: Rowman & Littlefield.

Bromley, S. (1994) *Rethinking Middle East Politics*, Cambridge: Polity Press.

Brown, B. (1990) 'The government of India', in M. Curtis, M. Needler and R. Kanet (eds), *Introduction to Comparative Government*, 2nd ed., New York: Harcourt, Brace Jovanovitch: 469–517.

Brown, D. (2000) *Contemporary Nationalism: Civic, Ethnocultural and Multicultural Politics*, London and New York: Routledge: pp. 70–88.

Bull, H. (1977) *The Anarchical Society. A Study of Order in World Politics*, London: Macmillan.

Bull, H. and Watson, A. (eds) (1984), *The Expansion of International Society*, Oxford: Clarendon Press.

Bulmer-Thomas, V. (ed.) (2001) *Regional Integration in Latin America and the Caribbean: The Political Economy of Open Regionalism*, London: Institute of Latin American Studies, University of London.

Burgess, J. (2003) 'Environmental values in environmental decision making', in N. Bingham, A. Blowers and C. Belshaw (eds), *Contested Environments*, Milton Keynes: the Open University: 251- 88.

Burnell, P. (1997) *Foreign Aid in a Changing World*, Buckingham: Open University Press.

Buzan, B. and Waever, O. (2003) *Regions and Powers: the Structure of International Security*, Cambridge: Cambridge University Press.

Byman, D. (2002) *Keeping the Peace: Lasting Solutions to Ethnic Conflict*, Baltimore: The Johns Hopkins University Press.

Callaghy, T. (1989) 'Toward state capability and embedded liberalism in the Third World: lessons for adjustment', in J. Nelson (ed.), *Fragile Coalitions: The Politics of Economic Adjustment*, Washington, DC/ New Brunswick: Overseas Development Council/Transaction Books: 115–38.

Calvert, S. and Calvert, P. (1989) *Argentina: Political Culture and Instability*, Basingstoke: Macmillan.

Cammack, P. (1997) 'Democracy and dictatorship in Latin America, 1930–80', in D. Potter, D. Goldblatt, M. Kiloh and P. Lewis (eds), *Democratization*, Cambridge and Milton Keynes: Polity Press in association with the Open University: 152–73.

Cardenal, R. (1990) 'The martyrdom of the Salvadorean Church', in D. Keogh (ed.), *Church and Politics in Latin America*, London: Macmillan: 245–62.

Cardoso, F. H. and Faletto, E. (1979), *Dependency and Development in Latin America* (trans. M. M. Urquidi), Berkeley, CA: University of California Press.

Carim, X. (1996) *South Africa and UNCTAD IX: New Beginnings?*, Pretoria: Institute of Strategic Studies, Occasional paper No. 7, August.

Carmen, R. (1996) *Autonomous Development: Humanising the Landscape: an Excursion into Radical Thinking and Practice*, London: Zed.

Castells, M. (1992) 'Four Asian Tigers with a dragon head: a comparative analysis of the state, economy and society in the Asian Pacific rim', in R. Henderson and J. Applebaum (eds), *State and Development in the Asian Pacific Rim*, London: Sage Publications: 33–70.

Castells, M. (1996) *The Rise of the Network Society* (The Information Age, Volume 1), Oxford: Blackwell.

Cawthra, G. and Luckham, R. (eds) (2003) *Governing Insecurity: Democratic Control of Military and Security Establishments in Transitional Democracies*, London: Zed.

Cerny, Philip (2003) 'Globalization and other stories', in A. Hulsemeyer (ed.) *Globalization in the Twenty-first Century: Convergence or Divergence?*, London: Palgrave: 51–66.

Cerny, P. (1998) 'Neomedievalism, civil war and the new security dilemma: globalization as durable disorder', *Civil Wars*, 1, 1: 36–64.

Cerny, P. (1999) 'Globalisation and the erosion of democracy', *European Journal of Political Research*, 36: 1–26.

Cerrutti, M. (2000) 'Economic reform, structural adjustment and female participation in the labour force in Buenos Aires, Argentina', *World Development*, 28, 5: 880–98.

Chabal, Patrick and Daloz, Jean-Pascal (1999) *Africa Works. Disorder as Political Instrument*. Oxford: James Currey.

Chandhoke, Neera (1995), *State and Civil Society. Explorations in Political Theory*, New Delhi: Sage.

Chang, K. and Ling, L. H. M. (2000) 'Globalization and its intimate other: Fillipina domestic workers in Hong Kong, in M. Marchand and A. Runyan (eds), *Gender and Global Restructuring: Sightings, Sights and Resistances*, London: Routledge: 27–43.

Chazan, N., Lewis, P., Mortimer, R., Rothchild, D. and Stedman, S. (1999) *Politics and Society in Contemporary Africa*, 3rd ed., Boulder, CO: Lynne Rienner.

Chenery, H. and Taylor, L. (1968) 'Development patterns among countries and over time', *Review of Economics and Statistics*, November: 391–416.

Chiriyankandath, J. (1993) 'Human rights in India: concepts and contexts', *Contemporary South Asia*, 2, 3: 245–63.

Chua, A. (2003) *World on Fire: How Exporting Free Market Democracy Breeds Ethnic Hatred and Global Instability*, New York: Doubleday.

Ciment, J. (1996) *The Kurds: State and Minority in Turkey, Iraq and Iran*, New York: Facts on File.

Cline, W. (1983) 'International debt and the stability of the world economy', *Policy Analyses in International Economics*, No. 4, Washington: Institute for International Economics, September.

Cline, W. (1991) 'Mexico: economic reform and development strategy', *Exim Review*, Special Issue, Tokyo: Export-Import Bank of Japan.

Cohen, A. (1969) *Custom and Politics in Urban Africa*, Berkeley, CA: University of California Press.

Cohen, D. and Soto, M. (2002) 'Why are some countries so poor? another look at the evidence and a message of hope', OECD Development Centre, Technical Papers, No. 197, October. Available at: www.oecd.org/dev/Technics

Collier, P. and Willem, J. (1999) 'Gunning argues financial liberalization has often been premature: The IMF's role in structural adjustment', WPS/99–18, June.

Collier, P., Dollar, D. and Stern, N. (2000) 'Fifty years of development', paper presented at Annual World Bank Conference, Paris, June 2000.

Cook, S. Juzhong, Z. and Shujie, Y. (eds) (2000) *The Chinese Economy Under Transition. Studies on the Chinese Economy*, London: St. Martin's.

Coomaraswamy, R. (1996) 'Comments', in A. Eide and B. Hagtvet (eds), *Conditions for Civilized Politics. Political Regimes and Compliance with Human Rights*, Oslo: Scandinavian University Press: 105–12.

Cox, H. (1966) *The Secular City*, New York: Macmillan & Co.

Cox, R. (ed.) (1997), *The New Realism. Perspectives on Multilateralism and World Order*, London/ Tokyo: Macmillan/United Nations University Press.

Cox, R. (1999) 'Civil society at the turn of the millennium: prospects for an alternative world order', *Review of International Studies*, 25, 1: 3–28.

Cox, R. (2002) *The Political Economy of a Plural World: Critical Reflections on Morals and Civilisation*, London: Routledge.

Cranston, M. (1973) *What are Human Rights?*, London: Bodley Head.

Cypher, J. (1990), *State and Capital in Mexico: Development Policy since 1940*, Boulder, CO: Westview.

Daddieh, C. (1995) 'Structural adjustment and regional integration: compatable or mutually exclusive?', in K. Mengisteab and B. I. Logan (eds), *Beyond Economic Liberalisation in Africa: Structural Adjustment and the Alternatives*, London: Zed Books: 243–71.

Dahl, R. (1971) *Polyarchy*, New Haven, CT: Yale University Press.

Davin, D. (1992) 'Population policy and reform: the Soviet Union, Eastern Europe and China', in S. Rai, H. Pilkington and A. Phizacklea (eds), *Women in the Face of Change: the Soviet Union, Eastern Europe and China*, London: Routledge: 79–104.

De Gregorio, J. and Jong, W.-L. (1999) *Economic Growth in Latin America: Sources and Prospects*, Global Development Network.

de Melo, J. and Panagariya, A. (1992) *The New Regionalism in Trade Policy*, Washington and London: World Bank and the Centre for Economic Policy Research.

De Soto, H. (2000) *The Mystery of Capital*, London: Black Swan.

De Waal, A. (2002) 'What's new in the "New Partnership for Africa's Development"?', *International Affairs*, 78, 3: 463–75.

Deaton, A. (with Dreze, J.) (2002) 'Poverty and inequality in India: a re-examination, *Economic and Political Weekly*, September 7: 3729–48.

DeFronzo, J. (1996) *Revolutions and Revolutionary Movements*, 2nd ed., Boulder, CO: Westview.

Dekmejian, R. K. (1982) 'Egypt and Turkey: the military background', in R. Kolkowicz and A. Korbonski (eds), *Soldiers, Peasants and Bureaucrats*, London: Allen and Unwin: 29–51.

Desai, Vandana, J. and Potter, R. (eds) (2002) *The Companion to Development Studies*, London: Arnold.

Deutsch, K. (1966) *Nationalism and Social Communication*, Cambridge, MA: MIT Press.

Deutsch, K. (1968) 'The impact of communications on international relations theory', in A. Said (ed.), *Theory of International Relations: The Crisis of Relevance*, New York: Prentice-Hall:

Deyo, F. (1987) *The Political Economy of the New Asian Industrialism*, Ithaca, NY: Cornell University Press.

Diamond, L. and Plattner, M. (eds) (1996) *Civil-Military Relations and Democracy*, Baltimore: Johns Hopkins University Press.

Dikerdem, M. A. (1987) 'Introduction', in M. A. Birand (ed.) *The Generals' Coup in Turkey: an Inside Story of September 12, 1980*, London: Brassey: 1–20.

Donnelly, J. (1998) *International Human Rights*, 2nd ed., Boulder, CO: Westview.

Donnelly, J. (1999a) 'The social construction of international human rights', in T. Dunne and N. J. Wheeler (eds), *Human Rights in Global Politics*, Cambridge: Cambridge University Press: 71–102.

Donnelly, J. (1999b) 'Human rights and Asian values: a defense of "Western" universalism', in J. R. Bauer and D. A. Bell (eds), *The East Asian Challenge for Human Rights*, Cambridge: Cambridge University Press: 60–87.

Dornbusch, R. (2001) 'Malaysia: was it different?', NBER Working Paper No. w8325.

Drake, P. W. and Silva, E. (eds) (1986) *Elections and Democratisation in Latin America*, San Diego: Center for Iberian and Latin American Studies, University of California.

Dreze, J. and Sen, A. (1989) *Hunger and Public Action*, London: Clarendon Paperbacks.

Dreze, J. and Sen, A. (1995) *India. Economic Development and Social Opportunity*, Oxford: Clarendon Press.

du Toit, P. (2003) 'Why post-settlement settlements?', *Journal of Democracy*, 14, 3: 104–18.

Duffield, M. (1998) 'Post-modern conflict: warlords, post-adjustment states and private protection', *Civil Wars*, 1, 1: 65–102.

Duffield, M. (2001) *Global Governance and the New Wars*, London and New York: Zed.

Duffield, M. (2002) 'Reprising durable disorder: network war and the securitization of aid', in B. Hettne and B. Odén (eds), *Global Governance in the 21st Century: Alternative Perspectives on World Order*, Stockholm: EGDI: 74–105.

Dyer, C. (2004) 'A light falls on Camp X-Ray', *Guardian*, January 20. Available online at: http://www.guardian.co.uk/guantanamo/story/0,13743,1126959,00. html

Eckersley, R. (1992) *Environmentalism and Political Theory: Towards an Ecocentric Approach*, New York: UCL Press.

ECOSOC (Economic and Social Council) (2003) *Official Records, Supplement No. 3, Commission on Human Rights. Report on the Fifty-Ninth Session (17 March – 24 April 2003)*, E/2003/23, E/CN.4/2003/135 Available at: http://www.unhchr. ch/html/menu2/2/sessions.htm

Edwards, S. (1995) *Crisis and Reform in Latin America: From Despair to Hope*, New York: Oxford University Press.

Ehrlich, P. (1970) *The Population Bomb*, New York: Ballantine.

EIA (Environmental Investigation Agency) (1998) *The Politics of Extinction: The Orangutan Crisis – The Destruction of Indonesia's Forest*, London: Environmental Investigation Agency.

Eisenstein, Z. (1997) 'Women's publics and the search for new democracies', *Feminist Review*, 57: 140–67.

Ekins, P. (1993) 'Making development sustainable', in W. Sachs (ed.), *Global Ecology: A New Arena of Political Conflict*, London: Zed: 91–103.

Elliott, L. (2001) 'Short joins push for new WTO talks', *The Guardian*, 19 March.

Elson, D. (1989) 'How is structural adjustment affecting women?', *Development*, 1: 67–74.

Elson, D. (1994) 'Micro, meso, macro: gender and economic analysis in the context of policy reform', in I. Bakker (ed.), *The Strategic Silence: Gender and Economic Policy*, London: Zed: 33–45.

Emerson, R. (1967) *From Empire to Nation: The Rise of Self-Assertion of Asian and African Peoples*, Cambridge: Harvard University Press.

Enloe, C. (1989) *Bananas, Beaches and Base. Making Feminist Sense of International Politics*, London: Pandora Press.

Entessar, N. (1992) *Kurdish Ethnonationalism*, Boulder, CO: Lynne Rienner.

Erwin, A. (1998) 'Trading with Latin America: defining policies for the future – keynote address', *Unisa Latin American Report*, 14, 2, July–December 1998.

Escobar, A. (1995) *Encountering Development: The Making and Unmaking of the Third World*, Princeton, NJ: Princeton University Press.

Evans, P. (1995), *Embedded Autonomy: States and Industrial Transformation*, Princeton, NJ: Princeton University Press.

Evans, P., Rueschemeyer, D. and Skocpol, T. (1985) *Bringing the State Back In*, Cambridge: Cambridge University Press.

Evans, T. (1998) 'Introduction: power, hegemony and the universalization of human rights', in T. Evans (ed.), *Human Rights Fifty Years On. A Reappraisal*, Manchester: Manchester University Press: 2–23.

Evans, T. (2001) *The Politics of Human Rights. A Global Perspective*, London: Pluto Press.

Falk, R. (1999) 'The challenge of genocide and genocidal politics in an era of globalisation', in T. Dunne and N. J. Wheeler (eds), *Human Rights in Global Politics*, Cambridge: Cambridge University Press: 177–94.

Falk, R. (2002) 'The post-Westphalia enigma', in B. Hettne and B. Odén (eds), *Global Governance in the 21st Century: Alternative Perspectives on World Order*, Stockholm: EGDI: 147–83.

Farouk-Sluglett, M. and Sluglett, P. (2001) *Iraq Since 1958: From Revolution to Dictatorship*. London: I. B. Tauris.

Ferguson, N. (2001) 'Welcome the new imperialism', *The Guardian*, October 31.

Ferraro, V. and Rosser, M. (1994) 'Global debt and third world development', in M. Klare and D. Thomas (eds), *World Security: Challenges for a New Century*, New York: St. Martin's: 332–55.

Fine, B. (1999), 'The development state is dead: Long live social capital', *Development and Change*, 30: 1–19.

Fine, J. and Yeo, S. (1997) 'Regional integration in sub-Saharan Africa: dead-end or fresh start?', in A. Oyejide, B. Ndulu and D. Greenaway (eds), *Regional Integration and Trade Liberalisation in Sub-Saharan Africa*, Basingstoke and New York: Macmillan and St Martin's: 429–74.

Finer, S. E. (1962) *The Man on Horseback*, London: Pall Mall.

Finer, S. E. (1985) 'Retreat to barracks: notes on the practice and theory of military withdrawal from seats of power', *Third World Quarterly*, 7, 1: 16–30.

Finger, M., (1993) 'Politics of the UNCED process', in W. Sachs (ed.), *Global Ecology: a New Arena of Political Conflict*, London and Atlantic Highlands, NJ: Zed: 36–48.

Fitch, J. S. (1998) *The Armed Forces and Democracy in Latin America*, Baltimore: Johns Hopkins University Press.

Folbre, N. (1992) 'Introduction: The feminist sphinx', in N. Folbre, B. Bergmann, B. Agarwal and M. Floro (eds), *Women's work in the World Economy*, New York: New York University Press: xxiii–xxx.

Foreign Policy (2003) 'Measuring globalization: who's up, who's down?' *Foreign Policy*, January/February: 60–72.

Frank, A. G. (1970) *Latin America: Underdevelopment or Revolution – Essays on the Development of Underdevelopment and the Immediate Enemy*, New York: Monthly Review Press.

Franko, P. (2003) *The Puzzle of Latin American Economic Development*, 2nd ed., Lanham, MD: Rowman & Littlefield.

Freedom House (2004) *Freedom in the World 2004*, New York: Freedom House. Available online at: http://www.freedomhouse.org/research/survey2004.htm

Freeman, M. (2002) *Human Rights. An Interdisciplinary Approach*, Cambridge: Polity.

Frieden, J. (1991) *Debt, Development, and Democracy: Modern Political Economy and Latin America, 1965–1985*, Princeton, NJ: Princeton University Press.

Friedman, F. (1996) *The Bosnian Muslims: Denial of a Nation*, Boulder, CO: Westview.

Fukuda-Parr, S. (2003) 'The human development paradigm: Operationalizing Sen's ideas on capabilities', *Feminist Economics*, 9, 2–3: 301–17.

Fuller, G. (1999) 'Turkey's restive Kurds: The challenge of multiethnicity', in L. Binder (ed.), *Ethnic Conflict and International Politics in the Middle East*, Gainesville: University of Florida Press: 224–44.

Gaddis, J. (1997) *We Now Know: Rethinking Cold War History*, Oxford: Oxford University Press.

Galtung, J. (1998) 'The Third World and human rights in the post-1989 world order', in T. Evans (ed.), *Human Rights Fifty Years On. A Reappraisal*, Manchester: Manchester University Press: 211–31.

Ganguly, S. (1997) *The Crisis in Kashmir: Portents of War, Hopes of Peace*, New York and Cambridge: Cambridge University Press and the Woodrow Wilson Center Press.

Gardezi, H. and Rashid, J. (1983) (eds) *Pakistan: The Roots of Dictatorship*, London: Zed Press.

Gastil, R. (1987) *Freedom in the World*, Westport, CT: Greenwood.

Gause, F. G. (1994) *Oil Monarchies: Domestic and Security Challenges in the Arab Gulf States*, New York: Council on Foreign Relations Press.

Gearty, C. (2001) 'Airy-Fairy', *London Review of Books*, 23: 23. Available at: http://www.lrb.co.uk/v23/n23/print/gear01_.html

Gellner, E. (1994) *Conditions of Liberty: Civil Society and its Rivals*, New York: Penguin.

Gerschenkron, A. (1962), *Economic Backwardness in Historical Perspective*, Cambridge: MA: Harvard University Press.

Ghai, Y. (1998) 'Rights, social justice, and globalization in East Asia', in J. R. Bauer and D. A. Bell (eds), *The East Asian Challenge for Human Rights*, Cambridge: Cambridge University Press: 241–63.

Gilberg, T. (1998) 'Ethnic conflict in the Balkans: comparing ex-Yugoslavia, Romania and Albania', in K. Christie (ed.), *Ethnic Conflict, Tribal Politics: A Global Perspective*, Richmond Surrey, Curzon: 61–86.

Gill, G. (2000) *The Dynamics of Democratization: Elites, Civil Society and the Transition Process*. New York: St. Martin's.

Gill, S. (ed.) (1997) *Globalisation, Democratisation and Multilateralism*, Basingstoke: Macmillan.

Gilpin, R. (1987) *The Political Economy of International Relations*, Princeton: Princeton University Press.

Glasius, M. and Kaldor, M. (2002) 'The state of global civil society: Before and after September 11', in M. Glasius, M. Kaldor and H. Anheir (eds), *Global Civil Society 2003*, Oxford: Oxford University Press: 3–33.

Glendon, M.A. (2002) 'The dialogue on religious freedom in the framing of the 1948 Universal Declaration of Human Rights', paper presented at 'Truth and Freedom. Towards a Common Understanding Among Muslims, Jews and Christians, Washington D.C., March 20–21. Available at: http://www.becketfund.org/other/DCConf2002/GlendonPaper.html

Gordon, R. (1990) *The Measurement of Durable Goods Prices*, Chicago: University of Chicago Press.

Gouldson, A. and Murphy, J. (1997) 'Ecological modernisation: restructuring industrial economies', in M. Jacobs (ed.), *Greening the Millennium: The New Politics of the Environment*, Oxford: Blackwell:74–86.

Graf, W. D. (1996) 'Democratization "for" the Third World: Critique of a hegemonic project', *Canadian Journal of Development Studies*, Special Issue: 37–56.

Grant, R. and Short, R. (eds) (2003) *Globalization and the Margins*, London: Palgrave Macmillan.

Gray, J. (1998) *False Dawn: The Delusions of Global Capitalism*, London: Granta Books.

Grieco, J. (1997) 'Systemic sources of variation in regional institutionalisation in Western Europe, East Asia and the Americas', in E. D. Mansfield and H. V. Milner (eds), *The Political Economy of Regionalism*, New York: Columbia University Press: 165–87.

Guardian (2004) 'The climes they are a-changin', 13 January.

Gürbey, G. (1996) 'The development of the Kurdish Nationalism movement in Turkey since the 1980s', in R. Olson (ed.), *The Kurdish Nationalist Movement in the 1990s: Its Impact on Turkey and the Middle East*, Lexington: The University of Kentucky Press: 9–37.

Gurr, T. (2000) 'Preface' and 'Long war, short peace: the rise and decline of ethnopolitical conflict at the end of the Cold War', in T. Gurr (ed.), *Peoples Versus States: Minorities at Risk in the New Century*, Washington, DC: United States Institute of Peace Press: 10–11 and 27–56.

Gyimah-Boadi, E. (1996) 'Civil society in Africa', *Journal of Democracy*, 7, 2: 118–32.

Gylfason, T. and Radetzki, M. (1991) 'Does devaluation make sense in the least developed countries?', *Economic Development and Cultural Change*, 40, 1: 1–26.

Haas, E. (1958) *The Uniting of Europe*, Stanford: Stanford University Press.

Haas, E. (1964) *Beyond the Nation-State*, Stanford: Stanford University Press.

Haas, E. and Schmitter, P. (1964) 'Economics and differential patterns of political integration: projections about unity in Latin America', *International Organisation*, 18, 3: 705–37.

Haggard, S. (1990) *Pathways from the Periphery: The Politics of Growth in Newly Industrializing Countries*, Ithaca, NY: Cornell University Press.

Haggard, S. and Kaufman, R. (1995) *The Political Economy of Democratic Transitions*. Princeton, NJ: Princeton University Press.

Hall, J. (ed.) 1995. *Civil Society: Theory, History, Comparison*, Cambridge: Polity.

Handelman, H. (2003) *The Challenge of Third World Development*, 3rd ed., Upper Saddle River, New Jersey: Prentice Hall.

Hardin, G. (1968) 'The tragedy of the commons', *Science*, no. 162: 1243–8.

Harik, I. and Sullivan, D. (eds) (1992) *Privatization and Liberalization in the Middle East*, Bloomington, IN: Indiana University Press.

Harstock, N. (1990) 'Foucault on power: a theory for women?', in L. J. Nicholson (ed.), *Feminism/Postmodernism*, London: Routledge: 544–54.

Harvey, C. (ed.) (1996) *Constraints on the Success of Structural Adjustment Programmes in Africa*, London: Macmillan.

Hausman, R. and Rodrik, D. (2003) 'Economic development as self-discovery', working paper, John F. Kennedy School of Government, Harvard University, NBER-IASE.

Haynes, J. (1996) *Religion and Politics in Africa*, London: Zed.

Haynes, J. (1997) *Democracy and Civil Society in the Third World. Politics and New Political Movements*, Cambridge: Polity Press.

Haynes, J. (1998) *Religion in Global Politics*, Harlow: Longman.

Haynes, J. (2002) *Politics in the Developing World. A Concise Introduction*, Oxford: Blackwell.

Hayward, T. (1995) *Ecological Thought: An Introduction*, Cambridge: Polity Press.

Held, D., McGrew, A., Goldblatt, D., and Perraton, J. (1999) *Global Transformations: Politics, Economics and Culture*, Cambridge: Polity Press.

Helleiner, E. (1994) *States and the Re-emergence of Global Finance: From Bretton Woods to the 1990s*, Ithaca: Cornell University Press.

Henry, C. and Springborg, R. (2001) *Globalization and the Politics of Development in the Middle East.* Cambridge: Cambridge University Press.

Herring, R. (1999), 'Embedded particularism: India's failed developmental state', in M. Woo-Cumings (ed.), *The Developmental State*, Ithaca, NY and London: Cornell University Press: 306–35.

Hettne, B. (1993), 'The concept of mercantilism', in L. Magnusson (ed.), *Mercantilist Economics*, Boston: Kluwer: 235–56.

Hettne, B. (1995) *Development Theory and the Three Worlds. Towards an International Political Economy of Development.* London: Longman.

Hettne, B. (1997) 'The double movement: global market versus regionalism', in R. Cox (ed.), *The New Realism. Perspectives on Multilateralism and World Order*, Tokyo: United Nations University Press: 223–44.

Hettne, B. (2003) 'Regional governance and world order: lessons from ASEM', paper for the conference East Asia and Europe: Experiments with Region Building, Paris: French Institute of International Relations, October 1–3.

Hettne, B. and Odén, B. (eds) (2002), *Global Governance in the 21st Century: Alternative Perspectives on World Order*, Stockholm: EGDI.

Hettne, B., Inotai, A. and Sunkel, O. (eds) (1999/2001) *Studies in the New Regionalism.* (Volumes I-V), Basingstoke: Macmillan.

Hettne, B., Inotai, A. and Sunkel, O. (eds) (1999) *Globalism and the New Regionalism*, Basingstoke: Macmillan.

Hettne, B., Inotai, A., and Sunkel, O. (eds) (2001) *Comparing Regionalisms: Implications for Global Development*, Basingstoke: Macmillan/Palgrave.

Higgott, R. (1997) 'Mondialisation et gouvernance: l'emergence du niveau regional', *Politique Etrangère*, 2: 277–92.

Hirschman, A. (1981) *Essays in Trespassing: Economics to Politics and Beyond*, Cambridge: Cambridge University Press.

Hirschman, A. (1984) 'A dissenter's confession: the strategy of economic development revisited', in G. Meier and D. Seers (eds), *Pioneers in Development*, Oxford, Oxford University Press: 85–118.

Hirst, P. and Thompson, G. (1996), *Globalization in Question: the International Economy and the Possibilities of Governance*, Cambridge: Polity Press.

Hobsbawn, E. (1994) *The Age of Extremes. The Short Twentieth Century 1914–1991*, London: Abacus.

Holland, A. (1997) 'Substitutability or why strong sustainability is weak and absurdly strong sustainability is not absurd', in J. Forster (ed.), *Valuing Nature: Economics, Ethics and Environment*, London and New York: Routledge: 119–34.

Holton, R. (1998), *Globalization and the Nation State*, Basingstoke: Macmillan.

Horowitz, D. (1991) *A Democratic South Africa? Constitutional Engineering in a Divided Society*, Berkeley and Los Angeles: University of California Press.

Horowitz, D. (2001) *The Deadly Ethnic Riot*, Berkeley and Los Angeles: University of California Press.

Hoskyns, C. and Rai S. (1998), 'Gender, class and representation: India and the European Union', *The European Journal of Women's Studies*, 5, 3/4: 345–65.

Hout, W. (1998) 'Theories of international relations and the new regionalism', in W. Hout and J. Grugel (eds), *Regionalism Across the North-South Divide*, London: Routledge: 14–28.

Howe, C. (1996) *The Origins of Japanese Trade Supremacy*, London: Hurst & Company.

Huff, W. G. (1995) 'The development state, government and Singapore's economic development since 1960', *World Development*, 23, 8: 1421–38.

Hunt, D. (1989) *Economic Theories of Development. An Analysis of Competing Paradigms*, London: Harvester/Wheatsheaf.

Hunter, W. (1998) 'Civil–military relations in Argentina, Brazil and Chile: present trends and future prospects', in F. Aguero and J. Stark (eds), *Fault Lines of Democratization in Post-Transition Latin America*, Miami: North–South Center Press: 299–322.

Huntington, S. P. (1968), *Political Order in Changing Societies*, New Haven, CT: Yale University Press.

Huntington, S. P. (1991) *The Third Wave: Democratization in the Late Twentieth Century.* Norman, OK: University of Oklahoma Press.

Huntington, S. P. (1993) 'The clash of civilizations', *Foreign Affairs*, 72, 3: 22–42.

Huntington, S. P. (1996) 'Reforming civil–military relations', in L. Diamond and M. Plattner (eds), *Civil–Military Relations and Democracy*, Baltimore: Johns Hopkins University Press: 3–12.

Hurrell, A. (1999) 'Power, principles and prudence: protecting human rights in a deeply divided world', in T. Dunne and N. J. Wheeler (eds), *Human Rights in Global Politics*, Cambridge: Cambridge University Press: 277–302.

Hurrell, A. (2001) 'The politics of regional integration in MERCOSUR', in V. Bulmer-Thomas (ed.), *Regional Integration in Latin America and the Caribbean: The Political Economy of Open Regionalism*, London: Institute of Latin American Studies, University of London: 194–211.

Hyden, G. (1997) 'Democratisation and administration', in A. Hadenius (ed.), *Democracy's Victory and Crisis*, Cambridge: Cambridge University Press: 242–59.

International Commission on Global Governance (1995) *Our Global Neighbourhood*, Oxford University Press: International Commission on Global Governance.

Isaacs, H. (1975) *Idols of the Tribe: Group Identity and Political Change*, New York: Harper & Row.

Ivins, M. (2002) 'The Dick and Dubya Show', *The Texas Observer*, 30 August. Available at: www.texasobserver.org/showArticle.asp?ArticleID=1008

Jackson, C. and Pearson, R. (eds) (1998) *Feminist Visions of Development*, London: Routledge

Jacobs, M. (1997) 'The quality of life: social goods and the politics of consumption', in M. Jacobs (ed.), *Greening the Millennium: The New Politics of the Environment*, Oxford: Blackwell, pp. 47–61.

Jalan, B. (2003) *The Indian Economy*, New Delhi: Penguin Books.

Janowitz, M. (1964) *The Military in the Development of New Nations*, Chicago: Chicago University Press.

Jefferson, T. (1950) '"Rough Draft" of the American Declaration of Independence', in J. P. Boyd (ed.), *The Papers of Thomas Jefferson*, Volume 1: *1760–1776*, Princeton, NJ: Princeton University Press: 243–47.

Johnson, C. (1982) *MITI and the Japanese Miracle: the Growth of Industrial Policy, 1925–1975*, Stanford: Stanford University Press.

Johnson, C. (1995) *Japan: Who Governs? The Rise of the Developmental State*, New York: W.W. Norton.

Johnson, C. (1999) 'The developmental state: Odyssey of a concept', in M. Woo-Cumings (ed.), *The Developmental State*, Ithaca, NY: Cornell University Press: 32–60.

Jones, T. (1976) *Ghana's First Republic 1960–1966: The Pursuit of the Political Kingdom*, London: Methuen.

Kabeer, N. (1994) *Reversed Realities: Gender Hierarchies in Development Thought*, London: Verso.

Kaldor, M. (1999) *New & Old Wars. Organized Violence in a Global Era*, Cambridge: Polity Press.

Kaldor, M. and Luckham, R. (2001) 'Global transformation and new conflicts', *IDS Bulletin*, 32, 2: 48–69.

Kamrava, M. (1992) 'Conceptualising Third World politics: the state-society see-saw', *Third World Quarterly*, 14, 4: 703–16.

Kamrava, M. (1998) 'Pseudo-democratic politics and populist possibilities: the rise and demise of the Refah Party in Turkey', *British Journal of Middle Eastern Studies*, 25, 2: 275–301.

Kang, D. (2002), 'Bad loans to good friends: Money, politics and the development state in South Korea,' *International Organization*, 56, Winter: 177–207.

Kaplan, R. (1994) 'The coming anarchy', *Atlantic Monthly*, February: 44–76.

Karl, T. L. (1986) 'Imposing consent: Electoralism versus democratization in El Salvador', in P. W. Drake and E. Silva (eds), *Elections and Democratization in Latin America*, San Diego: Center for Iberian and Latin American Studies, University of California: 9–36.

Kaufmann, R. and Stalling, B. (1989) (eds) *Debt and Democracy in Latin America*, Boulder, CO: Westview.

Keohane, R. (1984) *After Hegemony*, Princeton, NJ: Princeton University Press.

Keohane, R. and Nye, J. (1977) *Power and Interdependence: World Politics in Transition*, Boston: Little Brown.

Kerr, C. (1962) *Industrialism and Industrial Man. The Problems of Labor and Management in Economic Growth*. London: Heinemann.

Kim, Y.-S. (1997) 'Korea and the developing countries: lessons from Korea's industrialization', *Journal of East Asian Affairs*, 11, 2: 417–29.

Kindleberger, C. (1973) *The World in Depresssion, 1929–1939*, Harmondsworth: Penguin Books.

Kitching, G. (1982) *Development and Underdevelopment in Historical Perspective*, London: Methuen.

Klare, M. (2002) *Resource Wars: The New Landscape of Global Conflict*, New York: Owl.

Knack, S. and Keefer, P. (1994) 'Institutions and economic performance: cross-country tables', unpublished paper, cited in Barro and Sala-i-Martin (1994): 439–41.

Kofman, E. (2000) 'The invisibility of skilled female migrants and gender relations in studies of skilled migration in Europe', *International Journal of Population Geography*, 6: 45–59.

Kolkowicz, R. and Korbonski, A. (eds) (1982) *Soldiers, Peasants and Bureaucrats*, London: Allen & Unwin.

Korany, B., Brynen, R. and Noble, P. (eds) (1995) *Political Liberalization and Democratization in the Arab World*, Volume 1: *Theoretical Perspectives*. Boulder, CO: Lynne Rienner.

Korany, B., Brynen, R. and Noble, P. (eds) (1998) *Political Liberalization and Democratization in the Arab World*, Volume 2: *Comparative Experiences*. Boulder, CO: Lynne Rienner.

Krasner, S. (1983) *International Regimes*, New York: Cornell University Press.

Krasner, S. (1985) *Structural Conflict: the Third World against Global Liberalism*, Berkeley, CA: University of California Press.

Krueger, A. (2002a) *Economic Policy Reforms and the Indian Economy*, Chicago: University of Chicago Press.

Krueger, Anne O. (2002b) Summary of NBER address: 'Says Argentina needs sustainable monetary anchor, stronger banking system', *IMF Survey*, 31, 5: 1–3. Available online at www.imf.org.

Krugman, Paul (1994) 'The myth of Asia's miracle', *Foreign Affairs*, November/December: 62–78.

Lake, D. and Rothchild, D. (1998) 'Spreading fear: The genesis of transnational ethnic conflict', in D. Lake. and D. Rothchild (eds), *The International Spread of Ethnic Conflict*, Princeton, New Jersey: Princeton University Press: 3–32.

Lall, S (2001) *Competitiveness, Technology and Skills*, Cheltenham: Edward Elgar.

Lane, T. (1999) 'The Asian financial crisis: what have we learned?', *Finance and Development*, 36, 3: 4–11.

Laxer, G. and Halperin, S. (eds) (2003) *Global Civil Society and its Limits*, Basingstoke: Palgrave.

LCHR (Lawyers Committee for Human Rights) (2003) *Assessing the New Normal: Liberty and Security for the Post-September 11 US*. Available at: http://www.lchr.org/us_law/loss/assessing/assessingnewnormal.htm

Lensink, R. (1996) *Structural Adjustment in Sub-Saharan Africa*, London: Longman.

Levine, D. (1990) 'The Catholic Church and politics in Latin America', in D. Keogh (ed.), *Church and Politics in Latin America*. London: Macmillan: 9–28.

Lewis, A. (1954) 'Economic development with unlimited supplies of labour', *Manchester School*, 22, 2, reprinted (1958) in A. N. Aggarwal and S. P. Singh (eds), *The Economics of Underdevelopment*, New Delhi: Oxford University Press: 400–49.

Lewis, D. (2002) 'Civil society in African contexts: Reflections on the usefulness of a concept', *Development and Change*, 33, 4: 569–86.

Lewis, P. (1992) 'Political transition and the dilemma of civil society in Africa', *Journal of International Affairs*, 46, 1: 31–54.

Liddle, J. and Rai, S. (1998) 'Orientalism and feminism: The challenge of the 'Indian woman', *Women's History Review*, 25, 4: 495–520.

Lijphart, A. (1969) 'Consociational democracy', *World Politics*, 21, 2: 207–25.

Lijphart, A. (1977) *Democracy in Plural Societies: A Comparative Exploration*, New Haven, CT: Yale University Press.

Lijphart, A. (1999) *Patterns of Democracy: Government Forms and Performance in Thirty-Six Countries*. New haven, CT: Yale University Press.

Lindqvist, S. (2001) *A History of Bombing*, London: Granta Books.

Linz, J. and Stepan, A. (1996) *Problems of Democratic Transition and Consolidation: Southern Europe, South America, and Post-Communist Europe*. Baltimore: Johns Hopkins University Press.

List, M. and Ritberger, V. (1992) 'Regime theory and international environmental management', in A. Hurrell and B. Kingsbury (eds), *The International Politics of the Environment*, Oxford: Clarendon Press: 85–109.

Little, I., Scitovsky, T. and Scott, M. (1970) *Industry and Trade in Some Developing Countries: A Comparative Study*, London: Oxford University Press.

Little, I. M. D., Cooper, R., Corden, W. M., and Rajapatirana, S. (1994) *Boom, Crisis, and Adjustment: The Macroeconomic Experience of Developing Countries*, Oxford: Oxford University Press.

Locke, J. (1977) *Two Treatises of Government*, London: J. M. Dent & Sons Ltd (first published 1690).

Lovelock, J. (1979) *Gaia: a New Look at Life on Earth*, Oxford: Oxford University Press.

Lovelock, J. (1988) *The Ages of Gaia,* New York: Norton.

Low, L. (2001) 'The Singapore developmental state in the new economy and polity,' *The Pacific Review*, 14, 3: 411–41.

Luciani, G. (1995) 'Resources, revenues, and authoritarianism: beyond the rentier state?' in, B. Korany, R. Brynen, and P. Noble (eds), *Political Liberalization and Democratization in the Arab World*, Volume 1: *Theoretical Perspectives*. Boulder, CO: Lynne Rienner: 211–27.

Luckham, A. R. (1971) 'A comparative typology of civil-military relations', *Government and Opposition*, Winter: 8–34.

Luckham, R. (1995) 'Dilemmas of military disengagement and democratization in Africa', *IDS Bulletin*, 26, 2: 49–61.

Lukauskas, A. J. and Rivera-Batiz, F. (eds) (2001) *The Political Economy of the East Asian Crisis and its Aftermath: Tigers in Distress*. Northampton, MA and Cheltenham, UK: Edward Elgar.

MacDougall, A. Kent (2001) 'Lake Victoria: casualty of capitalism', *Monthly Review*, 53, 7: 38–42.

Machlup, F. (1977) *A History of Thought on Economic Integration*, London: Macmillan.

MacLean, S., Harker, H. J., and Shaw, T. (eds) (2001) *Crises of Governance in Asia and Africa*, Aldershot: Ashgate.

MacLean, S., Harker, H. J., and Shaw, T. (eds) (2002) *Advancing Human Security and Development in Africa: Reflections on NEPAD*, Halifax: CFPS.

Mahwood, P. (1989) 'State formation in tropical Africa', *International Politics and Science Review*, 10, 3: 209–37.

Makhan, V. (2002) *Economic Recovery in Africa: the Paradox of Financial Flows*, London: Palgrave Macmillan.

Malan, M. (2000) 'Civil–military relations in Africa: soldier, state and society in transition', in H. Solomon and I. Liebenberg (eds), *The Consolidation of Democracy in Africa*, Aldershot: Ashgate: 139–70.

Malik, I. (2002) *Kashmir: Ethnic Conflict, International Dispute*, Oxford and Karachi: Oxford University Press.

Marchand, M. and Parpart, J. (eds) (1995) *Feminism/Postmodernism/Development*, London: Routledge

Marshall, D. (1998) 'NAFTA/FTAA and the new articulations in the Americas: Seizing structural opportunities', *Third World Quarterly*, 19, 4: 673–700.

Martinussen, J. (1997) *Society, State & Market*, London: Zed.

Marty, M. and Scott Appleby, R. (1993) 'Introduction', in M. Marty and R. Scott Appleby, (eds), *Fundamentalism and the State. Remaking Polities, Economies, and Militance*, Chicago: The University of Chicago Press: 1–9.

Marx, K. and Engels, F. (1971) *The Communist Manifesto*, Moscow: Progress Publishers.

Marysse, S. (2003) 'Regress and war: the case of the DRC Congo', *European Journal of Development Research*, 15, 1: 73–98.

Mattes, R. (2002) 'South Africa: democracy without the people?', *Journal of Democracy*, 13, 1: 22–36.

Mattro, A., Roy, D. and Subramaniam, A. (2003) 'The AGOA and rules of origin: Generosity undermined?', *World Economy*, 26, 6: 829–51.

Mawdudi, A. A. (1980) *Human Rights in Islam*, Leicester: Islamic Foundation, 1980.

Mayer, A. E. (1999) *Islam and Human Rights. Tradition and Politics*, 3rd edn., Boulder, CO: Westview Press.

Mbaya, E. R. (1996) 'The compatibility of regional human rights systems with international standards', in A. Eide and B. Hagtvet (eds), *Conditions for Civilized Politics. Political Regimes and Compliance with Human Rights*, Oslo: Scandinavian University Press: 66–89.

Mbeki, T. (1999) 'Statement at the 35th Ordinary Session of the OAU Assembly of Heads of State and Governments', issued by the Office of the President, Algiers, Algeria, 13 July.

McDowall, D. (2000) *A Modern History of the Kurds*, 2nd ed., London: I. B. Tauris.

Meadows, D. and Meadows, D. (1972) *The Limits to Growth*, Washington, DC: Potomac Associates.

Medhurst, K. (1989) 'Brazil', in S. Mews (ed.), *Religion in Politics. A World Guide*, Harlow: Longman: 25–9.

Meier, G. (1984) 'Introduction: the formative period', in G. Meier and D. Seers (eds), *Pioneers in Development*, Oxford, Oxford University Press: 3–26.

Meier, G. (ed.) (2000) *Leading Issues in Economic Development*, 7th ed., Oxford: Oxford University Press.

Meier, G. and Stiglitz, J. (eds) (2001) *Frontiers of Development Economics*, New York: Oxford University Press.

Mengisteab, K. (1996) *Globalization and Autocentricity in Africa Development in the 21st Century*, Trenton: Africa World Press.

Mengisteab, K. and Logan, I. (eds) (1995) *Beyond Economic Liberalisation: Structural Adjustment and the Alternatives*, London: Zed.

Merchant, C. (1980) *The Death of Nature: Women, Ecology and the Scientific Revolution*, New York: Harper and Row.

Michalak, W. and Gibb, R. (1997) 'Trading blocs and multilateralism in the world economy', *Annals of the Association of American Geographers*, 87, 2: 264–79.

Mies, M. (1982) *Lace Makers of Narsapur: Indian Housewives Produce for the World Market*, London: Zed.

Mies, M., Bennholdt-Thomsen, V. and von Werlhof, C. (1988) *Women: The Last Colony*, London: Zed.

Mies M. and Shiva, V. (1993) *Ecofeminism*, London: Zed Books.

Minns, J. (2001) 'Of miracles and models: the rise and decline of the development state in Korea', *Third World Quarterly*, 22, 6: 1025–44.

Mittelman, J. and Pasha, M. K. (1997) *Out From Underdevelopment Revisited: Changing Global Structures and the Remaking of World Order*, Basingstoke: Macmillan.

Mkandawire, T. (2001) 'Thinking about developmental states in Africa', *Cambridge Journal of Economics*, 25: 289–313.

Mkandawire, P. T., and Soludo, C. S. (1999) *Our Continent, Our Future: African Perspectives on Structural Adjustment*, Trenton: Africa World Press.

Mkandawire, T. and Soludo, C. (eds) (2001) *Our Continent, Our Future: African Perspectives on Structural Adjustment*, Dakar: CODESRIA.

Moghissi, H. (1999) *Feminism and Islamic Fundamentalism. The Limits of Postmodern Analysis*, London: Zed.

Mohamad, M. (2002) 'Toward a human rights regime in Southeast Asia: charting the course of state commitment', *Contemporary Southeast Asia*, 24, 2: 230–51.

Mohan, R. (2004) *Facets of the Indian Economy*, New Delhi: Oxford University Press.

Mohanty, Talpade C., Russa, A. and Torres, L. (eds) (1991) *Third World Women and the Politics of Feminism*, Bloomington, IN: Indiana University Press.

Molyneux, M. (1998) 'Analysing women's movements', *Development and Change*, 29: 219–45.

Monshipouri, M. (2001) 'Promoting universal human rights: dilemmas of integrating developing countries', *Yale Human Rights & Development Law Journal*, 4: 25–61.

Moser, C. (1989) 'Gender planning in the Third World: meeting practical and strategic gender needs', *World Development*, 17, 11: 1799–1825.

Moser, C. (1993) *Gender Planning and Development. Theory, Practice and Training*, London: Routledge.

Moynihan, D. P. (1993) *Pandaemonoim: Ethnicity in International Politics*, Oxford: Oxford University Press.

Mshomba, R. (2000) *Africa in the Global Economy*, Boulder, CO: Lynne Rienner.

Muthien, B. and Taylor, I. (2002) 'The return of the dogs of war?: the privatisation of security in Africa', in T. Biersteker and R. B. Hall (eds), *The Emergence of Private Authority in Global Governance*, Cambridge: Cambridge University Press: 183–202.

Myrdal, G. (1968) *Asian Drama: An Inquiry Into the Poverty of Nations*, New York: Pantheon.

Naim, M. (2003) 'Five wars of globalization', *Foreign Policy*, January/February: 29–37.

Nelson, J. (ed.) (1989) *Fragile Coalitions: The Politics of Economic Adjustment*, Washington, DC/ New Brunswick: Overseas Development Council/Transaction Books.

Nerfin, M. (ed.) (1977) *Another Development: Approaches and Strategies*, Uppsala: Dag Hammarsköld Foundation.

Neufeld, M. (1999) 'Globalization and the re-definition of democratic governance', *Studies in Political Economy*, 58: 97–119.

Nove, A. (1972) *An Economic History of the USSR*, Harmondsworth: Penguin.

Nzo, A. (1997) 'South Africa will contribute to the strengthening of the activities of the Non-Aligned Movement', *Review of International Affairs*, 48, October: 3–4.

Nzomo, M. (1995) 'Women and democratization in Africa: what relevance to post-modernist discourse?', in M. Marchand and J. Parpart (eds), *Feminism/ Postmodernism/Development*, London: Routledge: 131–41.

O'Byrne, D. J. (2003) *Human Rights. An Introduction*, Harlow: Longman.

O'Connell, S. and Ndulu, B. (1999) 'Africa's growth experience: a focus on sources of growth', paper prepared for the AERC/Harvard Conference on African Economic Growth, March, 1999, and the Global Development Network Conference, Cairo, October 1999.

O'Donnell, G. (1973) *Modernization and Bureaucratic-Authoritarianism: Studies in South American Politics*, Berkeley: CA: Institute of International Studies.

O'Donnell, G. (1988) *Bureaucratic-Authoritarianism, Argentina, 1966–1973, in Comparative Perspective*, Berkeley, CA: University of California Press.

O'Donnell, G. (1994) 'Delegative democracy', *Journal of Democracy*, 5, 1: 55–69.

O'Hearn, D. (2003) 'Is trade an agent of development'?, in G. McCann and S. McCloskey (eds), *From the Local to the Global: Key Issues in Development Studies*, London: Pluto Press: 111–24.

Oliviero, M. and Simmons, A. (2002) 'Who's minding the store? Global civil society and corporate responsibility', in M. Glasius, M. Kaldor and H. Anheier (eds), *Global Civil Society 2003*, Oxford: Oxford University Press: 77–107.

Olson, G. (1976) *US Foreign Policy and the Third World Peasant*, New York; Praeger.

Oman, C. (1994) *Globalisation and Regionalisation: The Challenges for Developing Countries*, Paris: OECD.

Omoruyi, O. (1986) 'State creation and ethnicity in a federal (plural) system: Nigeria's search for parity', in D. Thompson and D. Ronen (eds), *Ethnicity, Politics, and Development*, Boulder, CO: Lynne Rienner Publishers: 119–28.

Onitri, H. M. A.(1997) 'Changing political and economic conditions for structural adjustment in sub-Saharan Africa', in A. Oyejide, B. Ndulu and D. Greenaway (eds), *Regional Integration and Trade Liberalisation in Sub-Saharan Africa*, Volume 1: *Framework, Issues and Methodological Perspectives*, London and New York: Macmillan and St Martins Press: 398–428.

Oteiza, E. and Sercovich, F. (1976) 'Collective self-reliance: selected issues', *International Social Science Journal*, 28, 4: 664–71.

Oucho, J. (2002) *Undercurrents of Ethnic Conflict in Kenya*, Leiden, Boston, Koln: Brill.

Overbeek, H. and Van der Pijl, K. (1993) 'Restructuring capital and restructuring hegemony: neo–liberalism and the unmaking of the post-war order', in H. Overbeek (ed.), *Restructuring Hegemony in the Global Political Economy*, London: Routledge: 1–27.

Oxhorn, P. (1995) 'From controlled inclusion to coerced marginalization: the struggle for civil society in Latin America', in J. Hall (ed.), *Civil Society: Theory, History, Comparison*, Cambridge: Polity: 250–77.

Parpart, J. and Shaw, T. (2002) 'African development debates and prospects at the turn of the century', in P. McGowan and P. Nel (eds), *Power, Wealth and Global Equity: an International Relations Textbook for Africa*, 2nd ed., Cape Town: UCT Press for IGD: 296–307.

Parpart, J., Connelly, M. and Barriteau, V. (eds) (2000) *Theoretical Perspectives on Gender and Development*, Ottawa: IDRC.

Parpart, J., Rai, S. and Staudt, K. (2001) *Rethinking Empowerment, Gender and Development in a Local/Global World*, London: Routledge.

Pellerin, H. and Overbeek, H. (2001) 'Neoliberal regionalism and the management of people's mobility', in A. Bieler and A. D. Morton (eds), *Social Forces in the Making of the 'New Europe': the Restructuring of European Social Relations in the Global Political Economy*, Basingstoke: Palgrave: 137–57.

Philip, G. (2003) *Democracy in Latin America*, Cambridge: Polity Press.

Pinkney, R. (1990) *Right-Wing Military Government*, London, Pinter.

Pinkney, R. (2003) *Democracy in the Third World*, Boulder, CO: Lynne Rienner.

Piro, T. (1998) *The Political Economy of Market Reform in Jordan*, Lanham, MD: Rowman & Littlefield.

Polanyi, Karl (2001 [1944; 1957]) *The Great Transformation: the Political and Economic Origins of our Time*, Boston: Beacon Press.

Ponte, S. and Gibbons, P. (2004) *Globalization and Economic Change in Africa*, London: Palgrave Macmillan.

Prebisch, R. (1984) 'Five stages in my thinking on development', in G. Meier and D. Seers (eds), *Pioneers in Development*, Oxford, Oxford University Press: 173–204.

Premdas, R. (1990) 'Secessionist movements in comparative perspective', in R. Premdas, S. W. R. de A. Samarasinghe and A. Anderson (eds), *Secessionist Movements in Comparative Perspective*, London, Pinter: 12–29.

Pripstein Posusney, M. (1997) *Labor and the State in Egypt: Workers, Unions, and Economic Restructuring*, New York: Columbia University Press.

Pritchett, L. (1998) 'Patterns of economic growth: hills, plateaus, mountains, and plains', World Bank Policy Research Working Paper, No. 1947, July.

Prunier, G. (1995) *The Rwanda Crisis: History of a Genocide*, New York: Columbia University Press.

Ra'anan, U. (1991) 'Nation and state: Order out of chaos', in *State and Nation in Multi-Ethnic Societies*, Manchester: Manchester University Press: 2–21.

Radelet, S. and Sachs, J. (1998) 'The East Asian financial crisis: diagnosis, remedies and prospects', HIID and USAID, Brookings Paper 1.

Rahman, M. (1996) *Divided Kashmir: Old Problems, New Opportunities for India, Pakistan and the Kashmiri People*, Boulder, CO: Lynne Rienner Publishers.

Rahnema, M. (1997) 'Introduction', in M. Rahnema and V. Bawtree (eds), *The Post Development Reader*, London and NJ: Zed.

Rai, S. (1997) 'Gender and representation: women MPs in the Indian parliament', in A.-M. Goetz (ed.) *Getting Institutions Right for Women*, London: Zed Press: 104–22.

Rai, S. (2002) *Gender and the Political Economy of Development: From Nationalism to Globalisation*, Cambridge: Polity Press

Rai, S. (ed.) (2003) *National Machineries for Women: Mainstreaming Gender, Democratising the State?*, Manchester: Manchester University Press.

Ramachandran, N. (2003), 'The Washington consensus fades into history', *Financial Times*, 3 August.

Randall, L. (ed.) (1997) *The Political Economy of Latin America in the Postwar Period*, Austin, TX: University of Texas Press.

RAND Corporation (2003) 'Headlines over the horizon, *Atlantic Monthly*, 292, 1, July/August: 84–90.

Ranis, G. (1991) 'Towards a model of development, in L. Krause and K. Kihwan (eds) *Liberalization in the Process of Economic Development*, Berkeley, CA: University of California Press: 59–101.

Rehman, J. (2003) *International Human Rights Law. A Practical Approach*, Harlow: Longman.

Reno, W. (1995), *Corruption and State Politics in Sierra Leone*, Cambridge: Cambridge University Press.

Reno, W. (1998) *Warlord Politics and African States,* London: Lynne Rienner.

Rial, J. (1996) 'Armies and civil society in Latin America', in L. Diamond and M. Plattner (eds), *Civil–Military Relations and Democracy*, Baltimore: Johns Hopkins University Press: 47–65.

Rich, P. B. (1986) *Race and Empire in British Politics*, Cambridge: Cambridge University Press.

Richards, A. and Waterbury, J. (1996), *A Political Economy of the Middle East*, 2nd ed., Boulder, CO: Westview Press.

Ricardo, D. (1973) *Principles of Political Economy and Taxation*, London: Dent.

Rist, G. (1997), *The History of Development*, London: Zed.

Robinson, F. (1998) 'The limits of a rights-based approach to international ethics', in T. Evans (ed.) *Human Rights Fifty Years On. A Reappraisal*, Manchester: Manchester University Press: 58–76.

Robinson, M. and White, G. (1999) *The Democratic Developmental State: Political and Institutional Design,* Oxford: Oxford University Press.

Robinson, W. (1995) 'Pushing polyarchy: the US-Cuba case and the Third World', *Third World Quarterly*, 16, 4: 631–47.

Robinson, W. (1996) *Promoting Polyarchy: Globalization, U.S. Intervention and Hegemony*, Cambridge: Cambridge University Press.

Rodrik, D. (1997) 'TFP controversies, institutions, and economic performance in East Asia', NBER Working Paper Series, No. 5914, National Bureau of Economic Research.

Romer, P. (1986) 'Increasing returns and long-run growth', *Journal of Political Economy*, 94: 1002–37.

Root, H. (2001}, 'Asia's bad old ways', *Foreign Affairs*, 80, 2: 9–14.

Rosenberg, J. (2000) *The Follies of Globalisation Theory*, London: Verso.

Rosenstein-Rodan, P. (1984) 'Natura facit saltum: Analysis of the disequilibrium growth process', in G. Meier and D. Seers (eds), *Pioneers in Development*, Oxford, Oxford University Press: 205–26.

Rostow, W. (1960) *The Stages of Economic Growth. A Non-Communist Manifesto*, Cambridge: Cambridge University Press.

Rothchild, R. and Olorunsola, V. (1983) 'Managing competing state and ethnic claims', in R. Rothchild and V. Olorunsola (eds), *State versus Ethnic Claims: African Policy Dilemmas*, Boulder, CO: Westview Press: 1–24.

Rowlands, J. (1997) *Questioning Empowerment: Working with Women in Honduras*, Oxford: Oxfam.

Roy, A. (2001) *The Algebra of Infinite Justice*, New Delhi: Viking.

Rueschemeyer, D., Huber Stephens, E. and Stephens, J. (1992) *Capitalist Development and Democracy*. Chicago, IL: University of Chicago Press.

Ruggie, J. (1998), *Constructing the World Polity. Essays on International Institutionalization*, London and New York: Routledge.

Rwegasira, D. G. (1998) 'Economic co-operation and integration in Africa: Experiences and the road ahead'. Unpublished paper for workshop entitled, 'Understanding new orders between old borders', Cape Town, South Africa, 30 January–1 February.

Sachs, J. (1989) *Developing Country Debt and the World Economy*, Chicago: Chicago University Press.

Sachs, W. (ed.) (1992) *The Development Dictionary: A Guide to Knowledge and Power*, London: Zed.

Sachs, W. (1993) 'Global ecology and the shadow of development', in W. Sachs (ed.), *Global Ecology: A New Arena of Political Conflict*, London and Atlantic Highlands, NJ: Zed: 3–22.

Sachs, W. (1999) *Planet Dialectics: Explorations in Environment and Development*, London and New York: Zed Books: 110–28.

Sadowski, Y. (1998), *The Myth of Global Chaos*, Washington: Brookings Institution Press.

Safa, H. (1995) *The Myth of the Male Breadwinner: Women and Industrialization in the Caribbean*, Boulder, CO: Westview Press.

Sahliyeh, E. (ed.) (1990) 'Religious resurgence and political modernization', in E. Sahliyeh (ed.), *Religious Resurgence and Politics in the Contemporary World*, Albany, NY: State University of New York Press: 1–16.

Said, A. and Simmons, L. (1976) 'The ethnic factor in world politics', in S. Said and L. Simmons (eds), *Ethnicity in an International Context*, New Brunswick, NJ: Transaction Books: 2–24.

Said, E. (1978) *Orientalism*, London: Routledge and Kegan Paul.

Sassen, S. (1995) *Transnational Economies and National Migration Policies*, Amsterdam: IMES/Het Spinhuis.

Sassen, S. (2002) 'Global cities and diasporic networks: microsites in global civil society' in M. Glasius, M. Kaldor and H. Anheier (eds), *Global Civil Society 2003*, Oxford: Oxford University Press: 217–38.

Schmitter, P. C. (1995) 'Transitology: The science and art of democratization', in J. S. Tulchin and B. Romero (eds), *The Consolidation of Democracy in Latin America*, London: Lynne Rienner: 11–41.

Schofield, V. (2000) *Kashmir in Conflict: India, Pakistan and the Unfinished War*, London: I. B. Tauris.

Schumpeter, J. (1950), *Capitalism, Socialism and Democracy*, 3rd ed., London: Allen & Unwin.

Schuurman, F. (1993) *Beyond the Impasse. New Directions in Development Theory*, London: Zed.

Shuurman, F. (2000) 'Paradigms lost, paradigms regained? Development studies in the twenty-first century', *Third World Quarterly*, 21, 1: 7–20.

Seckinelgin, H. (2002) 'Time to stop and think: HIV/AIDS, global civil society and people's politics', in M. Glasius, M. Kaldor and H. Anheier (eds), *Global Civil Society 2003*, Oxford: Oxford University Press: 109–136.

Seidman, R. (1978) *The State, Law and Development*, London: Croom Helm.

Sen, A. (1997) *Human Rights and Asian Values*, New York: Carnegie Council on Ethics and International Affairs.

Sen, A. (1999a) 'Human rights and economic achievements', in J. R. Bauer and D. A. Bell (eds), *The East Asian Challenge for Human Rights*, Cambridge: Cambridge University Press: 88–99.

Sen, A. (1999b) *Development as Freedom*, Oxford: Oxford University Press.

Sen, G. (1984), *The Military Origins of Industrialization and International Trade Rivalry*, London: Frances Pinter.

Sen, G. and Grown, C. (1988) *Development, Crises and Alternative Visions: Third World Women's Perspectives*, London: Earthscan.

Sen, G. (2002) 'Post-reform China and the international economy: economic change and liberalisation under sovereign control', The Globalsite, First Press. Available at: www.theglobalsite.ac.uk.

Senghaas, D. (1985), *The European Experience*: Berg Publishers.

Senghaas, D. (2002), *The Clash Within Civilizations: Coming to Terms with Cultural Conflicts*, London and New York: Routledge.

Serra, L. (1985) 'Ideology, religion and class struggle in the Nicaraguan revolution', in R. Harris and C. Vilas (eds), *Nicaragua: a Revolution under Siege*, London: Zed: 151–74.

Sesay, A. (1998) 'Africa, Non-Alignment and the end of the Cold War', in S. Akinrinade and A. Sesay (eds) *Africa in the Post-Cold War International System*, London: Pinter.

Shaw, T. (2004) 'Africa', in M. Hawkesworth and M. Kogan (eds), *Routledge Encyclopedia of Government and Politics*, 2nd ed., London: Routledge.

Shiva, V. (1989) *Staying Alive: Women, Ecology and Development*, London: Zed.

Shiva, V. (1999) 'Monocultures, monopolies, myths and the masculinization of agriculture', *Development Journal*, 42, 2: 35–8.

Shubane, K. (1992) 'South Africa: a new government in the making?' *Current History*, 91, 5: 202–7.

Shue, H. (1996) *Basic Rights: Subsistence, Affluence and US Foreign Policy*, 2nd ed., Princeton: Princeton University Press.

Simensen, J. (1999) 'Democracy and globalization: nineteen eighty-nine and the "Third Wave"', *Journal of World History*, 19, 2: 391–411.

Singer, H. (1984) 'The terms of trade controversy and the evolution of soft financing', in G. Meier and D. Seers (eds), *Pioneers in Development*, Oxford, Oxford University Press: 273–312.

Sklair, L. (2002) *Globalization. Capitalism and Its Alternatives*, Oxford: Oxford University Press.

Smillie, I., Gberie, L., and Hazleton, R. (2000) *The Heart of the Matter. Sierra Leone, Diamonds and Human Security*, Ontario: Partnership Africa Canada.

Smith A. D. (1992) 'Chosen peoples: Why ethnic groups survive', *Ethnic and Racial Studies*, 15: 436–56.

Smith, D. (ed.) (1974) *Religion and Modernization*, New Haven, CT: Yale University Press.

Smith, D. (1997) *The State of War and Peace Atlas*, London: Penguin.

Smith, J. (2002) 'An unappealing industry', *The Ecologist*, 32, 3: 40–1.

Söderbaum, F. and Taylor, I. (2001) 'Transmission belt for transnational capital or facilitator for development? Problematising the role of the state in the Maputo Development Corridor', *Journal of Modern African Studies*, 39, 4: 675–95.

Soderbaum, F. and Taylor, I. (eds) (2003) *Regionalism and Uneven Development in Southern Africa: the Case of the Maputo Development Corridor*, Aldershot: Ashgate.

Solomon, H. and Liebenberg, I. (eds) (2000) *The Consolidation of Democracy in Africa*, Aldershot: Ashgate.

Solow, R. (1970) *Growth Theory: An Exposition*, Oxford, Clarendon Press.

Soros, G. (2002) *On Globalization*, New York: Public Affairs.

Southall, A. (1970) 'The illusion of tribe', *Journal of Asian and African Studies*, 5, 1–2: 28–50.

Sowa, N. K. (1994) 'Fiscal deficits, output growth and inflation targets in Ghana', *World Development*, 22, 8: 1105–17.

'The Spirit of Cartagena', declaration adopted by UNCTAD at its eighth session held at the Convention Centre, Cartagena de Indias, Colombia, from 8 to 25 February, 1992. Available online at: http://www.inro.com.my/inro/cartagena.htm

Spivak, G. (1988) 'Can the subaltern speak?', in C. Nelson and L. Grossberg (eds) *Marxism and the Interpretation of Culture*, Basingstoke: Macmillan: 271–313.

Stepan, A. (ed.) (1973) *Authoritarian Brazil*, New Haven, CT: Yale University Press.

Staudt, K. (2001) 'The uses and abuses of empowerment discourse', in J. Parpart et al. (eds) *Rethinking Empowerment in a Global/Local World*, London: Routledge: 23–45.

Steans, J. and Pettiford, L. (2001) *International Relations: Perspectives and Themes*, Harlow: Pearson Education.

Stienstra, D. (2000) 'Making global connections among women, 1970–1999', in R. Cohen and S. Rai (eds) *Global Social Movements*, London: Routledge: 115–34.

Stiglitz, J. (1999) 'Back to basic: policies and strategies for enhanced growth and equity in post-crisis East Asia', speech given at the Shangri-la Hotel, Bangkok, Thailand, July 29, 1999.

Stiglitz, J. E. (2002) *Globalization and Its Discontents*, London: Penguin Books.

Stitcher, S. and Parpart, J. L. (1990) 'Introduction', in S. Stitcher and J. L. Parpart (eds.), *Women, Employment and Family in the International Division of Labor*, Philadelphia: Temple University Press: 1–9.

Sunstein, Cass R. (2001) *Designing Democracy: What Constitutions Do*, Oxford: Oxford University Press.

Syatauw, J. (1993) 'The Non-Aligned Movement at the cross-roads: the Jakarta Summit adapting to the post-Cold War era', *Asian Yearbook of International Affairs*, No. 3: 129–62.

Sylla, R. and Toniolo, G. (1991), *Patterns of European Industrialization: the Nineteenth Century*, London: Routledge.

Tandon, Y. (n.d.) *The Role of Foreign Direct Investments in Africa's Human Development*. Available at: http://attac.org/fra/list/doc/tandon.htm

Tatsuo, I. (1999) 'Liberal democracy and Asian orientalism', in J. R. Bauer and D. A. Bell (eds), *The East Asian Challenge for Human Rights*, Cambridge: Cambridge University Press: 27–59.

Taylor, I. (2001a) *Stuck in Middle GEAR: South Africa's Post-Apartheid Foreign Relations*, Westport, CT: Praeger.

Taylor, I. (2001b) 'The "Mbeki Initiative": towards a post-orthodox new international order?', in P. Nel, I. Taylor and J. van der Westhuizen (eds) *South Africa's Multilateral Diplomacy and Global Change: The Limits of Reform*, Aldershot: Ashgate: 59–75.

Taylor, I. (2002) 'Good governance or good for business? South Africa's regionalist project and the "African Renaissance"', in S. Breslin, C. Hughes, N. Phillips and B. Rosamond (eds), *New Regionalisms in the Global Political Economy: Theories and Cases*, London: Routledge: 190–203.

Taylor, I. (2003) 'Globalization and regionalization in Africa: reactions to attempts at neo-liberal regionalism', *Review of International Political Economy*, 10, 2: 310–30.

Taylor, I. and Nel, P. (2002) '"Getting the rhetoric right", getting the strategy wrong: "New Africa", globalisation and the confines of elite reformism', *Third World Quarterly*, 23, 1: 163–80.

Taylor, I. and Vale, P. (2000) 'South Africa's transition revisited: globalisation as vision and virtue', *Global Society*, 14, 3: 399–414.

Taylor, L. (1992) *Varieties of Stablization Experience. Towards a Sensible Macroeconomics in the Third World*, Oxford: Clarendon Press.

Teitelbaum, J. (2002) 'Dueling for *Da'wa*: state vs. society on the Saudi internet', *Middle East Journal*, 56, 2: 222–39.

Tester, K. (1992) *Civil Society*, London and New York: Routledge.

Thomas, C. (1998) 'International financial institutions and social and economic human rights: an exploration', in T. Evans (ed.), *Human Rights Fifty Years On. A Reappraisal*, Manchester: Manchester University Press: 161–85.

Thomas, C. and Reader, M. (2001) 'Development and inequality', in B. White, R. Little and M. Smith (eds), *Issues in World Politics*, Basingstoke: Palgrave: 74–92.

Thompson, L. and Leysens, A. (1996) 'Comments: South African foreign policy discussion document', unpublished paper, Department of Political Science, University of Stellenbosch.

Thompson, M. R. (2003) 'The Asia-Pacific after "Asian values": regional reactions to a globalized "good governance" discourse', paper delivered at the European Consortium of Political Research Conference, Marburg, Germany, September 18–21.

Tilly, C. (ed.) (1975) *The Formation of National States in Western Europe*, Princeton, NJ: Princeton University Press.

Tinker, I. (1976) 'The adverse impact of development on women', in I. Tinker and M. Bramsen (eds), *Women and World Development*: Washington, DC: Overseas Development Council: 22–34.

Tinker, I. (1997) 'The making of a field: advocates, practitioners and scholars', in N. Visvanathan, L. Duggan, L. Nisonoff and N. Wiegersma (eds), *The Women, Gender and Development Reader*, London: Zed: 33–42.

Todaro, M. (1994a) *Economic Development*, 5th ed., Oxford: Oxford University Press.

Todaro, M. (1994b) 'New growth theory', *Journal of Economic Perspectives*, 8, Winter: 3–72.

Todaro, M. (2000) *Economic Development*, 7th ed., New York, Addison-Wesley.

Toth, J. (1980) 'Class development in rural Egypt, 1945–1979', in T. Hopkins and I. Wallerstein (eds), *Processes of the World System*, Volume 3: *Political Economy of the World-System Annuals*, London: Sage: 127–47.

Toye, J. (1987), *Dilemmas of Development. Reflections on the Counterrevolution in Development Theory and Policy*, Oxford: Basil Blackwell.

Toye, J. (1993) *Dilemmas of Development*, 2nd ed, Oxford: Basil Blackwell.

Truong, Thanh-Dam (1999) 'The underbelly of the tiger: gender and the demystification of the Asian miracle', *Review of International Political Economy*, 6, 2: 133–65.

Truong, Thanh-Dam and Rosario, V. (1994) 'Captive outsiders: Trafficked women in the sex industry and mail-order-brides in the European Union', in J. Wiersma (ed.), *Insiders and Outsiders: On the Making of Europe II*, Kampen: Pharos.

Tulchin, S. and Romero, B. (eds) (1995) *The Consolidation of Democracy in Latin America*, London: Lynne Rienner.

Udayagiri, M. (1995) 'Challenging modernization: gender and development, postmodern feminism and activism', in M. Marchand and J. Parpart (eds), *Feminism/Postmodernism/Development*, London: Routledge: 44–83.

UNCTAD (1999) *World Investment Report 1999: Foreign Direct Investment and the Challenge of Development*, New York and Geneva: UNCTAD.

UNCTAD (2001) *World Investment Report 2001: Promoting Linkages*, New York and Geneva: UNCTAD.

UNDP (United Nations Development Programme) (2000) *Human Development Report 2000*, New York: Oxford University Press.

UNDP (United Nations Development Programme) (2002) *Human Development Report 2002*, Oxford, Oxford University Press.

UNDP (United Nations Development Programme) (2003) *Human Development Report 2003*, Oxford, Oxford University Press.

UNDP (United Nations Development Programme)/Arab Fund for Economic and Social Development (2003) *Arab Human Development Report 2003*, New York: UNDP.

United Nations, ESCAP (1998) 'Foreign direct investment in selected Asian countries: policies, related institution-building and regional co-operation', Development Papers, No. 19, New York: United Nations.

van den Berghe, P. (1987) *The Ethnic Phenomenon*, New York: Praeger.

Van der Pijl, K. (1984) *The Making of an Atlantic Ruling Class*, London: Verso.

van der Westhuizen, J. (2001) 'Marketing the Rainbow Nation: the power of South African music, film and sport industry', in K. Dunn and T. Shaw (eds) *Africa and International Relations Theory*, London: Palgrave: 64–81.

Varshney, A. (2003) *Ethnic Conflict and Civil Life: Hindus and Muslims in India*, 2nd ed., New Haven, CT: Yale University Press.

Viner, J. (1950) *The Customs Union Issue*, New York: Carnegie Endowment for International Peace.

Viswanathan, G. (1989) *Masks of Conquest. Literary Study and British Rule in India*, London: Faber & Faber.

Vogler, J. and Imber, F. (1996) *The Environment and International Relations*, London: Routledge.

Wackernagel, M. and Rees, W. (1996) *Our Ecological Footprint*, Gabriola Island, British Columbia: New Society Publishers.

Wade, R. (1990) *Governing the Market. Economic Theory and the Role of Government in East Asian Industrialization*, Princeton, NJ: Princeton University Press.

Wade, R. (1992) 'East Asia's economic success: conflicting paradigms, partial insights, shaky evidence', *World Politics*, 44, January: 270–320.

Walby, S. (1990) *Theorizing Patriarchy*, Oxford: Basil Blackwell.

Waldner, D. (1999) *State Building and Late Development*. Ithaca, NY: Cornell University Press.

Walicki, A. (1969), *The Controversy Over Capitalism. Studies in the Social Philosophy of the Russian Populists*, Oxford: Clarendon.

Wallace, T. with March, C. (1991) (eds) *Changing Perceptions, Writings on Gender and Development*, Oxford: Oxfam.

Wallbank, T. W. (1958) *A Short History of India and Pakistan*, New York: Mentor.

Walters, R. F. and McGee, T. G. (eds) (1997), *Asia Pacific – New Geographies of the Pacific Rim*, London: Hurst.

Waltz, K. (1979) *The Theory of International Politics*, New York: McGraw Hill.

Waring, M. (1988) *If Women Counted. A New Feminist Economics*, San Francisco: Harper & Row.

Waterbury, J. (1999) 'The long gestation and brief triumph of import-substituting industrialization', *World Development*, 27, 2: 323–41.

Watson, A. (1992), *The Evolution of International Society*, London: Routledge.

WCED (World Commission on Environment and Development) (The Brundtland Report) (1987) *Our Common Future*, Oxford: Oxford University Press.

Weale, A. (1992) *The New Politics of Pollution*, Manchester: Manchester University Press.

Weber, Maria (ed.) (2001), *Reforming Economic Systems in Asia: A Comparative Analysis of China, Japan, South Korea, Malaysia and Thailand*, Cheltenham, UK: Edward Elgar.

Weber, Max (1974), *The Protestant Ethic and the Spirit of Capitalism*, London: Allen & Unwin.

Weber, Max (1978) *Economy and Society*, Berkeley, CA: University of California Press.

Weinstein, W. (1972) 'Conflict and confrontation in Central Africa: the revolt in Burundi 1972', *Africa Today*, 19, 4: 26–9.

Weiss, L. (1998) *The Myth of the Powerless State*, Ithaca, NY: Cornell University Press.

Weller, M. (2002) 'International Criminal Court', *International Affairs*, 78, 4: 693–712.

Welzel, C., Inglehart, R. and Klingemann, H.-D. (2003) 'The theory of human development: a cross-cultural analysis, *European Journal of Political Research*, 42, 2: 341–80.

White, G. (1984) 'Developmental states and socialist industrialisation in the Third World', *Journal of Development Studies*, 21, 1: 97–120.

White, G. (1996) 'The Mexico of Europe? Morocco's partnership with the European Union', in D. Vandewalle (ed.), *North Africa: Development and Reform in a Changing Global Economy*, London: Macmillan: 111–28.

White, G. and Wade, R. (eds) (1988) *Developmental States in East Asia*, New York: St Martin's Press.

White, P. (2000) *Primitive Rebels or Revolutionary Modernizers?: The Kurdish National Movement in Turkey*, London: Zed.

Whyte, R. and Whyte P. (1982) *The Women of Rural Asia*, London: Westview.

Williams, R., Jr (2003) *The Wars Within: Peoples and States in Conflict*, Ithaca, NY and London: Cornell University Press.

Wolfensohn, J. (2004) 'Foreword', in World Bank, *World Development Report 2004: Making Services Work For Poor People*, Oxford: Oxford University Press for the World Bank.

Woo-Cumings, M. (1999) 'Introduction: Chalmers Johnson and the politics of nationalism and development', in M. Woo-Cumings (ed.), *The Developmental State*, Ithaca, NY: Cornell University Press: 1–31.

Wood, E. M. (2002) 'Global capital, national states', in M. Rupert and H. Smith (ed.), *Historical Materialism and Globalization*, London: Routledge: 17–39.

World Bank (1981), *Accelerated Development in Sub-Saharan Africa: An Agenda for Action*, Washington, DC: World Bank.

World Bank (1989a) *Sub-Saharan Africa: From Crisis to Sustainable Growth*, Washington DC: World Bank.

World Bank (1989b) 'East Asian crisis: an overview', in *East Asia: The Road to Recovery*, Washington DC: World Bank: 3–15.

World Bank (1993) *The East Asian Miracle Economic Growth and Public Policy*, New York: Oxford University Press.

World Bank (1994) *Adjustment in Africa, Reforms, Results and the Road Ahead*, Oxford: Oxford University Press.

World Bank (1997a) *China Engaged: Integration with the Global Economy China 2020*, Washington, DC: World Bank.

World Bank (1997b) *The State in a Changing World, World Development Report 1997*, Oxford: Oxford University Press.

World Bank (1998) *World Development Report 1998/1999*, Oxford: Oxford University Press for the World Bank.

World Bank (2001) *World Development Report 2000/2001*, Oxford: Oxford University Press for the World Bank.

World Bank (2003) *2003 World Development Indicators*, Washington, DC: World Bank.

World Bank (2004) *World Development Report 2004: Making Services Work For Poor People*, Oxford: Oxford University Press for the World Bank.

Xia, M. (2000) *The Dual Developmental State: Development Strategy and Institutional Arrangements for China's Transition*, Aldershot: Ashgate.

Young, A. (1994) 'The tyranny of numbers: confronting the statistical reality of the East Asian growth experience', *NBER Macroeconomics Annual 1992*, Cambridge, MA: MIT Press.

Young, C. (1976), *The Politics of Cultural Pluralism*, Madison: University of Wisconsin Press.

Young, K. (1997) 'Gender and development', in N. Visvanathan, N. Duggan, L. Nisonoff and N. Wiegersma (eds), *The Women, Gender and Development Reader*, London: Zed: 51–4.

Zartman, I. W. (1993) 'L'analyse politique du regionalisme', in S. Belaid and I. W. Zartman (eds), *Les experiences d'integration regionale dans les pays du tiers-monde*, Tunis: CERP-CEMA: 13–40.

index